KD 4430 CRO

THE CONSTITUT
REVOLUTI

23 D1760977

Alan Cromartie gives an innovative account of English constitutional
ideas from the mid-fifteenth century to the time of Charles I, showing
how the emergence of grand claims for common law, the country's
strange unwritten legal system, shaped England's cultural development. This is the first book of its type for at least a generation to
offer an interpretative framework that covers both the Reformation
and the Revolution; it makes a unique contribution both to the history of the English state and to the broader history of ideas. Though
he does not neglect the role of narrowly religious disagreements,
Dr Cromartie brings out the way that 'religious' and 'secular' values came to be intertwined: to the majority of Charles's subjects,
the rights of the clergy and the king were legal rights; the institutional structure of church and state was an expression of monarchical
power; obedience to the king and to the law was a religious duty.
A proper understanding of this cluster of ideas reveals why Charles
found England so difficult to control and why both parties in the civil
war believed that they were fighting for established institutions.

ALAN CROMARTIE is Reader in Politics at the University of Reading. His previous publications include *Sir Matthew Hale, 1609–1676*
(Cambridge, 1995).

WITHDRAWN
FROM STOCK
QMUL LIBRARY

WITHDRAWN
FROM STOCK
QMUL LIBRARY

IDEAS IN CONTEXT

Edited by Quentin Skinner and James Tully

The books in this series will discuss the emergence of intellectual traditions and of related new disciplines. The procedures, aims, and vocabularies that were generated will be set in the context of the alternatives available within the contemporary frameworks of ideas and institutions. Through detailed studies of the evolution of such traditions, and their modification by different audiences, it is hoped that a new picture will form of the development of ideas in their concrete contexts. By this means, artificial distinctions between the history of philosophy, of the various sciences, of society and politics, and of literature may be seen to dissolve.

The series is published with the support of the Exxon Foundation.

A list of books in the series will be found at the end of the volume.

THE CONSTITUTIONALIST
REVOLUTION

An Essay on the History of England, 1450–1642

ALAN CROMARTIE

CAMBRIDGE
UNIVERSITY PRESS

CAMBRIDGE UNIVERSITY PRESS
Cambridge, New York, Melbourne, Madrid, Cape Town, Singapore, São Paulo, Delhi

Cambridge University Press
The Edinburgh Building, Cambridge CB2 8RU, UK

Published in the United States of America by Cambridge University Press, New York

www.cambridge.org
Information on this title: www.cambridge.org/9780521788113

© Alan Cromartie 2006

This publication is in copyright. Subject to statutory exception
and to the provisions of relevant collective licensing agreements,
no reproduction of any part may take place without the written
permission of Cambridge University Press.

First published 2006
This digitally printed version 2009

A catalogue record for this publication is available from the British Library

Library of Congress Cataloguing in Publication data
Cromartie, Alan.
The constitutionalist revolution : an essay on the history of England, 1450–1642 / Alan Cromartie.
p. cm. – (Ideas in context ; 75)
Includes bibliographical references and index.
ISBN 13: 978 0 521 78269 2 (alk. paper)
ISBN 10: 0 521 78269 4 (alk. paper)
1. Executive power – England – History. 2. England – Kings and rulers – History.
3. Constitutional history – England. 4. Common law – England – History. I. Title. II. Series.
KD4430.C76 2006
342.4202′9 – dc22
2006001848

ISBN 978-0-521-78269-2 hardback
ISBN 978-0-521-78811-3 paperback

QM LIBRARY
(MILE END)

Cambridge University Press has no responsibility for the persistence or accuracy of URLs for external
or third-party Internet websites referred to in this publication, and does not guarantee that any
content on such websites is, or will remain, accurate or appropriate.

For Cait and Aideen

Contents

Acknowledgements

Research for this book began at Christ's College, Cambridge, where I benefited from the encouragement, advice, and practical kindness of my colleagues Susan Bayly, David Reynolds, and Quentin Skinner. It was written in the friendly atmosphere of Reading University Politics department, where I have been particularly grateful for the tolerance of successive heads of department (Richard Bellamy, Peter Woodward, and Bob McKeever), the support of my fellow theorists (Barry Holden, Tony Coates, Andrew Williams, Catriona McKinnon, and Paula Casal), and the much-tested patience of the administrators (Pat Hicks, Melanie Richardson, and Caroline Waters). It would not have been completed without a grant from the Arts and Humanities Research Council's enlightened Research Leave scheme, the assistance of librarians at Cambridge and Reading University Libraries and the British Library, the careful copy-editing of Jean Field, and numerous tactful reminders from Richard Fisher.

Introduction

Some civil wars are easily predicted. They split the polity concerned along an obvious fault-line created by race, geography, religion, patronage ties, or economic dealings. They happen where the centre is relatively weak, where sectional attachments trump wider loyalties. But there are other, more unusual conflicts in which the usual pattern appears to be reversed, in which the tug exerted by the values of the centre (or some interpretation of those values) creates new groups that cut across existing social structures. The English civil war was one such conflict. The English fought each other in 1642 because their precociously unified national culture turned out to have ambiguous political implications. Both sides maintained, apparently sincerely, that they were fighting for the king, the laws, and the established Protestant religion, but each side turned out to be loyal to different understandings of these concepts. The cluster of apparently shared values was powerful enough to split the nation's governing class and to produce both royalists and roundheads in virtually all areas of the country. The kind of war the English fought reveals the kind of country that they lived in.

A satisfying history of early modern England must make this kind of war intelligible. No such account is likely to be wholly secular, for legalism, monarchy, and Protestant religion were intertwined and mutually supportive: the rights of church and crown were legal rights; the institutional structure of church and state was an expression of monarchical power; obedience to the King and to the law was a religious duty. In any case, there is much evidence of narrowly religious motivation. Though Oliver Cromwell in retrospect maintained that what he later came to call 'religion' was 'not the thing at the first contested for',[1] such statements reflected a subsequent shift in perspective. Even in 1642, the nucleus of the parliamentarian party consisted of those who wanted church reform, while

---

[1] *The writings and speeches of Oliver Cromwell*, ed. W. C. Abbott, 4 vols. (Cambridge, MA, 1937–47), III, 586.

many of King Charles's most active supporters were certainly attracted to his cause by his determination to resist it. Both sides produced effective propaganda, in which they demonised their foes as Jesuits or Munster Anabaptists.

But there are limits to the power of any explanation that focuses upon religious motives. What might be termed a 'genuine' war of religion, a conflict generated by opposed theologies and modes of worship, would surely have been lost by parliament, if only because puritans had need of non-puritan allies. If puritanism is defined as principled belief in reform of the church, pursued by a distinctive group self-identified as 'godly', then puritans were, and would remain, a small minority. Although entrenched in certain areas (especially in some provincial towns, and in regions with a clothing industry), their strength was unevenly spread across the country. If, as has often been maintained, their doctrines were attractive to the literate 'middling sort', they found it much harder to influence both more and less sophisticated people. Unlike their enemies, who saw advantage in posing as defenders of folk custom, they had to work against the grain of popular tradition; but they also found themselves cut off from aristocratic and academic circles. They had no agreed coherent positive programme. It was striking, but hardly surprising, that none of the post-war puritan regimes were to acquire much legitimacy and that their military control of England had very little effect upon its culture.

Puritanism narrowly defined was thus a handicap to parliament, which was no doubt why the Houses' public statements during the crucial summer of 1642 were not overtly puritanical. One could of course coherently maintain that an unintended consequence of royal policy was to radicalise much moderate opinion, creating a temporary movement for puritan reform that went beyond the previously 'godly'. But the more loosely the idea of puritanism is used, the more it covers groups whose aspirations for the church were functions of their attitudes to monarchy and law. This is not to assert that such people had 'secular' motives (though some of them probably did), but only that their views about religion cannot be separated from their wider social values. The parliamentarian movement's political theory was blended with its anti-Catholic feeling in such a way that none of its supporters had any immediate need to choose between them. It is anachronistic to suppose that there was any necessary tension between these different strands of propaganda, because the threat of 'popery' was amongst other things a threat of secular oppression (just as the threat presented by the ultra-puritan sects – the favoured bogey of the royalists – was amongst other things a threat of democratic or anarchic licence).

This book sets out to recreate the intellectual world in which the aspirations of the godly fitted into a *political* solution to the crisis of the Stuart monarchy. From a sufficiently long-term perspective, that crisis can be understood as the result of two developments. The first was the emergence of a mode of government that both expanded and constrained the powers of the monarch. During the sixteenth century, the English crown vastly extended its reach – its capacity to motivate its servants – by an appeal to the prestige of English positive law; but in so doing, it provided means by which its power could be limited. The country's legalistic Reformation helped to encourage the belief that English common law was in a strict sense omnicompetent, that is, was capable of finding answers to every social and political question, including questions that concerned the powers of the church and the monarch. This high view of the common law in general strengthened kings, but as soon as royal policies conflicted with expectations of the legal system, it had the effect of stiffening resistance. By the later 1620s, it had produced a parliamentary deadlock that a much subtler king than Charles would have had difficulty in resolving.

The second long-term development was also the result of the unusual character of England's Reformation. In the religious sphere, the great peculiarity of England was not so much the vestiges of Catholic modes of worship as the survival, virtually unscathed, of a medieval institutional structure. One fruit of this survival was the latent disaffection of the godly; another was the attractiveness to the supporters of the *status quo* of a more Catholic theology. The greatest of these, Richard Hooker (1554–1600), succeeded in fusing defence of the church with regard for legal values, but later high churchmen adopted a more risky strategy. As their claims for the church became bolder, their politics became more absolutist. They regarded themselves and the crown as equally menaced by the aggression of the common lawyers, and looked to a powerful monarch to defend them. Though James was sympathetic, he rejected their political assistance; Charles by contrast went into alliance with an anti-erastian church, and in so doing, helped to doom both church and monarchy.

This book's account is focused on the history of law, but neither of these stories is comprehensible without the background presence of the other. The English constitutionalist tradition would hardly have developed as it did without the impulse given it by attitudes towards religious questions, but the effect of law upon religion was arguably almost as important. Together, they moulded the rational, rights-bearing self that has persisted and that shapes our present situation.

CHAPTER I

Fortescue's world

Any account of late medieval England must take some note of a surprising contrast. The kingdom's rulers were unfortunate (five out of Henry VIII's ten predecessors died violent deaths at the hands of their own subjects), but the society they tried to govern appears to have been increasingly well ordered. Its relative stability could even survive a uniquely unsuitable monarch. The regime of Henry VI suffered every disaster that could happen to a personal monarchy – foreign defeat, court faction, royal minority and lunacy, kidnapping, civil war, and usurpation – but the result was nothing like the Anarchy of Stephen. The Wars of the Roses were brief campaigns concluding in formal engagements; the houses that magnates erected were only minimally fortified; and few of them spent more than a tenth of their income on wages for retainers. There is not in fact much evidence that violence was endemic, or murder other than exceptional.[1] What really needs to be explained is not dynastic chaos, but the resilience of social order.

One cause of this resilience was surely the role of the gentry in county government. Before 1294, the senior central court, King's Bench, aspired to visit the counties on regular 'general eyres', thus bringing the whole panoply of royal law to the localities. After this mechanism was abandoned, the crown began to make more use of local notables. The history of county commissions of the peace – bodies intended to combine so-called 'sages de la ley' with landowners worth at least £20 a year – was virtually continuous from 1361; a century later, in 1461, their members in effect displaced the sheriffs as royal judges at a county level. There were and are two different ways of looking at these local magistrates. On one quite easily constructed view, their very existence weakened monarchy. Their emergence has been seen as symptomatic of the way in which a 'law state' turned into a 'war state', a country in which the demands of foreign warfare forced kings to

---

[1] P. C. Maddern, *Violence and social order: East Anglia 1422–1442* (Oxford, 1992), 5.

abandon performing a core royal function.[2] A 'strong' king would not have permitted this to happen. The exceptionally capable Henry V attempted to revive the earlier practice of sending King's Bench to project royal power in the localities; it was the new and insecure regime of Edward IV that witnessed the displacement of the sheriff.

On another view, however, the JP was the central mechanism of what, potentially at least, was an immensely powerful apparatus. The principal cause of the general eyre's collapse was the sheer weight of popular demand for its attention; the JP could handle indefinite amounts of trivial business without administrative overload. What was more, one great advantage of commissions of the peace was that they gave the more important gentry a certain stake in the idea of law. Thus William Worcester's *The Boke of Noblesse*, a work that reached its final form in 1475, regretted the high value that was set on legal knowledge:

knightis sonnes esquiers and of othir gentille bloode, set hem silfe to singular practik . . . as to learn the practique of law or custom of lande, or of civile matier, and so wastyn gretlie theire tyme in such nedelese besinesse, as to occupie courtis halding, to kepe and bere out a proud countenaunce at sessions and shiris halding . . . And who can be a reuler and put hym forthe in such matieris, he is, as the worlde goithe now, among alle astatis more set of than he that hathe despendid 30 or 40 yeris [in the wars].[3]

This perception was no doubt exaggerated (it may indeed have been a generalisation from Worcester's pushy acquaintances, the Pastons), but its expression at this date, less than four years from Tewkesbury and Barnet, is nonetheless both striking and suggestive.

The legalistic character of English social life was perfectly consistent with a large role for aristocratic power – indeed it explains how a governing class that was threaded with patronage networks could stop its disagreements escalating. Some law-suits are perhaps best understood as a symbolic substitute for battle; this was probably why the Pastons spent at least 600 marks – to say nothing of time, trouble, political capital, and travel costs – on the struggle for a property, East Beckham, that may have been worth 20 marks a year.[4] The obvious shortcomings of the medieval law did not prevent it structuring such quarrels. A powerful man could resort to self-help or intimidating juries – a jury was an admirable method

[2] R. W. Kaeuper, *War, justice, and public order* (Oxford, 1988).
[3] *The Boke of Noblesse: addressed to King Edward IV on his invasion of France in 1475*, ed. J. G. Nichols (1860), 77. Spelling of quotations has been modernised, unless (as here), there might be some loss of the author's intended meaning.
[4] Colin Richmond, *The Paston family in the fifteenth century: the first phase* (Cambridge, 1990), 114.

of ratifying 'facts upon the ground' – but these are best seen as irregular moves within or around a respected legal process: as gamesmanship which presupposed a rulebook. Even the apparently slow pace of standard court procedures had the important practical advantage of offering ample time for arbitration.⁵ The law both shaped and tamed the gentry's squabbles, whatever other methods were used to settle them.

A faith in legal processes affected even national politicians. Thus Richard duke of York could write to the council (probably in October 1450), denouncing unnamed enemies in legalistic terms. His letter was a kind of memorandum 'to your highe and noble discrecion, and the trewe lordes of the kinges counsele', complaining of 'grete injuries, coloured threasons and oppressions maignetened by highe astates, the enstimiable extorcions and the sophisticall subverting of the kinges lawes'. These had led to the loss of King Henry VI's 'enheritaunce of his reaume of France', to 'rising and rebellions' at home, and 'shamefull rebuke in the conseyte of straun-geres'. York demanded that 'suche personnes detecte and charged with threason and crymis, beyng aboute the kinges personne, maybe arrested, to be determined and juged after the forme of lawe'. He went on to offer a vivid account of law's centrality:

And it is to be advertised in the correccions of the highe and noble discrecion that a king or alorde lawlesse ys as afisshe watirlesse, for lawe causith the king inheritable to the croune. Lawe causith every astate and degree to kepe ordinate reule, and the king is sworne to his lawe and to defende his people, and so under your highe correccion hit is conseyved, who that subvertith or hath subverted the lawe, hit is the most threason on earthe that can be thoughte, for they impovereth here prince in unlawfull askinges of his inheritaunce and demaynes.⁶

The purpose of this missive was not philosophical – Richard and his advis-ers were attempting a political manoeuvre – but its ingenious rhetoric is useful evidence of what was thought politically appealing. Its strategy was to conflate the King's 'inheritance of France' with 'the inheritance and domains' *unlawfully* asked by suitors: misgovernment was redescribed as illegality; misdeeds were characterised as crimes; and crimes in turn were characterised as treasons. 'Discretion' was repeatedly referred to, but the discretionary action sought was just an ordinary legal process: York was arguing that the law must take its course.

---

⁵ Edward Powell, *Kingship, law, and society: criminal justice in the reign of Henry V* (Oxford, 1989), 274.
⁶ M. L. Kekewich, C. Richmond, A. F. Sutton, L. Visser-Fuchs, and J. L. Watts, *The politics of fifteenth-century England: John Vale's Book* (Stroud, 1995), 187–8.

Appeals to legal processes were not confined to Yorkists. In a text composed in 1459 (usually known as 'Somnium Vigilantis'), one of Henry VI's supporters could assert that

all controversies and debates civil or criminal, real or personal, ben decided by the king's laws without maintenance or wilful interruption of the course of justice, and in case that any thing fall of the which determination is not expressed in the common law, then the prince must be asked and enquired and by his exceeding auctorite and prudence of his council an expikan shalbe made thereupon, and so that no thing may be done by singular will and senceall affection.[7]

Here, just as in York's letter, the King was presented as standing outside law, but royal power dissolved, upon further inspection, into a right to set the law in motion. An 'expikan' may be an 'explication' or an unusually illiterate spelling of Aristotle's word *epieikeia* (a concept that will be discussed below), but it seems to refer to some kind of impersonal process.

The claims so confidently made in these essentially propagandist texts are evidence, if any is required, that late medieval Englishmen had an ideal of government by law. As heirs to seventeenth-century disagreements, we naturally seize on such pronouncements as the essential stuff of political theory, but in the late Lancastrian period, they seem to have been made quite casually. They suggest that the law's prestige was worth invoking, but that the King's relationship to law was not politically sensitive: that politicians with some transient reason for stressing the supremacy of legal processes were not afraid that over-stating matters would leave them vulnerable to criticism.

Part of the explanation of their insouciance was that the law was something the king *did*. In calling for the rule of law, these writers were calling for kingship, not undermining it. Upholding the law – 'doing justice' to his people – should have been one of Henry's central functions: as York pointed out, it was a royal duty to which the monarch had been sworn by his coronation oath; conversely, 'denial of justice' had been prohibited by Magna Carta. A true king, that is, one who acted rightly – the word *rex* was often derived from *recte agendo*[8] – was one who acted to promote the common weal of the community. Dispensing remedies through known procedures, assisted by appropriate counsellors, was an important aspect of his function. As we shall see, this was the view of kingship that seems to underlie the scattered comments of the few English writers of legal treatises.

[7] J. P. Gilson, 'A defence of the proscription of the Yorkists', *English Historical Review* 26 (1911), 518.
[8] *Isidori Hispaliensis episcopi etymologiarum sive originarum libri xx*, ed. W. M. Lindsay, 2 vols. (Oxford, 1911), Book I, chapter xxix.3.

Although it long pre-dated the translation of Aristotle's work *The Politics* (a treatise not available in Latin before the later thirteenth century), it harmonised neatly with Aristotelian thinking; an Aristotelian king, as opposed to a tyrant, was someone who possessed the moral habits (in medieval terminology, the 'virtues') encouraging promotion of the common interest. Thus the constraints on kingship were the constraints internal to a role, expressed through habits that the role demanded.

One side of Aristotelian thought had a republicanising tendency. As Aristotle had explained, a law was better than a human ruler because it was 'intellect without desire'; to use the *Somnium*'s phrasing, it was a process without 'will and senceall affection'. But as Aristotle also pointed out, a rule of law would generate hard cases; the common good demanded an agent equipped with the virtue of *epieikeia*, the equity that 'rectified' the law's unpalatable consequences. This was indeed the Aristotelian reason for thinking that the rule of the best man should be preferred to that of the best laws. The point was well explained by Giles of Rome (?1243–1316), whose *De regimine principum*, a mirror for princes developed from Aristotelian materials, was the most popular 'political' work in fifteenth-century England.[9] The idea was readily assimilable, because medieval Englishmen expected justice tempered by 'discretion'. At English coronations, the monarch was asked 'Will you cause (*facies*) equal and right justice and discretion in mercy (*misericordia*) and truth to be done in all your judgements, to the utmost of your powers', to which the reply was 'I will do so' (*faciam*).[10]

The charges by which Henry IV had justified deposing Richard II show the importance of this undertaking. They quoted this part of the oath before complaining that Richard acted 'without any pity (*absque omni misericordia*)' in his behaviour to the banished Henry. A further indication of the relevant patterns of thought is found in the best-known of all these charges: the claim that Richard had maintained that he could make and change the laws at will. The full charge runs as follows:

The same king not wishing to conserve or protect the just laws and customs of the realm, but to enact according to the decision of his will whatever might occur to his desires, from time to time, and often when the laws of the realm were expounded and declared to him by judges and others of his Council and when he should have displayed justice to those who sought it according to those laws,

---

[9] *The governance of kings and princes: John Trevisa's Middle English translation of the De regimine principum of Aegidius Romanus*, ed. D. C. Fowler, C. F. Briggs, and P. G. Remley (New York, 1997), 378.

[10] S. B. Chrimes and A. L. Brown (eds.), *Select documents of English constitutional history 1307–1485*, (1961), 4.

said explicitly, with a harsh and shameless countenance, that his laws were in his mouth and sometimes in his breast, and that he could make and change the laws of his realm by himself. And seduced by that opinion, he did not allow justice to be done to many of his subjects, but by threats and fears forced many to desist from the pursuit of ordinary justice.[11]

The anxiety expressed here is superficially familiar; Richard's opponents were alarmed by what their seventeenth-century descendants would demonise as 'arbitrary power'. But the immediate context is subtly alien. Two features of Richard's assertions were particularly shocking: their flat rejection of appropriate counsel; and their denial of his aid to subjects who approached him for assistance. Both these unkingly elements of his behaviour derived from an imbalance in his personality: the dominance of a will (*arbitrium*) that was the prey of momentary desires. Though one of King Richard's offences was a disregard for rules, his failure to do 'justice' was an aspect of a more general failure to be royal.

One way of describing the intellectual changes that are the principal subject of this book is as a shift away from this conception: a move, in fact, from personal to rule-bound monarchy. Medieval conceptions of kingship required the king, from time to time, to over-ride existing regulations. The notion of kingship involved, to be sure, respect for 'laws and customs', but it was not exhausted by this duty; the habits befitting a monarch included the 'discretion' and the 'mercy' demanded by particular situations. If some medieval writers thought that 'law' could 'make' the king, they seem to have been thinking of *lex naturalis*; at all events, no other human being had the authority to define the limits of his power. Constraints on his behaviour were, as it were, internal to a picture of the monarch as someone directed by reason, not by will. During the Stuart period, by contrast, it came to be held that monarchical power could be defined by ordinary judges: that much the same procedures that settled disagreements about property in land could settle conflicts between king and subjects. An arbitrary power was not so much a power swayed by passion (although the phrase retained this connotation) as one that escaped the scrutiny of lawyers.

The claim that ordinary law defines the monarch's power will be referred to in this book as 'constitutionalism'. Seventeenth-century Englishmen of constitutionalist sympathies were naturally prone to discover this claim among their ancestors, but (as we shall see) their ability to do so was actually the product, not the cause, of the transition that needs explanation.

[11] Ibid., 189.

Although the details of the shift are complex, its essence can be simply formulated. The faith that the English developed in 'law' was faith in the tradition of behaviour, generally known, of course, as 'common law', evolved by a small group of royal servants. These royal servants came to feel that their professional learning was adequate to any situation: that their particular form of royal justice incorporated royal *epieikeia*. This strange belief did not emerge until the Tudor period, but some of the materials from which it was constructed had been supplied by Sir John Fortescue (*c.*1390–1479). The starting point for any exploration of the process must be a brief description of his professional world.

I

The law that Fortescue described and practised consisted in the methods and traditions of two courts: King's Bench, which originally dealt with those suits to which the monarch was himself a party; and Common Pleas, which dealt with litigation between subjects, especially suits concerned with debt and real property. Although King's Bench was notionally superior – its suits were fictionally *coram rege*: before the king himself – professional tradition owed much more to Common Pleas. It was Common Pleas that was observed by students, it was Common Pleas whose business was reported in the professional texts we know as 'Year Books', and Common Pleas whose advocates (known as 'serjeants') supplied the judges of both jurisdictions.

One way of thinking about common lawyers was as members of a small professional guild whose craft could only be picked up by living and working among them. This was probably the reason why four 'Inns', which may have started as mere lodging houses, had come to acquire some educational functions, to the point where being a member of an Inn was constitutive of professional status. Living alongside students at these 'Inns of Court' in Holborn helped generate a corporate life that centred round their training, so much so that the law's articulation was intimately linked to its transmission. The importance of this corporate life to lawyers can be inferred from the fact that invisible pressures eventually led all four Inns to adopt broadly similar structures;[12] as members had no personal financial interest in seeing that fresh students were recruited, the spread of best practice presumably owed something to a developing professional ethos.

---

[12] For some of the complexities of this process, see A. W. B. Simpson, *Legal theory and legal history: Essays on the common law* (1987), 17–52.

After the initial period of study (normally seven years), the stages of professional life involved the adoption of successive roles in the training of the rising generation: an 'utter barrister' of a given Inn was somebody entitled to stand outside the 'bar' (the rail enclosing students at the post-prandial learning exercises); a 'bencher' was a man who had given a 'reading' (a sort of lecture series on a statute), and was therefore entitled to sit down and preside. Notes on readings and the subsequent discussions appear to have had roughly the same status as notes upon courtroom events, so the shape acquired by law on these occasions had a significant effect on its development.[13] Even the true professional elite had some involvement in these practices. When lawyers became serjeants, they had to leave their Inns, but judges themselves on occasion returned in order to participate at readings. In any case, the court of Common Pleas conducted all its business under the eyes of students (who sat in a special area called the 'crib'),[14] so everything it ever did had a potentially didactic function.

What students learned was 'common erudition', the consensus of the judges, court officials, and leading advocates. This was something more complex than knowledge of precedent and less determinate than a list of rules; it was knowledge of the ways of the profession and of the possibilities inherent in courtroom procedures.[15] Outside the minds of lawyers, it was to be found, if anywhere, in books 'of years and terms' (later known as the Year Books), the law reports compiled from the later thirteenth to the early sixteenth century. These volumes appear to have started as records of discussions over 'pleading', the art of presenting a problem in such a way as to provide the judges with a single point (the 'issue') for decision. The fact that some of what was said was purely hypothetical in nature meant that the Year Books were much less a record of what the court had done than of the way in which the court was thinking; they often record *dicta* and exchanges without revealing context or the outcome of the case. Even in early Tudor times, the purpose of courtroom discussion was not so much (as we would say) to 'settle' legal questions as to allow consensus to emerge; when difficult decisions were unavoidable, they were usually made by the whole of the profession in the informal meeting of judges and serjeants referred to (because of its customary location) as the Exchequer Chamber.

---

[13] J. H. Baker (ed.), *The reports of Sir John Spelman*, 2 vols., Selden Society 93–4 (London, 1977–8), II, 124.

[14] J. H. Baker (ed.), *Readings and moots at the Inns of Court in the fifteenth century*, II, Selden Society 105 (1990), xxvi.

[15] E. W. Ives, *The common lawyers of pre-Reformation England* (Cambridge, 1983), 155–61.

It followed that the lawyers were not entirely bound by precedent. Though precedents were naturally referred to,[16] they were no more than evidence of the law, and they were never in themselves decisive. What the court did (what else could it have done?) was adjust the claims of policy, common sense, morality, and professional tradition, with special attention to the need to keep its practice as a whole consistent; the last consideration underlay the common claim that 'mischief' was to be preferred to 'inconvenience' (a technical term connoting contradiction).[17] The necessarily protean concept describing this activity was 'reason'. 'Reason' was a ubiquitous criterion, generally used quite unselfconsciously, by which the court decided what was law and what was not; doctrines 'encounter reason' were unacceptable, while arguments could be endorsed as cogent by saying they were 'reason' or 'bon reason'. The sheer pervasiveness of such expressions makes it quite hard to estimate their force; to the extent that 'reason' was constitutive of what lawyers did, it was incapable of definition by someone speaking in a courtroom setting. What can be said for certain is that its routine use within the law suggested ways of thinking about legal principles. In ordinary non-legal usage, the word could mean 'justice', and to an educated man it probably suggested *ratio recta*, the abstract rationality that underpinned all valid legal systems.[18] Even among the lawyers, these connotations were of course exploited. On one well-known occasion, a judge confronted with the claim that a privilege was 'as old as the common law' replied by saying simply that 'common law has existed since the creation of the world'.[19] If what he meant by 'common law' was reason as applied to social problems, this was a quite intelligible statement.

But the concept's main advantage was probably the scope it gave for flexibility; whenever the court was reminded that 'law is reason', or else that 'common law is common reason', the speaker had some motive for stretching or reversing legal doctrine.[20] There is no need to think about such claims as 'jurisprudence'; they were permissible rhetorical moves, not scientific theories about the system's status. Use of this type of language

---

[16] The uniquely detailed Year Book of 5 Edward IV is full of references to precedents; this suggests that their absence from more concise reports tells us more about the purpose of a Year Book than it does about professional practices (*Select cases in the Exchequer Chamber before all the Justices of England*, II: 1461–1509, ed. M. Hemmant, Selden Society 64 (1945), xxi–xxii).

[17] Norman Doe, *Fundamental authority in late medieval English law* (Cambridge, 1990), 161–3 and nn.

[18] Ibid., 108–11.

[19] *Year Books of Edward IV: 10 Edward IV and 49 Henry VI*, ed. N. Neilson, Selden Society 47 (London, 1931), 38.

[20] For an exchange of just this type involving Fortescue, see YB M 19 Henry VI, fo. 5, pl. 10.

was an important part of a sophisticated social practice; it may be, indeed, that the very success of common law considered as a practice discouraged raising the disturbing questions of second-order legal theory. At all events, fourteenth- and fifteenth-century lawyers showed very little interest in such matters. Besides whatever could be gleaned from study of the Year Books or from a layman's smattering of civilian principles, somebody curious about the status of the system was limited to a treatise literature that was already largely obsolete, deriving from the late twelfth-century 'Glanvill' (*c.* 1188) and the thirteenth-century 'Bracton' (?1225–60).

From the perspective of political thought, the interest of these pre-Year Book writers lies in their monarchist presuppositions. Within their intellectual world, the law of imperial Rome was hegemonic; to speak of English practices as 'law' was to conform them to a scheme established by the Romans. When judged by Roman standards, their picture of law was remarkably free of any impulse towards populism, that is, of any tendency to trace authority to an expression of the people's will. What was remarkable about their thought was its comparative neglect of the idea of custom. In Roman terms, the principles of King's Bench and Common Pleas were obviously examples of *ius non scriptum*, the sort of law, civilians said, that usage confirmed (*quod usus comprobavit*).[21] It was not so clear, however, that *all* examples of such law in England were covered by the Latin word *consue-tudo*, a word that normally referred to strictly *local* usage. It was, of course, accepted that *general* customs, the immemorial customs that happened to be observed throughout the realm, were part of the main body of common law doctrine, but no one seems to have believed that all of common law was general custom. Bracton does state that 'civil law', the strictly positive part of human law, 'may be called customary law (*ius consuetudinarium*)',[22] but he was slow to use the word even when talking about laws peculiar to England.

There were probably two grounds for this reluctance. The first was that custom connoted a principle developed by non-lawyers or anyway a pattern of behaviour that pre-existed recognition by professionals.[23] In England, the direction of this process was reversed, for common law largely consisted in knowledge about 'writs', which were in essence administrative procedures

---

[21] *Justinian's Institutes*, ed. P. Krueger, tr. P. Birks and C. McLeod (1987), 1.2.9.

[22] *Bracton on the laws and customs of England*, ed. G. E. Woodbine, tr. S. E. Thorne, 4 vols. (Cambridge, MA, 1968), II, 27.

[23] For a useful survey, see Donald R. Kelley, '"Second nature": the idea of custom in European law, society, and culture' in *The transmission of culture in early modern Europe*, ed. A. Grafton and A. Blair (Philadelphia, 1990), 131–72.

afforded by the monarch through his servants. The second was that custom was as it were penumbral to law proper; the classic Roman statements of the role of *consuetudo* as supplementing, or resembling, or repealing *lex* all presupposed the existence of the latter. This was probably the reason why Glanvill and Bracton set out to claim the title *lex* for the main body of their principles.

Thus Glanvill stressed that common law was in its essence royal legislation, invoking, as he did so, a notion subsequently found unEnglish. The laws that he spoke of were covered, he maintained, by the civilian principle (conventionally referred to as the *Lex Regia*) that what pleases the prince has the force of law. They had been promulgated, after all, 'on the subject of doubts to be settled in council, by the advice of magnates and with the concurring [*accedente*] authority of the prince'. He added that 'if merely for lack of writing, they were not deemed to be *leges*, then surely writing would be seen to supply to *leges* a force of greater authority than either the justice of him who decrees them or the reason of him who establishes them'.[24] It is revealing of his attitudes that he instinctively derived the justice and reason of laws from the good qualities of legislators, which meant, in this context, the king and his advisers. He may even have been consciously rejecting an alternative, more populist tradition. A civilian who was lecturing in England perhaps a decade later felt able to advance the view that 'a *consuetudo* [based on reason] can abrogate *lex*, just as *lex* can abrogate *consuetudo*. For the force of *lex*, like the force of *consuetudo*, is the will of the people. *Lex* does not derive its authority from writing.'[25] A striking and surprising clue to the political attitudes of English common lawyers was their indifference to this line of thought.

In the form in which it has come down to us, 'Bracton' inherits Glanvill's emphases. Bracton took Glanvill's reference to the *Lex Regia*, but added a further reference to the *Digest*, this time to Papinian's statement that *lex* 'is a general precept, the pronouncement of judicious men (*prudentes*) . . . the general agreement of the commonwealth (*communis rei publicae sponsio*)'.[26] His principal adjustment to his sources, a

---

[24] *The treatise on the laws and customs of the realm of England commonly called Glanvill*, ed. G. D. G. Hall (Oxford, 1993), 2.

[25] *The teaching of Roman law in England around 1200*, ed. F. de Zulueta and P. Stein (Selden Society supplementary series 8 (1990), 12).

[26] *The Digest of Justinian*, ed. T. Mommsen and P. Krueger, tr. A. Watson, 4 vols. (Philadelphia, 1985), 1.3.1. The sentence is quoted in full at *Bracton*, ii 22.

concession to the fact of noble power, was to refer to 'magnates' instead of *prudentes*:

[In England] law derives from nothing written, [but] from what usage has approved (*quod usus comprobavit*). Nevertheless, it will not be absurd to call English laws *leges*, though they are unwritten, since whatever has been rightly decided and approved with the counsel and consent of the magnates and the general agreement of the commonwealth (*communis rei publicae sponsio*), with the previous authority of the King or prince, has the force of *lex*. England has also many *consuetudines*, varying from place to place, for the English have many things by *consuetudo* which they do not have by *lex*, as in the various counties, cities, boroughs and vills.[27]

'Bracton' thus held that common law had all the characteristics appropriate to *lex*, including, crucially, royal authority, except for having been committed to writing. He thought of *consuetudo*, like the Romans, as something supplementary to law, and the whole thrust of his argument was to assert that English law was *lex*. He noted that 'custom, in truth, in regions where it is approved by the practice of those who use it, is sometimes observed as and takes the place of *lex*. For the authority of custom and long use is not slight.'[28] But this characteristic conflation of well-known civilian tags omitted any reference to *Digest* 1.3.32, where custom was explicitly regarded as an expression of the people's will.

It seems unlikely, then, that the Bractonian view of custom would have encouraged populist conclusions in anyone not predisposed to draw them. But Bracton did have a significant influence on early modern constitutionalism, if only through the statement, much quoted from the sixteenth century onwards, that 'the King ought not to be under man, but under God and *lex*, because *lex* makes the King'.[29] In the form in which it has come down to us, his treatise has three arguments that might be used to justify this doctrine. The only undoubtedly populist one was also the most absolutist; in a notoriously difficult sentence, Bracton appears to have maintained that the king was under law, on the grounds that the *Lex Regia*, by which he enjoyed his legislative power, was after all an instance of a *lex* made by the people.[30] A second, rather different argument (contained in the probably spurious 'Addicio De Cartis') was that the leading barons were in some sense the equals of the king and that they therefore had the right to 'put the bridle' on him.[31]

---

[27] *Bracton*, II 19. [28] Ibid., II 22. [29] Ibid., II 33. [30] Ibid., II 305. [31] Ibid., II 110.

Both these ideas had fairly obvious failings; the first was hardly a constraint on monarchs, while the second was a virtual invitation to opportunistic baronial rebellion. A third, however, was more promising:

The king himself ought not to be under man but under God and under *lex*, because *lex* makes the king. Let him therefore bestow upon *lex* what *lex* bestows on him, namely lordship (*dominatio*) and power. For there is no king where will rules rather than *lex*.[32]

This passage treats the rule of 'law' as built into the concept of kingship; though lordship and power are intrinsic to the office, true kingship, on this moralistic view, does not consist in arbitrary decisions. Bracton went on to offer a revealing parallel:

And that he ought to be under *lex* appears clearly in the analogy of Jesus Christ, whose vice-gerent on earth he is, for though many ways were open to him . . . he would not use the power of force but the reason of justice. Thus he willed himself to be under *lex* that he might redeem those who live under it. For he did not wish to use force but judgement.[33]

Thus kingship involves *voluntary* submission to the law; in appealing to legal procedures, one appeals to a manifestation of monarchy at its best, but one is necessarily admitting that kings are quite free to behave in a different fashion.

One reason for discussing these cryptic passages is that they were frequently quoted by seventeenth-century English politicians; another is that they disclose a crucial difference between conventional medieval thinking and early modern constitutionalism. When Bracton wrote, there was nothing extreme in the notion that *lex* in some broad sense created kingship; this principle was no constraint while *lex* received a broad interpretation allowing appropriate scope for the monarch's discretion.[34] If *lex* incorporated the tempering influence of *lex naturalis* whenever the positive law of the land might lead to some injustice, then it was virtually a truism. This was probably how Bracton understood it. His most elaborate treatment of the topic began by noting that the king, as the vicar of God on earth, enjoyed a power only to do right – the power to do injury deriving not from God, but from the devil. A king was called *rex* so long as he ruled well, 'tempering his power by *lex* which is the bridle of power'. But Bracton seems not to have felt the least discomfort at moving from insisting that the king 'ought

[32] Ibid., II 33.   [33] Ibid., II 33.
[34] Cf. John of Salisbury, *Policraticus: of the frivolities of courtiers and the footprints of philosophers*, ed. and tr. C. J. Nederman (Cambridge, 1990), 30–1.

properly to yield to *lex* what *lex* has bestowed on him, for *lex* makes him king', through noting that kings needed 'wisdom' in the exercise of justice, to speaking of discretionary 'mercy'.[35]

When 'law' became identified with a determinate body of procedures, this kind of intellectual slide became more difficult. It was thus of some importance that late medieval law grew steadily more technical and rigid. The law of the Year Books had passed from the hands of clerical judges like Bracton into the care of serjeants and ex-serjeants – professionals shaped by a lifetime devoted to practice – who naturally saw themselves as the custodians of 'forms of action'.[36] During the fifteenth century, in what may be a further sign of growing ossification, professionals started suggesting that some of their learning could be embodied in exceptionless rules. By the last quarter of the century, the Year Books frequently referred to 'maxims', 'grounds', or 'principles' of the law: fixed rules it was impossible to challenge.[37] This way of talking about law is echoed in Littleton's *Tenures* (*c*. 1480), the astonishingly lucid presentation of common law about real property that was the period's only legal treatise, and in *De laudibus legum Angliae* (*c*. 1470), Sir John Fortescue's encomium to the system. Fortescue went so far as to suggest that maxims formed the axiomatic basis of legal reasoning; their detailed application was a matter for the judges, but they could, at least in principle, be learned by intelligent laymen.[38]

From a narrowly professional perspective, this drift towards a rule-based law was doubtless an advance, but it also unavoidably encouraged appeal to extra-legal mechanisms. In any monarchy whose law is relatively rigid, the king's most senior ministers are bound to be plagued by subjects with petitions, many of whom will plausibly allege that their problems require a kind of intervention that supplements existing court procedures. A natural dynamic is likely to create new institutions by which such irregular cases can be handled. The most important English institution of this type was the 'equitable side' of Chancery. It was not at all surprising that the Lord Chancellor acquired this role: as the crown's most senior servant, he was deluged with petitions; and Chancery, his department, was a secretariat, the office charged with issuing common law writs. It was, it followed, reasonable enough that he should have the duty of helping litigants to whom the major courts denied assistance. Precisely because common lawyers were

---

[35] *Bracton*, II 305–6.
[36] S. F. C. Milsom, *Historical foundations of the common law*, 2nd edn (1981), 36.
[37] Peter Stein, *Regulae iuris: from juristic rules to legal maxims* (Edinburgh, 1966), 160; Doe, *Fundamental authority*, 156.
[38] Sir John Fortescue, *De laudibus legum Angliae*, ed. S. B. Chrimes (Cambridge, 1942), 20–4.

attached to their procedures, they seem in general not to have objected to the appearance of this jurisdiction.[39]

The exact chronology is still obscure, but the origins of the equitable side appear to be found in the later 1300s. Unlike the 'Latin' or common law side of the court, it dealt with its business in English and in writing, and its procedures could be seen as primarily 'administrative' in flavour. Its characteristic weapon, the 'sub poena' writ, enabled Chancellors to enforce their will by threatening people with substantial fines. The *subpoena* was first devised in the 1350s, when its employment by the Chancellor was barely distinct from its use by the king's council.[40] In consequence, one tenable position, articulated in the later Year Books, maintained that Chancellors had no power over the rights contended for before them, but only over the persons of the various litigants;[41] their power was not conventional jurisdiction, but only an authority to levy certain pains.

Attitudes to this use of royal power appear to have been tinged with some suspicion, especially as it first became firmly established towards the end of Richard II's reign; his successor Henry IV offered some reassurance by passing a statute in 1403 preventing Chancellors from taking action in cases that a common law judgement had settled. In 1415, a petition of the Commons complained that the Chancellor meddled in 'matters determinable by your common law', but Henry V was not prepared to offer legislation on the subject.[42] In about 1430, a litigant with a grievance could maintain that 'there may none accion be mayntened in that court that is terminable at the comyn lawe',[43] but there seems to have been no serious further attempt to regulate the Chancellor's behaviour.

As we shall see, anxiety about equitable procedures recurred in some subsequent times of political tension. For most of the fifteenth century, however, the Chancellor's equitable jurisdiction appears to have been generally accepted. It was, in principle, a 'court of conscience', applying principles of natural justice in the light of individual circumstances (the putative uniqueness of each case explains why not till 1544 did Chancellors begin to keep decree rolls).[44] Though it was largely staffed by canonists, and the Chancellor was generally a churchman, most advocates before it were members of the Inns and judges were consulted in difficult cases. The

[39] Milsom, *Historical foundations*, 82–93.
[40] W. M. Ormrod, 'The origins of the *subpoena* writ', *Historical Research* 61 (1988), 11–20.
[41] YB 27 Henry VIII fo. 15, pl. 6; cf. 22 Edward IV fo. 37, pl. 21.
[42] *Rotuli parliamentorum ut et petitiones et placita in parliamento*, 6 vols., 1767–77 vol. IV, 84.
[43] *The Armbrugh Papers*, ed. C. Carpenter (Woodbridge, 1998), 115.
[44] Franz Metzger, 'The last phase of the medieval Chancery', in Alan Harding (ed.), *Law-making and law-makers in British history* (1980), 87.

jurisdiction rested on a general consensus that there were numerous cases beyond the scope of law and that non-legal methods of conflict resolution were often perfectly appropriate; thus when Fortescue, as Chief Justice, was helping to resolve a Chancery matter, he took it as axiomatic that 'we are to argue conscience here, not the law'.[45]

It has been plausibly maintained that the best way to think about the early Chancery was simply as the royal way of offering non-legal arbitration and that the Chancellor was not restricted to special areas of expertise; what suits in Chancery had in common was simply that the Chancellor had opted to accept them.[46] There were, however, certain operations requiring cancellarial intervention. The one that bulked the largest in every gentleman's imagination was surely his role in enforcing enfeoffments to uses. One failing of the common law, in a country with an active land market, was its absolute prohibition on leaving real property by will. Most landowners evaded this by enfeoffing some part of their property to uses, in other words by granting it to a body of trustees, a group who then became its legal owners, but who held it 'to the use of' the true proprietor. This common device had the further substantial advantage that property that was enfeoffed to uses was immune from all the feudal obligations (most notably, and onerously, wardship) attending ordinary inheritance.

The appearance of a mechanism supplementing law was not in itself a recipe for conflict; a rule-bound system arguably needed the sort of flexibility the Chancellor provided. It was only if law had unlimited power to supplement itself that clashes became unavoidable. On one occasion in the fifteenth century, a claim of this type was explicitly advanced. According to Justice Yelverton, in 1468,

We will do now in this case as the Sorbonnists and civilians do when a new case comes, for which they have no law before . . . they resort to the law of nature which is the ground of all laws, and according to that which is suggested by them to be more beneficial for the commonwealth, etc., they do, and so now will we do.[47]

This statement assumed some importance in early seventeenth-century speculations precisely because it was virtually unique. The idea was in no way remarkable (it can be found in local custumals),[48] so the fact that it found little echo in the Year Books is interesting and significant;

---

[45] Quoted in J. H. Baker, *An introduction to English legal history*, 3rd edn (1990), 124.
[46] J. B. Post, 'Equitable resorts before 1450', in E. W. Ives and A. H. Manchester (eds.), *Law, litigants, and the legal profession* (1983), 70.
[47] Doe, *Fundamental authority*, 71.   [48] Ibid., 72.

judges were evidently quite reluctant to characterise their actions in these terms.

The problem with Yelverton's dictum was that it left no space outside the judges' jurisdiction; the danger of ending up with such a theory may indeed have discouraged reflection on the system's character. The only picture of law that judges needed was one that created a gap just large enough between procedures and their justification to offer some scope for revision of existing principles. Fortescue's practice as a judge provides us with an interesting example. He once robustly told the court that:

> Sir, the law is as I have said, and has been always since the law was first begun, and we have many courses and forms, which are held for law, and have been held and used because of reason, although the same reason may not be readily remembered; but by study and labour it may be found; and if any such course or form is and has been used contrary to reason, it is no harm to amend it.[49]

The idea of law as rational thus seems to have functioned for Fortescue in two quite different ways: both as a guarantee that rules had reasons; and as a licence to amend those rules where they were found unsatisfactory.

The ambiguity was a fruitful one; by the early years of Henry VII's reign, a law that was thought of as reason could even be seen as in some sense approving the Chancellor's extra-legal operations. Petitioners to Chancery could encourage a certain conflation by making their appeal to 'reason and conscience', and judges could pick up this kind of language. Thus in a Chancery case involving fraud, a common law judge could remark that it was 'good reason and conscience that the party will be restored [to his possessions], and if he cannot be by common law, then it is good learning (*bon science*) that he should be by conscience'.[50] The very development of the *subpoena* as an instrument for controlling a feoffee was known to be partly attributable to judges; it was not until the time of Henry VI that a *subpoena* could be sent to the heir of a feoffee 'and on that point *the law* was changed by Fortescue Chief Justice'.[51]

Unfortunately for historians, Fortescue left no treatise that addressed this sort of question. The writings he did leave behind him were not attempts at legal theory, but pamphlets stimulated by a crisis in the nation's politics, of which only one, *De laudibus legum Angliae*, acquired an extensive readership. The importance of these writings to our story has little to do with Fortescue's intentions; as the rest of this chapter will show, Fortescue's

---

[49] YB 36 Henry VI fos. 25–6, pl. 21.   [50] YB P 7 Henry VII fo. 11, pl. 2.
[51] *Reports of cases by John Caryll*, ed. J. H. Baker, 2 vols., Selden Society 115–16 (1998–9), II, 396.

mind was nothing if not fertile, but his strictly political theory was not so very different from Bracton's – which is to say that it was moralistic and altogether focused on the monarch. What readers found in Fortescue, however, was unimpeachable authority – the word of a Chief Justice – for a range of near-republican opinions.

II

Fortescue worked for almost twenty years (1442–61) as Henry VI's Chief Justice of King's Bench, but all his writings were produced in the unsettled period that followed, when he was titular Lord Chancellor and one of the exiled Margaret of Anjou's most prominent advisers. Besides some slight or fragmentary pieces, they included three contrasting major works: *De natura legis naturae* (*c.* 1463), a tract on the succession, which he probably wrote in political exile in Scotland; *De laudibus legum Angliae* (*c.* 1470), his panegyric on the laws of England, which he undoubtedly composed in France; and the interesting untitled memorandum that has been known since 1885 as *The Governance of England* (*c.* 1474), which was advice addressed to Edward IV after the final triumph of the Yorkists. Fortescue's works have often been presented as if they were examples of 'common law thinking', but it would be more cautious to describe them as pamphlets written by a common lawyer. Both *De natura* and *De laudibus* were after all the products of a member – perhaps, to some extent, the effective leader – of a faction in a desperate situation. As might have been expected, the view of law that he produced was shaped by the needs of his party, so much so that he demonstrably altered his position about the system's range of competence.

In the political debate in which he was engaged, the principal question at issue was whether females could transmit a claim to inherit the throne: the Yorkists were descended through two women from Edward III's second son; the Lancastrians were descended from his third son, John of Gaunt, but all the intervening links were male. Though he had earlier employed a range of arguments, Fortescue's best-known writings concentrated on this particular consideration. The earliest of his pamphlets, *Of the title of Edward earl of March*, was written in early 1462. Here he appealed to English 'law and custom' to show the invalidity of any claim transmitted through a woman, but he also maintained that even if it were granted that Henry IV was simply a usurper, this point had long ceased to be relevant. His grandson's title was confirmed by four undoubted facts: God's permission, the approbation of

the papacy, the consent of the people of England (including the Yorkists),
and long possession of the kingly power.[52]

But Fortescue later abandoned these ideas. By the time he composed
De natura, which was probably in 1463, Edward was more secure upon his
throne and arguments from possession had ceased to favour the Lancastrians.
It made much more sense to adopt a legitimist standpoint, to argue,
that is, that no power on earth could weaken or efface king Henry's title. He
therefore chose to make a sharp distinction between the natural principles
deciding succession to kingship and the internal laws of particular nations:

> Before the time of Moses, there was no human *lex* besides some *consuetudines*
> brought in by men in certain territories, which could not have begun the kingly
> office, since *consuetudo* only grows from repeated acts and length of time, so that it
> could not have begun the rank of king; and the decrees (*constitutiones*) of princes,
> which only bind subjects, could not have set up (*constituisse*) the kingly eminence
> which knows no superior . . . nor ought the ordinances of men by which some
> of them are erected into kings deservedly be called decrees but acts of the law of
> nature.[53]

Fortescue's motive for this change of heart was surely a simple political
calculation; Lancastrians needed arguments that could not be eroded by prescription. But this expedient shift of ground had long-term consequences,
not least in requiring his picture of law to place a novel emphasis on custom.

As a Lancastrian partisan, Fortescue must have feared the claim that
unwritten law, as declared by royal judges, was evidence of nature's law for
England (and therefore that the judges had the authority to validate the
Yorkist usurpation). A claim of this sort was implicit in everyday practice,
for when the common lawyers spoke of 'reason', it is unlikely that they
knew if they were appealing to natural or positive law; the tendency of this
whole way of talking, not least in the judicial work of Fortescue himself, was
to erase or blur the difference. But Fortescue the Lancastrian propagandist
had opted to depict all legal rules as *either* natural *or* positive. As the former
type of rule was universal – a part of every nation's legal system – it followed
that legitimate rules peculiar to England must all be positive in character.
The consequence of making a rigid distinction between natural and man-
made principles was thus to force the bulk of English law into the category
of *consuetudo*.

[52] *Sir John Fortescue, Knt, his life, works and family history*, ed. Thomas Fortescue, Lord Clermont, 2 vols.
(London, 1869), 1, 69*. For a similar but more detailed account of these works see Alan Cromartie,
'Common law, counsel and consent in Fortescue's political theory' in *The fifteenth century* 4 (2004),
45– 67.
[53] Fortescue, *Works*, 1 72–3.

De laudibus put this theory to work. When Fortescue was trying to show that English law was better, at least for the English, than any comparable legal system, he confidently stated that all of its rules were natural, or, custom, or statute. For the purposes of a comparison, the law of nature could be disregarded, on the grounds that its rules were identical everywhere (he noticeably did not try to argue that judges in England interpreted it better).[54] The wisdom of statute could be relied upon, because the statutes had been made by the assent of the whole realm gathered in parliament.[55] Everything else was custom, and English custom's suitability was shown by the fact that no conqueror had changed it, not even the Romans 'who judged almost the whole of the rest of the world by their laws'.[56]

Thus Fortescue's need to distinguish 'laws of nature' from more parochial legal principles affected the way he presented those legal procedures peculiar to England. But his decision to cram legal rules into the category of *consuetudo* demanded, in turn, an unusual picture of custom. As we have seen, an obstacle to seeing common law as *consuetudo* was that it was, if anything, the custom of the lawyers, not the people. Fortescue managed to avoid this problem by leaving out any suggestion that unwritten but positive law had been produced by popular consent; his claim that English custom was superior rested entirely on the observation it had never actually been altered. But though he gave no comfort to populist claims about the ultimate origins of custom, his later readers tended to ignore what doubtless seemed to be an oversight. This was because they read his views within the context of a larger doctrine, a theory of the character of English monarchy.

This doctrine of course has a label that was given it by Fortescue himself: *dominium politicum et regale*. All three of his main works – the 'Yorkist' *Governance* as much as the earlier 'Lancastrian' *De natura* – gave somewhat disproportionate attention to the idea that the best rule is not '*regale tantum*' (merely regal), but what he called '*politicum*' as well; and that 'regal and politic lordship' is beneficial to the lord as much as to his subjects. The nub of the distinction between the two forms appeared to be that regal and politic rulers could neither tax nor legislate without the consent of their people. He presented these ideas as 'incidental'[57] to the ideas advanced in *De natura*, but they were clearly central to his opinions about government; *De laudibus* referred four times to *De natura*'s text, each time to its proof that 'regal and politic' rule was in the personal interests of the monarch.[58]

[54] Fortescue, *De laudibus*, 38.   [55] Ibid., 40.   [56] Ibid., 38.   [57] Fortescue, *Works*, I 63.
[58] Fortescue, *De laudibus*, 26, 34, 80, 90.

In both *De laudibus* and *The Governance*, the contrast was considerably enlivened by an appeal to patriotic feeling. He broke with the tradition of Glanvill and Bracton by treating the *Lex Regia* as something alien. In Fortescue's opinion, it was acceptance of the principle *quod principi placuit legis habet vigorem* that accounted for the misery of France. The unfortunate French peasantry had been impoverished by the demands of royal tax collectors. In prosperous England, however, security of property explained the country's wealth, its military prowess, and the existence of a class of honest, independent jurymen. It seems unlikely that these claims were just a tactical expedient. An exiled propagandist had every incentive to argue for moderate government, but the first third of *The Governance*, addressed to his victorious enemies, was devoted to exactly the same point.

There can be little doubt, then, that Fortescue was genuinely committed to the ideal of regal and politic lordship. But the precise sense of the phrase is difficult to grasp, partly because its classic definitions, which dwell on the need for consent to laws and taxes, are subtly but significantly misleading. Scholars who think of common law as rules worked out by popular agreement have naturally jumped to the conclusion that Fortescue valued consent for its own sake. The truth is slightly different, for though consent was certainly important to his thought, the type of consent that he valued was consent in parliament, consent that was a sign that kings had taken appropriate counsel.

Appreciation of this point is crucial to a proper understanding of Fortescue's political position, but demonstrating it is not straightforward. One reason his work is so easy to misread is that he introduced his terms in a confusing context. The first appearance of the phrase was part of his attempt to meet a dangerous objection. As he was trying to maintain that the succession to a monarchy should be determined by the law of nature, he had to show that monarchy itself was natural. Like any Christian who supported kingship, he needed to explain away a well-known Old Testament passage: Samuel's description of 'the law (*ius*) of the king who is to rule over you', who would 'take your fields and your vineyards and your best olive groves, and give them to his servants'. As such behaviour contravened the principle of doing as one would be done by, this 'law of the king' was in conflict with natural law.[59]

Fortescue's answer was the standard one that Samuel's remarks were a prediction of the behaviour of the tyrant Saul, not a description of the rights of kings in general. Though Saul was not strictly entitled to act oppressively, God punished the ungrateful Israelites by giving him the sort

[59] Fortescue, *Works*, 1 74.

of powers that allowed him 'to do wrong, freed (*absolutus*) from all bonds of human law';[60] what made God's act a punishment was that other forms of monarchy existed. It was in the context of his proof that not all kings enjoyed the powers of Saul that Fortescue first mentioned *dominium politicum et regale*. He noted that Aquinas (1224–74) had praised two different types of government, *dominium politicum* and *dominium regale*, and that Giles of Rome had spelled out the distinction. Fortescue cited Giles as having stated that 'he is head of a regal government, who is so according to the laws which he himself lays down, and according to his will, but he is head of a political government, who governs the citizens according to the laws which they have established'.[61]

He went on, however, to qualify this statement:

But that there is a third kind of government, not inferior to these in dignity and honour, which is called the political and regal, we are not only taught by experience and the histories of the ancients, but we know has been taught in the teaching of the said St Thomas also. For in the kingdom of England the kings do not make laws, nor impose subsidies on their subjects, without the consent of the Three Estates of that Realm. Nay, even the judges of that kingdom are all bound by their oaths not to render judgment against the laws of the land, although they should receive the commands of the sovereign to the contrary. May not then this form of government be called political, that is, regulated by the administration (*dispensatio*) of many . . . ?[62]

Here Fortescue was making a rather narrow point: there could exist a government with regal *and* political elements, and England was an obvious example.[63] He went on to mention two further instances: imperial Rome was part political because the imperial office was not hereditary; the Israelite theocracy was part political because its ruling magistrates, the judges, were bound to account for their actions to the people.

Both of these facts were taken from the Thomist work he cited, the treatise *De regimine principum*, a text he understandably believed to represent the teachings of Aquinas. He had no way of knowing that this was a composite work by dissimilar authors. The opening eighteen chapters, which seem to have been composed by Thomas himself, were firmly monarchist in sympathy, but the rest of the work, which is usually said to have been produced by Ptolemy of Lucca (*c.* 1264–1327), is markedly republican in feeling. Fortescue took material from both portions. Thus he noted the view, expressed in the opening chapters, that monarchy was preferable because it resembled God's rule in his creation; but he also cited Ptolemy's

---

[60] Ibid., 1 83.   [61] Ibid., 1 77.   [62] Ibid., 1 77.
[63] Felix Gilbert, 'Sir John Fortescue's dominium politicum et regale', *Medievalia et humanistica* 2 (1944), 92–3.

opinion that sinless human beings would be ruled politically.[64] The notion of *dominium politicum et regale* was amongst other things a brave attempt to reconcile such inconsistencies.

He found the word *politicus* in Ptolemy's material, where it was derived from *polus* meaning 'many', and used, of course, to mean 'republican'; the simplest distinguishing feature of republics was that they were controlled by more than one person. In Ptolemy's view, all types of legitimate ruler were bound to govern for the public good, but a further distinguishing feature was that republican regimes were strictly bound by law, unlike their regal counterparts, who were allowed to exercise discretion.[65] Not even monarchs were allowed to levy unnecessary taxes, so Samuel's famous prophecy was not a description of kingship, but of a despotism.[66] Thus a political regime had to respect its subjects' property, but a regal one could tamper with property rights whenever the collective good made this desirable. All these ideas are found in Fortescue. The aspect of Ptolemy's theory that he did not accept, perhaps because he simply failed to grasp it, was Ptolemy's claim that communities could flourish without a single person's leadership.

Though Fortescue mentioned other forms in passing, he fully accepted the teaching of Aquinas that monarchy was the most natural; at times, indeed, he came close to suggesting that no community could do without it.[67] He seems to have thought of republican Rome as a sort of mutant kingdom, in which a pair of consuls shared the functions of the king; this was doubtless why he leapt to the conclusion that the Republic had collapsed 'by division that fille betwene the consuls for lakke of an hed'.[68] Given this firm commitment to government by kings, the role that he found for the many was necessarily auxiliary. Thus Fortescue invoked the role of the Blessed, who were to rule as 'senators' with Christ, and play a part in judging men and angels.[69] His clearest single statement on the subject was his advice to merely regal kings:

But you, O king, who rules regally, make it your business, as far you can, to rule politically also. For polity (*politia*) is so called from *polus*, which is plurality, and *ikon*, ministration (*administratio*), as it were a system of government served (*ministratum*) by the advice of many. Manage the common weal of your realm by the advice of many.[70]

---

[64] Fortescue, *Works*, 1 72, 84; cf. Thomas Aquinas, *Opuscula omnia necnon opera minora*, ed. J. Perrier, 3 vols. (Paris, 1949), 1, 227, 286–7.
[65] Aquinas, *Opera minora*, 1 362.   [66] Ibid., 1 332.
[67] Fortescue, *Works*, 1 80; *De laudibus*, 30; *The governance of England: otherwise called The difference between an absolute and limited monarchy*, ed. Charles Plummer (Oxford, 1885), 112.
[68] Fortescue, *Governance*, 347.   [69] Fortescue, *Works*, 1 84.   [70] Ibid., 1 85.

He went on to adduce the way in which 'the kingdom (*regnum*) of the Romans, long regulated by the counsel of three hundred and twenty senators, grew from very small into the greatest empire in the world'; and the contrast between Solomon, who prayed for a teachable heart, and Rehoboam who 'despising the advice of the wise, lost more than ten parts of his father's kingdom'. The moral of this story was that 'the opinion of a king, whoever he may be, is not sufficient to rule a kingdom, without the support of counsellors, even though that king were son of Solomon'.[71] Where kingdoms were concerned, at any rate, political rule was rule employing counsel.

This principle explains the next two chapters, in the first of which even political kings were informed it was sometimes fitting to govern regally. Not every case was covered by existing 'statutes and customs', so those that remained were left to the royal discretion. What was more, *epieikeia* required the occasional use of an absolute power (*potestas absoluta*), 'not indeed so that [a ruler] might release (*solvere*) a perfect law, but rather so that he might himself better fulfil the law of his kingdom by reason of the law of nature, which is natural equity'.[72] The only limit on this power was a significantly worded warning: 'let a king ruling politically be careful that he does not enact new laws without consulting the chief men of his kingdom, repudiating laws of his own kingdom that are pregnant with justice'.[73] The following chapter went further. He noted that 'there are however very many other circumstances in which it is sometimes permissible and expedient for a king ruling politically to use a regal violence (*regaliter saevire*) on certain of his people'.[74] In case of a rebellion or invasion, it might be perfectly acceptable for monarchs to act as Samuel had predicted, taking their children and their property in order to provide for public safety. Precisely because kingship had been ordained to serve the common good, kings had a right to over-ride their subjects' privileges.

This was the passage that led S. B. Chrimes to abandon the Victorian conception that Fortescue believed in 'constitutional monarchy' (defined as monarchy 'controlled by some other co-existent power'). Chrimes thought it better to describe such kings as 'limited', that is, as 'absolute except in certain spheres delimited by law and custom'.[75] But even this modified formula is misleading, because it suggests that the different spheres were clearly demarcated: that there was an established list of limitations on political monarchs. In fact, from God's perspective, political and regal kings

---

[71] Ibid., I 85. [72] Ibid., I 85. [73] Ibid., I 86. [74] Ibid., I 86.
[75] S. B. Chrimes, *English constitutional ideas in the fifteenth century* (Cambridge, 1936), 339 n.

had virtually identical rights and duties. Neither could wilfully remove the subject's property; both were enjoined to use *epieikeia* whenever a general law appeared deficient in a particular case; both could and should ignore the law in an emergency. The difference between the two was captured by a simple principle: that a political ruler was strictly obliged to take counsel whenever doing so was practicable. Where taking advice was impracticable, this principle had a corollary: political kings should act like regal ones, that is, they should use their discretion, guided by their perception of the common interest. Fortescue showed no interest, however, in distinguishing the numerous occasions when acting on advice was practicable from the minority when it was not.

On this interpretation, then, the role of Fortescue's concept of the political was to identify and to commend a form of monarchy that took advice. The notion that obsessed him was not consent but counsel; members of parliament were councillors, and the need for parliamentary approval for royal legislation was really just an aspect of the need to take advice. This reading is supported by his later treatises, at least when their details are carefully examined. *De laudibus* praised the written laws of England precisely because of the counsel they embodied. In merely regal kingdoms, the king's laws were sometimes damagingly self-interested, while at other times

> by the inadvertence of princes of this type and by the inertia of their counsellors, their statutes are issued so ill-advisedly that they deserve the name of corruptions rather than of laws. But the statutes of England cannot arise in this way, since they are issued not only by the will of the prince, but also by the assent of the whole realm, so that they cannot do that harm to the people or fail to secure their advantage. It must be supposed that those laws are filled with foresight, too, and wisdom, since they are not issued by the foresight of one or of a hundred counsellors only, but of more than three hundred chosen men – such a number as the senate of the Romans was ruled by.[76]

The passage is not easy to translate, but Fortescue's main emphasis is clearly on the wisdom of a process; the chapter heading states that 'Here he shows with what solemnity statutes are issued in England.' He may conceivably have thought that the wisdom of the process derived from the representation of various interests, but this idea is nowhere unambiguously stated.

Analogous points can be made about another famous passage: the trenchant opening of *The Governance*:

---

[76] Fortescue, *De laudibus*, 40 (translation much amended).

Ther bith ii kyndes off kyngdomes, of the wich that on is a lordship callid in laten *dominium regale*, and that other is callid *dominium politicum et regale*. And thai diversen in that the first kynge mey rule his peple bi suche lawes as he makyth him selfe. And therfor he mey sett uppon thaim tayles and other imposicions, such as he wol hym self, with owt thair assent. The seconde kynge mey not rule his peple bi other lawes than such as thai assenten unto. And therfore he mey sett uppon thaim non imposicions with owt thair owne assent.[77]

At first sight this looks like an unambiguous statement of the supreme importance of popular assent, but further research casts doubt upon this theory. Fortescue went on to explain that 'this diversite is wel taught by Seynt Thomas . . . but yet it is more openly tredid in a boke callid *compendium moralis philosophiae*, and sumwhat bi Giles [of Rome]'.[78] The best place to look for his underlying theory is thus in the *Compendium* he referred to: an edifying work by Roger of Waltham (fl.1300) whose main concern was with the kingly virtues. Here we find a most significant *lacuna*; both Giles and Thomas maintained that political rule is rule in accordance with laws laid down by others, but Roger, who was said to make the essence of the point 'more openly', appears to have no teaching on the subject.

There were, however, two important questions that Roger discussed more openly than Thomas. One was the monarch's attitude to private property. In a passage the Chief Justice must have found congenial, Roger gave an interesting exposition of the idea (derived from Seneca) that 'under a good king, the king possesses power (*imperium*); individuals property (*dominium*)'.[79] But Roger's presentation of this view did not involve him making a distinction between two different forms of government; he never suggested some kings have a right to take away their subjects' property that is denied to other, more limited monarchs. It seems more likely Fortescue was thinking of Roger's thorough treatment of the advantages of taking counsel, a passage that is found in the same chapter as the account (which Fortescue had drawn on in *Of the title of Edward earl of March*)[80] of how a usurpation can become legitimate. Fortescue later quoted a tag that Roger used in his discussion, the admittedly commonplace claim that there is safety in much counsel: *ubi multa consilia, ibi salus*.[81] Though the idea arose quite naturally from Roger's treatment of the kingly virtues, it was a plausible intellectual bridge from his more moralistic emphases to Fortescue's own stress on institutions.

[77] Fortescue, *Governance*, 109.   [78] Ibid., 109.
[79] Bodleian Library, Laud Misc. MS 616, fo. 35v.   [80] Fortescue, *Works*, I 69*.
[81] Fortescue, *Governance*, 144. Roger actually has it in the form 'salus est ubi multa sunt consilia' (Laud Misc. MS 616, fo. 55r). The discussion of usurpation is at fos. 51v–52.

This left one final problem. Fortescue needed to explain why certain kings were more constrained than others. *De laudibus* accounted for this fact by pointing to the origins of kingship: Fortescue postulated that 'no people ever by its own will embodied itself as a kingdom' except in order to possess 'more safely' themselves and their possessions.[82] It followed that a monarchy created by the people enjoyed a strictly instrumental power, a power that had 'issued from the people' for 'the protection of the law, and of their bodies and goods'. The point was illustrated by an interesting version of a near-universal simile:

> As in the body natural . . . the heart is the source of life, having in itself blood which it transmits to all the members of the body, whereby they grow and live, so in the body politic the purpose of the people is the source of life, having in it the blood, namely political forethought for the interest of that people, which it transmits to the head and all the very members of the body, by which the body is fed and grows.[83]

The safeguard that the people instituted was not so much consent *per se* as the provision of 'political forethought'.

During the early modern period, this passage was extensively misused; it is probably not fanciful to see its influence behind Locke's claim that government's sole purpose was to protect 'lives, liberties and estates'. But nothing could be more remote from the tenor of Fortescue's thinking. The idea that certain governments were founded by consent was advanced to explain an exceptional situation: the existence of some monarchs who had an *obligation* to take counsel. All of the earliest monarchies had been set up by force, and all of the successors of such monarchs enjoyed the powers of their ancestors. Thus the fact that neither St Louis 'nor eny of his progenitors' had ever taxed 'without the assent of the iii estates' did nothing to erode the principle that they were kings 'dominio regali'.[84] Nor did the fact that England had frequently been conquered – a point that Fortescue had stressed when dealing with the antiquity of custom[85] – affect its original status as a political and regal lordship.

III

Within the history of legal theory, the importance of *De laudibus* rests largely on its concept of a 'maxim'. Fortescue may have been the first to think that English law could be described, in principle, as a deductive system;

---

[82] Fortescue, *De laudibus*, 34.   [83] Ibid., 30.
[84] Plummer, *Governance*, 113.   [85] Fortescue, *De laudibus*, 38.

he was also unusual in stating, if only for political purposes, that the majority of English *leges* ought to be classified as *consuetudo*. These were significant shifts in attitude. But Fortescue did not maintain that the 'maxims' that could summarise the system were the unmediated fruit of custom; nor did he anywhere suggest that the customs that he spoke of were the expression of the people's will. He did believe that custom resulted from reiterated actions,[86] but the actions that he was referring to were probably the actions of the judges; he gave no sign, in other words, of going beyond the Year Book commonplace that the usage of the judges made the law. His theory's subsequent career as one of the sources of English populism would surely have astonished its inventor.

Fortescue's true affinity was not with populists, but with earlier Aristotelians like Giles, for whom the limitations on the monarch were as it were internal to their view of monarchy. Fortescue's interesting innovation was his idea that an appropriate council – a carefully constructed *institution* – was an objective safeguard against royal misbehaviour; but his stress upon parliament's wisdom had nothing to do with regard for the will of the people. His emphasis on counsel was not, indeed, particularly likely to favour the long-term survival of parliaments and parliament-like bodies. A permanent 'privy' council, such as the *Governance* had recommended, was after all better equipped to use government experts than cumbersome occasional assemblies. As it happened, this was roughly what happened in France. It was perfectly compatible with 'absolutism' to hold that monarchs were obliged to govern in their subjects' interests; to stick to the law of their kingdoms so long as doing so was beneficial; to live off an ordinary income provided by inalienable lands; and to refrain from taxing without the assent of national assemblies. All of these propositions were endorsed by Jean Bodin (1530–96), who was certainly the thinker with the deepest influence on the small group of English absolutists. All that an 'absolutist' really needed was something that Fortescue's theory provided: the right to make exceptions to the usual legal rules, whenever, in the king's sincere opinion, the good of the whole realm demanded them.

As it happens, the practical weakness of safeguards of Fortescue's type was to receive a perfect illustration soon after he composed the *Governance*. In 1474–5, his newly acquired master, Edward IV, managed to tax without consent through a 'benevolence', a nominally voluntary levy. A further benevolence followed in 1481–2. Though Richard III curried favour with his subjects by passing a statute against this unpopular practice, it

---

[86] Fortescue, *Works*, I 72.

proved impossible to stop by act of parliament. In 1491–2, Henry VII had no difficulty in raising yet another of these levies.[87] Only in 1525, when Henry VIII was rebuffed in his quest for an 'Amicable Grant', was such an exaction successfully resisted. Even then, we have no real evidence that the objections that were raised were constitutionalist in character.[88]

The only source recording such objections, the chronicle composed by Edward Hall, was a work by an intelligent common lawyer who probably started to write his account at least a decade later. Hall stated the complaints in credible detail, mentioning that the London corporation appealed to Richard's statute, while the clergy maintained that 'never king of England did ask any man's goods but by an order of the law'.[89] But he also recorded that Wolsey was able to reply that 'when it was moved in council, how to make the king rich, the king's council, and especially the judges said, he might rightfully demand any sum by commission, and that by the assent of the whole council it was done'.[90] As Hall approached the topic from a lawyer's point of view and as he clearly disapproved of Wolsey, it is interesting that he refrained from comment. He did not suggest that the judges had failed in their duty, nor did he hint that Wolsey had somehow frightened them into submission.

It would have been unreasonable to do so. Down to the 1520s, the judges remained essentially crown servants who had a special expertise in certain established procedures. Whatever their political opinions, it is unlikely any of them believed that government was tied to those procedures in every conceivable future situation. They doubtless knew of Fortescue's ideas, but nothing in Fortescue's writings enabled them to claim that any particular liberties enjoyed by Englishmen should be immune from royal interference. In short, they had developed no criterion that could define a privileged sphere within which kingship was controlled by judges. That was to be the achievement of St German.

---

[87] R. Virgoe, 'The benevolence of 1481', *English Historical Review* 104 (1989), 25–45.
[88] G. W. Bernard, *War, taxation and rebellion in early Tudor England* (Brighton, 1986), 150–3.
[89] *Hall's chronicle* (1809), 698, 696.   [90] Ibid., 700.

CHAPTER 2

St German's world

If the last chapter's arguments are basically correct, then fifteenth-century England had a legalistic culture, but not, in the narrower sense of the word, a 'constitutionalist' politics. The achievement of the Tudors was to extend the reach of law still further, until it threatened to subsume all aspects of the role of monarchy. In doing so, they built upon what foreigners saw as an enviable position. As Giovanni Botero (1544–1610) reported in 1592,

> In England the nobility possess few castles or strong places environed with walls and ditches, neither have they jurisdiction over the people. The dignities of dukedoms, marquesses and earldoms are no more but mere titles, which the king bestoweth on whom he pleaseth, and peradventure they possess never a penny of revenue in the place from whence they take their titles.[1]

This had probably long been Italian conventional wisdom. Almost a hundred years before, a Venetian had reported, with the same implied surprise, that territorial names were meaningless: 'the jurisdiction, both civil and criminal, and the fortresses remain in the hands of the crown'.[2] Italian travellers were not wrong to seize upon this simple observation, for nothing about England was more striking than the sheer feebleness of noble power. After the battles of Bosworth and of Stoke (in both of which the rebels enjoyed the aid of foreign mercenaries), the military capacity of even the greatest magnates appears to have been rather unimpressive; from the great Cornish rising of 1497 to the rebellion of the Northern Earls in 1569, every significant revolt depended on appealing to 'the commons'. But as the monarchy itself possessed no standing army, its largely unchallenged grip upon the nation can hardly have depended on the threat of violence. A much more significant asset than any fortresses was its monopoly of jurisdiction.

[1] Giovanni Botero, *The travellers breviat* (1601), 18–19.
[2] *A relation or rather a true account of the island of England*, tr. C. A. Sneyd, Camden Society 37 (1847), 37; cf., in Mary's reign, *Two Italian accounts of Tudor England*, tr. C. V. Malfatti (Barcelona, 1953), 48.

The steady intensification of English government depended on exploiting this advantage, enhancing royal capacity to interfere in the localities
by further involving the gentry in the processes of law. There is room for
disagreement about the timing of the crucial shift, but at some time in the
sixteenth century, the magistrate replaces the 'good lord' as the main pillar
of the social order. Though it makes sense to speak of the two Henrys as
making use of an 'affinity', a network of personal supporters at least analogous to that of a great nobleman, Elizabeth seems to have had no need
of such an instrument; the impersonal legal relation created by commissions of the peace (a relation that the government could terminate at will)
was evidently a better way of mobilising local notables. This great political
success had cultural preconditions, for it required some gentlemen, some
of the time, to interest themselves, unpaid, in trivial administrative duties.
In acting as the agents of the royal government, they doubtless bolstered
their prestige in their communities, but 'prestige' is simply a label for what
needs to be explained: the attractiveness of the idea of a particular type of
social role. Part of the explanation must be that a conception of a good
magistrate became an element of their conception of what it was to be a
gentleman.

Such attitudes enjoyed support from English humanists, but humanist
writers, by their own account, were simply building on existing values. Thus
Sir Thomas Elyot's *The boke named the governour* (1531) was a humanist
advice-book aimed at amateur crown servants. Though Elyot expressed
admiration for Erasmus's advice to Charles V, *On the education of a Christian
prince* (1516), his focus of attention was not the prince himself, but 'sundry
mean authorities, as it were aiding him in the distribution of justice'. Elyot
was able to assume that formal legal training was the appropriate coda to a
gentry upbringing, so much so that he worried about those philistines who
'put their children at the age of 14 or 15 years old to the study of the laws
of the realm of England'.[3] He was not alone in hating the bad Latin and
worse French encountered in a legal education. In about 1540, one writer
wanted lawyers to have knowledge of 'other sciences and arts liberal', and
drew up a scheme to raise their cultural level by codifying common law
in Latin.[4] The point of this whole project was that regard for common
law was a non-humanist phenomenon that humanist thinkers needed to
adapt to.

A little later in the century, some humanist-influenced people were less
ambivalent. A handbook published in 1555, *The institution of a gentleman*,

---

[3] Sir Thomas Elyot, *The boke named the governour*, ed. H. H. S. Croft, 2 vols. (London, 1883), I, 25,
132.
[4] British Library Royal MS 18 A 50 (quotation at fo. 7v).

stressed that it was 'a very meet office for a gentleman to be called to the ministration of the law, and so according to his knowledge therein to proceed in the degrees of the same'. Rather than being idle, the gentry should 'be studious in the laws . . . and although they practise not the law so called, yet ought they to have knowledge therein for the better furtherance of their neighbours' just causes'.[5] The author, whose profession is not difficult to guess, was probably going a little beyond conventional opinion, but legal knowledge of a basic type does seem to have been regarded as increasingly important. In the good-humoured dialogue called *Cyvile and uncyvile life* (1579), it is the spokesman for uncivil life who advocates a training at the Inns, but even his adversary concedes that 'both the laws civil and common are studies most excellent', like 'all learnings that tend to action in the state'.[6] Such works simply took it for granted that education at the Inns was in itself a mark of gentry status. Laurence Humphrey's *The nobles, or of nobility* (1561) and John Ferne's *The blazon of gentrie* (1586) were dedicated to the Inner Temple. The world William Worcester imagined, in which nobility derived from knowledge and 'practique of law', appeared to have become reality.

The growth of constitutionalist habits was obviously closely related to this much larger, more mysterious process; it is easy to see that a group of social actors who grasped their own authority as legal would have been ready to project this view on monarchy. What none of this really explains, though, is why such people reverenced *common* law: that is, the professional learning of the judges, embodied in the usage of King's Bench and Common Pleas. The law that local magistrates devoted much time to enforcing was not, for the most part, common law but statute; as a later common lawyer was to put it, 'a justice of peace is a statute creature, and ought to act no farther than the statutes empower him'.[7] Whatever the lawyers were prone to imply, the points of law tackled in learning exercises had virtually no relevance to problems that a justice might encounter. At the time Sir Thomas Elyot was writing, it could not even be maintained that common law proper had growing social impact. For much of the first four decades of the Tudor period, the business of the two great courts was actually declining, in part because of vigorous competition from other, more informal types of justice. Wholesale replacement of these courts was probably unlikely, but the professional elite was threatened by external interference. The subsequent development that needs to be explained is how

[5] *The institution of a gentleman*, 2nd edn (1568), sig. Cv, C3.
[6] *Cyvile and uncyvile life* (1579), sig. C3v.
[7] B. H. Putnam, *Early treatises on the practices of justices of the peace in the fifteenth and sixteenth centuries*, Oxford studies in social and legal history 7 (Oxford, 1924), 55.

their esoteric erudition survived, recovered, and acquired a new centrality, a status as the science of the English common weal.

I

The story begins in the reign of King Henry VII, a foreign-educated prince with an extremely tenuous hereditary claim. In spite of some imaginative visual propaganda, Henry appears to have been unsuccessful in fostering dynastic loyalty. The surname Tudor still meant very little and the frequent reversals of fortune of the last half-century had evidently encouraged some pragmatic attitudes. The Venetian quoted earlier had been told that 'should there be no direct heir, and the succession be disputed . . . heretofore it has always been an understood thing, that he who lost the day lost the kingdom also'.[8] As late as 1504, a well-informed group could discuss the next succession without so much as mentioning Henry's children.[9]

The king's peculiar governmental style did little to improve the situation. He chose not to involve his leading subjects in the shared enterprise of war with France; he also left no evidence that he possessed the temperament or presence to build authority by personal contact. Instead, he terrorised the titled peerage (and even the spiritual lords) by forcing them, as individuals, to enter into bonds for good behaviour. As the Spanish ambassador put it, King Henry was 'not a great man', partly because his character was marred by avarice.[10] There seems no good reason for doubting the ancient consensus that the spirit of his rule was legalistic, that he distrusted magnate power and set out to control it by threatening nobles with financial ruin, and that his favoured ministers were able bureaucrats, often of fairly modest origins. It is consistent with this general picture that his single most important innovation was the institution of a 'Privy Chamber', a private space within the court within which he conferred with his closest advisers, most of them secular or canon lawyers.[11]

If this traditional picture is broadly justified, it tends to confirm that the peerage, his principal victims, lacked either the will or the power for resistance. One anecdote suggests a marked deficiency in both. In 1497,

---

[8] *Relation*, 46.

[9] G. R. Elton, *The Tudor constitution: documents and commentary*, second edn (Cambridge, 1982), 5–6.

[10] *Calendar of letters, despatches, and State Papers relating to the negotiations between England and Spain*, 11 vols. (1862–1916), I, 178.

[11] David Starkey, 'Intimacy and innovation', in Starkey (ed.), *The English court: from the Wars of the Roses to the Civil War* (Harlow, 1987), 71–118.

at the height of the reign's most serious popular rising, Lord Bergavenny and the earl of Suffolk were sharing the same bed while on campaign when they were told the rebels were approaching. In this crisis Bergavenny blurted out 'if a man will do aught what will ye do now it is time', but was frustrated by the earl, who foiled his incipient treason by stealing his shoes. Perhaps the most interesting aspect of this ludicrous vignette was not so much Bergavenny's remark as Henry's subsequent response to his behaviour. When Henry learned the details (which curiously was not till 1506), he briefly sent his subject to the Tower, but his real revenge took the form of a fine for retaining imposed by King's Bench in the autumn of 1507.[12]

This use of law was typical of Henry's style of rule, especially at the end of his long reign. So far as we know, his contemporaries and subjects found his objectives odiously transparent; he seems to have been the target of the remarks in More's *Utopia* (1516) about the heaping up of gold and the abuse of law to work injustice.[13] But legalistic tyranny is hardly worth the candle unless two demanding conditions are fulfilled. The first is that 'law' as a process must be under the tyrant's control; the second is that 'law' as an ideal must have some genuine purchase on his subjects. Both these conditions seem to have obtained. The informative Venetian who noted the royal monopoly of justice believed that 'every officer of justice, both civil and criminal, has the power of arresting anyone, at the request of a private individual';[14] he also thought that 'if the king should propose to change any old established rule, it would seem to every Englishman as if his life were taken from him', adding, however, that 'I think the present King Henry will do away with a great many, should he live ten years longer.'[15]

Here the Venetian was perhaps mistaken, for Henry had little incentive to revolutionise the legal system, which he was more than capable of using to promote his interests. A rational king had no motive for damaging his courts by mounting an assault upon their most revered procedures. A much more likely future involved the indefinite extension of various extra-legal institutions, 'conciliar' jurisdictions whose power could be invoked when common law was found too cumbersome. It was therefore not surprising that the reaction that occurred immediately after his death involved the

---

[12] C. G. Bayne and W. H. Dunham (eds.), *Select cases in the council of Henry VII*, Selden Society 75 (1956), xxix–xxx.
[13] Sir Thomas More, *Utopia: Latin text and English translation*, ed. G. M. Logan, R. M. Adams, and C. H. Miller (Cambridge, 1995), 88–90.
[14] *Relation*, 33.   [15] Ibid., 37.

abolition of some 'bye-courts', apparently largely concerned with revenue matters.

According to the council register, these were courts 'of none authority', which ultimately threatened the king's 'right and title . . . for the king's highness cannot be entitled by record but by matter of record in court of authority'. The register further explained that 'all such matters had afore such by-officers be void and of none effect by the king's laws'.[16] At this point, we seem to have entered a fairly familiar world, a world in which the king must act by record. But closer scrutiny reveals a less familiar picture. To begin with, it appears significant that the important statements here are all tautologies: transactions not by record are not by record; things done outside or contrary to the common law are done outside or contrary to the common law. No principled reason was offered why the conception of a court of record should not be extended so as to include these novel jurisdictions. A crucial argument for abolition was a worry of a rather humbler nature about the 'great losses to our sovereign lord of such profits as should grow to his highness by means of his seals in his courts of record if the law might have his due course'.[17] It is hard to exclude the suspicion that common law here was essentially a 'course' – that is, a mode of government procedure – successfully stifling the growth of other courses.

The clearest commentary upon this posthumous reaction is a text by its most celebrated victim: the lawyer Edmund Dudley's *The tree of commonwealth*. Dudley was a distinguished common lawyer, enjoying an 'oracular legal reputation in fifteenth-century Gray's Inn',[18] but he had been imprisoned, and would be executed, as one of the old King's most rapacious servants. The reporter John Spelman described him as a man who did not 'pay any attention to the common weal but only to fulfilling the covetous intent of the said King'.[19] A famous petition from prison confessed to this charge in circumstantial detail,[20] but it is not so interesting, for present purposes, as his extremely moralistic treatise. Worries about this work's 'sincerity' hardly detract from its significance. A man who composes a book under sentence of death may see it as his testament (a final statement of his true beliefs) or as an opportunity to plead for clemency (a chance to tell the authorities what they would like to hear). But whether *The tree of commonwealth* was an expression of Dudley's own convictions or of the attitudes that he imputed to his gaolers, it offers a uniquely detailed picture of what could be implied by 'commonwealth'.

[16] B. P. Wolffe, *The crown lands 1461 to 1536: an aspect of Yorkist and early Tudor government* (1970), 162–3.

[17] Wolffe, *Crown lands*, 163.   [18] Baker, *Spelman*, II 49.   [19] Ibid., I 175.

[20] C. J. Harrison, 'The petition of Edmund Dudley', *English Historical Review* 87 (1972), 82–99.

'Commonwealth' was a word (or phrase) that captured the suggestions of the Latin word (or phrase) *respublica*. This fortunate coincidence explains its prevalence; not everyone who spoke of 'common weal' was influenced by humanist conceptions, but this everyday vernacular expression must greatly have eased the reception of classical ideas. Its use was bound to reinforce a view of government as instrumental to the common good. As William Worcester had noted, in a passage that explicitly expounded Cicero, *respublica* was 'the grounde of welfare and prosperite of alle maner peple'; an officer in a *respublica* was 'governoure of a comon profit'.[21] It is suggestive that the term gained currency as a political slogan at roughly the time of the duke of York's claim to the throne.[22]

During the sixteenth century, the notion played a growing role in legal argument. As early as 1514, the lawyer and law-publisher John Rastell included some remarks upon the subject in the sententious preface of a volume of reports:

What thing so ever that common weal be it must needs be the thing which of himself is a good thing and whereunto some goodness naturally is annexed sithin that God which is the foundement of all goodness hath naturally given to every man a common and an universal love and zeal to the same or else it were not digne nor worthy to be called a common good thing or a common weal but rather a common evil.[23]

Though Rastell was a scholar and a friend of Thomas More, there is no need to think of such ideas as 'humanist'; they were the common possession of educated Tudor Englishmen. There is no reason to believe that Dudley had much interest in 'good letters', but his treatise presupposes the same pattern of conceptions.

The tree of commonwealth's noteworthy features include an edifying Augustinian piety; it is interesting to see a pre-Lutheran layman stress that 'if we will rejose ourselves of our good deeds or works, let us reiose only in God and his grace, whereby and by whom we have done it, and not in the good deed'.[24] But what is most suggestive in his views about the church is the way they were set in the context of his 'commonwealth' ideas. The clergy surface in his text as a potential problem to be dealt with, and as a problem, what is more, demanding the personal attention of the monarch: 'if there be any manner of grudge between his subjects

---

[21] *Boke of Noblesse*, 56–7.
[22] C. Coleman and D. Starkey, *Revolution reassessed: revisions in the history of Tudor government and administration* (Oxford, 1986), 20.
[23] *Liber assisarum*, ed. Johannes Rastell (1514), 'Prologus'.
[24] Edmund Dudley, *The tree of commonwealth*, ed. D. M. Brodie (Cambridge, 1948), 72.

of the spiritualty and his subjects of the temporalty for privilege or liberties that were a great help to [public concord] to have it stablished and
reformed: and no man can do it but the prince'.[25] Still more suggestively,
Dudley was hostile to clergymen who wielded any form of secular power.
It is true he had a motive to dissociate himself from Henry VII's ordained
bureaucrats, but it is nonetheless a little startling to find him seriously
recommending that 'none of them be in any temporal office, nor executors thereof, for thereby most commonly is destroyed the church and the
office'.[26]

Opinions like these were a part of the background to the reforms of
the next generation. Dudley cast further light upon this background by his
attention to the role of law. If only for practical reasons, he thought that the
monarch should 'suffer [his nobles] not to revenge their own quarrels, old
or new, by force or by violence. For if men be at their own liberties therein
beware the prince in a while.'[27] Although he presumed that his master was
perfectly free to set up new procedures, he nonetheless advised him to work
through the existing mechanisms:

> Let it not be seen that the prince himself, for any cause of his own, enforce or
> oppress any of his subjects by imprisonment or sinister vexation, by Privy Seal or
> letters missives, or otherwise by any of his particular counsellors, but to draw them
> or extract them by due order of his laws. For though the matter be never so true
> that they be called for, though their pain or punishment should be sorer by the
> due order of the law, yet will they murmur and grudge by cause they are called
> by the way of extraordinary. Wherefore the most honourable and sure way for the
> prince to have his right of his subjects, to punish them for their offences, shall be
> by the due order and course of his laws. And let the subjects never be letted and
> interrupted by his writing, tokens, messages, or commandments to his judges or
> other officers to have the straight course of his laws.[28]

This was not a constitutionalist position. The king was advised against
selfish interference with the law; it is not at all clear what Dudley would have
said in circumstances when some legal rule conflicted with royal perceptions
of the public interest. The king was certainly adjured to moderate the law
in applying 'the great number of penal laws and statutes made in his realm
for the hard and strait punishment of his subjects'.[29] Unlike Fortescue,
moreover, Dudley seems not to have believed in any variety of *obligation*,
however unenforceable and 'moral', that bound a monarch, other things
being equal, to do such things as take appropriate counsel or stick to the
provisions of positive law.

[25] Ibid., 41.   [26] Ibid., 25.   [27] Ibid., 41.   [28] Ibid., 36–7.   [29] Ibid., 41.

Thus Dudley thought about the law as one of the tools that a monarch could make use of. He was, however, writing at a moment at which this tool's utility was steadily increasing. As the work of J. H. Baker has established, the period 1490 to 1550 saw common law escape from the ossification imposed by its limited list of accepted procedures.[30] One likely explanation of this creativity was that the senior court, King's Bench, was strongly motivated to be ingenious. The bread-and-butter business of the lawyers, litigation over debt and real estate, was in effect reserved for Common Pleas. At a time when they faced growing competition from the more flexible conciliar courts, there was thus a structural reason why King's Bench officers were inclined to be aggressively inventive.[31] In particular, they encouraged the development of the 'bill of Middlesex', a streamlined procedure based upon the fiction that the defendant lurked (*latitat*) within that county. But the most telling symptom of the novel attitudes was the extension of the use of 'action on the case', an action that could be employed whenever the judges decided a wrong had been suffered for which no other remedy existed.[32] The legal potential of 'case' had been grasped by fifteenth-century lawyers – as Justice Fairfax noted in 1481, 'the *subpoena* will be less often used than today if we pay attention to such actions on the case'[33] – but vigorous exploitation of its capacities was delayed until the following century. As the developments concerned were relatively slow and only cumulatively lucrative, it may be unduly reductive to think of judges and officials as driven by their personal financial interests. Some part was presumably played by the disinterested conviction that common law supplied the means to serve the common good.

All explanations of these shifts are largely speculative, but it seems reasonable to suppose that the increased self-confidence of lawyers had something to do with the rise of legal printing. Considering the small size of the profession (there were probably approximately fifty barristers), the early sixteenth-century common lawyers produced and consumed large quantities of print. The earliest printed edition of Littleton's *Tenures* had been produced in 1481, at roughly the same moment as the earliest abridgement of the statutes. Thereafter legal printing was both continuous and copious; by about 1560, the industry had published at least 260 Year Book volumes.[34]

---

[30] See especially the important monograph disguised as the introduction to vol. II of J. H. Baker (ed.), *The Reports of Sir John Spelman*, 2 vols., Selden Society 93–4 (1977–8).
[31] Marjorie Blatcher, *The court of King's Bench, 1450–1550* (1978).
[32] J. H. Baker, *The Oxford history of the laws of England*, 12 vols. (Oxford, 2003–), VI, 751–3.
[33] P 21 Edward IV, f. 23, pl. 6 quoted in A. K. Kiralfy, *The action on the case* (1951), 9.
[34] H. S. Bennett, *English books and readers 1475 to 1557* (Cambridge, 1970), 81–3.

Print gave the law a fixity it previously lacked, and therefore helped encourage the illusion that it could be recovered from works of reference. If any book compounded the illusion, it was Anthony Fitzherbert's great *Magnum abbreviamentum* (1514–17), a work much later supplemented by Sir Robert Brooke's similar *La graunde abridgement* (1573). These *Abridgements* were essentially commonplace books of a type that many lawyers manufactured; for want of other finding aids, they assembled notes and extracts from the Year Books under loose alphabetical headings. A scholarly lawyer would treat them as a fallible guide to the sources, but there was an obvious temptation to use them as a simple substitute. Over time, they were bound to promote the idea that the Year Books were in essence a repository of rules, the somewhat unwieldy expression of a 'system' that could in principle be reconstructed in a more visibly coherent form.

This appears to have been Fitzherbert's own belief. In the Preface to his *La novel natura brevium* (1534), his updating of the classic guide to writs, he echoed Fortescue's idea that law should be treated by students as based upon maxims:

In every art or science there are certain rules and foundations, to which a man ought to give credit, and which he cannot deny. In like manner, there are divers maxims and fundamentals in the knowledge of the common laws of the land which a man ought for to believe very necessary for those who will understand the same law, especially at the beginning of their studies; for upon these fundamentals the whole law doth depend.[35]

Thus law was in essence a teachable body of knowledge. If lawyers became more ready to suppose that they possessed the expertise to settle social problems, it may be because their self-conception changed. A student of the common law was not just being socialised into a way of thinking; he was acquiring access to a list of propositions that was potentially, at least, a science of the English common weal.

In due course, this new attitude would motivate some lawyers to undertake heroic feats of learning, but even in the short term, it seems to have had some practical results. Its impact was felt first in church-state relations. Not every sign of tension in this sphere was necessarily a sign of anticlericalism. It was, no doubt, the judges' role to know whatever precedents existed of kings resisting papal interference; Chief Justice Huse (d. 1495) was often to be cited as if he were a proto-Anglican, but he was merely doing his job when he recalled, in 1485, that Edward I 'had written to the Pope by advice of his council that he had no persons above him in temporal affairs, seeing

---

[35] Anthony Fitzherbert, *The new natura brevium* (1652), sig. A4.

he was immediately subject to God'.[36] In the next generation, however, the lawyers became increasingly aggressive whenever they believed that clerical practice conflicted with the public interest. Thus when Dudley referred to 'privilege and liberties' that monarchs ought to 'stablish and reform', he was probably thinking of something that struck the visiting Venetian as a scandal: the abuses that arose from sanctuary.[37] The first step in the crown attack upon this privilege took place in 1486, when judges decided that only the king could grant a right of sanctuary for treason.[38] This judgement was politically expedient, but even in the absence of government pressure, the leading common lawyers appear to have favoured reform. By 1495, Huse was holding that kings were unable to grant such privileges, apparently on the grounds that they were not for 'common profit'.[39]

A number of comparable straws in the wind suggest a shift in attitudes towards the English church. J. H. Baker has detected 'a widespread belief' among early sixteenth-century litigants 'in the superiority of the secular over the ecclesiastical wherever the former had some colour of jurisdiction'.[40] Their expectations drew support from the behaviour of the common law judges, especially their growing willingness, from the 1480s onwards, to invoke the penalties for *praemunire*. The statute of *praemunire* was originally aimed at those who needlessly appealed to Rome, but early Tudor judges systematically applied it in conflicts with the bishops' courts in England.[41] The consequence was a sharp decline in church court business. In 1482, the diocesan court at Canterbury heard 636 cases, but forty years later, in 1522, it handled just 223.[42] The clash of jurisdictions led judges into some surprising claims; they were prepared, for instance, to say that a denial of the duty to pay tithes was just an error, not a heresy.[43] This was an understandable position, but it involved a serious encroachment on church authority in points of doctrine.

The same point arose in the case of Dr Standish (1515), who was accused of heresy for saying that God's law allowed lay trial of criminal clergy (a practice that had been condemned by the recent Lateran council). The reporter John Caryll noted with approval that Standish had said that this practice 'may well stand with the laws of God and with the liberties of Holy Church . . . for they are things which advance the public weal of the whole realm, which public weal ought to be favoured in all the laws in the world'.[44]

---

[36] H 1 Henry VII, fo. 10, pl. 10.   [37] *Relation*, 34–5.   [38] Ives, *Common lawyers*, pp. 245–6.
[39] Baker, *Spelman*, II 342.   [40] Ibid., II 66.
[41] R. H. Helmholz, *Roman canon law in Reformation England* (Cambridge, 1990), 25–6.
[42] Ibid., 31.   [43] Edward Coke, *The third part of the institutes of the laws of England* (1644), 42.
[44] J. H. Baker (ed.), *Reports of cases by John Caryll*, 2 vols., Selden Society 115–16 (2000), II, 684.

He also noted Henry VIII's pronouncement that 'we are king of England, and the kings of England in times past have never had any superior but God alone'.[45] What was most interesting in this affair was not so much Henry's own statement (which from his own perspective was a response to clerical aggression) as the significance, in Caryll's mind, of Standish's appeal to public welfare. Four years later, Caryll reported Chief Justice Fyneux's view that privilege of sanctuary for more than forty days was 'something so much in derogation of justice and against the common weal of the realm that it is not allowable by the law'.[46] Fyneux even maintained that 'the law of God and the law of the land are all one. Both the one and the other prefer and favour the common and public weal of the land.'[47]

It must have been this growing professional confidence that made the experience of Wolsey so traumatic. At exactly the moment that lawyers had come to think that common law defined the common weal, they faced a brilliant Chancellor who seems to have despised them. Wolsey's alleged contempt for law and lawyers may well have been partly a matter of perception, but the perception is well documented. The parliament which he summoned in 1523, and which he encouraged to busy itself with 'commonwealth' reforms, addressed itself to 'the abusions of the temporal law'.[48] Though his promise to teach a delinquent common lawyer 'the new law of Star Chamber' was a joke reserved for private correspondence,[49] contemporaries could and did notice a marked high-handedness. The articles against him at his fall were to state that 'the said Lord Cardinal hath examined divers and many matters in the Chancery, after judgement thereof given at the common law' and that 'the same Lord Cardinal hath not only given and sent injunctions to the parties [in common law suits approaching judgement], but also sent for your judges, and expressly by threats commanding them to defer the judgement, to the evident subversion of your laws, if the judges would so have ceased'.[50] As modern scholarship has pointed out, these charges give a rather misleading impression; to begin with, his most important innovations were not in fact in Chancery but Star Chamber. The current orthodoxy holds that Wolsey was irascible, and possibly too ready to listen to plaintiffs, but that his conduct as a judge was 'at best creative, at worst competent'.[51] Above all, it stresses that Wolsey's

[45] Ibid., II 691.   [46] Ibid., II 708.   [47] Ibid., II 711.

[48] John Guy, 'Wolsey and the parliament of 1523' in *Law and government under the Tudors*, ed. C. Cross, D. Loades, and J. J. Scarisbrick (Cambridge, 1988), 8.

[49] *Letters and papers, foreign and domestic*, ed. J. S. Brewer, 23 vols. (1862–1932), II, 1539.

[50] Baker, *Spelman*, II 79.

[51] John Guy, *Christopher St German on chancery and statute*, Selden Society. Supplementary series 6 (1985), 69.

judicial performance was similar to that of his precursors and that of his successor Thomas More (who actually handled more business and who was faced with similar objections). The somewhat hysterical character of the complaints against him thus seems to tell us less about the Chancellor's behaviour than it does about the assumptions of his critics.

The most important fruit of the new confidence of common lawyers was probably a new approach to uses. Hostility to uses was partly the result of policies adopted by Henry VII. Henry's lawyers were keen to wring money from the various perquisites arising from his status as the country's feudal landlord; they therefore had a motive for systematic study of the 'prerogative', that is, of the king's feudal rights. In consequence, his reign saw 'an attempt to organise a coherent body of legal doctrine . . . around the so-called statute *Prerogativa Regis*'.[52] Any such body of doctrine was bound to see the use as an obnoxious form of tax evasion.

During the 1520s, the Inns of Court developed two approaches to this problem, both of them based on fairly strong assumptions about the system's rationality.[53] One sought to assimilate the use into the common law. It noted that uses were based upon trust, that any rational system would allow for such arrangements, and that the word 'use' had appeared in statutes. The other approach set out to turn the clock back. It treated the use as an alien intrusion into a previously harmonious system, an intrusion, what was more, that was essentially a fraud. The most elaborate statement of this view was Thomas Audley's reading of 1526. In Audley's view,

notwithstanding that these uses were at first imagined for good purpose . . . nevertheless for the greater part they were pursued and connived at of ill purpose, to destroy the good laws of the realm, which now by reason of these trusts and confidences is turned into a law called conscience, which is always uncertain and depends for the greater part upon the whim (*arbitrement*) of the judge in conscience; by reason whereof no man is certain of knowing his title to any land.[54]

Audley's words appear remarkably courageous, so much that one wonders if the text that we possess may not post-date the fall of Thomas Wolsey. But if his line of argument attacked the minister, it nonetheless promoted the monarch's interests. He had shown that there existed a body of respectable opinion that was quite happy to support the crown in its pursuit of fiscal feudalism.

The government's subsequent actions revealed a willingness to grasp its opportunity. In 1535, when Thomas Audley was Lord Chancellor and

---

[52] J. M. W. Bean, *The decline of English feudalism, 1215–1540* (Manchester, 1968), 236.
[53] For the next three paragraphs, see Baker, *Spelman*, II *195–203*.   [54] Ibid., II *198*.

Thomas Cromwell Master of the Rolls, it obtained a judicial decision to the effect that land enfeoffed to uses could not be passed by will. It seems to have won acceptance for the simple argument that 'it is against the nature of land to pass in such a way'.[55] As the decision cast in doubt the basis of much private property, it gave the king the leverage that he needed to force his parliament to pass the unpopular Statute of Uses (1536). This measure confirmed the status of property rights based on wills, but only in return for a concession: that the beneficial interest created by the use was henceforth to be treated as an ordinary title to land. In other words, the common law swallowed the use, while the government destroyed, at least for a moment, a well-established method of circumventing feudal obligations.

The episode is an important one, if only as an excellent example of the potential of the law for the legitimation of royal policies; but it is less significant to our story than an extraordinary work produced in the years preceding this alliance. One fruit of the resentment that Wolsey occasioned may well have been a new determination, in energetic figures such as Audley, to show that law could benefit the monarch. Another, more subtle, response was Christopher St German's *Doctor and student*.

II

St German's *Dialogus de fundamentis legum Anglie et de conscientia* was published in Latin in 1528, when its author was approaching seventy; the English version published two years later bore the title *Hereafter followeth the first dialogue in English betwixt a doctor of divinity and a student in the laws of England of the grounds of the said laws, and of conscience* (1530). As the title suggests, this remarkable book set common law within a larger context: the Doctor's role was to expound the viewpoint of a moral theologian, while the Student explained the practices of lawyers. Its instant and lasting commercial success owed much to a triumph of literary skill over rebarbative material. St German not only devised for himself an enviably transparent English prose, but also found ways of exploiting the dialogue form for his expository purposes: when he allowed his speakers to endorse each other's points, he artfully concealed much repetition; when he permitted them to disagree, he economically conveyed the existence of a problem that he was still unable or reluctant to resolve. He thus achieved great clarity on points of principle, while veiling many aspects of their detailed application.

<hr>

[55] Ibid., I 229.

St German was so old and his thinking so complex that it is difficult to believe that all of the latter developed under Wolsey. There is no doubt, however, that the *First Dialogue* was topical. As the prologue to the Latin version put it, 'the present dialogue shows what are the principles or grounds of the laws of England, and how conscience ought in many cases to be formed in accordance with those same principles and grounds'; he also promised to discuss 'when English law ought to be rejected or not on account of conscience'.[56] He may have had further objectives, especially in relation to the church, but this was a fair summary of his central argument; what he was offering to provide was an intellectual framework within which the Chancellor's powers could be debated. The striking innovation of this framework was the centrality he gave to custom.

St German thought that English law derived from six distinguishable sources: the law of reason, the law of God, general customs, maxims, particular customs, and statutes. These categories looked conventional enough, but an investigation of their contents reveals a novel intellectual structure. It was one thing to admit, with Fortescue, that the vast bulk of common law was custom; it was another to work out in detail the implications of this principle. The achievement of St German's legal theory was to align a picture of the law as *consuetudo* with the behaviour of his profession. Where Fortescue thought of natural law as a short list of rules that was a part of every legal system, St German set out to expand the concept's range so it approximated to the common lawyer's 'reason'. As the English version noted,

It is not used among them that be learned in the laws of England to reason what thing is commanded or prohibit by the law of nature and what not: but all the reasoning in that behalf is under this manner: as when anything is grounded upon the law of nature: they say that reason will that such a thing be done and if it be prohibit by the law of nature they say it is against reason or that reason will not suffer that it be done.[57]

Fortescue's law of nature was what St German chose to call 'the law of reason primary', prohibiting such outrages as 'murther that is the death of him that is innocent, perjury, deceit, breaking of the peace and many other like'.[58] This law did not 'command or prohibit anything save what any man who has reason, as a mere man, knows ought to be commanded or prohibited by reason'.[59] St German also recognised, however, a 'law of

---

[56] Christopher St German, *St German's doctor and student*, ed. T. F. T. Plucknett and J. L. Barton, Selden Society 91 (1975), 3.
[57] Ibid., 31–3.   [58] Ibid., 33.   [59] Ibid., 33.

reason secondary general', supplemented by a 'law of reason secondary particular'. The former was deduced from the existence of 'the law or general custom of property',[60] an institution humans had invented, but one that was diffused throughout the world. This law explained why theft was illegal in England. The 'law of reason secondary particular' consisted in deductions from 'divers customs general and particular' and 'divers maxims and statutes ordained in this realm'.[61]

St German's 'secondary law of reason general' was thus a rational response to a universal custom; his 'secondary law of reason particular' was a rational response to a more local positive law, in this case to the customs of the English. He seems to have been anxious to discourage the idea that every feature of the law of England could be worked out *a priori* from natural principles. The Student stressed that 'the law of reason is not of such strength and virtue that a knowledge of it would be equivalent to a knowledge of all English law', and the Doctor was made to reaffirm the point:

Although many things in English law are derived from the highest practical reason, nevertheless thou dost not pretend that the law of England can be said to be in all respects the law of reason (as some would maintain) . . . For as thou hast said above [some laws] can be changed by a statute made contrary to them; and thou affirmest that something that can be changed was certainly never the law of reason primary.[62]

Thus 'reason' in the broad judicial sense was not to be confounded with reason in the narrow sense of primary natural law. St German was perfectly happy to admit that actions inconsistent with natural law proper were altogether illegitimate, but he thought it was hard to distinguish such rules from rules that were based on unwritten but positive law, that is to say, on customs and on maxims.

In St German's view, most English legal rules consisted in 'customs of old time used through all the realm, which have been accepted and approved by our sovereign lord the King and his progenitors and all their subjects'; these were, he thought, 'the customs that properly be called the common law'.[63] St German stressed that though such general customs were not unreasonable, they could not 'be proved only by reason' and they could all be changed by parliament.[64] The important implication was that the general customs had just the same kind of authority as statutes. The same could be said, more strikingly, of 'maxims'. As we have seen, appeals to 'grounds' or 'maxims', principles that were taken to be unchallengeable, were a feature of late fifteenth-century Year Books. To Fortescue, who had

[60] Ibid., 33.   [61] Ibid., 35.   [62] Ibid., 74–5.   [63] Ibid., 45–7.   [64] Ibid., 57

supplied the only existing theory of their status, they offered a way for amateurs to know a legal system that was derived from natural law, custom, and statute.

St German alluded to Fortescue's treatment of maxims, but his own thoughts on the subject were rather different. To him, they were more than pedagogic aids; they were themselves examples of positive law 'of the same strength and effect in law as statutes be'. There was no need to offer 'any reason why they were first received for maxims'; the practice of assigning 'reasons or consideration why such maxims be reasonable' was an expository device that was meant to assist future lawyers 'to the intent that other cases like may the more conveniently be applied to them'.[65] The only real distinction between a maxim and a general custom was that the general customs 'were known through the realm as well to them that be unlearned as learned', while maxims were 'only known in the king's courts or among them that take great study in the law of the realm'.[66] St German thus asked his readers to accept that much of English law was really custom – that is, 'accepted and approved by the king and his progenitors and all their subjects' – in spite of the fact that its details were virtually unknown to all but the most learned of the lawyers. This incoherence was the price he paid for severing the common law proper from reason. His probable motive for taking this step emerged from his discussion of the role of Chancery.

III

In the early Tudor period, the court of Chancery was still the forum in which the Chancellor, acting for the king, displayed the monarchical virtue of *epieikeia*: a concept defined by St German, conventionally enough, as 'no other thing but an exception of the laws of God or of the law of reason from the general rules of the law of man: when they by reason of their generality would in any case judge against the law of God or the law of reason'. He gave his definition a more unusual twist by suggesting that 'if any law were made by man without any such exception expressed or implied it were manifestly unreasonable'.[67] In the context of the kind of disagreements occasioned by Wolsey's behaviour, this view of *epieikeia* cut both ways. On the one hand, it suggested the need for an additional jurisdiction that could correct the common law's procedures by reference to natural principles; but on the other it implied that equitable exceptions were actually a part of positive law.

[65] Ibid., 59. [66] Ibid., 59. [67] Ibid., 97.

St German was not a mere government hack, but his defence of Chancery was seen by the authorities as helpful. *Doctor and student* was put out by Thomas Berthelet, the royal printer, and Wolsey offered him a post as Master of Requests.[68] As Wolsey should have realised, however, St German was, in some respects, politically unreliable. Wolsey might have been struck, to begin with, by a significant silence. The little tract *Diversite de courtz* (1523), the only printed treatise on the subject, had echoed a well-known passage in the Year Books by drawing a distinction between an 'ordinary' and 'absolute' power, the former being exercised in line with positive law, the latter 'in all the ways by which the truth of the matter can be known'.[69] The notion of an 'absolute' power was obviously politically suggestive, but St German never mentions the idea.

This silence was consistent with the important fact that *Doctor and student* placed limits on the Chancellor's intervention. Not every rule with unfair consequences required correction from outside the system. The judges were entitled, for example, to disregard the letter of a statute where it evidently frustrated the intention of its makers. At times, the law had made express provision for the inequities that it created; a maxim that had unfair consequences could be corrected by another maxim. But even on occasions when the rigour of the law had generated manifest unfairness, the Chancellor's power to step in was not unlimited; the tag *nullus recedat a cancellario sine remedio* – let no one return from the Chancellor without a remedy – was thus at best misleading. The sphere from which the Chancellor was excluded was extensive. Given that the very existence of property depended on convention, it was entirely reasonable that human convention should govern its transmission (by demanding, for example, that payment should be proved by a receipt). What was more, there was a public interest in the stability of property rights which justified the rule that a common law judgement could not be overturned by Chancery.[70]

These principles were defensible enough, but as St German readily admitted, they offered rather little practical guidance. It was unclear when common law could deal with a problem on its own and when the Chancellor should act by issuing a *subpoena*. He summed up the whole question by remarking that

---

[68] Guy, *St German on chancery*, 14.

[69] *Diversite de courtz* (London, 1523), sig. A6v; YB T 9 Edward IV, fo. 14, pl. 9. The YB uses the word 'ordinata', which suggests that the distinction is theological in origin.

[70] St German, *Doctor and student*, 107.

thus it appeareth that sometime a man may be excepted from the rigour of a maxim of the law by another maxim of the law. And sometime from the rigour of a statute by the law of reason and sometime by the intent of the makers of the statute, but yet it is to understand that most commonly where any thing is excepted from the general customs or maxims of the laws of the realm by the law of reason the party must have his remedy by a writ that is called *subpoena*.[71]

This was an interesting taxonomy of ways of relaxing the rigour of positive law, but it cast no light at all upon the question of whether a *subpoena* could be issued in any given unprecedented case.

Perhaps the most interesting feature of St German's legal theory was his acceptance of the implication that the learning surrounding the issue of *subpoenas* was in effect a part of positive law. He noted that 'it is oft times argued in the law of England where *subpoena* lyeth and where not: and daily bills be made by men learned in the law of the realm to have *subpoenas*'. These arguments left no trace in the common law records because they were conducted before the Chancellor. St German nonetheless believed they had a legal status, for

the Lord Chancellor must order his conscience after the rules and grounds of the laws of the realm, in so much as it had not been much inconvenient to have assigned such remedy in the Chancery upon such equities for the vii ground of the law of England, but for as much as no record remaineth in the kings court of no such bill ne of the writ of *subpoena* or injunction that is sued thereupon, therefore it is not set as for a special ground of the law, but as a thing that is suffered by the law.[72]

The distinction between common law and Chancery equity was thus dependent upon record-keeping.

This aspect of St German's thought was greatly clarified in two of his unpublished later writings: the 'Replication of a Serjeant at the laws of England' and 'A little treatise concerning writs of *subpoena*'. The former was a brief attack on *Doctor and student*'s treatment of the subject, taking the form of dialogue between the Student and an unnamed Serjeant. Although it is anonymous, it was written in a style much like St German's, with what looks like a touch of parodic over-statement in its depiction of the Serjeant's views. But its authorship is not of much importance, compared to the picture that it gives of the position against which St German had defined his jurisprudence. Underlying the serjeant's objections was a conception of the law as a fixed repertoire of remedies by which the king himself was

---

[71] Ibid., 103.   [72] Ibid., 105.

limited; the *subpoena* could not possibly be valid because it could not
be located in registers of writs.[73] A remarkable statement grounded this
position in the restrictions on the monarchy:

I marvel much what authority the Chancellor hath to make such a writ in the king's
name, and how he dare presume to make such a writ to let the king's subjects to
sue his laws, the which the king himself cannot do right wisely, for he is sworn the
contrary, and that is said *hoc possumus quod de jure possumus.*[74]

Some of the Serjeant's arguments would doubtless have occurred to any
writer making a comparable case. He insisted, for example, that any resort
to discretion diminished law's predictability 'and the more uncertain that
the law is in any realm, the less and the worse it is for the common weal of
the realm'.[75] The Chancellor appealed to conscience, but conscience was
'a thing of great uncertainty, for some men think if they tread upon two
straws that lie across, that they offend in conscience'.[76] Rather less obvious,
perhaps, was his depiction of the lay reformer:

I may liken my Lord Chancellor, that is not learned in the laws of the realm, to him
that standeth in the vale of the White Horse, far from the horse, and beholdeth
the horse; and the horse seemeth and appeareth to him a goodly horse, and well
proportioned in every point. And then, if he come near to the place where the
horse is, he can perceive no horse, nor no proportion of any horse.[77]

The Serjeant was giving expression to the thought that proper understanding of a detail of the law depends on a grasp of its function within
an ordered whole. The germ of this idea was the common law saying that
'mischief' was to be preferred to 'inconvenience'; its fruits would ultimately
include a prominent theme of Burke's conservatism. The Serjeant used it
to maintain that the apparent flaws within his system were the delusions
of the ill-informed and that existing remedies were adequate to cope with
any wrong, 'for the law commandeth all thing that is good for the common
wealth to be done, and prohibiteth all thing that is evil and that is against
the common weal'.[78] He even asserted that 'if ye therefore follow the law
truly, ye cannot do amiss, nor yet offend your conscience, for it is said, *quod
implere legem est esse perfecte virtuosum* (to fulfil the law is to be perfectly
virtuous)'.[79] The Student made the obvious objection that the law that the
scriptures referred to was in fact the law of God, but the Serjeant affirmed,
undaunted, that 'the law of man is made principally to cause the people to
keep the law of God; and so me seemeth that if ye follow the law of the

---

[73] Guy, *St German on chancery*, 102.   [74] Ibid., 100.   [75] Ibid., 101.   [76] Ibid., 101.
[77] Ibid., 102.   [78] Ibid., 102.   [79] Ibid., 103.

realm truly, ye shall not need to leave the law for conscience'.[80] He went on to complain that 'these uses began by an untrue and a crafty invention'[81] and that the result of Chancery interference was 'such an uncertainty that no man can be sure of any lands . . . but every man's title shall be by this mean brought into the chancery'.[82]

The Serjeant may be a straw man, but straw men are not very useful to a polemicist unless they resemble a possible opponent; as we shall see, some later common lawyers appear to have held a similar position. What was more, the views imputed to this common law extremist were actually in some respects quite close to St German's opinions. St German's reply to his onslaught, 'A little treatise concerning writs of *subpoena*', did not deny that 'common law', when taken in a broad sense, ought to dictate the conduct of crown servants; it simply denied that the system was exhausted by the procedures of the two great courts. To begin with, the Chancellor's equitable powers resembled the powers of King's Bench and Common Pleas in being founded on a general custom: 'no man ought to marvel what authority the Chancellor hath to make such a writ of *subpoena* in the king's name; for the old custom, not restrained by any statute, warranteth him by reason of his office so to do after certain grounds'.[83]

St German accepted the Serjeant's basic premise that English law was grounded on the law of God and nature 'for else it were a very gross law, and far insufficient, and also against reason in many things', but he thought that the word 'law' should be construed as covering the remedies supplied by Chancery.[84] Thus common law judges knew perfectly well that purchasers without receipts were entitled to enjoy their purchases, but it was not a judge's place to offer this kind of assistance:

the judges of the common law know as judges by the grounds of the law that the payment sufficiently dischargeth the debt in reason and conscience, as the Chancery doth, but yet they may not by the maxims and customs of the law admit the only payment for a sufficient plea . . . for that they may not break the grounds and principles of old time used in the courts where the action is taken. But the common law pretendeth not that the maxim stretcheth not [*sic*] to all courts *nor to the whole common law*, but to certain courts, according to the custom before time used . . . And so it is ofttimes seen that several courts hath several customs, and *the law* suffereth them all.[85]

St German thus probably shared the Serjeant's proto-Burkean view of the coherence of the legal system; but he coped with the Chancellor's equitable

[80] Ibid., 103.   [81] Ibid., 104.   [82] Ibid., 105.   [83] Ibid., 108.   [84] Ibid., 110.
[85] Ibid., 111 (my italics).

powers by treating them as a resource afforded by that system, within a sphere delimited by custom.

To a casual modern reader, the Serjeant's fulminations suggest post-prandial conservatism; they seem the sort of attitudes more likely to be cherished than defended. But in fact a not dissimilar position was carefully set out by John Hales in 'An oration in commendation of the laws', a manuscript treatise submitted to the king in about 1540. Hales was the archetypical *bien-pensant* humanist, the man who inadvertently de-stabilised the Somerset regime by an ill-advised crusade against enclosures; it tells us something interesting about the common law that someone with his temperament should think that it deserved a panegyric. The primary purpose of his work appears to have been to argue for codification, which he was sure could be achieved without substantive losses: 'what were their laws that we now call civil before the noble Emperor Justinian's time but customs unwritten and answers and opinions of learned men'. He was the first of many whose confidence in the details of the system was partly Protestant and nationalistic: 'whereupon at the first did the Romans ground their laws but upon the XII Tables fett [*sic*] from the Greeks? Have not we better principles the ten of commandments of God the very exposition of the law [of] nature?'[86] He went out of his way to praise Sir Thomas Audley (the then Lord Chancellor) not only for his 'learning in the laws, but for the knowledge that he hath in God's word'.[87]

What nonetheless concerned Hales about Chancery's behaviour was that 'because most of the masters thereof [i.e. the Masters in Chancery] be civilians, some will say that our laws be tempered by the civil'.[88] He responded by distinguishing two types of equity. One was the general rule of *aequum et bonum*, which he called 'arithmetic' equity. This was 'the matter and ground of all laws positive which hath respect [to] and helpeth the thing that happeneth generally'.[89] The other was 'geometric' equity, which remedied general rules in particular cases. This latter type of equity was not a part of any legal system. Hales offered a traditional example:

The civil law commandeth and willeth that if I give my knife . . . to another to keep, he shall re-deliver that when I ask it. This is reason. But if in the mean season I fall out of my wit, then saith the civil law ye may keep it, for it is to be thought I would kill myself therewith. And this exception they take for an example geometric, whereunto I agree not for this is but an inferior law.[90]

---

[86] British Library, Harleian MS 4990, fo. 17–17v.   [87] Ibid., 44.   [88] Ibid., 44.   [89] Ibid., 42.
[90] Ibid., 42–42v.

The right of retaining the weapon was grounded on 'another law, which is he doth the hurt which giveth the occasion thereof' or on the 'general law both of nature and God which saith thou shalt not kill'.[91] It followed that 'there is no equity geometric in the example but two contrary laws'.[92] Hales went on to maintain that it was better 'to suffer one private injury than a common mischief', using St German's instance of the purchaser who loses his receipt. There were, however, occasions when circumstances would demand the Chancellor's intervention: 'upon a false and untrue surmise of the party not known to the laws equity geometric will help in another court, that is to say, in the Chancery, the circumstances examined'.[93]

The importance of Hales and St German is not that their ideas were 'typical' (a judgement we are not, of course, in any position to make), but that their writings demonstrate awareness of some emergent possibilities. Close reading of their treatises reveals a subtle difference between them in their divergent attitudes to rules. Hales thought that Chancery was not a rule-based jurisdiction; it was the jurisdiction that coped when rules broke down. St German thought it did appeal to rules – to laws of God and nature – although the area in which the Chancellor could do so was ultimately limited by custom. In other words, St German thought that there were *laws* outside the common law. This difference deserves some attention because it implied a divergence between their views of monarchy. Both men believed that power to control the national church was inherent, by the law of God, in monarchs; but their underlying positions were incompatible. As Hales subsumed the law of God into the body of the common law, he thought of Royal Supremacy as quite straightforwardly a common law doctrine: 'this law of declaration of the king's majesty to be the supreme head in earth of the church of England is not new. But a confirmation of the old laws of this realm, grounded and consonant with the law of nature and the word of God.'[94] St German believed that 'the king's grace hath now no new authority by that that he is confessed by the clergy and authorised by the parliament to be the head of the church of England. For it is but only a declaration of his first power by God committed to kingly and regal authority and no new grant.'[95] But the 'kingly and regal authority' referred to in this passage is royal authority outside the sphere of common law; it is an example of Fortescue's *ius regale*. The only passage in St German's writings in which he actually refers to Fortescue's political theory provides a confirmation of this reading:

---

[91] Ibid., 42v.   [92] Ibid., 42v–43.   [93] Ibid., 43v–44.   [94] Ibid., 31v–2.
[95] *A treatyse concerninge the power of the clergye and the laws of the realm*, sigs. Gv–G2.

There be two manner of powers that kings and princes have over their subjects: the one is called *ius regale* that is to say a kingly governance: and he that hath that power may with his counsel make laws to bind his subjects and also make declaration of Scripture . . . the other is called *ius regale politicum*, that is to say a kingly and politic governance. And that is the most noble power that any prince hath over his subjects and he that ruleth by that power may make no laws to bind his subjects without their assent.[96]

The important power of declaring scripture is mentioned as an attribute of 'kingly', but not of 'kingly and politic' governance.

The difference between Hales and St German corresponded, of course, to a tension within the ideas appealed to by Henry VIII's regime. During the 1530s, Henry repeatedly appealed to his 'imperial' rights, rights annexed to his crown by either God or nature. But when he made use of parliament and lawyers in order to declare these royal powers, he tended, as it were, to naturalise them: to encourage their absorption into ordinary law. Henrician legislation on the Supremacy provides examples of this kind of slippage; but the same kind of tension is perceptible elsewhere. Thus the 'Act for recontinuing of certain liberties and franchises heretofore taken from the crown' (1536), the statute that effectively completed the king's monopoly of jurisdiction, noted that 'divers of the most ancient prerogatives and authorities of justice appertaining to the imperial crown of this realm' had been lost to the crown by 'sundry gifts' of Henry's predecessors. The opening clause of the statute provided that 'the whole and sole power and authority' to pardon should be 'united and knit to the imperial crown of the realm, as of good right and equity it appertaineth'.[97] But the 'good right' that the statute so vaguely declared was hard to distinguish from a right that parliament conferred.

The most revealing instance of this process was Henry's famous Act of Proclamations (1539), a statute suggesting that thought about law in its connection with the regal power had reached new levels of self-consciousness. A letter from Thomas Cromwell to his conciliar colleague the duke of Norfolk suggests this was a new development. At the time when it was written (in 1531), the crown felt a need to stop merchants exporting the coinage. Thomas Cromwell and others consulted the government's lawyers, who offered conflicting opinions on the subject, 'but finally it was concluded that the statutes should be insearched to see whether there were any statute or law able to serve for the purpose'.[98] In the end a 'good statute' was found, but in the mean time Cromwell asked another kind of question:

---

[96] *An answere to a letter*, 5v–6.   [97] Elton, *Tudor constitution*, 37–8.
[98] *Life and letters of Thomas Cromwell*, ed. R. B. Merriman, 2 vols. (Oxford, 1902), I, 409–10.

If in case there were no law nor statute made already for any such purpose what might the king's highness by the advice of his council do to withstand so great a danger like as your grace alleged . . . to the which it was answered by my Lord Chief Justice that the king's highness by the advice of his council might make proclamations and use all other policies at his pleasure as well in this case as in any other like . . . and that the said proclamations and policies so devised by the king and his council for any such purpose should be of as good effect as any law made by parliament or otherwise which opinion I assure your grace I was very glad to hear.[99]

What is most striking in this glimpse of government in action is the apparent absence of an intellectual framework for coping with this kind of difficulty: although the government recognised its need to find a 'law', it seems to have had no particular preconceptions about the form this 'law' would be likely to take. All parties may have been unsure if the Chief Justice seriously meant that the effect of such a proclamation was legally identical to statute (and thus enforceable at common law) or if he was simply admitting that this extraordinary course of action was in some vaguer sense legitimate (and thus enforceable by some conciliar jurisdiction).

The Act of Proclamations dispelled this innocence. In the version first considered by the Commons, it may have conferred on royal proclamations precisely the same authority as statutes, but there exists some evidence that this original draft met with unprecedented opposition.[100] The statute that eventually emerged was a considerably more modest affair, incorporating safeguards for every type of private property; but its reflections upon 'regal power' were nonetheless revealing. It noted that some subjects, 'not considering what a king by his regal power may do', had shown contempt for royal proclamations 'for lack of a direct statute and law to coarct offenders to obey'; and also that 'sudden causes and occasions' often required 'speedy remedies' without 'abiding for a parliament'. Lastly, it mentioned 'that his Majesty (which by the kingly and regal power given to him by God may do many things in such cases) should not be driven to extend the liberty and supremacy of his regal power and dignity by wilfulness of froward subjects'.[101]

This final assertion was probably meant as a threat, but the wording of the statute did offer some comfort to anybody worried about extra-legal power. It could be taken to restrict the exercise of such a power to real emergencies. The preamble's concluding words offered support to this interpretation:

---

[99] Ibid., I 410. [100] R. W. Heinze, *The proclamations of the Tudor kings* (Cambridge, 1976), 153–71. [101] Elton, *Tudor constitution*, 27–8.

It is therefore thought in manner more than necessary that the king's highness of this realm for the time being, with the advice of his honourable council, should make and set forth proclamations for the good and politic order and governance of this his realm . . . for the defence of his regal dignity, and the advancement of his commonwealth and good quiet of his people, as the cases of necessity shall require, and that an ordinary law should be provided, by the assent of his Majesty and Parliament, for the due punishment, correction and reformation of such offences and disobediences.[102]

As it happens, the 'ordinary law' that eventually passed turned out to be of little practical use, if only because the conciliar court entrusted with enforcement was much too cumbersome to be effective. The importance of the episode lies in its revelations about perceptions of monarchical power. It shows that the king was believed to possess some extra-legal powers – of which the 'speedy remedies' appropriate to an emergency were probably the paradigm example – but it also shows awareness of the possibility of bringing such powers within the reach of ordinary law. Whether this constitutionalising process would ultimately limit monarchy depended, of course, on the attitudes of judges. Here we enter much more difficult terrain, for the attitudes in question are more difficult to study than simple propositional beliefs. The best approach, as we shall see, is through the history of the Reformation.

---

[102] Ibid., 28.

CHAPTER 3

Reformation and the body politic

The sharp-eyed Venetian who visited in 1497 thought that the English people had 'various opinions concerning religion'.[1] He had probably heard of the Lollards, but otherwise we do not know precisely what he meant; we can be sure, however, that if variety is a sign of vigour, English religious culture was extremely vigorous, not least because its intellectual leaders showed some capacity for self-criticism. The Standish affair was an excellent example: Standish was a Franciscan with a friar's indifference to merely institutional privileges, while the leader of his critics, the abbot of Winchcombe, was not a comical reactionary, but a reformer of another type, 'the most distinguished English monk' of the early Tudor period.[2] It was entirely fitting that a serious-minded monk should favour the reception of the canons of the recent Lateran council.

In the first part of the reign of Henry VIII, an obvious feature of this lively scene was the support of church and state for humanist endeavours. William Warham, the archbishop of Canterbury, was a significant patron of Erasmus, as was Richard Fox, the bishop of Winchester, who may for a time have been Henry VII's most influential servant. In his retirement from politics, Fox was also the founder of Corpus Christi, Oxford, a college he provided with a lecturer in Greek. Henry VII's widow, Margaret Beaufort, set up two Cambridge colleges in close association with John Fisher, while Wolsey went out of his way to attract the great Spanish humanist Juan Luis Vives to England. Henry VIII chose a noted Greek scholar, the humanist Thomas Linacre, as his personal physician; appointed Erasmus's close friend Cuthbert Tunstall to the plum bishoprics of London and Durham; and made Sir Thomas More Lord Chancellor. When Oxford was divided, in 1518, between the factions known as 'Greeks' and 'Trojans' (a party that

---

[1] *A relation or rather a true account of the island of England*, tr. C. A. Sneyd, Camden Society 37 (1847), 23.
[2] David Knowles, *The religious orders in England*, 3 vols. (Cambridge, 1959), III, 91.

wished to encourage the study of Greek and one that saw it as unnecessary),
Henry ensured the triumph of the 'Greeks'.

A fashionable interest in the latest scholarship did not invariably imply
reformist inclinations: we know that Warham's piety, for instance, was
utterly conventional in nature.[3] But it was rather difficult to offer support for good letters without at the same time granting some respectability to an 'Erasmian' critique of the existing order. The authorities thus
encouraged distaste for those mechanical devotions that could be stigma-
tised as 'superstitious'; a high valuation of knowledge of the scriptures;
intensified respect for secular duties; and a contempt for the traditional
methods, based as they were in Aristotelian logic, of Western academic
institutions. According to Erasmus, these attitudes were ideally united
in the leading English humanist John Colet (*c.* 1467–1519);[4] but none
of them prevented his rise in the church. Colet out-did Erasmus in his
contempt for Aristotelian methods, but his famous Oxford lecture course
on Romans, combining literal interpretation with an unusual Christian
Platonism, did nothing to stop him becoming the dean of St Paul's
or being asked, in 1510, to preach the opening sermon to that year's
Canterbury Convocation. Nor does anybody seem to have objected to
his use of this last establishment position for a denunciation of the
clergy for being excessively concerned with perquisites like tithes and
mortuaries.

At one time, Colet's sermon was routinely used by scholars as proof
of the decadent state of the country's religion. More recent Reformation
scholarship has tended to reveal a different picture; there is impressive
evidence that a wide range of traditional devotions continued to attract
support from all but a small minority of people.[5] Such evidence has perhaps
been pushed too far; an oddity of English history-writing is that expressions
of lay zeal, which have often been supposed, in other contexts, to be a sign of
'rising expectations' that would be satisfied by Protestantism, are generally
seen, when encountered in England, as nothing but a barrier to reform.
It has long been clear, however, that Protestants were very few in number
(except in a few parts of the South-East) until at least the reign of Edward
VI and that it is misleading to speak of 'Anglicans' – of principled believers
in an English compromise – before the last years of Elizabeth. Where
most historians have been less successful has been in specifying the relation

[3] M. J. Kelly, 'Canterbury jurisdiction and influence during the episcopate of William Warham, 1503–
  32', unpublished Cambridge PhD dissertation (1963), 38–9.
[4] *The correspondence of Erasmus*, tr. R. A. B. Mynors (Toronto, 1988), VIII, 232–44.
[5] Eamon Duffy, *The stripping of the altars: traditional religion in England, c. 1400–c. 1580* (Yale, 1992).

between the abstract notions of intellectuals and the religious practices of the majority.

One influential school has avoided the problem by privileging the type of source (wills, churchwardens' accounts, and best-selling devotional manuals) that gives the impression of registering popular practice. It postulates that the patterns of behaviour that were the norm in 1525 ought to be grasped as a coherent system that was the passive object of an alien assault. This may be, for some purposes, a valuable approach, but its adoption is anachronistic, if only in ignoring that sixteenth-century concept: 'superstition'. To grasp the web of practice as a system that stood or fell as a coherent whole was to have attained a clarity of vision that was a product of the Reformation. It is revealing that a favourite source of these revisionist historians is an effective piece of propaganda – a detailed evocation of arrangements at early sixteenth-century Long Melford – by an Elizabethan recusant.

In fact, a major weakness of the early Tudor church was its confusion on doctrinal matters. As Colet's life and thinking showed, the leaders of the church were open-minded, but readiness to favour new religious attitudes made orthodoxy harder to determine. In any case, lay piety was changing; it is, for example, suggestive that no traditional monastic house (excluding friaries) had been established anywhere in England in the whole period since 1450.[6] Moreover, there was some degree of regional divergence in behaviour. The fifteenth-century boom in church construction was still continuing in northern parts, but it seems to have died away in southern England. In Lancashire during the 1520s, almost 80 per cent of testators made bequests for intercessions; in the archdeaconries of Buckingham and Lincoln, the proportion was approximately a quarter.[7]

The primary agent of religious change in this extremely fluid situation was not, as it turned out, a Lutheran heresy, but a revaluation of lay authority that formed a part of the revaluation of labour in an ordinary 'calling'. Intellectuals who prized the life of action (including the vocation of a ruler) were led to aspire to a political order in which intensive public regulation would minimise vice, superstition, and above all idleness. It may be that these 'Erasmian' objectives were not particularly original – we know that small communities in late medieval England found reason, intermittently, for proto-puritan attempts to discipline their members[8] – but humanist

---

[6] Robert Whiting, 'Local responses to the Henrician Reformation', in *The reign of Henry VIII: politics, policy and piety*, ed. D. MacCulloch (London, 1995), 205.
[7] Ibid., 214.
[8] M. K. McIntosh, *Controlling misbehaviour in England* (Cambridge, 1998).

recovery of ancient civic values gave intellectuals a special motive to hope for more government efforts to stimulate virtue. One reason that Henry succeeded in altering his church was that he could present his policies as a fulfilment of these aspirations.

Another was that English kings could operate through existing institutions. Over much of Western Europe – especially the territories in Switzerland and the Empire in which the Reformation first emerged – the church as an organisation was a major obstacle to humanist schemes of cultural renewal. It figured as the patron of popular superstition and monastic idleness, and its internal structure (which overlapped political boundaries) posed problems for reforming governments. In England, however, things were different. The ecclesiastical provinces of Canterbury and York were co-extensive with the English nation, and kings controlled episcopal appointments. Thomas Wolsey had further enhanced the king's control by wielding the near-papal powers of a legate *a latere*, an office he used, anticipating Cromwell, to perform a visitation of both the provinces and even to dissolve some monasteries. All parties thus had reasons for preserving the church's bureaucratic apparatus. The few but well-connected Protestants, who came to include the Primate of All England, could hope to turn it into an instrument for spreading Protestantism; the king could use its malleability to maximise his scope for religious manoeuvre.

In his dealings with the leaders of the church, Henry was helped by three considerations. The first was that his government's policies (attacks on superstition, promotion of Bible-reading, even suppression of the monasteries) were not in principle objectionable to many Catholic Erasmians, whatever might be said about the methods by which those policies were implemented. The second was that his critics had no obvious sticking-point; the abiding weakness of conservatives (apart from a few rigorous papalists) was that they had no clear criterion by which they could exclude collaboration. The third was that a high view of the king's authority had a tremendous positive appeal, which drew upon, but went beyond, the standard humanist desire to attach a religious importance to secular duties. The English were hardly unusual in looking to the magistrate to settle their religion. They were unique, however, in that their breach with Rome was over a claim about royal *jurisdiction* and in that subsequent developments encouraged stress upon this disagreement. The great advantage of the radicals, even in periods of adversity, was their ability to claim that their antagonists were really 'papists', that is, adherents of a foreign power. Their arguments were ultimately successful; in the end, it was the acceptance by some conservatives that a conservative future *must* be papist that forced them to abandon the national church. But though the Royal Supremacy to some extent explained the Protestants' triumph, it also gave the English Reformation a lastingly unusual character.

I

King Henry had always been hostile to any social force or institution that might be thought to qualify his crown's 'imperial' status, his status, that is, as a monarch who had no temporal superiors. At the time of the Standish affair, he regarded himself as 'wishing to maintain the right of our crown and of our temporal jurisdiction'.[9]innovations. But such behaviour was not at all unprecedented; Richard II had set store by his 'imperial' status and even passed an anti-papal statute declaring that the crown of England 'hath been so free at all times that it hath been in no earthly subjection, but immediately subject to God in all things touching the regality of the said crown'.[10]

During the 1530s, though, Henrician policy broke with this tradition. What Henry was really attempting in that decade was less an expansion in temporal jurisdiction at the expense of its church counterpart than a total integration of every kind of visible coercion, including the act of excommunication. Henry was not asserting a power of external supervision; instead, he was maintaining that all varieties of jurisdiction had a common because royal origin. He had arrived at this idea by February 1531, the month in which he startled the convocation of the southern province by demanding recognition as 'sole protector and supreme head of the English church and clergy' and even as enjoying the 'cure of souls'.[11] When the York convocation protested, a letter in Henry's name to Cuthbert Tunstall explained his underlying theory. The convocation's protest seems not to have survived, but the northern clergy evidently distinguished between the temporal and the spiritual, 'whereof the one, ye say, [Christ] committed to princes, the other *sacerdotibus* [to priests]'. Henry thought that the clergy's own evidence subverted any claim to be immune from royal jurisdiction: 'for princes ye allege texts which show and prove obedience due to princes of all men without distinction, be he priest, clerk, bishop, or layman, who make together the church'. The king's responsibilities were virtually unbounded. It was

---

[9] Caryll, *Reports*, II 691.   [10] 16 Richard II c.5.
[11] John Guy, 'Henry VIII and the praemunire manoeuvres of 1530–31', *English Historical Review* 97 (1982), 495.

the monarch's duty to bear the sword 'against him also that in any wise breaketh God's laws; for we may not more regard our law than God nor punish the breach of our laws, and leave the transgression of God's laws unreformed'.[12] Though Henry acknowledged that the sacraments, 'whereby grace is of [God's] infinite goodness conferred upon his people', escaped the control of any temporal head, the clergy were free of royal authority only 'for the time they do that, and in that respect'. If the incorrect performance of ministerial duties caused a scandal, the conduct complained of fell within the cognizance of monarchs.[13]

The workings of Henry's own sharp, if uncritical, mind can be recovered from his annotations upon the manuscript now known as the Collectanea satis copiosa. This somewhat unfocused collection of anticlerical materials, which probably reached its present form in 1532,[14] includes some quite traditional conciliarist ideas, but Henry's underlinings and marginalia reveal the different tendency of his opinions. He marked a couple of passages on the superiority of councils but his purpose in so doing was probably more anti-papal than pro-conciliar. The claims that most excited him were those that assigned a positive role to kings in church affairs or that excluded churchmen from any role in matters temporal. He underlined a passage comparing a king in his kingdom to 'the soul in the body' and 'God in the world'.[15] He also singled out the biblical excerpt in which Jehoshaphat, the King of Judah, is said to have issued orders to the Levites about the principles that governed judgements; his approving marginal comment was 'an instruction (*praeceptum*) to the priests'.[16]

The Collectanea refer to the traditional notion of 'two swords', contrasting purely corporal pains inflicted by the state with spiritual ones inflicted by the church, but there are signs that Henry was, if anything, a 'one-sword' theorist. Thus he underlined the biblical quotation that 'in those days there was no king in Israel, but each man did that which seemed right to him' – a state of affairs that the Collectanea attributed to the absence of a higher kingly power 'by whose sword they might be coerced from vices'.[17] He twice drew attention to Christ's admonition to Peter that those who take the

---

[12] David Wilkins (ed.), *Concilia Magnae Britanniae et Hiberniae a synodo Verulamensi A.D. 406 ad Londiniensem*, 4 vols. III, 763.

[13] Ibid., III 764.

[14] British Library, Cotton MS Cleopatra E 6. Current scholarly consensus acknowledges that some at least of Henry's annotations must post-date the Submission of the Clergy (1532), but insists that the earlier part of this particular collection had a decisive impact upon Henry during the later months of 1530. It seems just as likely, however, that Henry's views derive from other sources; his marginalia impose some fairly coherent principles of selection upon material with no single message.

[15] Cleopatra E 6, fo. 26v.   [16] Ibid., 24.   [17] Ibid., 25–25v.

sword will perish by it.[18] 'The sword' was thus a matter for the lay authorities. Moreover, the residual scope for excommunication could never be a threat to secular power. Henry underlined a passage disapproving of clergymen who shunned the monarch's friends, and added a marginal comment – 'a most beautiful privilege' (*pulcherrimum privilegium*) – to one that pronounced that a tenant-in-chief should be immune from excommunication till the king or (in his absence) the king's court had been consulted.[19]

From one perspective, what was happening was just a stretching of the commonplace that things promoting temporal happiness were properly a part of the temporal sphere (the Collectanea quoted from Aquinas, but statements of this general type could doubtless have been found in almost any writer touched by Aristotelianism). The lengths to which the monarch took this ordinary idea are probably explained by his involvement in a debate that focused on the *act* of legislation. The House of Commons's recent 'Supplication against the Ordinaries' complained of the church making 'laws, constitutions, and ordinances, without your knowledge or most royal consent, and without the assent or consent of any of your lay subjects'.[20] The complaint was superficially familiar: a memorable passage in Bracton described the barons responding 'with one voice' to the new Roman principle that marriage could legitimise a bastard, allegedly by saying that 'we do not wish to change the laws of England which have hitherto been used and approved'.[21] More recently, the Standish case evoked a claim that alien law required a reception and that the English nation could modify its principles by usage. But the emphasis on such earlier occasions had been on temporal results of some particular piece of legislation. What was novel in Henry's position in the thirties was his denial that the church *qua* church had any power to legislate at all.

Henry had somehow come to think that any institution that both made laws and punished their infraction was of its very nature a purely temporal phenomenon. As his adviser Edward Fox was to explain in 1534, 'the common gloss doth interpret the sword to mean power in judgments', but 'neither the scripture of the evangelists nor of the Apostles do give [the clergy] judicial power nor court to make examination or determination of punishment'.[22] Thus the church as a political organisation, an organisation equipped with laws and courts, was constituted by the monarchy. This

---

[18] Ibid., 29v., 72v.   [19] Ibid., 41.
[20] Gerald Bray (ed.), *Documents of the English Reformation* (Cambridge, 1994), 52.
[21] Bracton, *Laws and customs*, IV 296.
[22] Edward Fox, *The true dyfferens betwen ye regall power and the ecclesiasticall power*, tr. Henry Lord Stafford (1548), 68a.

principle was pushed to extraordinary lengths. It might have been thought, for example, that bishops had inherent jurisdiction over such crimes as heresy committed by their clerical inferiors, even if it were granted that such a power, in a Christian state, was subject to the monarch's supervision. But Henry's government disdained such compromise positions. The definitive Act of Supremacy (1534) declared that all the crimes committed by the clergy were the *immediate* concern of monarchs. Henry was to enjoy 'full power and authority from time to time to visit, repress, redress, reform, order, correct, restrain and amend all such errors, heresies, abuses, offences, contempts and enormities, whatsoever they be, which by any manner spiritual authority or jurisdiction ought or may lawfully be reformed, repressed, ordered, redressed, corrected, restrained or amended'.[23]

In the event, this power of visitation was exercised by a layman, Thomas Cromwell, from 1536 to 1540. It is true that the emergence of a lay 'vicegerency' may have been something of an accident, the result of Cromwell keeping the powers that he acquired in order to dissolve the monasteries.[24] But the fact that such an outcome could be semi-accidental revealed the extent of the collapse of the ideal of a self-governing clergy. By the end of the reign, the regime made a positive virtue of the admission of laymen to sacred offices. The parliament of 1545 empowered married laymen to exercise all 'censures and coercions' in the church, including the act of pronouncing the penalty of excommunication. The draftsman appears to have seen this remarkable step as a natural implication of Henry's settlement, because he thought the church law to the contrary was 'directly repugnant to your Majesty of Supreme Head [*sic*] of the church and prerogative royal, your grace being a layman'.[25]

As this revealing statement showed, the Headship was not a sacerdotal function. By making the king central to the church of England's life, Henry admittedly did much to sacralise his office, thus easing the mutation that transformed 'His Grace' King Henry into 'His Most Sacred Majesty' King James. But the indispensable core of Henrician theory, his claim to power within the church and not just over it, derived from a view of his function in the community; the metaphor of 'Headship' demanded a body, and it was his *natural* connection with that body, the people of England considered as Christian believers, that was the essence of Supremacy. As we shall see, this point had some importance for the development of parliament. It also

[23] Elton, *Constitution*, 365.
[24] F. D. Logan, 'Thomas Cromwell and the vicegerency in spirituals: a revisitation', *English Historical Review* 103 (1988), 658–67.
[25] 37 Henry VIII c.17.

helped to ensure the speedy failure of the attempt to introduce political Lutheranism.

The classic English statement of the Lutheran position was the biblical translator William Tyndale's *The obedience of a Christian Man* (1528). Tyndale reminded readers that 'thou shalt find in the English chronicle, how that King Adelstone caused the holy Scripture to be translated', but this was the only moment in his work at which he admitted that the king might have religious functions. Tyndale's principal concern was to rebut the prelates' accusation that Protestants were revolutionary, so he emphasised that the duty of obedience was 'not to be understood in bowing the knee and putting off the cap only' but also promoting the rulers' 'worship, pleasure, will and profit in all things, counting them worthy of all honour . . . remembering that thou art their good and possession'.[26] It is easy to see why Anne Boleyn is said to have given a copy to her lover.

But it is also evident that Tyndale's way of thinking was not a possible ideological basis for Henry's move against the papacy. Tyndale's conception of authority followed the early Luther's in its indifference to law and virtue. He thought of worldly power, in other words, as something authorised by providence 'to take vengeance of evil-doers, that others might fear',[27] something that strictly speaking had no relevance at all to the religious lives of proper Christians. From a purely religious perspective, it was the actions of *bad* kings that might be salutary. A Christian thought of tyrants as 'the rod and scourge wherewith God chastiseth us; the instruments wherewith God searcheth our wounds', but the activities of virtuous kings did not impinge on his behaviour: 'he now that is renewed in Christ keepeth the law without a law written, or compulsion of any ruler or officer, save by the leading of the spirit only'.[28] The ruler's function was extremely narrow: 'in time of judgement he is no minister in the kingdom of Christ; he preacheth no Gospel, but the sharp sword of vengeance', which was why it would be wrong for royal judges 'to break up into the consciences of men'.[29]

The weakness of this theory was its atomistic vision; both the leading of the spirit and the vengeance of the king addressed themselves to isolated individuals. Tyndale's analysis of secular power as providentially sanctioned violence discouraged more positive attitudes to social interaction. His view of the church's life was just as meagre. His only mention of the sacraments was a jeer at superstitions surrounding baptism – 'if aught be left

[26] William Tyndale, *Doctrinal treatises and introductions to different portions of the holy scriptures*, ed. Henry Walter, Parker Society 32 (Cambridge, 1848), 149, 168.
[27] Ibid., 185.   [28] Ibid., 197, 185.   [29] Ibid., 203.

out ... How tremble they! How quake they'[30] – and the one ministerial duty in which he showed much interest was evangelical preaching. A country in which church and state were both such well-developed and coherent institutions was never likely to accept such doctrines. In the event, rejection of the Lutheran position was exemplified by the fate of Robert Barnes, whose work *A supplication unto King Henry the VIII* (1531) originally included a long section explaining that 'the constitutions of men' were not in conscience binding. The second edition of 1534 omitted the whole passage. But when Barnes and his fellow Lutheran William Jerome were burned for heresy in 1540, Jerome is said to have maintained that magistrates lacked the authority to make 'that thing which of itself is indifferent to be not indifferent'. In this, he followed 'Dr Barnes' book where he teacheth that men's constitutions bind not the conscience.'[31]

As it turned out, the king was not content with such an impoverished view of the royal position. Nor did he wish to sweep away the institutional church; some of the spoils from the monastic lands went into the creation six new bishoprics equipped with the same apparatus of deans, chapters, and church courts as any of their medieval predecessors. From the letter to Tunstall onwards, his arguments worked by identifying 'the church' with the community of English Christians (as opposed to just its clerical personnel) and treating his role in governing that church as one department of his general duty of working to promote the common weal. In consequence, the famous opening passage of the Act in Restraint of Appeals (1533) was less concerned with kingship than with *England*:

Whereas by divers sundry old authentic histories and chronicles it is manifestly declared and expressed that this realm of England is an empire, and so hath been accepted in the world, governed by one supreme head and king having the dignity and royal estate of the imperial crown of the same, unto whom a body politic, compact of all sorts and degrees of people divided in terms and by names of spiritualty and temporalty, be bounden and owe to bear next to God a natural and humble obedience.[32]

What is most interesting about this text is its unnecessary radicalism, a radicalism still more marked in the unpublished draft material. As G. R. Elton long ago discovered, the opening passage can be found in all surviving versions. Study of this material also shows that 'An Act in Restraint of Appeals' would have been a misnomer for the measure that the government

---

[30] Ibid., 277.
[31] W. D. J. Cargill Thompson, 'The sixteenth-century editions of *A supplication*', *Transactions of the Cambridge Bibliographical Society* 3 (1960), 141.
[32] Elton, *Tudor constitution*, 353.

intended. The statute's original purpose was not just to restrain appeals from the English church court system, but to create a novel mechanism, a court of appeal from the Archbishop's court composed of crown-appointed civil lawyers.[33] As Elton realised, this was a symptom of a revolution that cannot be accounted for as part of the monarch's campaign for an annulment. If Henry's only purpose had been to see to it that his 'Great Matter' was handled by the loyal Thomas Cranmer, he could perfectly well have accomplished this objective by an assertion of the adequacy of the existing clerical arrangements.

What made his new claims possible was evidently the new disposition, exemplified in Dudley's *The tree of commonwealth*, to see the running of the church as simply a part of the problem of governing the English polity. The exploitation of this new assumption by Henry's more conservative defenders suggests the extent of its general acceptance. It appears in the defences of the Supremacy by Stephen Gardiner and Richard Sampson, two loyal servants of the crown with no desire for further innovation. Perhaps because neither aspired to produce a new theology, both chose to organise their thoughts as an 'oration' on obedience, and both linked the notion of Henry as the 'head' with a picture of the people as his 'body'. The more elaborate, Stephen Gardiner's, presented the recent religious revolution as the result of an appeal to 'the perfect line and plummet of God's word', but Gardiner's argument was not entirely scriptural. He treated his master's reforms as the fulfilment of a duty: 'must every man', he asked, 'in his own private care seek the kingdom of God and must the prince in his administration neglect it?'[34] The reason for the clergy's exemption from his rule was that 'good men were afraid lest any king should wax too holy', so that 'they invented a fine devise, thinking it a witty part to appoint a king his office so as he take no thought whether his people (*cives*) be good or not'.[35] A significant part of the basis of the Supremacy was thus the obligation of the monarch to foster virtue in his 'citizens'.

A glance at the statutes reveals beyond reasonable doubt that the Henrician government of the succeeding decade took this more general duty extremely seriously. Whatever view is taken of Thomas Cromwell's conscious purposes, he clearly regarded social legislation as something of considerable importance. As early as 1531, he was involved in making plans for moral reformation. He seems to have been in contact with St German,

---

[33] G. R. Elton, 'Evolution of a Reformation statute', *English Historical Review* 64 (1949), 178, 185–8.
[34] Pierre Janelle, *Obedience in church and state: three political tracts by Stephen Gardiner* (Cambridge, 1930), 69, 105.
[35] Ibid., 105.

who drafted for him an elaborate scheme of reform, combining predictable measures to prune the powers of church courts with schemes for using public works to banish idleness. William Marshall, his most active propagandist, found time to translate into English *The form and manner of subvention or helping for poor people devised and practised in the city of Ypres* (1535), a humanist-influenced Poor Law scheme most notable for banning mendicancy.

This moral concern was not entirely new (Cromwell may actually have picked it up from his admired patron Thomas Wolsey), but it was applied to real social problems with a new energy and thoroughness. It was probably not just coincidence that the Act in restraint of Appeals was followed, in the printed statute book, by a compendious sumptuary law that aimed to avoid the 'detriment of the common weal, the subversion of good and politic order', and the impoverishment of foolish persons inclined to 'pride the mother of all vices'.[36] Cromwellian legislation included a Poor Law designed to correct the idleness of vagrants and a Sheep Law to tackle the problem that exercised so many humanists: the avarice of 'depopulating' landlords. The former bill was brought into the Commons by the king, who 'would not, he said, have them pass on it ... because his grace giveth in the bill, but they to see if it be for a common weal to his subjects'.[37] When the Lower House passed a version of the latter, Cromwell himself described it to his master as 'the most noble profitable and most beneficial thing that ever was done to the commonwealth of this your realm', a benefit such 'as never was seen in this realm sithen Brutus time'.[38] The English crown was taking its duties as a 'head' with an unprecedented seriousness, and the programme it was trying to implement was basically humanist in nature.

II

One reason that this programme was so difficult to resist is that its roots were not in a conventional sense 'religious'; no theologian had explored the logical ramifications of the adoption of such arguments. No one except Sir Thomas More appears to have foreseen the status it would ultimately give to parliament; the parliamentary Supremacy on which so much was subsequently to hinge was really a by-product of other impulses. During the 1530s, clerical conservatives could even find some grounds for optimism.

---

[36] 24 Henry VIII c.13.   [37] G. R. Elton, *Reform and renewal* (Cambridge, 1973), 123.
[38] Merriman, *Letters*, I 373.

Some parts of the Act in restraint of Appeals (in its moderate final version) suggested a kind of English Gallicanism, an assertion of the liberties of England's hierarchy against the threat of papal interference. The statute recorded, for instance, that

when any cause of the law divine happened to come into question or of spiritual learning, then it was declared, interpreted and shewed by that part of the said body politic called the spiritualty, now being usually called the English church, which always hath been reputed and also found of that sort that both for knowledge, integrity and sufficiency of number, it hath been always thought and is also at this hour sufficient and meet of itself, without the intermeddling of any exterior person or persons, to declare and determine all such doubts and to administer all such offices and duties as to their rooms spiritual doth appertain.[39]

This was not the only passage that seemed to reserve to the clergy some measure of their old autonomy. For example, the preamble also stated that 'the laws temporal for trial of propriety of lands and goods and for the conservation of the people . . . was [*sic*] and yet is administered, adjudged, and executed by sundry judges and administers of the other part of the said body politic called the temporalty, and both their authorities and jurisdictions do conjoin together in the due administration of justice the one to help the other.'[40] This was consistent with a two-swords theory. So was the new provision that appeals should terminate in the archbishop of the relevant province, while cases involving the monarch himself should have a separate appeals procedure, ending in the Upper House of Convocation.[41]

Though these politic concessions were no more than a stay of execution (the court of appeal originally envisaged was duly established in 1534), lay power in the church was not yet total. The Act for the Submission of the Clergy (1534) provided for a commission of thirty-two (half clergymen, half laymen) with power to revoke existing canons where these conflicted with the temporal law, but it confirmed that future canon law was a matter for the King-in-Convocation;[42] the fact that the church was now subject to the monarch was not, in itself, a reason for the clergy to be subjected to the laity. What was more, as intelligent clerics were quick to realise, the image of a body politic implied a degree of functional specialisation. Gardiner was careful to maintain that government of the church was a matter for the Apostles and their successors. His fellow conservatives, Tunstall and John Stokesley, explained to the exiled papist, Reginald Pole, that 'Christian

[39] Elton, *Tudor constitution*, 353.   [40] Ibid., 353–4.   [41] Ibid., 357, 358.
[42] 25 Henry VIII c.19.

kings be sovereign over the priests and may command the priests to do their offices . . . and ought . . . to see that all men of all degrees do their duties.' As the body politic simile made clear, it did not matter that the King could not himself perform the priestly functions: 'it is not requisite in every body natural, that the head shall exercise either all manner of offices of the body, or the chief office of the same'; the appropriate analogy was with 'a captain of great armies, which is not able, nor never could peradventure shoot or break a spear by his own strength'.[43]

Even Gardiner and Tunstall, however, found the Supremacy difficult to present without supporting some degree of Protestantisation. In appealing to the 'literal sense' of the Bible, they could hardly not encourage the idea that scripture's meaning had to be recovered from the obscurity produced by centuries of self-interested glosses. What was more, the unavoidable effect of letting the monarch determine the details of church government and worship was to re-orient religious thinking in ways that were likely to favour the reformers. A distinction between the secular and the sacred was replaced by a distinction between the rules that human beings could alter and those that they could not, between arrangements fixed by God and 'things indifferent'. If given ceremonial practices (the lighting of candles, for instance) could be enjoined or banned by local usage, it followed that they fell into the latter category; so far from being intrinsically sacred, they were simply the product of custom, to be tested and, if necessary, rejected by reference to the English common weal. The underlying thought was well explained in a letter that the archbishop wrote to Henry just after the full establishment of the Supremacy:

as the common laws of your grace's realm be not made to remit sin, nor no man doth observe them for that intent, but for a common commodity, and for a good order and quietness to be observed among your subjects; even so were the laws and ceremonies first instituted in the church for a good order, and remembrances of many good things, but not for remission of our sins.[44]

But though the assumptions Cranmer was promoting were utterly destructive of traditional piety, his argument's practical effect was still ambiguous. If most of the institutions of the old spiritual sphere had no more status than the common law, it could equally be argued that at least they were no less legitimate; if canon law was royal legislation, then it could claim equality with common law and statute. One possible view of these questions was frankly expressed by Lord Chancellor Thomas Audley in private conversation with Stephen Gardiner. As Gardiner later remembered,

---

[43] *A letter written by Cuthbert Tunstall* (1560), sig. D4v, C4, C5v.
[44] *The works of Thomas Cranmer*, ed. Edmund Cox, 2 vols. (Cambridge, 1846), II 326–7.

'it seemed to me strange that a man authorised by the king (as, since the king's Majesty hath taken upon him the supremacy, every bishop is such one) could fall into a *praemunire*'. Audley's reply was simple:

'Look [upon] the Act of Supremacy, and there the king's doings be restrained to spiritual jurisdiction; and in another act it is provided that no spiritual law shall have place contrary to a common law or act of parliament. An this were were not', quoth he, 'you bishops would enter in with the king and by means of his Supremacy order the laity as ye listed. But we will provide', quoth he, 'that the *praemunire* shall ever hang over your heads, and so we laymen shall be sure to enjoy our inheritance by the common laws and acts of parliament'.[45]

From one point of view, as Audley realised, King Henry seemed to have behaved with some shortsightedness, missing an opportunity to liberate his instrument, the church, from the external curbs that were imposed by parliament.

The usual explanation of his curious restraint, by no means confined to followers of Elton, has been to postulate in Thomas Cromwell an unexplained commitment to ruling by statute, perhaps because he entertained 'Marsilian' beliefs. But though Marsilius of Padua (?1275–?1342) had worked out a theory that Cromwell might have used, there are good grounds for thinking that 'Marsilian' ideas were utterly unacceptable in England. Most of *Defensor pacis* was translated by Cromwell's propagandist William Marshall, but Marshall carefully censored Marsilius's distinctive populism. Marsilius saw the Emperor (to whom he gave the right of controlling the church), as representative of the 'legislator', by which he meant the people; Marshall identified this force with English monarchy. Though Marshall not infrequently referred to parliament in contexts where the Latin had spoken of the whole community, his general conception of the assembly's role was as the *setting* of the monarch's action.[46]

There is no need, however, to treat the rise of parliament in English political thinking as the expression of a *theory*. It can more plausibly be seen as the result of tactical adjustments by less-than-visionary politicians. From a practical political perspective, the royal supremacy was best presented as a response to an appeal for 'commonwealth' reform or as a barrier against encroaching foreign law. Both trains of thought involved a novel stress on parliament. An early expression of the first was 'An act concerning the restraint of the payment of annates' (1532). After rehearsing inconveniences arising from these levies, the statute pronounced that 'it is considered and

[45] *The letters of Stephen Gardiner*, ed. J. A. Muller (Cambridge, 1933), 392.
[46] S. Lockwood, 'Marsilius of Padua on the royal ecclesiastical supremacy', *Transactions of the Royal Historical Society*, 6th series, I (1991), 89–119.

declared by the whole body of this realm now represented by all the estates of the same assembled in this present parliament that the king's highness before Almighty God is bound as by the duty of a good Christian prince, for the conservation and preservation of the good estate and commonwealth of this his realm' to do all he could to stop this damaging practice. Here parliament's capacity to represent 'the whole body of the realm' gave it the standing to pronounce about the common weal.[47]

An example of the second line of thought was 'An Act for the exoneration of exactions paid to the see of Rome' (1534), a statute that showed how the king could appeal to popular consent. It made the expected assertion that the Supremacy was a position that 'the prelates and clergy of your realm representing the said church in their synods and convocations have recognised'. But it also held that valid English law consisted either in measures 'ordained within this realm for the wealth of the same' or 'such other as by sufferance of your Grace and your progenitors the people of this your realm have taken at their free liberty by their own consent to be used among them.' In the latter case, they were to be obeyed 'as the accustomed and ancient laws of this realm originally established as laws of the same by the said sufferance, consents, and custom'. The obvious corollary was that laws that had been taken up by popular consent could surely be dispensed with by the same mechanism. It was therefore understandable that parliament should be the appropriate body to delegate a power of dispensation. There followed an assertion of parliamentary supremacy incorporating roughly the same tensions as Henry's subsequent Act of Proclamations:

It standeth therefore with natural equity and good reason that in all and every such laws human, made within this realm or induced into this realm by the said sufferance consents and custom . . . your royal Majesty and your lords spiritual and temporal and commons, representing the whole state of your realm in this your most high court of parliament, have full power and authority not only to dispense, but also to authorise some elect person or persons to dispense with those and all other human laws of this your realm.[48]

Where dispensation was concerned, the enactment's primary purpose was quite narrow – it aimed to transfer the power to dispense with canon law from the Pope to the archbishop of Canterbury – but the underlying theory raised the possibility of statutes either conferring or removing unlimited power to tinker with positive law.

---

[47] 23 Henry VIII c. 20.   [48] Elton, *Tudor Constitution*, 360–1.

Thus whether or not the king or Thomas Cromwell were committed to a constitutional theory, they had good reason to make use of acts of parliament. But though their course of action was near-inevitable, it had significant long-term consequences. At every turn, Henrician legislation embodies the paradox noted in chapter 2: that Henry found it difficult to use his parliament in order to declare his royal powers without also simultaneously implying that the assembly had the right to limit or extend them. There was, in fact, a natural dynamic which led the body that declared the Royal Supremacy to be regarded as creating it.

III

This tendency was not, as yet, embodied in a propositional doctrine. If anyone had had a proper *theory* of parliamentary Supremacy, pre-dating Henry's legislative programme, it would surely have been Christopher St German. But careful reading of St German's claims suggests a surprising indifference to the subject. The outline of St German's views about church-state relations was laid out with his usual clarity. *Doctor and Student* named 'the law of God' as one of the six sources of the English legal system, but the whole tendency of his ideas was to minimise this category's extent. The Doctor and the Student both accepted that this variety of law consisted in rules given by revelation 'for obtaining of the felicity eternal'.[49] The purpose of this definition was to exclude a type of law we shall encounter in another context, 'the laws such as those in the Old Testament showed by revelation of God for the political rule of the people the which be called judicials'.[50]

St German's view, in other words, was that the nature of a given rule should be decided by its subject matter; laws made by man suppressing heresy, including 'divers laws made by the common people',[51] were nonetheless a part of God's law proper, but 'all the laws canon be not the laws of God. For many of these be made only for the political rule and conversation of the people.'[52] This was a momentous distinction, whose implications would be worked out further when it was taken up by Richard Hooker. St German pointed out the most immediately important when he went on to state that 'the goods of the [clergy] may no more be called spiritual than the goods of the [laity] for they be things mere temporal and keeping the body'.[53] The ultimate basis of such property lay in the custom of the human race

---

[49] St German, *Doctor and student*, 21.   [50] Ibid., 21.   [51] Ibid., 23.
[52] Ibid., 23.   [53] Ibid., 23.

by which the first and natural arrangement – community of goods – had been succeeded by appropriation

The intended effect of this theory was probably to show that much, if not most, of canon law was not divine but human. Conversely, many principles *not* found in canon law were actually divine in character, including God's law that the king was the head of the church: parliamentary recognition of the royal supremacy conferred on Henry 'no new power', for he already enjoyed 'all such power over his subjects spiritual and temporal as to a king belongeth by the law of God'.[54] The only qualification to this basic principle was that 'yet the recognition is not to all intents void, for by reason thereof the power of the king is more evidently known'. This royal power was limited, however, for he was not entitled 'to take upon him any authority that our Lord gave only to his apostles or disciples in spiritual ministration to the people'.[55] But even spiritual ministration did not escape the monarch's supervision. He had responsibilities arising from his duty to do justice, 'and therefore if bishops were negligent in doing their ministration to the people the king might command them to do it; and that were more honour to him than to do it himself'.[56]

These moderate principles would have been accepted by a conservative like Cuthbert Tunstall. On this conservative foundation, though, St German erected a radical ecclesiology. Though the universal power of the Apostles was wholly governed by the law of God, the power of their successors, that is, bishops, was power 'within a certain circuit, but that appointment was only by the power and law of man, and not by the immediate power of God'.[57] The clergy were even denied the ultimate authority about doctrinal matters. Where the interpretation of scripture was concerned, they might, to be sure, be consulted as expert advisers 'like as it is convenient in doubts of physic to ask counsel of doctors of physic', but it was best not to consult them on questions affecting the interests of their order.[58] The ultimate authority within a given realm was an appropriately counselled monarch:

it seemeth that kings and princes whom the people have chosen and agreed to be their rulers and governors and which have the whole voices of the people may with their council spiritual and temporal make exposition of such scripture as is doubtful so as they shall think to be the true understanding of it and none but they and that their subjects shall be bound even by the law of God to follow their exposition.[59]

[54] *An answere to a letter*, sig. A3. [55] Ibid., A3v. [56] Ibid., A4v. [57] Ibid., A8.
[58] Ibid., G–G2. [59] Ibid., G5.

St German did not argue that 'councils spiritual and temporal' had to be representative assemblies; it was the 'kings and princes', not the council, who had been 'chosen' as the people's ruler. In any case, as we have seen, those princes who ruled by Fortescue's *ius regale* enjoyed the same religious rights and duties. Although St German did remark that parliament 'representeth the estate of all the people within this realm, that is to say of the whole Catholic church thereof', his purpose in so doing was simply to discredit Convocation, 'which representeth only the state of the clergy'.[60] The last appeal of all was to a council composed of 'kings and princes and such as they will appoint under them to bear voices therein seeing that they have the power and voice of the whole people of Christendom'.[61]

This casts an interesting light upon the nature of St German's thinking. It has always been tempting for scholars to suppose that he was in essence a thinker who had a theory about parliament. But closer reading of his works does not support this view; the effective omnicompetence of statute was simply a corollary of other ideas to which he was committed. The obvious comparison is quite informative: Fortescue was a writer about counsel, and the nation's 'common council', parliament, was therefore very important to his theory; St German was a writer about law and equity, and therefore saw the character of statute as being, at best, a secondary issue. So far as we know, he was never himself an MP, and he never showed an interest in parliament's procedure. In *Doctor and Student*, the statutes were listed sixth and last in his catalogue of sources of the law, and his only real comment on their nature was that they were made 'in such cases where the law of reason, the law of God, customs, maxims ne other grounds of the law of England seemed not to be sufficient to punish evil men and to reward good men'.[62] In other words, their usual contribution was to increase the penalties for conduct that was anyway illegal.

It was important to St German's theory that statute *could* change virtu- ally the whole of common law, but only because such a power was logically implied by his belief that common law was largely positive. Unlike his pre- decessor Fortescue, he never claimed that parliament's composition was any guarantee that it was wise; indeed, the Student complacently remarked, in the spirit of some later common lawyers, that law in certain spheres could be developed 'without any estatute made in that behalf. And peradventure the laws and the conclusions therein be the more plain and the more open.'[63] The only treatise that he wrote in which the assembly's role was really

---

[60] Ibid., G6–G6v.   [61] Ibid., G6v.   [62] *Doctor and student*, 73.   [63] Ibid., 261.

central was the so-called 'New Additions' of 1531, which 'treat most specially of the power of parliament concerning the spiritualty and the spiritual
jurisdiction'.[64] As might have been expected, this work attributed broad
powers to statute in matters previously deemed spiritual, including a power
for 'the king and his parliament' to choose between two claimants to the
papacy itself.[65] But careful scrutiny of the 'New Additions' confirms our
picture of his attitudes. The force of the whole argument is not that parliament has characteristics – such as wisdom guaranteed by representation –
entitling it to power over churchmen, but simply that most features of
ecclesiastical law can actually be changed by human agents.

   A couple of further details illuminate St German's true position. The
chapter about choosing between popes includes an elaborate story about
an episode involving a Pictish monarch called Neitanus. Neitanus had sent
for and welcomed a ruling by St Colfride about the date for celebrating
Easter 'and it is not to think that he did this intending to give sentence
therein by his own authority for that belonged not to him, but he did it
to know the truth and that he might thereupon show his favour to the
better part'. Neitanus was said to be seated 'among his lords' when he
received the message from St Colfride, but otherwise the whole thrust of
the story suggests a personal Supremacy. This personal Supremacy did,
however, have limitations. St German also thought this a good moment to
tell a story of 'the blessed man saint Theodore, then archbishop of Canterbury' collecting his clergy together to reaffirm the Trinitarian doctrines of
'the holy and universal five synodals'; on occasion, at least, deference was
due to the authority of national synods and properly constituted general
councils.[66]

   Thus even the most articulate and fearless of all non-Protestant Henrician
thinkers still fell a long way short of advocating a parliamentary Supremacy;
the practice of settling religion by act of parliament preceded the emergence
of a theory. But the character of Henry's Reformation did give the king a
motive for a high view of the law, especially of parliamentary statute, and for
encouraging such a view in others. As he himself is said to have pronounced,
in a privilege case of 1542,

we be informed by our judges that we at no time stand so highly in our estate
royal as in the time of parliament, wherein we as head and you as members are
conjoined and knit together into one body politic, so as whatsoever offence and
injury (during that time) is offered to the meanest member of the House is to be
judged as done against our person and the whole court of parliament.[67]

[64] Ibid., 315.   [65] Ibid., 327.   [66] Ibid., 329.   [67] Elton, *Tudor constitution*, 277.

Needless to say, these rightly famous phrases involve a now familiar type of ambiguity, especially when they are read in context. Henry was acting to protect the privilege from arrest of one George Ferrers, a member of the Commons who was also, as it happened, a royal servant. This latter fact enabled the monarch to maintain that 'he, being head of the parliament and attending in his own person on the business thereof' had exactly the same right as other members of claiming privilege for his attendants.[68] If this argument were taken seriously, it guaranteed immunity from arrest to an indefinite number of such 'servants'. The celebrated statement that 'we at no time stand so highly in our estate royal as in the time of parliament' was doubtless deliberately handsome, but it was not intended to recognise a royal limitation; it was less a claim that kingship was parliamentary than that the houses of parliament were royal. It complimented individual members by stressing their intimate link with the monarch's own person. It typified much else in Henry's reign in that its implications – which were constitutionalist – were hidden in its praise of monarchy.

[68] Ibid., 277.

CHAPTER 4

Commonwealth and common law

From 1540 onwards, successive English rulers appear to have exercised a choice between two strategies. During the 'Catholic' phases of the next thirty years, the final part of Henry's reign and the whole of his daughter Queen Mary's, the crown made use of parliament at its convenience, but it also enjoyed considerable success in levying non-parliamentary taxes. It was only in the period's 'Protestant' phases, under the two Edwardian dukes and Queen Elizabeth, that there emerged a bias towards law-bound government. So far as we know, this shift owed almost nothing to Protestantism among common lawyers; if the profession as a whole had a religious preference, it lay in a conservative direction.[1] The likely explanation of the new respect for law is that it reflected the Protestants' perception of the exigencies of their position: the Catholic governments fought wars that gave them excuses for cutting legal corners; the Protestants too fought wars in France and Scotland, but they appear to have judged themselves to be too insecure to take their opportunities of using 'regal' power.

Both types of ruler had to face the problems that were caused by Henry's extravagant quest for martial glory. In October 1542, Henry invaded Scotland, apparently as a preliminary to a more cherished military project: the invasion of France he undertook in 1544. But in December 1542 the unexpected death of the Scots king created a dangerous vacuum in Scottish politics necessitating further intervention. There was an obvious danger that the Queen Mother, Mary of Guise, would marry the child-Queen Mary to the dauphin, with the result that England's northern neighbour would be absorbed into its enemy. The unsuccessful war to stop this marriage taking place was to persist till 1551. The problem was compounded, in 1544, by Henry's unfortunate triumph in capturing

---

[1] R. M. Fisher, 'The Inns of Court and the Reformation 1530–1580', unpublished Cambridge PhD dissertation, esp. 200–40.

Boulogne, which gave the French a grievance that encouraged their Scottish ambitions.

In consequence, the interests of England dictated an alliance with the Habsburgs, partly in order to preserve the continental foothold and partly to stop the French controlling Scotland. This strategic situation barely altered until the final victory of the Scottish Reformation and the complete abandonment of English hopes of re-acquiring Calais. But friendship with the Habsburgs demanded a conservative religious policy. These were the grounds on which Sir William Paget (1505–63), the self-described 'Cassandra' of the Somerset regime, appears to have advised religious caution.[2] At the very least, prudence suggested maintaining a belief in Real Presence (a 'Lutheran' as opposed to a Reformed theology) as the official English orthodoxy – which was why the risk-averse Elizabeth liked to pretend to foreigners that England's church was Lutheran in its doctrine.

In the last years of Henry's reign, the government's behaviour seems to have been shaped by these considerations. Aggression on the Continent was matched, in church affairs, by an apparent halt to Reformation. Meanwhile, the demands of war improved the king's position. The revolutionary change in perceptions of parliament's status had not increased its influence on foreign policy. Its power in this area appears to have been, if anything, declining: in the parliament of 1523, the young Thomas Cromwell had referred to Tournai and Thérouanne, his sovereign's recent continental conquests, as being 'ungracious dogholes';[3] during the 1540s, no MP dared to echo this defensible opinion. But the most impressive symptom of Henry's dominance was his ability to raise taxation even without his parliament's approval. As early as 1542, he had exacted a Forced Loan of £112,000. The parliament of 1543 was persuaded to turn this loan into a grant; the parliament of 1545 voted a subsidy and two fifteenths, to be paid in two yearly instalments, that brought in £270,000 (a sum that happened to be roughly equal to the aggregate parliamentary taxation that was collected in his father's reign). In the same year, he expunged the shame of the Amicable Grant by raising a benevolence of an additional £120,000. In a perfect illustration of the potential usefulness of 'regal' power in military matters, a London Alderman who had objected was conscripted and despatched to fight the Scots. Even this was not the end of royal exactions. In the last year of Henry's life, some richer taxpayers were compelled to pay

[2] 'The letters of William, Lord Paget of Beaudesert, 1547–63', ed. B. L. Beer, *Camden Miscellany* 25 (1974), 22–4.
[3] *Life and letters of Thomas Cromwell*, ed. R. B. Merriman, 2 vols. (Oxford, 1902), I, 39.

a 'contribution' on the same scale as the benevolence.[4] The crown appeared to have escaped from Fortescue's 'political' restrictions.

Perhaps the most striking feature of the regimes of the Edwardian dukes was their refusal to make use of Henry's precedents. Though Somerset chose to adopt the quasi-regal title Lord Protector and though his style of government was notably high-handed, he made no attempt to tax without consent. He even showed a noticeable reluctance to levy parliamentary taxation. One of Paget's reproachful letters to his master casts light upon the Lord Protector's thinking. According to Paget, the parliament then sitting (he was writing at Christmas 1548) had been expecting to be asked to vote a subsidy, while 'as for matters of religion, your grace thought they might if need were be ordered by the king's majesty's authority'.[5] In the event, though, Somerset switched tactics: no tax upon income was asked for, but the Edwardian Prayer Book of 1549 was authorised by parliamentary statute. There is no pressing reason to believe that this was a symptom of principled adherence to legalistic modes of government. Instead, it offers evidence of two distinct political calculations: first, that religious progress was not achievable without legitimacy of a type that only the Houses of parliament could provide; and secondly, that godly reformation was, for whatever reason, a more important task than rescuing the government's finances.

The Lord Protector had already made a number of remarkable concessions. At the beginning of the reign, he acquiesced in the provisions of 1 Edward VI c.12, a statute which explained in its preamble that nothing was more to be wished 'betwixt a prince the supreme head and ruler and the subjects whose governor and head he is' than love inspired by royal clemency. It tactfully acknowledged that Edward's predecessor had enacted 'certain laws and statutes which might seem and appear to men of exterior realms and many of the king's Majesty's subjects very strait sore extreme and terrible', though under the circumstances of the time, they were 'not without great consideration and policy moved and established'. In the more 'calm and quiet' time of Edward, such measures were no longer necessary.[6] The statute went on to repeal all felonies created since the death of Henry VII, all new Henrician treasons, the Act of Proclamations, and every statute 'touching, mentioning, or in any wise concerning religion or opinions'.[7]

---

[4] R. Hoyle, 'War and public finance', in D. MacCulloch (ed.), *The reign of Henry VIII: politics, war and piety* (Basingstoke, 1995), 92–3.
[5] Paget to Somerset 25 December 1548, ed. B. L. Beer in *Huntington Library Quarterly* 34 (1971), 282.
[6] Elton, *Tudor constitution*, 64–5.   [7] Ibid., 66.

This was, no doubt, a gesture, whose practical impact was relatively slight except in preventing religious persecution. But it was of a piece with other gestures by which a regime with shallow social roots sought to establish its legitimacy. Henry had left the government of the country to sixteen councillors and twelve deputies. When every allowance has been made for the vicissitudes of politics, the state of the church, and the small size of the nobility, it still seems quite extraordinary that only three of them had been ordained; that half to two-thirds of their number had nonetheless had some experience of university-level education; and that only one was born into the peerage.[8] New men with a new social role were likely to clutch at the notion of a project by which their rule could be legitimated. As conciliar rule by such people was a persistent feature of the next sixty years, it was not altogether surprising that two of the great clichés of the period were the ideas that virtue was true nobility and that the best way of acquiring statecraft was by the diligent reading of civil histories. It was also not surprising that they showed interest in displaying virtue by implementing programmes of humanist reform.

I

In a famous phrase that echoed a humanist joke about the ignorance of the parish clergy, Henry allegedly explained to his last parliament that 'some be too stiff in their old mumpsimus, others too busy and curious in their new sumpsimus'. The criticisms are not quite evenhanded:[9] the allusion implied humanist commitments, while the adjectives, when carefully inspected, endorse the idea of a continuing process; 'stiffness' implies a hostile view of immobility, but 'busyness' and 'curiosity' (words subsequently frequently applied to puritans) suggest a legitimate action carried on in an improper or over-eager spirit. The quip was not in fact conservative; like much in Henry's 'Catholic' phase, it was consistent with the view that his reforming policy was a continuing process.

Even in the early 1540s, the government progressively established principles that logically demanded further action, especially through its growing stress on regulating worship. The mildly evangelical Bishops' Book of 1538 permitted the faithful 'to kneel before [images], and to offer unto them, and to kiss their feet and such other things', but only as a service 'to God and in his honour, or in the honour of the holy saint or saints'; the revised version

---

[8] W. K. Jordan, *Edward VI: the young king* (London, 1968), 81, 84.
[9] Peter Marshall, 'Mumpsimus and sumpsimus: the intellectual origins of a Henrician bon mot', *Journal of Ecclesiastical History* 52 (2001).

of these words in the broadly conservative King's Book of 1543 omitted any mention of offerings or kissing of feet, and even of doing honour to the saints, and stressed that 'such things be not nor ought to be done to the image itself, but to God, and in his honour although it be done afore the image, whether it be of Christ, of the cross, or of our lady or of any other saint'.[10] The committee that drafted these words was mostly 'Catholic' in composition, but it had brought the statues on the rood screen, the most important single group of images in the church, within the scope of the assault on popular superstition. The King's Book also paved the way for abolishing the chantries by its denial that a human prayer could help specific souls in purgatory.[11] The next year, Thomas Cranmer set a useful precedent by issuing an English Litany; by 1545, the government's regulation of private devotions extended to the issue of a *Primer*, a volume collecting essential liturgical texts, 'for the avoiding of the diversity of primer books'.[12] At a significant moment in 1546, during the celebrations that followed peace with France, Henry even apparently hinted that the next step, as he saw it, was the replacement of the Mass with a communion service.[13]

If any text could illustrate the problems of conservative non-papists, it was the Catholic John Bekinsau's *De supremo et absoluto regis imperio* (1546). Like Gardiner's treatment of the theme more than a decade earlier, Bekinsau's argument was based upon the principle that magistrates have a natural right and duty to use their powers to discourage vice.[14] Bekinsau thought some ceremonies were genuinely *adiaphora* (and therefore to be settled by the monarch), but he made it clear that other important questions, including aspects of liturgical practice, were decided by traditions of the universal church that had been handed down from the Apostles.[15] His difficulty was the lack of any clear criterion by which to protect the practices he favoured from abolition by the government. From the perspective of the educated, the popular religion that is memorably described in Eamon Duffy's *The Stripping of the Altars* was after all largely a matter of things indifferent. The logical foundation of Bekinsau's case, the natural role of governments in disciplining their communities, was also the foundation of Edward's much more radical Reformation.

[10] *Formularies of faith put forth by authority during the reign of Henry VIII*, ed. C. Lloyd (Oxford, 1856), 136, 300.

[11] *Formularies*, 375–7.

[12] Diarmaid MacCulloch, *Thomas Cranmer: a life* (New Haven, CT, 1996), 335.

[13] J. J. Scarisbrick, *Henry VIII* (1968), 472–8.

[14] Joannes Bekinsau, *De supremo et absoluto regis imperio* (1546), fo. 5–5v.

[15] Bekinsau, *De imperio*, 18–18v.

This was the opportunity of Cranmer and his allies. Around the time of Henry's death, Cranmer became committed to denying the corporal Presence, but it was not till 1552 that the official liturgy embodied a full Reformed doctrine. In the mean time, the government's programme – the iconoclastic visitations, the secularisation of the chantries, even the English-language services – was different only in degree from Henry's policies. Where questions of church-state relations were concerned, the continuities were obvious. As we have seen, Henry's last parliament enabled married laymen to excommunicate. The first religious statute passed by Edward cemented the secular grip on jurisdiction by forcing the courts of the prelates to act in the name of the king. It also abolished, as a needless fiction, the election of bishops by cathedral chapters.[16] The culmination of this early phase was the first Act of Uniformity (1549), a parliamentary statute whose very name implied the primacy of a desire for order.

Four centuries of confessional religion have tended to obscure the fact that it was possible to see such measures as a desirable reconstitution of national religious harmony in relatively unimportant matters. In February 1548 William Paget had reminded Somerset

to appoint the number of learned men as well for consideration of the laws which are to be continued and which abrogated as also for the decent orders to be observed in the church and staying all things unto the parliament time, then with advise and consent of the body of the realm and the learned men, to continue or alter such things as upon great and deep consideration . . . shall be thought convenient, and agreeable both to God's law and to preservation of the policy of the realm.[17]

This was the essence of Henricianism in its equation of the 'decent orders' with other laws that were to be considered and in its appeal to the wisdom of 'the body of the realm and learned men'. There is little doubt, moreover, that Paget genuinely believed that all the mooted changes were 'things indifferent'. A characteristically pessimistic letter, correctly if dismally noting that 'we have no money at all to speak of', stressed the extreme importance of 'feigning friendship' with the Emperor.[18] But it also said, apparently sincerely, that 'the things that hitherto you have passed' (including the new vernacular Communion) 'be but forms and fashions of service and ministration of the sacraments which is and hath been diverse in diverse places in Christ church and ordered and altered as pleaseth the governors'.[19]

In Edward's reign, as in the 1530s, religious reform could be perceived as an integral part of a still broader social transformation. Somerset's own

---

[16] 1 Edward VI c.2.   [17] 'Paget letters', 15.   [18] Ibid., 23, 24.   [19] Ibid., 24.

commitment to this project was so pronounced that he alarmed his colleagues and advisers and that impressionable historians discerned a Glad-
stonian statesman. It is true that the best discussion of his 'government
policy' reveals a man obsessed with conquering Scotland, a task that he
hoped to accomplish by the expensive strategy of building and maintaining garrisons. But even this revisionist account concedes that his motives
included 'a keen wish to appear a virtuous and dynamic ruler'.[20] It follows that his policies were shaped by his opinion – and the opinion of his
supporters – of what would count as 'virtuous and dynamic'.

In some Protestant eyes, doctrinal and social reform were virtually inex-
tricably linked; to several famous preachers of the period – Latimer, Hooper,
Lever – the promotion of the usual list of 'commonwealth' reforms (especially those addressing idleness) was a symptom of a spiritual renewal. It
would have been odd if the duke had made no gesture to satisfy these
influential people. But as it happens, the evidence suggests that his commitment to their views was genuine, for even his Scottish policy was shaped
by their delusions. His forts were not intended to hold the country down,
nor even to levy tribute from the people, but to supply support to local
allies;[21] he must have expected those allies to grow rapidly in numbers, presumably because he thought that any rational person would soon embrace
the 'godly' cause (as his propaganda frequently described it)[22] of marriage
between Edward and Queen Mary. This expectation presupposed an optimistic judgement of the attractiveness of godliness. The same somewhat
pig-headed attachment to reform gave England his notorious Vagrancy Act,
a statute that attempted to abolish idleness by turning persistent vagrants
into slaves.[23]

In the minds of some, such nostrums were connected with an ideal
conception of the body politic. Thus the anonymous Edwardian writer
of a dialogue entitled 'A discourse of the commonweal of this realm of
England' chose to locate his dialogue at a session of the Commission of the
Peace at which 'I and my fellows [the speaker is a 'Knight'], the Justices
of the Peace . . . had declared the king's highness commission touching
enclosures'.[24] According to John Hales, who was the architect of such
commissions, one part of the purpose of commonwealth reform was to assist
the missionary endeavour: 'if there be any way or policy of man to make the

---

[20] M. L. Bush, *The government policy of Protector Somerset* (London, 1975), 160.
[21] Ibid., 27.
[22] Stephen Alford, *Kingship and politics in the reign of Edward VI* (Cambridge, 2002), 193.
[23] 1 Edward VI c.3.
[24] *A discourse of the commonweal of this realm of England*, ed. M. Dewar (Charlottesville, VA, 1969), 15.

people receive, embrace, and love God's word, it is only this, – when they shall see that it bringeth forth so goodly fruit, that men seek not their own wealth, nor their private commodity, but, as good members, the universal wealth of the whole body'.[25] But this pragmatic attitude concealed a much more visionary conception. In 1540, he had claimed that English common law had its foundation in the Ten Commandments. In Somerset's time, he hoped that England's body politic would undergo a mystic transformation. The aim of the government's programme was

> to remove the self-love that is in many men, to take away the inordinate desire of riches wherewith many be encumbered, to expel and quench the insatiable thirst of ungodly greediness wherewith they be diseased, and to plant brotherly love among us, to increase love and godly charity among us, to make us know and remember that we all, poor and rich, noble and ignoble, gentlemen and husbandmen, and all other of whatsoever state they be, be but members of one body mystical of our saviour Christ.[26]

This vision of fraternity was doubtless a limiting case, but humanist concern for social order was a significant political force that had a lasting influence on English government. Although Northumberland's regime was understandably less ostentatious, it legislated against new enclosures and made a useful Poor Law (which Mary permitted to lapse). The only comparable laws enacted under Mary appear to have owed nothing to government action; they may, however, have received some principled support from Protestants. In the parliament of 1555, Northumberland's Secretary of State, the young Sir William Cecil, is known to have made two different interventions. One (which was undeniably courageous) was in defence of the religious exiles, whose property the government then wished to confiscate; the other was in favour of a law protecting tillage.[27] Both stands were the natural expressions of his humanist Protestantism.

During the lengthy period in which Cecil governed England as Queen Elizabeth's chief minister, there was undoubtedly a vogue for Ciceronian 'commonwealth' ideas.[28] It is, however, more difficult to specify the link (if it existed) between this intellectual mood and constitutionalist expectations. One theory with considerable appeal is that the obvious prevalence of Ciceronianism encouraged de-personalisation of government power. Cecil's

[25] Diairmaid MacCulloch, *Tudor church militant: Edward VI and the Protestant Restoration* (1999), 50.
[26] Ethan H. Shagan, *Popular politics and the English Reformation* (Cambridge, 2003), 278.
[27] Conyers Read, *Mr Secretary Cecil and Queen Elizabeth* (London, 1955), 109–12.
[28] Markku Peltonen, *Classical humanism and republicanism in English political thought, 1570–1640* (Cambridge, 1995).

habit of carrying a copy of *De officiis* was hardly in itself a sign of crypto-republicanism, but it expressed devotion to the English common weal that could in theory be detached from a commitment to the rule of monarchs. At a rather general level, two possibilities may be distinguished. The first is that some people were assisted by their Ciceronian language to grasp their situation in broadly republican terms. As we shall see, this did in fact occur, with the important consequence that a conception of their state as a mixed monarchy became available to English thinkers. But it is hard to demonstrate that the adoption of this way of talking on some occasions, for some purposes, diminished the practical purchase on the English of notions and attachments that such language found difficulty in accommodating. The second possibility, which seems much more attractive, is that the stress of humanist Reformers on the idea of social discipline encouraged a new emphasis on virtue. It introduced a bias towards aristocracy (a form of government in which the rulers were in a position to discipline each other), especially as practised within sub-state institutions: towns, synods, guilds, and even congregations.

This latter bias had played a part in More's *Utopia* (1516), which may well be the only book by any Englishman, of any period, whose title page identifies its author as 'Under-Sheriff of London' (its dedicatee, Peter Giles, was Town Clerk of Antwerp). Book One – the so-called Dialogue of Counsel – addresses the problems of counsellors to *princes*, that is, of those who work outside this useful, civic context and are obliged, in consequence, to make some compromises. In the mid-Tudor period, this aspect of the work was not forgotten; the title page of the earliest English translation (of 1551) described it as 'translated into English by Raphe Robinson Citizen and Goldsmith of London at the procurement and earnest request of George Tadkow Citizen and Haberdasher'.

This kind of civic-mindedness was more than a projection of the *polis* on the realities of Northern Europe; it drew on attitudes we have abandoned. The rhetoric of common weal could be deployed in any institution that had a vigorous collective life, including institutions that were presumably untouched by Ciceronianism. The Elizabethan Company of Armourers, for example, could be said 'to have a master God be praised the which hath taken as great pains as ever any man did that was in office I think this hundred years. And all for the common wealth of his company not seeking his own commodity but the commodity of the whole company.'[29] Our impulse, on reading this passage, to say that the idea of 'wealth' is not

---

[29] Ian Archer, *The pursuit of stability: social relations in Elizabethan London* (Cambridge, 1991), 143.

political, is really, of course, the fruit of an assumption that the political must be connected with the state. A world where this assumption was rejected was a world in which authority was, as it were, secreted by a wide range of social practices. The obvious subversive potential of such an attitude (a potential all too obvious to Elizabeth and James) was that the authority of sub-state bodies might undermine the power of the monarch.

These points have been sketched, not explored, because the prominence of this way of talking is hardly controversial; the problem lies in guessing the effect of such ideas on people who habitually invoked them. Here, a degree of caution seems appropriate. There cannot be much doubt that the succession of anomalous monarchs from 1547 to 1603 – a child, a Habsburg by marriage, and a brilliant but indecisive spinster – helped to condition English attitudes, but Patrick Collinson's useful phrase 'monarchical republic' has had a certain tendency to misdirect attention. The lecture in which the phrase was initially coined points, somewhat tentatively, to Cecil's capacity to plan for a brief interregnum in the not unlikely event of Elizabeth's murder. But it also quite properly stresses that Cecil's plan was a response to an anomaly; the later Tudor monarchs were so obviously strange that the assumptions that they generated were liable to be effaced by masculine and adult government.[30]

This was a helpful insight, because what really needs to be explained is less the intermittent prevalence of a republicanising way of talking than its relation to another trend: the steadily growing imaginative purchase of the idea of English monarchy. One clue is Cecil's anxiety, when working out his interregnum scheme, to embody his plans in a statute that would give conciliar rule the character of an 'ordinary power'.[31] A preference for ordinary measures could undermine the crown's authority, as when the learned magistrate William Lambarde (1536–1601) '[wished] that absolute power should not be extended where ordinary laws may effect our desires'.[32] But Lambarde's sententious addresses to Kentish quarter sessions reveal some rather complex attitudes. On the one hand, he was confident that England's constitution was a mixture; that the liberties she currently enjoyed had been secured by armed rebellion; and that without the rule of law 'the very life and soul of the commonwealth itself cannot long be maintained'.[33] On the other, he invariably told his listeners that service to law was a

---

[30] Patrick Collinson, 'The monarchical republic of Elizabeth I' in *Elizabethan essays* (1994).
[31] Ibid., 56.
[32] Paul Slack, *From reformation to improvement* (Oxford, 1999), 53.
[33] *William Lambarde and local government; his Ephemeris and twenty-nine charges to juries and commissions*, ed. Conyers Read (Ithaca, NY, 1962), 188, 79, 143.

service to the queen, because (to quote a typical expression) 'it pleaseth her highness to use us as the mouth of her laws'.[34] Whatever else it was, the classical republican ideal was an ideal of government by 'laws'; but England was a country in which every law was royal.

II

In this king-saturated mental world, one source of respect for the positive law of the land was the fact that it determined who was monarch. All three of Henry's children were placed on the throne by his will, a document whose power to settle the question rested in turn on a Henrician statute, the 1544 Succession Act. All three, furthermore, required some legislation to clarify the terms on which they governed. In Edward's case, this took the form of another Henrician statute, a measure that empowered a former child-monarch who had attained the age of twenty-four to abolish some or even all the statutes that had been passed in his minority. As this was a power that could be exercised at any subsequent moment in his reign, the statute was a significant expansion, along the lines of the Act of Proclamations, in the capacities of English kingship. In 1547, the government found it prudent to pass a further Act declaring that King Edward's laws were nonetheless as valid, in the mean time, as any previous royal legislation.[35]

Over the course of Edward's reign, his rule became, if anything, more legalistic in its character. One reasonable hypothesis is that a certain pressure towards regularity was the predictable result of rule by a collective. Paget maintained, implausibly, that 'my Lord Protector nor none of the Privy Council meddle with no private matter whose soever it be, but only with matters of estate, leaving all other things to their ordinary course of justice'.[36] As clerk of the body, he must have known that this was just a pious aspiration, but its adoption does suggest a shift in norms of conduct. After the fall of Somerset in 1549 no single person formally inherited his powers; Northumberland sensibly cloaked his *de facto* position by calling himself 'Lord President of the Council'. In these new circumstances, the quasi-regal status of the council had the capacity to breed a fairly sharp distinction between the legal and non-legal spheres. At the start of the Northumberland regime, Paget drew up an 'Advice to the king's council' including the recommendation 'that none of the king's privy council shall in no wise speak or write for his friend in any matter of justice between party and party', on the grounds that 'the request of a councillor is in

---

[34] Ibid., 69.   [35] 28 Henry VIII c.17; 1 Edward VI c.11.   [36] 'Paget letters', 49.

a manner a commandment'.[37] The principle perhaps explains why 1551 is the probable date of a landmark in the history of Star Chamber: the abandonment by this 'conciliar' court of any direct jurisdiction over real property.[38]

But this emergent regularisation of government conduct was the sort of thing likely to happen in a minority; similar aspirations were expressed in the minority of Henry VI.[39] It could hardly be expected to survive a reasonably strongwilled adult sovereign. When Edward and Northumberland successfully browbeat the council and the judges into altering the succession in favour of Lady Jane Grey, they gave a foretaste of the likely shape of a mature Edwardian regime. It was, at best, an accident that their successful disregard for statute should in the end have reinforced its power. The same could be said of some of Mary's actions. Mary came to the throne in the first place because the vast majority of the English, including a number of prominent Protestants, rejected her brother's illegal attempt to disinherit her. This was not the last occasion in her reign on which she accidentally encouraged common law, but if her rule had lasted rather longer, it might have had quite different results.

As many historians have noted, Mary could not abolish her own Supremacy without employing the same means that her father had used to create it. Some Protestants indeed maintained that she invalidated her own writs by failing to style herself the Head of the Church when she was summoning her parliament. Arrangements for including her husband Philip within the scope of English treason law and for the regulation of his power in the event of a minority also required that she make use of statute. But though these facts were not irrelevant to the development of English thinking, they had relatively little short-term bearing upon the actual nature of the country's government; as in her father's final years, parliament's theoretical position was no guide at all to the practical balance of power. Nor was the fact that government was organised around a privy council.

Unlike her younger sister, Mary has never been accused of being a subtle woman. Her strict Roman Catholic beliefs were both unpopular and undisguised, and she had no capacity to dazzle. She also suffered from the fact that her immediate Catholic adherents – those who had helped to organise her stand against Jane Grey – lacked the administrative capacity

[37] Elton, *Tudor constitution*, 98.
[38] J. A. Guy, *The court of Star Chamber and its records to the reign of Elizabeth I*, Public Record Office Handbook 21 (1985), 57.
[39] *Archeion, or a discourse upon the high courts of justice in England*, ed. C. H. McIlwain and Paul L. Ward (Cambridge, MA, 1957), 77–80.

of counsellors inherited from Edward. Given that Englishmen were not accustomed to government by any kind of woman, let alone a politically inexperienced spinster, it was a great achievement on her part to force her council to accept her principal personal policy objective: a marriage with her cousin Philip of Spain. This achievement was particularly striking as there is every reason to suppose that even religious conservatives disliked it; its most formidable opponent was Stephen Gardiner, who was the council's leading Catholic.[40]

Her personal success in this battle of wills was only one sign of the strength of her position. Much has been made of troubles within her parliaments, including the notorious episode in which the Protestant Sir William Kingston forcibly barred the exit from the Commons in order to secure a vote he wanted. But the Venetian envoy Michieli, who is our major source for this event, was in no doubt that England was in our terms an 'absolutist' state. In the formal Report on the country that he composed in 1556, he saw the very principle of privy council rule as being 'Turkish'; to the mind of a republican Venetian, it was self-evidently deplorable that any single person should have the right to choose her own advisers. Though Michieli did believe that parliament had once been a constraint, in the days when English rulers were 'civil and political chiefs, rather than lords and monarchs as they now are', he regarded the modern assembly as a formality.[41] The facts on balance justified this pessimistic judgement.

This is not to deny that the Marian regime provoked some novel oppositional thinking. Worries about absorption into Philip's wider empire were likely to encourage legalistic attitudes, if only because agitation against Philip (which was not necessarily tinged with Protestantism) almost inevitably involved appealing to the liberties of England. But Mary was nonetheless able to establish precedents that a determined queen could have exploited to undo the Edwardian concessions. During her first three years upon the throne, her government gave scattered indications of unEdwardian disregard for legal niceties: a non-parliamentary duty on the import of sweet wine; rough treatment of Protestant bishops;[42] the impression of a foreigner that Chancery heard cases after judgement.[43] But the true measure of her strength and willingness to use it was her

[40] D. Loades, *The reign of Mary Tudor: politics, government and religion in England, 1553–58*, 2nd edn (1991), 71.

[41] *Calendar of state papers and MSS relating to English affairs existing in the archives of Venice*, ed. Rawdon Brown, 6 vols. (1864–84), VI, part ii, 1052–3.

[42] Norman Jones, *Faith by statute: parliament and the settlement of religion 1559* (London, 1982), 103–5.

[43] *Two Italian accounts of Tudor England*, ed. C. V. Malfatti (Barcelona, 1953), 49.

response to the demands of wartime. At the end of the reign, when fighting against France (in the course of the pro-Habsburg war that lost the country Calais), she made more concentrated use of extra-legal power than any of the other Tudor monarchs. Her government raised a substantial Forced Loan that was never to be paid back; it drew up a new Book of Rates that more than doubled English customs duties; and it showed readiness unique in English history to keep the peace by means of martial law.[44]

III

The events of Mary's reign revealed the strength of the monarch's position; the events, or non-events, of her cleverer sister's created attitudes and expectations that helped promote a legalistic style of government. This is not to say, however, that the returning Protestant regime was ever completely constrained by its legal procedures; when necessary, it could be just as ruthless as any of its Catholic predecessors. Though Mary regulated the militia by two elaborate parliamentary statutes, Elizabethan military officials routinely imposed non-statutory duties on members of these amateur armed forces.[45] After the Northern rising of 1569, more than 600 rebels were hanged by martial law (a handful of the prosperous received a jury trial, but only because a conviction was a prerequisite for confiscation of real property).[46]

The very existence of such power was not, as yet, especially controversial. Thus though there were regular complaints about the *misuse* of the power of dispensation, the Elizabethans recognised the need for this kind of discretion. That paradigm case of 'extraordinary' power, the Chancellor's equitable jurisdiction, appears to have been exercised with caution, but the conventional theory of his activities continued to resemble Fortescue's. As William Lambarde put it, the king must 'either reserve to himself or refer to others a certain sovereign and pre-eminent power, by which he may both supply the want and correct the rigour of that positive or written law'.[47] It may be that an interest in extraordinary power was actually encouraged by the tightening grip of ordinary procedures, if only because emphasis on regularity was likely, in the end, to draw attention to the significance of the

[44] Loades, *Reign of Mary*, 331.
[45] Lindsay Boynton, *The Elizabethan militia 1558–1638* (1967), 11.
[46] *Memorials of the rebellion of 1569*, ed. C. Sharp (1840), 163, 127, 188.
[47] Lambarde, *Archeion*, 43; Edward Hake, *Epieikeia: a dialogue on equity in three parts*, ed. D. E. C. Yale (New Haven, 1953), 139–40.

exceptions.[48] If ordinary royal power was legal, then occasional irregular proceedings must be expressions of non-legal power: of what was increasingly frequently referred to as royal *absolute* prerogative.

Thus Sir Thomas Smith's *De republica Anglorum*, the standard description of English institutions as they existed in the 1560s, gave quite a generous account of what a king or queen could do unaided. The monarch had 'absolutely in his power the authority of war and peace', the power to make foreign policy, and the right to choose his personal privy council.[49] In time of war, moreover, he had power of life and death, a power that was sometimes used 'before any open war in sudden insurrections and rebellions'. In what was almost certainly a reference to Mary, Smith noted that this practice was not 'allowed of by wise and grave men', but he did not suggest a mechanism by which an abuse of this type could be prevented.[50]

It would, in other words, be most misleading to imply that anyone desired a revolution that stripped the queen of extra-legal power. It was, however, politically important that the regime's most dedicated servants took pride in their regard for legal values. At the opening of the parliament of 1571, the Speaker of the Commons felt able to assert that Elizabeth had 'given free course to her laws, not sending or requiring the stay of her justice by her letters or privy seals, as heretofore sometime hath been by her progenitors used'.[51] He probably exaggerated somewhat, but there is evidence to suggest that the boast was not unfounded; if anything was new in Elizabeth's reign, it was a willingness to respect judicial independence. During the 1560s, for example, the judges made some use of *habeas corpus* to rescue prisoners of conciliar courts. Moreover, they succeeded, after 1581, in discouraging the issue of 'protections', documents that permitted named individuals immunity from civil litigation.[52]

One reason for respecting law was fairly obvious. No follower of Elizabeth's had legitimist beliefs, if only because the queen was Henry's bastard (declared so by a Protestant archbishop). Edward and Mary could rely on other arguments, but the Elizabethan claim depended utterly on Henry's will, which in its turn depended on his last succession statute. In consequence, her supporters were committed to the view that the identity of England's monarch could be determined by a parliament. In the duke

[48] W. H. Dunham, 'Regal power and the rule of law: a Tudor paradox', *Journal of British Studies* 3 (1964), 53–5.

[49] Sir Thomas Smith, *De republica Anglorum*, ed. Mary Dewar (Cambridge, 1982), 85.

[50] Smith, *De republica*, 85–6.

[51] T. E. Hartley (ed.), *Proceedings in the parliaments of Elizabeth I*, 3 vols. (1981–95), I, 199.

[52] J. H. Baker (ed.), *Reports from the lost notebooks of Sir James Dyer*, 2 vols., Selden Society 109–10 (1993–4), I, lxxix–lxxxi, lxxxiii–v.

of Norfolk's treason trial in 1571, the queen's Solicitor-General was led to deplore the idea that 'the judgement of the right of the crown of this realm is reduced to an universal law, which they call *ius gentium*, and the discerning thereof exempted from the laws of this realm'.[53] From 1571 to 1603 it was high treason to deny the queen's power 'with and by the authority of the parliament of England . . . to make laws and statutes of sufficient force and validity to limit and bind the crown of this realm and the descent, limitation, inheritance and government thereof'.[54]

In the first decade of Elizabeth's reign, this view was surprisingly readily accepted. The brilliant Catholic lawyer Edmund Plowden, a man of rigorously papist views, devoted the Christmas vacation of 1566 to writing a manuscript treatise proving Mary Queen of Scots to be the Queen's legitimate successor. Although he made some technical objections to the validity of Henry's will (an instrument which pointedly ignored the Stuart line), he voluntarily conceded that the question was something that a statute could determine.[55] His argument depended on the notion, which he was later to expound in printed law reports, that kings have two capacities because they have two bodies: a 'body natural' and a 'body politic'. Plowden argued that deficiencies in the body natural, such as infancy, or illness, or (in the case of Mary) alien status could not affect the body politic; Henry VII's much more serious defect of having been attainted as a traitor proved not to be a bar to his accession.[56]

What was revealing about Plowden's treatise was the unnecessary elaboration with which he discussed the whole notion of a body politic. One sign of the impact of Henry's Reformation was that a common lawyer who opposed religious change was nonetheless committed to its central metaphor. Plowden informed his readers that just as the body natural had 'members' (i.e.limbs) of various sorts 'so hath this body politic for his subjects who be of divers degrees and sorts be his members and they be incorporate to him and he to them and they both make a perfect incorporation. And the office of this body politic of the king is to govern well and the office of the subject is to obey.'[57] Plowden appears to have been a little uncertain of the relationship between the body and its members; at times, he appeared to suggest that the 'corporation' of king and subjects was conceptually distinct from the 'body politic of the crown'.[58] But at all events, the monarch was a creature of the law; a corporation could exist by

---

[53] W. Cobbett and T. B. Howell, *A complete collection of state trials*, 32 vols. (1809–26), i, 1016.
[54] Elton, *Tudor constitution*, 76.   [55] British Library, Harleian MS 849, fo. 31v.
[56] Ibid, 16.   [57] Ibid., 2   [58] Ibid., 17.

letters patent or by common law, and the king's body politic was 'founded without letters patent by common law only'.[59] Moreover, its characteristics were dictated by its purpose, for 'other action than good government and direction the law of the realm doth not ascribe or appoint to the body politic of the king of this realm'.[60]

Elizabeth thus worked with the cultural grain in building her regime, in theory, upon respect for England's legal system. In practice, she may have been equally constrained by the shared moral attitudes of those through whom she governed. At the beginning of the reign, the young Elizabeth surprised observers by choosing to rule her kingdom through a faction: against the expectations even of Protestants, she dispensed with two thirds of her predecessor's council, while all but one of her new councillors were connected by blood, marriage, or household service to her or her adviser William Cecil. As Cecil was returning to his previous post as Secretary of State, the regime looked, if anything, like a revival of Northumberland's. Even the council's leading Catholic, Lord Treasurer William Paulet, marquess of Winchester, was originally a Northumberland appointment. Soon afterwards, this impression was strongly reinforced, because Elizabeth had the misfortune to fall in love with the future earl of Leicester, the duke's charismatic but married second son. Elizabeth thus governed through a clique with whom she had close personal connections.

If this was a deliberate decision, then it was vindicated by events, because the establishment that she created allowed her to maintain a grip on government policy. The narrowness and coherence of this group did, however, have some awkward consequences, if only because the perspective of these servants was often rather different from their sovereign's. One source of intermittent strain was that her leading followers were relaxed about rebellion. Virtually all the councillors she initially appointed had played some part in the Lady Jane Grey usurpation or one of the subsequent plots to unseat Mary. In the course of the reign, they repeatedly supported armed resistance against the monarchs of France, Spain, and Scotland. This was no doubt the reason why the respectable Sir Thomas Smith could blandly remark that evil rule was often followed by rebellion 'whereof the judgement of the common people is according to the event [= outcome] and success; of them which be learned, according to the purpose of the doers and the estate of the time then present'.[61]

Some Protestants under Mary held the more extreme position that even 'private subjects' could commit tyrannicide, but once Elizabeth was on

---

[59] Ibid., 7.　　　[60] Ibid., 2.　　　[61] Smith, *De republica*, 52.

the throne, this theory was in general indignantly rejected. As archbishop Matthew Parker pointed out,

If such principles be spread into men's heads, as they now be framed and referred to the judgement of the subject, of the tenant, and of the servant, to discuss what is tyranny and to discern whether his prince, his landlord, his master, is a tyrant, by his own fancy and collection supposed, what lord of the council shall ride quietly minded in the streets among desperate beasts?[62]

Parker was worried about theories that vested the right to judge tyrants in the people; he did not deny the existence of special circumstances in which rebellion might be laudable. Few of his generation of moderate Protestants appear to have had a principled objection to a position – such as Calvin's own – permitting certain magistrates the right to armed resistance. When Elizabeth visited Oxford in 1566, the academics staged a disputation on the theme 'Whether it may be permitted to a private man to take up arms against an evil prince' – a formulation that suggests that individuals with a 'public' status had a potentially superior claim.[63]

During this early period, it was in fact the government's own defenders who seem to have been most inclined to limit monarchy. Their type of thinking was of course encouraged by the embarrassment of the Queen's gender, an embarrassment that had recently been deepened by Knox's notorious *A first blast of the trumpet against the monstrous regiment of women* (1558). It is well known that even John Aylmer's official response, *An harborowe for faithful subjects* (1559) made tacit concessions to masculine misgivings. A combination of his classical reading with worries about the dangers of a woman's government led Aylmer to the novel view that England's constitution was a mixture: 'the regiment of England' was 'not a mere monarchy . . . nor a mere oligarchy, nor democracy', but a regime 'the image whereof, and not the image but the thing indeed, is to be seen in the parliament house, wherein you shall find these three estates: the king or queen which representeth the monarch; the noblemen which be the aristocracy; and the burgesses and knights the democracy'. The closest analogy, he thought, was Sparta. The wisdom of this arrangement led him to congratulate 'those that in Henry VIII's days would not grant him that his proclamations should have the force of statute'. It followed that the rule of queens was relatively harmless, 'for first it is not she that ruleth but the

---

[62] Matthew Parker, *Correspondence of Matthew Parker D.D.*, ed. J. Bruce (Cambridge, 1853), 61.
[63] *The progresses and public processions of Queen Elizabeth*, ed. John Nichols, 3 vols. (London, 1823), I, 241–3.

laws, the executors whereof be the judges appointed by her, her justices of the peace and such other officers'.[64]

Some of the same anxiety had shaped Sir Thomas Smith's account in his famous *De republica Anglorum*. Smith thought that women should not rule 'except it be in such cases as the authority is annexed to the blood and progeny'. Even then, it was 'by common intendment understood that such personages never do lack the counsel of such grave and discreet men as be able to supply all other defaults'.[65] Like Aylmer, Smith showed interest in a mixed constitution that had a certain bias towards aristocracy, that is, in the sort of arrangements that were realised in England in periods when parliament was sitting. In what became a standard formulation of parliamentary omnicompetence, Smith noted that the assembly had the power of 'establishing forms of religion' and that 'all that ever the people of Rome might do either in *centuriatis comitis* or *tributis*, the same may be done by the parliament of England, which representeth and hath the power of the whole realm both the head and the body. For every Englishman is intended to be there present.'[66] There is no mystery about Smith's motives: if parliament were not, in fact, effectively omnipotent in England, then Elizabeth was a heretic and bastard, and the rightful queen of England was Mary Queen of Scots. But the longevity of a regime with such a large investment in this notion was bound to have some long-term consequences.

In time, Elizabeth's establishment grew old, rich, and increasingly averse to further changes, but most of the great crises of the traditional narratives of the period had something to do with a clash between their values and those of their inflexible employer. Elizabeth's major political successes – not marrying, not settling the succession, not altering any part of her religious settlement – involved her in resisting near-consensus in this group and its supporters in the House of Commons. Elizabeth's victory on all these questions casts the burden of proof on those scholars who are inclined to emphasise the limits on her power. Her tendency to steer well clear of difficult decisions did, however, have its disadvantages: Elizabethan government was competent and cheap, but it was never very innovative. Its remarkable achievement was to fight in several theatres against the greatest European power without at any moment approaching bankruptcy; its striking limitation was its comprehensive failure to find a new way of exploiting the nation's resources. The obvious opportunity not taken was that of exploiting Queen Mary's courageous precedent by a revision of the Book of Rates.

[64] John Aylmer, *An harborowe for true and faithful subjects* (Strasburg, 1559), sigs. H2v–H4.
[65] Smith, *De republica*, 64–5.   [66] Ibid., 79.

Elizabeth did make some use of extra-legal power, but she did so sparingly and timidly. Her greatest political problems were caused by her 'monop-olies', but the most onerous of her exactions were probably local military rates (including the levy on coastal areas that was already known as Ship Money). She raised Forced Loans of moderate size to ease her cash flow problems, but only one of them was never repaid (it nonetheless stayed on the government's books as a *loan* until at least as late as 1620).[67] What she conspicuously failed to do was raise the yield of parliamentary taxes or find a realistic substitute. In an inflationary age, the nominal level of direct taxation during the 1590s was roughly the same as in Henry's final years[68] – this in spite of the fact that the country had since become richer and that the enemy it faced was a menace to its national survival. In conse-quence, it has been estimated that Elizabeth was extracting some 3 per cent of English national income at a time when Philip II was taking about 10 per cent of the income of Castile.[69] The best way of accounting for this failure of government nerve is to turn back to the idea of law.

IV

Protestant humanist ideas have attracted much attention, especially in con-nection with the history of English political theory. The same cannot as yet be said of later sixteenth-century legal thinking. The period's manuscript reports are still very largely unstudied and the complex interaction of law and politics has barely been attended to at all. But though many of the details are still poorly understood, a few rather general conclusions can be drawn. To begin with, most Elizabethan lawyers appear to have shared St German's general outlook; they understood the common law as composed of determinate rules, the bulk of which derived from general custom. His masterpiece's cogency was probably not the sole reason for the spread of his ideas; it may be better to regard St German's influence as one of the symptoms of a larger shift: the gradual transformation of *nostre erudition*, the common lawyers' way of doing things, into a less flexible body of determinate principles, created by judicial precedent.

As might have been expected, one of the agents of this shift was printing, which made available new ways of reaching out to non-professional readers. During the final decade of the reign of Henry VIII, increasing interest was being shown in the recovery and presentation of common law considered as

---

[67] F. C. Dietz, *English public finance 1558–1641* (New York, 1932), 81n.
[68] Penry Williams, *The Tudor regime* (Oxford, 1979), 74.
[69] Ralph Davis, *The rise of the Atlantic economies* (London, 1973), 211.

a *system* that could, at least in principle, be set out in a printed publication. The achievements of Sir Anthony Fitzherbert may have encouraged this new attitude and given a certain impetus to the complaints that surfaced in the 30s about the common lawyers' lack of 'method'. Someone who thought that common law could be reduced to maxims, as Fortescue appeared to have shown by precept and Littleton by example, had reason to hope that 'some expert and learned man would take upon him to set forth plainly, sincerely, and faithfully the whole course of laws used in this realm of England'.[70]

Another manifestation of this impulse was an increasing interest in legal history as an essential key to understanding. At the beginning of the century, Fitzherbert thought that Bracton was 'of no authority', but references by later English judges were soon to become increasingly respectful.[71] Their purpose was not, or not solely, to gild their judgements with a show of learning. In about 1540, the editor of Bracton's follower 'Britton' explained that 'the antiquities and first principles of every learning (especially of the laws of this realm) are most in price esteemed and to be set by'. His object in printing the treatise was practical, not antiquarian; he thought that 'the brief, pithy, and substantial writings' of the first common lawyers supplied students with the background they required for a full comprehension of the year books, which 'for lack of good grounds plainly expressed' had 'so amazed, dulled, and discouraged many noble wits learning the same'.[72] A roughly contemporary editor of the most ancient statutes explained that 'in the same [statutes] if they be well sought is contained a great part of the principles and old grounds of the law. For by searching the great extremities of the common laws before the making of the statutes and remedies provided by them, a good student shall soon attain to a perfect judgement.'[73]

The evident presupposition of these developments was that the law was something which could be written down. But a feeling that the law's unwritten status was in a sense a mere anomaly did nothing to discourage hostility towards civilians. In about 1545, when Fortescue's *De laudibus* was first printed, the Epistle to the Reader described it as a work 'from which you may easily see that our laws excel not only the constitutions of the Roman Caesars, but also those of every other nation, in prudence, justice

---

[70] *Institutions in the lawes of Englande* (?1540), sig. G6.

[71] D. E. C. Yale, 'Of no mean authority: some later uses of Bracton' in *Of the laws and customs of England*, eds. M. Arnold, T. Green, S. Scully, and S. White (Chapel Hill, NC, 1981), 383–96.

[72] *Britton* (1540), 'To the reader'.

[73] *The great charter called in latyn Magna Carta with divers olde statutes* (?1540), 'To the reader'.

and equity'. The first great political crisis of Edward's reign revealed that such claims had come to be widely accepted. The then Lord Chancellor, Thomas Wriothesley, had been in the habit, like his predecessors, of acting through Masters in Chancery who were trained as Roman lawyers. At the start of the new reign, he had renewed the powers of these Masters by issuing a warrant on his own authority. At this point, 'divers students' petitioned the council in terms that blended Fortescue's ideas with Henry VIII's imperial pretensions:

> whereas the imperial crown of this realm of England and the whole estate of the same have been always from the beginning a realm imperial, having a law of itself called the common laws of the realm of England, by which law the kings of the same have as imperial governors thereof ruled and governed the people.[74]

The students' tactics were themselves revealing of a high estimate of common law, because the phrasing hints at an inversion of the established government position. Henry had thought that England, as an Empire, ought to be free of alien legislation; here the existence of autonomous law was treated as an argument for Edward's imperial status.

The students' central argument came straight from Fortescue. Their principal assertion was that the common law

> as well before the conquest as since hath been accepted from time to time and allowed as most apt and meet of all other, as well for the maintenance of the prerogative royal as for the good governance and true obedience of the people and subjects of the same; insomuch as neither the conqueror ne any other governor thereof have either before his time or sithence at any time altered or changed the same laws for any other. By and under which common laws . . . the kings subjects be preserved under the kings majesty in your lives, honours, goods, chattels, and all other things that you have and do enjoy therein.[75]

These laws consisted in 'certain rules and grounds confirmed and approved by reasons and judgements thereupon by great deliberation given, the reports whereof remain in writing for every man willing to study';[76] the Masters in Chancery, by contrast, acted 'according either to the . . . law civil or their own conscience; which law civil is to the subjects of this realm unknown'.[77] The interest of this episode is that the common lawyers were successful in forcing the Lord Chancellor's dismissal. The council had non-legal grounds for wishing to be rid of Wriothesley (he was Somerset's most formidable opponent), but the fact that the lawyers could offer them an adequate excuse was a significant development.

---

[74] *Acts of the Privy Council*, new series, ed. J. R. Dasent, 32 vols. (London, 1890–1907), II, 48–9.
[75] Ibid., II 49.   [76] Ibid., II 49.   [77] Ibid., II 50.

The students' phrasing gave no indication that they believed that common law had somehow been engendered by the people. But during the next generation, professionals began to stress this aspect of the system. In Anthony Fitzherbert's *Magnum abbreviamentum* (1514–17) the title 'custom' was concerned with purely local customs; but his emulator Brooke's *La graunde abridgement* (compiled at some time before Brooke's death in 1558) reported a fifteenth-century judge as stating that 'the common law is the general custom of the realm'. The importance of this statement was not so much the claim that law was custom – which can be paralleled within the Year Books[78] – as the fact that the word 'custom' appears to have been grasped as populist. This involved Brooke in an interesting minor distortion. Although the Year Book passage that he cites is concerned with the custom of London, the dictum he refers to is not concerned with custom, but with the narrower concept of *prescription*. It states that there are two kinds of prescription, one which is purely local and one 'which runs throughout the realm, and that is properly law'.[79] Brooke thus misrepresents his source; the statement that some prescriptive rights are properly common law does not imply that common law is, as a whole, prescriptive.

Brooke's treatment of this Year Book tag was a small indication of the shift to stressing the role of popular consent in the establishment of institutions. This may explain the limits that came to be imposed upon Star Chamber. To modern scholars it seems obvious that the authority of Wolsey's court was quite straightforwardly derived from its 'conciliar' nature – it could impose itself on litigants because it *was* the council. But most Elizabethan common lawyers preferred to trace its powers to a statute of Henry VII's, a measure that set up a jurisdiction to cope with magnate criminality (significantly, this was Plowden's view).[80] William Lambarde commanded the learning to reject this vulgar error, but he himself encouraged a similar idea when he maintained that action on the case, the most important mechanism of reason-based professional innovation, was 'warranted' by parliamentary statute.[81] Belief in popular consent as the criterion of legitimacy was being read back into the country's past.

One sign that people were impressed by parliamentary power was that they placed increasing stress on parliament's historical intentions. During the Middle Ages, a judgement and a statute were not utterly distinct. A statute could be said to be a parliamentary 'judgement'; conversely, the judges were happy to state that they were 'making law'. When interpretative

[78] YB 2 Henry IV, fo. 18, pl. 6.   [79] Brooke, *Abridgement*, 206; YB P 7 Henry VI, fo. 33, pl. 27.
[80] L. W. Abbott, *Law reporting in England, 1485–1585* (London, 1973), 205–6.
[81] Lambarde, *Archeion*, 84, 39.

difficulties arose, the judges appealed to the 'equity' of the statute without much reference to known facts about its origins. But in the Elizabethan period there was a growing willingness to think historically. The statutes were increasingly approached as rational (though fallible) responses to problems that had been discerned in pre-existing law.

This development was brilliantly discussed by Samuel Thorne in an edition of a student notebook that had been owned by Thomas Egerton (who was later, as Lord Ellesmere, a controversial Lord Chancellor). As Thorne perceived, the notebook marked a moment of transition from the medieval emphasis on finding out the 'equity' of the statute to a more modern notion of 'intention'. One way of grasping what was happening was as a shift in the interpretation of Aristotelian *epieikeia*. The notion of *epieikeia* had an ambiguity: some people thought that equitable judgements involved an appeal beyond the positive law to universal natural principles, but others saw them as an application of the intentions of the legislator, that is, of what the legislator would have wanted done in an unusual set of circumstances. The notebook's theory still leaned towards the former view; one reason that it was important to know the common law was that the unwritten law could offer guidance about the substance of the reasonable. His notebook explained that

those statutes that come in increase of the common law . . . shall be taken by all equity, for since the common law is grounded upon common reason it is good reason that that which augmenteth common reason should be augmented.[82]

But Egerton did not maintain that common law was perfect; he recognised that statute could reform 'a common law that was slavish and could not be defended by reason, as that of Magna Carta, ca.18, that taketh away the common law that did forbid a man to devise his goods. And as this ground is for statutes abridging common law, so is it for those statutes that do abridge the king's prerogative. Magna Carta 27 & 31.'[83]

This was, of course, where abstract legal theory could intersect with practical political concerns. The more the English thought of law as fixed and fallible, and of statute as having unlimited power to transform it, the more their present rights and obligations depended on the principles to which the people had, in fact, consented. The first clear evidence of such ideas was a debate about Queen Mary's title, at least as remembered, some two decades later, by the learned Protestant lawyer William Fleetwood.

---

[82] *A discourse upon the exposicion and understandinge of statutes*, ed. S. E. Thorne (San Marino, CA, 1942), 143.
[83] Ibid., 161.

In the novel situation in which 'the king' was actually a woman, Stephen Gardiner had drafted legislation confirming the monarch's enjoyment of her predecessors' powers. The Protestant Ralph Skinner objected that

If we by a law do allow unto her Majesty all such preeminences and authorities in all things as any of her most noble progenitors kings of England ever had, enjoyed, or used, then do we give to her Majesty the same power that . . . William the Conqueror had.[84]

If the episode was accurately remembered, it marked an important transition in English attitudes. Fortescue's view of England as a political and regal lordship was not in any real sense dependent upon the details of its history; the nature of the polity had been established, once for all, by the free action of the band of Trojans in choosing to have Brutus as a monarch. This meant that Fortescue ignored the statute laws, from Magna Carta onwards, by which the crown had limited its power. The fact that William was a conqueror was so far from disturbing his position that it supplied him with his argument for the high quality of English custom (William and others *might* have changed unwritten positive law, but they had seen good reason not to do so). Skinner's assumptions were quite different. He evidently thought of limitations on the crown as things that had developed over time, presumably as a result of tacit or explicit royal concessions, and that could readily be swept away by a single piece of ill-phrased legislation.

It is conceivable, of course, that Skinner's remarks were really a projection of Fleetwood's own political concerns: in other words, that they have more to tell us about the 1570s than about the reign of Mary. But Mary's conduct did evoke some other arguments that draw upon roughly the same set of ideas. The most dangerous of Mary's achievements, from the standpoint of her more suspicious subjects, were certainly her precedents for levying impositions, that is, non-parliamentary customs duties. At the beginning of Elizabeth's reign, the judges discussed an imposition on cloth 'not granted by parliament but assessed by Queen Mary of her absolute power'.[85] They seem to have come to no definite conclusion, but the fact that the matter got as far as a judicial conference was in itself of some significance; in an episode foreshadowing the early Stuart constitutional cases, an important 'absolute' prerogative was being scrutinised by common lawyers.

The printed report is unhelpful, but an important argument survives in manuscript, apparently from the pen of Edmund Plowden. Plowden chose to divide the question into two. The first essential point to be decided

---

[84] British Library, Harleian MS 6234, fo.21.
[85] Sir James Dyer, *Les reports des divers select matters* (1688), 165b.

was 'whether the English merchants by the laws of England may freely pass out of this realm in their persons with all manner of merchandise except such as be restrained by especial Acts of Parliament'; the other was 'whether in generality the king by his prerogative may now set an impost or custom on the said merchants other than hath been heretofore used and granted by sundry Acts of Parliament'.[86] Plowden took it for granted both questions could be tackled by reference to ordinary professional materials. He answered the first by pointing to the wording of a writ, which stated that by 'the common course of the common law' every man was allowed to leave the kingdom, though he thought that the same point could be inferred from several relevant medieval statutes.[87] So far as the second was concerned, he pointed to the royal undertaking by 25 Edward I c.5 to levy no 'aids, tasks, or prises but by the common assent of all the realm and for the profit thereof saving the ancient aids and prises due and accustomed'.[88]

The question was never definitively settled, perhaps because government pressure was exerted; it was probably unthinkable in practice that any regime would willingly surrender a source of income on the scale of Mary's Book of Rates. The trend of judicial opinion is easier to gauge from the less urgent but related case of a privilege Mary granted to Southampton. In recognition of the fact that Philip had first landed at the Solent, Mary had chosen to celebrate her wedding by granting the port a monopoly on the trade in Malmsey wine. This privilege was to be enforced by levying treble custom on those who imported the wine through other places. In Mary's time, the merchants acquiesced, but in the first year of Elizabeth's reign, there was a legal challenge to the custom. In 1561, the matter was considered by all the judges, most of whom thought the privilege was illegal 'in respect of the principal matter of the restraint in the landing of malmseys at the pleasure and liberty of the denizens and aliens, which was against the laws, customs and statutes of the realm'. The judges invoked two separate lines of thought; they appealed to a list of statutes made from Magna Carta onwards in which the king had promised not to act without consent, but they also mentioned the idea that 'the above prohibition is private and not public'. This was, of course, a claim that cut two ways: it ruled out grants *intended* to benefit named private individuals, but it confirmed the monarch's power to make such grants for public purposes. In the event, a compromise was found (Southampton's privilege was confirmed by Act of Parliament, but only against merchants who were aliens), and some thought that the episode

---

[86] British Library, Hargrave MS 27, fo. 84.   [87] Ibid., 84.   [88] Ibid., 85.

had clarified the law about the royal capacity to make such grants to private individuals.[89]

The case had two interesting features. One was its confirmation that judges were now thinking much like Plowden, that is, that they presumed they had the competence to settle such a question. The second was that they felt comfortable invoking the idea of public good. In the reign of Henry VIII and even earlier, the common weal had played some part in legal literature, but 'in all the book cases . . . the role of the common-wealth ideal was merely to explain existing principles of law, not to indicate new answers'.[90] Here the related notion of a 'public prohibition' appears to be the basis of a prospective rule. The point is greatly clarified by an exchange in parliament in 1571. The subject was a privilege that had been granted to a corporation – the Merchant Adventurers of Bristol – and later confirmed by a parliamentary statute. The MP Francis Alford 'said he might not speak of the prerogative aptly for he was not learned in the law, but made some remembrance of what he had there seen concerning the Act of parliament for Southampton, whereby it appeared that without an Act of Parliament her Majesty's letters patents were not sufficient'.[91] The debate appears to have turned, in part, on the interpretation of 'the statute which authoriseth all merchants to travel by sea *nisi publice prohibentur*'.[92] The lawyer John Popham gave it as his opinion that

concerning the prerogative . . . it was most clear her Majesty might thereby create at her pleasure corporations of bodies politic; yet that the prince by her own grant might establish any such trade privately or peculiarly to appertain to any one company, it could not be, as the case of Southampton did assure and the common opinion of the learned is on that part of the Great Charter of England which ever is construed to the public commodity and is not meant to the avail of any private company or body, which he meant upon these words of the statute *nisi rex publice* etc.[93]

He also complained that the statute had been obtained by fraud, omitting a proviso in the royal letters patent 'that the guild should not have continuance except it were to the commodity of the city', and 'desired the Act of parliament to be reversed and to leave the letters patent in force, to have their validity according to the law'.[94]

What was most interesting here was his presupposition, foreshadowing future arguments about monopolies, that the requirements of the common weal (of Bristol or the realm) were something for the judges to determine. This marked a stage in the continuing process (which was to culminate,

[89] Ibid., 92–92v.   [90] Baker, *Spelman*, II 35.   [91] Hartley, *Proceedings*, I 210.
[92] Ibid., I 210   [93] Ibid., I 211.   [94] Ibid., I 211.

as we shall see, in the thought of Edward Coke), by which opinions about common weal became more central to judicial thinking. This tendency had important consequences, for if the law were competent to judge the common good, then it was competent to judge the extra-legal measures that had traditionally been justified by reference to such considerations. The law and absolute prerogative had thus become direct competitors. As another exchange in the same session showed, this made relations between crown and subjects considerably more difficult to handle.

The occasion was a modestly worded complaint by the MP and lawyer Robert Bell about 'licences and the abuse of promoters'.[95] These royal licences were dispensations that Elizabeth had granted to 'projectors' (the people later demonised as being 'monopolists'). Perhaps by prearrangement, Bell was at once supported by John Popham. It was highly characteristic of Elizabeth's regime that Bell and Popham were both establishment figures: Bell was the Speaker of the House of Commons in the next parliament, while Popham eventually became Chief Justice. Bell seems to have intended his remark in a spirit of constructive criticism; the diarist who records the episode reported that 'he seemed (as was said) to speak against her prerogative; but surely so orderly did he utter what he spake as such who were touched might be angry, but justly to blame him it might not be'.[96]

Thus their practical objections to misuse of royal power were almost certainly not meant as a demand for constitutional changes. But it was a notable feature of the new political world that their behaviour could be described in terms of a zero-sum conflict with the monarch. This could be seen from an embarrassing speech made some days later by Sir Humphrey Gilbert, who described Bell's intervention as 'a vain device to be thought of and perilous to be treated, since that it tended to the derogation of the prerogatives imperial'. In an interestingly impersonal formulation, he asked 'what difference is it to say the Queen is not to use the privilege of the crown, and to say she is not Queen . . . We are (said he) to give to a common constable the right and regard of his office, which if we shall deny her, what is it else than to make her worse than the very meanest.'[97] Gilbert combined these loyal words with a more equivocal statement that

If we should in any sort meddle with these matters, her Majesty might look to her own power and thereby finding her validity to suppress the strength of the challenged liberty, and to challenge and to use the same her own power any way, and to do as did Louis of France who delivered his crown there out of wardship (as

[95] Ibid., 1 202.   [96] Ibid., 1 207.   [97] Ibid., 1 224.

he termed it), which the said French king did upon the like occasion. He also said other kings had absolute power, as Denmark and Portugal, where, as the crown became more free, so are all the subjects thereby rather made slaves.[98]

V

Within a setting like the House of Commons, Gilbert's challenge was, as yet, unanswerable. But within the professional world of the lawyers themselves, ideas were being developed that could absorb the royal absolute power within the sphere of legal processes. As usual, we are not in a position to say that such conceptions were becoming typical, but we can point to three elaborate texts that illustrate the emergence of new possibilities. The first, most interesting, and most fruitful was the first part of Plowden's *Commentaries* (1571). Plowden's reports are usually approached as an uncomplicated rendering of later sixteenth-century legal doctrines; but like the *Reports* of Edward Coke (which took them as a model), they can also be read as a form of political action. Although the author took great care to establish his concern for accuracy (invariably noting, for instance, if he happened to miss a portion of discussion), his method, by his own account, left plenty of scope for shaping by selection. He had, he said, 'for the most part reported cases in a summary way, collecting together the substance . . . without reciting . . . arguments verbatim'. It was Plowden, however, who judged what was substantial, there being 'few arguments so pure as not to have some refuse in them'. The upshot was that 'I have expressed the matter intended truly, and for the most part in the words of the party who spoke it, sometimes indeed in other words added by myself showing the matter more fully.'[99]

The consequence of these methods was a volume of reports that harped continually on certain questions. In case after case, he reverted to two topics. The first was statutory interpretation, which he treated as demanding reconstruction of the intention of the legislator. He took it for granted that 'the letter of the law is the body of the law, and the sense and reason of the law is the soul of the law, *quia ratio legis est anima legis*'.[100] This soul should be identified with the intention of the legislator, which was to be identified by 'equity which is called by some epichaia, which often puts an exception to the generality of the text for some reasonable cause'.[101] This was 'a necessary ingredient in the exposition of all laws'.[102] He quoted Aristotle to show that 'in order to form a right judgement when the letter

[98] Ibid., 1 224–5.   [99] Edmund Plowden, *The commentaries or reports* (1761), 'Preface'.
[100] Ibid., 465.   [101] Ibid., 465.   [102] Ibid., 466.

of a statute is restrained, and when enlarged by equity, it is a good way, when you peruse a statute, to suppose that the law-maker is present', partly because 'while you do no more than the law-maker would have done, you do not act contrary to the law, but in conformity to it'.[103]

The second was the king's political body, a theme addressed in celebrated works by F. W. Maitland and Ernst Kantorowicz, both of whom used the *Commentaries* to illustrate what they supposed was ordinary professional opinion. It is a pity that neither of these great scholars had access to Plowden's tract on the succession, which uses similar material for an avowedly polemical purpose, because this would have stimulated curiosity about the extent to which the law reported was shaped by the private ideas of its reporter. One point to which they might have given more weight is that the doctrine Plowden was expounding was not, strictly speaking, a doctrine of two capacities. Plowden taught that the king had two capacities *because* he had two bodies, the former being his ordinary body, the latter 'a body that cannot be seen or handled, consisting of policy and government and constituted for the direction of the people, and management of the public weal'.[104] In the reports as in the tract, this meant that the political powers enjoyed by English monarchs were properly rights granted by the English common law.

Plowden's originality lay in his combination of what are sometimes thought to be two widely divergent conceptions. On the one hand, he believed that law is something that is made by human beings – he casually referred to 'the founders of our law'[105] – but on the other, he was confident that it included principles that would be adequate to cope with any situation. Unwritten law consists in rules, but even rules must be applied by reason:

there are two principal things from whence arguments may be drawn, that is to say, our maxims, and reason which is the mother of all laws. But maxims are the foundations of the law and the conclusions of reason and therefore they ought not to be impugned, but always to be admitted; yet these maxims may by the help of reason be compared together and set one against another (although they do not vary) where it may be distinguished by reason that a thing is nearer to one maxim than to another, or placed between two maxims.[106]

There was normally, it followed, scope for judgement in application of these principles. Moreover, legal principles included the notion that rules could be suspended when circumstances made this necessary; necessity could dispense with 'common custom of the realm' and even with the 'ordinary

---

[103] Ibid., 467.   [104] Ibid., 213.   [105] Ibid., 368.   [106] Ibid., 27.

course of the common law'.[107] But if 'necessity' were a legal concept, then regal powers that rested upon necessity were part of the expanding sphere that judges supervised.

In Plowden's thought, much scope for judicial discretion was created by the need to make presumptions about the intentions of the legislators. In this connection, his most pregnant statements were a succession of *dicta* from the great case of *Willion* v. *Berkeley*. The case turned in part on the question of whether the monarch was bound by the statute *De donis conditionalibus*, a law in which 'the king' was not actually mentioned. A judgement put into the mouth of Chief Justice Dyer asserted that she fell within its scope, on the grounds that the statute corrected an abuse – 'which being a common error was taken for the common law' – that had the effect of frustrating the donor's intentions.[108] Thus a priority discerned within the common law (at least if the system were rightly understood) had made the statute binding on the monarch.

The best-known passage in the whole report was an account of arguments attributed to counsel in which a version of this point was repeatedly expounded. It had apparently been said that 'in general statutes made for the safety of inheritances, or for the public good, the expositors of them have construed them according to the course of the common law', bearing in mind the principle that 'the law hath so admeasured [the king's] prerogatives that he shall not take away nor prejudice the inheritance of any'.[109] If the concept of inheritance was strictly understood, then this was not at all a new idea; there was a sense in which the law existed for the protection of 'inheritances', that is to say of property which could not be devised, which was for the most part property in land. Plowden was able to cite Fortescue, who noted that the king was free from tolls, but not from so-called 'toll-traverse', which was for 'crossing or going over another's soil or freehold'. But elsewhere in the passage, the notion of inheritance was used with colloquial looseness: Plowden could write of 'every man' as an 'inheritor' of a law 'which belongs to a common person'.[110] It was by no means clear which laws could be said to 'belong' to the people, but the criterion appealed to seemed to involve a judgement about the public good; when he said that the statutes binding on the monarch were 'those which concern the reality or inheritance, *or the public good of the realm*',[111] the last phrase evidently added something. The report was thus a landmark in the process by which an essentially specialised legal system acquired the pretensions of a science of common weal.

---

[107] Ibid., 9.   [108] Ibid., 251–2.   [109] Ibid., 236.   [110] Ibid., 236.   [111] Ibid., 237. My italics.

It had some influence on a more explicit work: a treatise on the royal prerogative addressed to William Cecil, now Lord Burghley, by the presbyterian barrister James Morrice. Morrice's treatise had its origins in a Middle Temple reading of 1579, but by his own admission he had rewritten it, no doubt with an eye to the concerns of its distinguished reader. He frequently made reference to the 'New Commentaries', and noted that the king was bound by statute 'when as common right and equity is by act of parliament restored, and wrong and injury by common error crept in for law is abolished'.[112] Where Morrice departed from Plowden was in his more explicit populism. His ultimate assumptions were derived from Fortescue:

The ancient customs and usages of the realm (whereof the king's prerogatives are a principal part) be called the common laws by which the same is governed not commencing about the time of King Henry I (as this ignorant Italian [Polydore Vergil] would have many of them) but (as Mr Fortescue that great and learned judge affirmeth) have been continued and used within this realm in the ancient reigns and governments of the Britons Romans Danes and Saxons and last of all in the time of the Normans received and allowed.[113]

Unlike Fortescue, however, Morrice appears to have thought of law in its entirety as the product of a popular agreement:

Forasmuch as the sovereign rule and absolute authority of one passing the sacred bonds of justice hath oftentimes burst forth into hateful tyranny and insolent oppression. And for that good kings and princes are neither by nature immortal, nor of themselves being men immutable, another state of kingdom and better kind of monarchy hath been by common assent ordained and established. Wherein the prince (not by licentious will and immoderate affections but by the law that is by the prudent rules and precept of reason agreed upon and made the covenant of the commonwealth) may justly govern and command and the people in due obedience may safely live and quietly enjoy their own.[114]

But though the king of England could not change the laws at will, he was more than 'a Venetian Duke or Spartan king'. To see how much more, it was necessary 'to search out and discuss what right and prerogatives the ancient common laws, or as Mr Saunders late Lord Chief Baron said, the commons of this realm in times past have given to the king'.[115]

Here was evidence of a decisive shift towards a populist account of English institutions. What makes the shift impressive is that Morrice was addressing the Queen's chief minister and that he clearly understood the government's point of view. He criticised Brooke, for example, for claiming that the king could not require an extra-judicial opinion from his judges. In Morrice's

---

[112] British Library, Egerton MS 3376, fo.16   [113] Ibid., 47.   [114] Ibid., 4v.   [115] Ibid., 5v, 7.

view, it was 'no small part of the justices' allegiance expressed in their oath faithfully and lawfully to counsel and advise the king in his affairs'.[116] He also disliked Brooke's statement that monarchs could not personally take recognisances 'for what is this but greatly to estrange his Majesty from the government'.[117] It is this obvious readiness to take the monarch's side that makes his theory so significant. Though Morrice probably had no intention of undermining personal monarchy, he nonetheless seems to have taken it for granted that even the Queen's most extensive discretionary powers had been conferred on her by common law.

There was, however, one important question that Morrice's treatise failed to address. Though he made the conventional admission that the Lord Chancellor enjoyed both absolute and ordinary power, he did not trouble to explore the question of the relationship between the law and equity. But even this dangerous question was soon to receive an interesting discussion from someone who treated the Chancellor's power as based on English custom. During the Lent vacation of 1581, the Middle Temple Reader, Serjeant Snagg, decided to lecture on Magna Carta's concept of *lex terrae*, which he believed was 'as it were, the sum of all the charter'.[118] Part of the interest of Snagg's work was his evident sensitivity, foreshadowing seventeenth-century controversies, to questions concerned with the origins of law. He thought it was important to deny that common law was introduced by Normans or even by Saxons. He also wanted to defend post-conquest baronial risings as rebellions 'not only of the people, that did rise without reason, but of divers of the nobility of the best sort . . . and all their cause was, but to be restored to their ancient laws and liberties'.[119]

This interest in the details of the past superficially resembled Fortescue's, but its underlying assumptions were quite different. Fortescue saw the status of the kingdom as a *dominium politicum et regale* as something forever established by its founders. As a result, he was relaxed about the Norman conquest; the reason that the antiquity of custom could guarantee its wisdom was that the unchanged character of English unwritten law reflected a series of judgements by successful conquerors, men who had the capacity to change the laws of England but sensibly decided not to do so. Snagg, by contrast, thought of conquest as a problem. The period from William I to Henry III was a time, he believed of will-government in kings, concluding only when the latter's charter established that 'how far the prerogative

---

[116] Ibid., 36v.   [117] Ibid., 27v.
[118] Robert Snagg, *The antiquity and original of the court of Chancery and authority of the Lord Chancellor of England. Being a branch of Serjeant Snagg's Reading* (London, 1654), 11.
[119] Ibid., 4, 6.

should go, and what is right and justice common to all, is referred to be decided *per legem terrae*'.[120] Snagg's view of events was supported by a reference to Bracton, whose author was said to be 'one of the chief that were appointed (as it is delivered by tradition) to find out again the ancient laws of the land'.[121] He quoted Bracton's statement that law makes the king and used it to draw a political conclusion: 'if the law of the land made the king, there was none before it; but kings we find by all stories to be of great antiquity here in this land and so by consequence the law must [be]'.[122]

Snagg's basic conviction was that

Our law is the ancient custom of the country or land, and of that antiquity, that there is no record nor matter that can show the commencement thereof, nor any man can tell it, but it was before all memory of man that remaineth in the world, consisting of maxims, general grounds and rules, received, approved, and allowed as good, just, and necessary for the government of this land, begun when this land first became a commonwealth under a king.[123]

Where Fortescue had stressed the forbearance of *kings* who had decided not to change the customs, Snagg thought that the *lex terrae* was 'the ancient custom of the land that all people of several nations that at several times inhabited here liked best of'.[124] It followed that popular usage constituted monarchy. This was a momentous pronouncement, the explicit formulation of a theory that would hereafter organise most understandings of the legal past. It was the more significant, as Snagg himself had grasped, because it brought the Chancellor's power within the legal sphere. Snagg was troubled that the Chancellor 'had most to do and bare the greatest rule; and yet gave his judgement (as it seemed to me) as pleased himself, whatsoever the law of the land required in the case'.[125] This observation left him 'in a maze, not seeing at first how it could stand with the Great Charter that referred all judgement *ad legem terrae*', but his fundamental legal theory provided him with a natural solution:

I found that the custom of the land, which is that *lex terrae*, allowed of that authority also, as of the rest; and that it was also a species of that general, the law of the land, which was the ancient custom of the realm.[126]

Snagg did not deny the traditional case for the provision of equitable procedures; he agreed it was 'impossible but some particular cases must fall out' in which a strict adherence to the letter of the law would necessarily lead to some injustice.[127] He even defended the King's Bench *latitats* (which

[120] Ibid., 12. [121] Ibid., 14. [122] Ibid., 15. [123] Ibid., 17. [124] Ibid., 16.
[125] Ibid., 20. [126] Ibid., 20–1. [127] Ibid., 21–2.

were encountering much criticism from the conservative staff of Common Pleas) on the grounds that 'no law can prescribe the king a form to proceed in justice for those causes that be before himself'.[128] He was not, in other words, a pedantic believer in the superior wisdom of well-established rules, but he was eager to attack the theory that the office of Lord Chancellor 'had been besides the law, erected out of the absolute authority that the conquerors claimed'.[129] Discretion remained an element of the system, but it was a manifestation of positive law, not a suspension of its principles. In short, Snagg had developed a fully constitutionalist position.

[128] Ibid., 57.   [129] Ibid., 31.

CHAPTER 5

Puritans and Anglicans

The readings of Morrice and Snagg are evidence of a new kind of thinking about the common law's capacities. It was probably not just coincidence that both were produced by puritans of presbyterian leanings. From the perspective of such men, a constitutionalist approach was the most natural response to an anomaly: the fact that though Elizabeth in general deferred to the law, there was one sphere of national life – the church – in which she placed some emphasis on extra-legal power. By 1571, her spokesman Sir Nicholas Bacon felt able to tell parliament that 'by religion we do not only know God aright but also how to obey the king or queen whom God shall assign to reign over us, and that not in temporal causes, but in spiritual or ecclesiastical, in which wholly her Majesty's power is absolute'.[1]

As Bacon's audience must have realised, this somewhat shrill assertion was a piece of crown aggression, for there was every reason to believe that further reform of religion was parliament's responsibility. In its earliest formulations, Elizabeth's Supremacy was markedly less 'personal' than her father's. At the beginning of the reign, she cautiously placated both Protestant and Catholic opinion by dropping the title 'Supreme Head' in favour of the less offensive 'Supreme Governor', while her Injunctions put a moderate gloss upon the oath that recognised this status, describing it, in essence, as an acknowledgement of 'sovereignty and rule over all manner of persons . . . so as no other foreign power shall or ought to have any superiority over them'.[2] On the official view, then, the purpose of the Governorship was simply to exclude the papacy.

Two further features of the settlement suggest a wish to minimise her personal involvement. One was the fact that the church courts continued to be formally the bishops'; the government omitted to revive the Edwardian statute instructing the clergy to act in the name of the monarch. This

[1] Hartley, *Proceedings*, I 198.
[2] Gerald Bray, *Documents of the English Reformation* (Cambridge, 1994), 347.

was not, as we shall see, a trivial matter. The other was that powers of visitation were placed on a statutory basis. King Henry's Supremacy statute had simply, by its own account, declared existing powers; Elizabeth's was more ambiguous, but it could plausibly be read as making a *new* law to the effect that any jurisdiction for dealing with 'errors, heresies, schisms, abuses, offences, contempts and enormities' should 'for ever, by authority of this present parliament, be united and annexed to the imperial crown of this realm'. A further provision previously thought needless allowed 'your Highness, your heirs and successors, kings *or queens* of this realm' to delegate this power to a royal commission.[3] Anxiety about Elizabeth's gender thus tended to bring the church further under parliament's control.

This was unfortunate for the queen, because her idiosyncrasies in this particular sphere made clashes with the Commons almost inevitable. Elizabeth's religion was doubtless in a broad sense Protestant, but it was more conservative than that of her immediate followers; it should perhaps be seen as a survival of moderately reformist Henrician thinking into a much more polarised late sixteenth-century world. Even the settlement obtained in 1559 may well have gone beyond her personal wishes. We know that the Commons considered a 'Lutheran' scheme (which was probably based upon the Book of 1549) as well as the more radical one (a re-issue, with minor conservative revisions, of the Prayer Book of 1552) eventually embodied in a statute.[4] Though William Cecil undoubtedly favoured the latter, Elizabeth's behaviour was more equivocal. When she made her Easter communion in 1559, she formally assented to the words 'This is the body of Christ' before reception of the sacrament (an act required in 1549, but pointedly omitted in 1552).[5] The Injunctions that she subsequently issued not only insisted on standards of clerical dress that had obtained in 1548 (a policy allowed for in the Prayer Book), but also established the principle that she could disregard a Prayer Book rubric: the Prayer Book insisted that ministers use ordinary bread for communion; Elizabeth chose to over-ride the statute by enforcing her own preference for wafers.

This trivial disagreement prefigured more serious clashes. In every single parliamentary session from 1566 to 1593, there was some attempt to bring in legislation by which to remedy what were seen as clerical abuses. On J. E. Neale's account, these episodes were stirrings of a puritan 'opposition'; but the work of G. R. Elton and M. A. R. Graves has shown that many

---

[3] Elton, *Tudor constitution*, 374. My italics.
[4] Roger Bowers, 'The Chapel Royal, the first Edwardian Prayer Book, and Elizabeth's settlement of religion 1559', *Historical Journal* 43 (2000), 334–5.
[5] Jones, *Faith by statute*, 122.

'opposition' leaders were really 'men of business' with close links to the council. In fact, they were probably both; a parliamentary session was an opportunity for a well-organised establishment to put unusual pressure on the monarch. Cecil himself had used this mechanism to give unwanted counsel to the queen when trying to persuade her to get married. Those members who went much too far, by advocating presbyterianism, were still in principle engaged in much the same type of activity.

All this suggests a simple and appealing theory, tracing the origins of 'opposition' to tensions at the heart of government. In the religious sphere, Elizabeth could not rely upon her own supporters, so she was forced to get her way by making use of extra-legal power. She had good reason to believe that making use of statute encouraged the spread of what, to her, were dangerous assumptions; when she made the mistake, in 1571, of passing a statute punishing those clergy who would not sign the thirty-six 'doctrinal' articles, she inadvertently gave rise to what was to prove the tenacious belief that parliament had power over doctrine. She therefore circumvented the assembly by appealing to the wisdom of the bishops (who were relatively easy to control) as the appropriate authorities in matters that were broadly spiritual. Because her Stuart successors adopted comparable attitudes, the period as a whole gave shape to a familiar world: puritans had a motive to appeal to legal values; while the upholders of the *status quo* had reason to present themselves as friends of monarchy. The characteristic alignments of English politics, in which high churchmen, by and large, were also royalist, while puritans were broadly legalistic, could thus be traced back to the 1560s.

The model can indeed be taken further. If any group in later Tudor England was heir to the humanist project of sacralising ordinary life, it was the godly magistrates of communities like Norwich or Bury St Edmunds. Such people had excellent grounds for tracing the legitimacy of their under-takings to the inherent wisdom of their measures – or perhaps to an imag-ined godly monarch. This was the way of thinking that led Sir Francis Knollys, Elizabeth's most puritan councillor, to identify two factions among the gentlemen of Oxfordshire, one of which 'leaned passionately to the strict observance of the ceremonies of the Book of Common Prayer', while the other 'did passionately lean to the strict observation of the dutiful main-tenance of her Majesty's supreme government'.[6] The 'dutiful maintenance of her Majesty's government' appears, if anything, to have excluded respect for her religious preferences.

---

[6] John Strype, *The life and acts of John Whitgift D.D.*, 4 vols. (Oxford, 1822), I, 604.

Knollys was registering the existence of two novel social roles. One was the puritan-baiter, the opponent of the godly, who used the liturgy to undermine them; the other was the gentleman who acted as their patron and protector. In areas where puritans were strong, the very existence of a group committed to further reform created opportunities for English politicians from Robert Dudley, earl of Leicester, downwards to draw support by offering them favour. There were places where this role was so attractive that it became hereditary in certain families; the Hampdens of Buckinghamshire, for example, were still performing it in 1700 (by which time they were known, of course, as 'Whigs'). Conversely, those suspicious of Protestantism became the natural allies of conformists; by the mid-1570s, the embattled conservative bishop of radical Norwich was welcoming the assistance of crypto-Catholics.[7]

Of course, religious groupings may well have been shaped in their turn by older interests and loyalties, but the *idea* of politics that hinged on godliness was evidently perfectly familiar, so much so that the pattern could be projected on more traditional contests for local dominance.[8] This way of understanding local quarrels can be connected, in its turn, with the appearance of a novel concept: the increasingly prominent notion of 'popularity' (the bogey, that is, of deliberate appeal to the mob). The term was found useful by the conformist Whitgift, whose anti-presbyterian *The defence of the answer to the Admonition* (1574) may well have introduced it to the language; the first recorded use of 'popular' (a straightforward Anglicisation of the Latin party label *popularis*) occurred just five years later in 1579.[9] The ready acceptance of both words thereafter suggests the need to characterise a new phenomenon.

Some such model perhaps underlay Neale's detailed work on parliamentary history. It cannot be refuted by showing that some 'opposition' manoeuvres enjoyed the full approval of privy councillors; the fact that puritans enjoyed some tacit support in high places made their audacity intelligible, but not, from the monarch's perspective, less alarming. Although what enabled the godly to act as they did was that they saw their actions as far from radical, the attitudes shaped by those actions could nonetheless have long-term and subversive consequences.

---

[7] Diarmaid MacCulloch, *Suffolk and the Tudors: politics and religion in an English county 1500–1600* (Oxford, 1986), 193–5.

[8] John Craig, *Reformation, politics, and polemics: the growth of Protestantism in East Anglian market towns, 1500–1610* (Aldershot, 2001), esp. 150–1.

[9] *Oxford English Dictionary*, s.v. 'popularity' and 'popular'.

Elton's assault on Neale's interpretation was thus to some extent beside the point. The model is, however, too schematic in its suggestion that convinced conformists were necessarily inclined to ultra-monarchism. Puritan invocation of the law helped change the style of English politics, but the relationship of law to prospects for religious revolution was actually of some complexity. The increasingly high claims of common lawyers made law a powerful instrument for clever partisans, but they were also ultimately fatal to any kind of clericalist programme, including the realisation of presbyterianism; to the extent that common law defined the common weal, it was an obstacle to any doctrine that claimed a similar authority. In the Elizabethan period, the hierarchy appreciated this; though they were naturally keen to cast themselves as monarchy's defenders, they were still, for the most part, too prudent to abandon legal values.

Thus though the monarch's preferences did, in the end, give shape to the alignments of subsequent political history, the developments involved were quite protracted. But by the time that James came south, the sheer longevity of her settlement had brought about some cultural consequences that even a more radical successor might have experienced difficulty reversing. In other Protestant countries, the state 'confessionalised'; it acquired a corps of intellectuals united by the shibboleths of their official doctrine. In England, this failed to happen, partly because acceptance of the Supremacy supplied an adequate basis for consensus, partly because the likely orthodoxy, a presbyterian high Calvinism, could be presented as a threat to English institutions.

The result was a temptation to rationalise some oddly mixed arrangements in terms that sat uneasily with Calvinist religion. Though, in the estimation of its leaders, the Church was a full member of the Reformed camp in the Protestant world, its semi-Catholic practices and purely Catholic institutional shape created pressure for a drift towards Catholicism. The Elizabethan hierarchy would have been horrified at the suggestion that they were pursuing a *via media* (though they might have agreed with their leading defender John Jewel that they were saddled with a 'leaden mediocrity'),[10] but the strange church that they presided over continuously allowed the space for non-Reformed beliefs and practices. In time, as we shall see, the lines of thought encouraged by these anomalies made lasting consensus unsustainable.

[10] *The Zurich letters*, ed. Hastings Robertson (Cambridge, 1842), 23.

I

Under the circumstances of 1559, Elizabeth's misfortune is simply summarised: she wanted a Henrician church – no doubt a little modified in a Protestant direction – but there were no Henrician intellectuals. The government would have liked co-operation from figures like Nicholas Heath, the archbishop of York, who was initially retained upon the royal council,[11] and the veteran Erasmian Cuthbert Tunstall, who spent his final days in Lambeth Palace, more as a guest than as a prisoner.[12] The refusal of such moderates to reject the papacy meant that the only group of English clergy through whom the church could credibly be run were men of unambiguously Reformed opinions.

Such people would probably not have accepted their posts if they had seriously supposed that the surviving ceremonies would last indefinitely. The archbishop of York, Edwin Sandys, noted the famous 'ornaments' proviso by which the paraphernalia of worship were to be left as they had been in 1548, but took this to mean 'that we shall not be forced to use them, but that others in the mean time shall not convey them away'.[13] Few if any of these bishops, left to themselves, would have enforced the surplice, especially as the objectors to the garment were disproportionately found among the most impressive of the clergy. Nor would they have followed Elizabeth in her occasional campaigns against the 'prophesyings', gatherings of local ministers in which the queen herself discerned potential for sedition, but most of her bishops saw only an innocent means of raising local intellectual standards.

There was, of course, a rational case for her behaviour. An elderly William Paget was still advising those prepared to listen of the supreme importance of sustaining the alliance with the Habsburgs.[14] At a time when Calais had been lost and France had a presence in Scotland, his views had only gained in cogency, especially as Cecil estimated that 'scantly a third'[15] of the country's JPs could be relied on in religious matters. In such a situation, there was a great deal to be said for being seen to be conservative. The greater degree of ritual Elizabeth encouraged in her chapel had the advantage, among other things, of giving this impression to Catholic nobles and ambassadors. Even much later in the reign, when Protestants had become more numerous, there were compelling

---

[11] Wallace MacCaffrey, *The shaping of the Elizabethan regime* (1969), 33.
[12] Parker, *Correspondence*, 77–8.   [13] Ibid., 65.
[14] *A collection of state papers . . . left by William Cecill*, ed. S. Haynes, 2 vols. (1740), I, 208–9.
[15] Conyers Read, *Mr Secretary Cecil*, 321.

reasons for accepting an undemanding standard of lay conformity. The government's anti-Catholic strategy was shaped by what had happened in 1570, when the emergence of a large-scale problem of principled refusal to attend church services had coincided with the bull by which the Pope attempted to depose the English queen. This made it sensible to stress that recusancy was a form of temporal disobedience with minimal religious justification.

Elizabeth therefore resorted to moderate Henrician arguments, professing herself contented with 'the authority . . . by the laws of God and this realm always due to our progenitors', authority that in some periods had been 'more clearly recognised by all the estates of the realm, as the like hath been in our time'. She did not claim the right to settle doctrine, but she was bound, she said, to see to it that God's law was observed and 'consequently to provide, that the church may be governed and taught by archbishops, bishops, and ministers according to the ecclesiastical ancient policy of the realm, whom we do assist with our sovereign power'. No one was to be troubled for 'matter of faith', so long as their behaviour was 'not manifestly repugnant and obstinate to the laws of the realm, which are established for frequentation of divine service'.[16]

There is some reason to believe that these arguments struck home; one of the problems of the mission priests was the existence of good Catholics who treated church attendance as a matter of civil obedience.[17] Not surprisingly, then, the government stuck to its story, denying that its actions represented a case of persecution for religion.[18] Use of coercion was reserved for those who declined to go to church at all or who assisted in the Catholic mission, whether by sheltering priests or hearing Mass. Although, from 1581, such crimes were regarded as treason, there was never any question of treating popery as heresy. In practice, intermittent non-communicant attendance was perfectly acceptable to the authorities, even when the conformity involved was offered only by the head of an otherwise Catholic household.

The advantage of these features of England's settlement was that they made available, to those whose consciences were solaced by them, a highly conservative picture of the church. They also eased relations with Catholics abroad; it was important to Elizabeth that she should be able to tell the

---

[16] *Queen Elizabeth's defence of her proceedings in church and state*, ed. W. E. Collins (1942), 42, 43.

[17] Alexandra Walsham, *Church papists: catholicism, conformity, and confessional polemic in early modern England* (1993), 53, 57.

[18] [William Cecil], *The execution of justice in England for maintenance of publique and Christian peace* (1583).

Emperor that 'we do not follow any new or foreign religions, but only that approved by the mind and voice of the most famous Fathers'.[19] Essentially Henrician arguments, appeals to the Fathers and to the scope of 'things indifferent', were thus inevitably a part of the defence of England's settlement.

This situation by its very nature encouraged general arguments for continuity. For example, a defender of the ceremonies could note 'how much our ancient fathers increased Christ's Church by such godly policy. Hence it was, they plucked not down all the Jewish synagogues and heathenish temples, but turned them to the service of God.'[20] The same proto-Anglican writer pointed out that even Calvin had allowed some weight to the desirability of decency and order and stressed 'what difference there is now when those things are set forth for comeliness and order, and the time when such like were enforced as the service of God'. This was a Henrician distinction, implicit (it has been suggested) in Cranmer's policies, that had remained available to anyone who wanted to invoke it.[21] During the reign of Edward, Nicholas Ridley, then bishop of London, had turned it against his colleague John Hooper of Gloucester, who had a proto-puritan objection to wearing vestments at his consecration. Ridley had characterised St Paul as using ceremonies 'to bear with [Jewish] weakness, and so to win them unto Christ', though he thought that such behaviour would be wrong 'if so be he that do the same . . . believeth that the thing is necessary to be retained'.[22] But though this line of argument was fairly well established, it was also manifestly incoherent: if a conservative populace was being encouraged to believe in continuities, then it was being encouraged to believe that the importance of the ceremonies extended beyond comeliness and order; if Mass had been idolatrous, then the surviving vestments were invitations to idolatry.

This point was naturally felt most keenly by those with the greatest attachment to the theology to which the church was notionally committed. For the next three generations, the major distinguishing feature of 'puritanism' was the fanaticism and ostentation of its commitment to official values: puritans were regarded as 'zealous', 'precise', and 'busy' in demeanour; and their enemies paid tribute to their virtue by slandering it as

---

[19] John Strype, *Annals of the Reformation and establishment of religion and various other occurrences in the Church of England during Queen Elizabeth's happy reign*, 4 vols. (Oxford, 1824), I–II, 574.

[20] *A briefe examination for the time of a certain declaration lately put in print in the name and defence of certain ministers in London* (1566), n.p.

[21] See above, 72.

[22] *The writings of John Bradford, M.A.*, ed. A. Townsend, 2 vols. (Cambridge, 1848–53), II, pp. 392, 384.

mere hypocrisy. Increasingly, and unsurprisingly, such Protestants regarded the church's hierarchy as a corrupting obstacle to their activities. There was an evident absurdity in forcing the church's most effective clergy, in things admittedly 'indifferent', to act against their consciences or cease their ministry. The scandal of the bishops' role in the enforcement of the ceremonies encouraged scepticism about their usefulness. It was entirely understandable that ultra-Protestant dissatisfaction should take the form of presbyterianism.

First-generation Protestant reformers, including John Calvin himself, had been relaxed about the role of bishops, but his successor Beza notoriously took a stricter line. The fundamental reason for this shift in attitude lay in a controversial aspiration for morally demanding government. The bishops were seen as a hindrance to something that some writers saw as vital to the church: the 'discipline' imposed by the free use of the spiritual sword. It would be quite wrong to assume that this development was inevitable. Wherever the claims of discipline were pressed, lay magistrates were naturally suspicious, while even among the clergy this way of thinking met with some resistance; as English conformists were able to point out, the Zurich ministers who rejected it were just as Reformed, in their own estimation, as Beza.[23]

There was, however, an existing strand of English theological opinion that was at least potentially receptive to a high view of excommunication. The Strasburg theologian Martin Bucer (d.1551), who spent his last days lecturing at Cambridge, was the earliest major thinker in the Reformed tradition to put church discipline on a par with preaching of the Word and the administration of the major sacraments. It was probably under Bucer's influence that Matthew Parker's 'Eleven Articles', a formulary drawn up by the archbishop at the beginning of Elizabeth's reign, referred to the church as 'the spouse of Christ, wherein the word of God is truly taught, the sacraments orderly administered according to Christ's institution, and the authority of the keys duly used'.[24] In 1563, Alexander Nowell's standard catechism held that 'the chief and necessary marks of the visible church' were preaching of the word, invocation of God, and administration of the sacraments, but he thought that the church's well-being additionally demanded 'such a form of ecclesiastical discipline that it shall not be free for any that abideth in that flock publicly to speak or do anything wickedly or in heinous sort without punishment'; it was, it followed, most regrettable that the

[23] Thomas Cooper, *An admonition to the people of England* (1589), 83–4.
[24] Bray, *Documents*, 349.

corruption of the times, especially among 'the rich and men of power' meant that this salutary institution 'can hardly be maintained in churches'.[25]

This intellectual fashion was the natural terminus of one side of the Reformation process; Reformers who demanded a truly disciplined community would treat their civil duties with religious seriousness, but they were also likely to find it obvious that spiritual means of coercion were intrinsic to church life. The result was that even conformists attached significance to the belief that excommunication was an *ecclesiastical* procedure. From a strictly Henrician standpoint, the act of excommunicating someone was an expression of royal jurisdiction, which could, in consequence, be exercised by anybody that the king entrusted with the task; but most of the Elizabethan clergy rejected this unpalatable doctrine. Instead, they insisted on a two-swords theory by treating the *act* of excommunication as properly a matter for the church, which drew authority, in this respect, from Christ's own institution. Thus even if the church was seen as coextensive with the English people, it still enjoyed a type of power *qua* church that was not owed to civil government. This apparently small shift was quite important, because it opened up a gulf between the clergy's teaching and the assumptions of the laity.

Throughout the period between the Reformation and the civil wars, most educated laymen distinguished jurisdiction *in foro interno* (that is, whatever power over conscience was exercised by preaching or through the sacraments) from jurisdiction *in foro externo* (that is, the visible exercise of a coercive power). The former derived immediately from God; the latter from the civil magistrate. But though lay attitudes remained unaltered, the bishops quite quickly adopted a different standpoint. As early as 1566, Robert Horne, the bishop of Winchester, presented a more complicated doctrine. He chose to divide external (or what he called 'cohibitive') jurisdiction into two different types, of which one was delegated by the state, while the other:

consisteth in the exercise of excommunication, and circumstances thereunto required by Christ's institution: the which power or jurisdiction belongeth to the church only, and not to the prince, bishop, or priest, for no man hath authority to excommunicate but the only church and those who receive authority thereunto by commission from the church.[26]

[25] *A catechism written in Latin by Alexander Nowell dean of St Paul's together with the same catechism translated into English by Thomas Norton*, ed. G. E. Corrie (Cambridge, 1853), 175.
[26] Robert Horne, *An answeare made by Rob. bishoppe of Wynchester to a booke entituled the declaration of such scruples* (1566), 105v.

A generation later, Hooker felt able to dismiss as nothing but 'absurd' the idea that a lay monarch could excommunicate.[27]

There was thus a near-consensus among the English clergy that any tolerably Christian church would be equipped with power to excommunicate: a power doubtless exercised under lay supervision, and with the assistance of the corporal pains that were provided by the magistrate, but nonetheless inherent in the church as opposed to the state. To anybody of this way of thinking, the state of the church's court system, with excommunication by lay civilians and large-scale crypto-papal dispensation by the archbishop of Canterbury himself, was one of its most scandalous shortcomings.

Even before the settlement of 1559, the leading proto-puritan Thomas Sampson had believed that want of discipline in the church would be a reason for refusing office.[28] Not all continental Reformers were sympathetic to this kind of scruple, but Sampson and others could rely on allies in Geneva. As Calvin's successor Beza wrote in 1566, 'I once thought that the matter was only about caps and I know not what other externals, but I afterwards understood that the controversy was of a far different character.' He was particularly appalled at ordination by unaided bishops, at the light use of excommunication 'even on account of suits relative to money and the like', at the fact that English midwives were permitted to baptise, and at the archbishop's power of dispensation.[29]

Nothing, it followed, could be less surprising than the emergence, in the 1570s, of an explicitly presbyterian movement with great appeal to intellectuals. A church with a rigorous system of excommunication by lay elders was the best way to supersede transitional arrangements that seemed to be inherently corrupting. The mystery, if anything, is why this mechanism found so little lay support, and why the establishment of 'the discipline' had dwindled, by the last years of the reign, into a distant radical aspiration. The answer may be that abolishing the bishops was not, for most people, an end in itself so much as an all-purpose cure for everything that hindered the spread of godliness, but especially for the shortage of adequate preachers. In consequence, the movement's fatal weakness was the priority assigned to maintenance of a public ministry. This doubtless explains why some 'moderate' intellectuals turn out, upon closer inspection, to favour presbyterian church order; while virtually no 'extremists' abandoned the church to establish their own congregations.

---

[27] *The Folger Library Edition of the Works of Richard Hooker*, ed. W. Speed Hill 7 vols. (1977–98), III, 422.
[28] *Zurich letters*, I.   [29] *Zurich letters*, second series (Cambridge, 1845), 129.

Commitment to the project of a national Reformation gave puritanism an anti-sectarian bias. By 1585, the movement's principal theorist, Thomas Cartwright, was vigorously defending continued membership of the church of England against the criticism of separatists.[30] As he carefully explained to his enemy Whitgift, he thought it was 'unlawful for any, in regard of that which is to be reformed in it, by way of schism to depart from the unity of the church'. Revealingly, he saw the intended further Reformation as the fulfilment of existing law

it being ordained by statute of all the late princes of the land that have departed from the church of Rome, that the canon law (by which this church is for the most part governed) should by a number of learned and grave men be revised.[31]

Cartwright's appeal to law was not unique. One of the most effective of puritan tracts took the form of *An abstract, of certaine acts of parliament: of certaine her Majesty's injunctions: of certaine canons, constitutions, and synodalles provinciall* (1583) purporting to show that many conformist abuses were actually illegal and uncanonical. In the short term, this tactic had great promise, but such polemical victories were costly; they reinforced the power of ideas and ways of thinking that ultimately favoured the conformists. The density of government and the prestige of law provided a structure within which to manoeuvre, but the same structure left no space for altogether novel institutions. In Scotland, introduction of lay elders could seem an attractive extension of local governance; in England, where both church and state were much more vigorous, it threatened the existing mechanisms.

This was probably the underlying reason why puritanism, which seemed so strong when it appealed for sympathy for conscience, attracted much less lay support when it proposed significant social changes. From 1571 to 1587, members of parliament who brought in bills designed to enact a presbyterian programme were one by one arrested and imprisoned. Puritan sympathisers on the council, who showed no hesitation in helping ministers against their clerical superiors, displayed much less enthusiasm for the promotion of the broader programme to which their godly protégés were actually committed. Perhaps the best example of this inconsistency was the Lord Treasurer Sir Walter Mildmay, the founder of Emmanuel College, Cambridge, a college whose earliest Master, the formidable presbyterian Laurence Chaderton, created what was in effect a godly seminary. Mildmay's undoubted sympathy with puritan ideas did not prevent him making a devastating speech against the so-called 'Bill and Book' of

---

[30] Thomas Cartwright, *Cartwrightiana*, ed. A. Peel and L. H. Carlson (1951), 49–58.
[31] British Library, Lansdowne MS 68, fo.139.

1587, the last and bravest serious attempt to implement the presbyterian programme.

Mildmay's objections started with the general conservative point that 'to make void so many laws, old and new, in one general short law, before every one of them be considered is utterly unmeet'.[32] He went on to ask a succession of practical questions: what would replace the function of existing existing episcopal courts in suits about wills, marriages and tithes? Would tithes indeed continue to exist? If not, how would the clergy be maintained? What sanctions were to be attached to excommunication? What would replace the various forms of clerical taxation, of which First Fruits and Tenths alone (which were disproportionately raised from the rich offices to be abolished) amounted yearly to £20,000?[33] How could the mechanism of election – 'being mere popular' – be expected to produce a learned clergy, given that the same 'will bring with it contentions, factions, and confusions amongst the vulgar people' and that 'the lord or chief of the town being evil given, the common multitude that depend upon them [sic] either for love or fear, will choose none other than he shall like of'?[34] The sheer complexity of the issues raised showed the extreme unlikelihood, except in revolutionary conditions, of comprehensive changes in the church's government.

But an additional safeguard of the existing order lay in another type of argument. Mildmay was troubled by the thought that

the pastors and doctors upon occasions rising amongst them may assemble themselves with the rest of the ministers in that country, or province, and so further . . . assemble all in a synod or national council, and there make orders without the licence, knowledge, or authority of the queen. How dangerous that will be, and what inconveniences are like to ensue upon such meetings, all men of judgement may see very apparently.[35]

The remedy for any grievances was simply to appeal to the queen 'for by act of parliament made in the first year of the queen there is left unto her Majesty sufficient authority . . . to reform, alter, add, or diminish so much and in such sort as her Majesty by advice of learned and wise men shall think convenient'.[36]

Mildmay's testimony is useful because he cannot possibly be thought to have been biased against puritans. His colleague Sir Christopher Hatton, who was committed to episcopacy, delivered a more aggressive speech in which he ruthlessly drew out the discipline's subversive implications.

---

[32] Hartley, *Proceedings*, II 345.   [33] Ibid., II 346–9.   [34] Ibid., II 348.
[35] Ibid., II 348.   [36] Ibid., II 350.

Hatton noted that *ius patronatus* was to be exercised by the lay elders, 'which toucheth us all in our inheritances' and, yet more seriously, that 'we are bound to surrender out of our hands our abbey lands and such other possessions as have at any time belonged to the church'. But the most important part of his objections concerned the threat that he perceived to the Supremacy, a threat deriving, in effect, from the revival of a two-swords theory:

For although it be said . . . that the sovereign Majesty is placed by God in highest authority under him within their dominions over all persons and causes as well ecclesiastical as civil, yet mark how the book interpreteth itself: for sooth their dominion they speak of is this, that the sovereign must see and command the ordering of them, as God hath appointed by his word. He must not make any himself by his ordinary authority, but see others make them: which is not a sovereign authority *in causas*, but *in personas*; and is called *potestas facti, non iuris.*[37]

He went on to draw attention to a dismaying possibility:

For who knoweth how far they will proceed, if her Majesty do neglect their excommunications? Is it not, think you, very well known what outrageous assertions are made in your chief presbytery men's books? Doth not her Majesty understand what is set down hereof in these books, *De iure regni apud Scotos, De iure magistratuum in subditos, Vindiciae contra tyrannos?*

From Hatton's perspective, such presbyterians were just as pernicious as Roman Catholics: 'for I pray you wherein differ these men in this cause from the papists? The Pope denieth the supremacy of princes, so do in effect these. The Pope yieldeth unto them only *potestatem facti, non iuris; in personas, non causas*: no more do our reformers in this point.'[38]

The difference between Mildmay's views and Hatton's was not in their opinion of the foreseeable results of presbyterianism; they had identical anxieties about the damage to the legal fabric involved in radical changes to church order. They also felt a similar commitment to the established principles of the Supremacy. But where Mildmay saw the godly as misguided, Hatton thought of them as consciously subversive. Much the most lasting legacy of intellectual presbyterianism was the conviction of the high conformists that they were the intended prey of a conspiracy. In the end, nothing the puritans achieved approached the practical effects of the anxieties that they created.

---

[37] Ibid., II 336.   [38] Ibid., II 338.

II

The strength, and the great weakness, of puritanism was the simplicity of its arguments; to be a puritan was to believe that God's instructions were perspicuous, at least in the sphere of church government and worship. The essence of their case thus needed no development; there was little to be said to an opponent who disregarded the plain sense of scripture. There were, to be sure, two different types of reason for wanting further Protestantisation. Some radicals thought that any non-scriptural practice was a presumptuous instance of 'will-worship'. More moderate spirits centred their objections upon the inappropriateness of given ceremonies to a particular pastoral situation; their views were really based upon a judgement that English culture was too Catholic for Catholic survivals to be wholly innocent. But neither position demanded much intellectual work. Both groups could concentrate upon their mission of converting the ungodly, secure in the knowledge that no one conscientious was likely to challenge their ultimate objectives.

Conformism, by contrast, was unstable; it rationalised a number of continuing processes, each of which tended, in the end, to lead the hierarchy away from a conventional Reformed position. The nature of these processes is relatively easy to discern, but their chronology is controversial, in part because the scholarship of the last generation has seen an understandable reaction against an Anglo-Catholic stress on continuities. The quite correct insistence that nobody respectable was looking for a *via media* has tended to obscure the mechanisms that actually promoted such an outcome. In consequence, it has tended to obscure an event of great importance to wider intellectual history: the birth of the conservative rationalism that in the end transformed the national culture.

One obviously important influence was the survival, virtually unscathed, of the church's governmental apparatus. To be a bishop was to have a complex social role involving privileges and obligations that were not necessarily affected by adopting a Reformed theology. Bishops had lands and courts and even troops at their disposal (there were separate episcopal militias) and they could quite legitimately feel that these advantages assisted them in the promotion of the true religion. One reason that episcopacy had less appeal in Scotland was that the bishops were so weak that they facilitated 'sacrilege', that is, diversion of the church's wealth for wholly non-religious purposes; a bishop could be just a figurehead enabling local aristocrats to take his episcopal income. In England, there were transfers from the bishops to the crown, but the high status of the church's leaders was generally an asset to the clergy. In any case, it was seriously argued that clerical wealth was spent on worthy causes, especially the public good of hospitality.[39]

From the perspective of an active bishop, some other apparent abuses seemed quite defensible. Laymen were shocked at excommunication for trivial offences; a bishop might retort that the sheer triviality of the disputes involved made disobedience inexcusable. Laymen were critical of pluralism; a bishop might see an arrangement of this kind as an irregular but useful means of finding income to support a preacher.[40] Such bishops could identify with predecessors with analogous problems, in the antiquarian Matthew Parker's case by sponsoring a lavish publication: a volume made up of biographies of all his predecessors whose very form implied a myth of continuity.[41]

Even at the high-water mark of English Reformation, in the last years of the reign of Edward VI, the urge to defend the resources of the institutional church was capable of creating bitter conflict between the Protestant bishops and Protestant laymen. This was the principal reason for a setback with far-reaching consequences: Northumberland's decision to veto Cranmer's code of canon law, the *Reformatio legum ecclesiasticarum*, a code which would have stopped church dignitaries from making lengthy leases of church lands.[42] This episode was a foretaste of the future, for Cranmer's *Reformatio* was not (as some puritans later supposed) a revolutionary document; though it incorporated some Protestant doctrinal principles, the law it sought to codify was largely derived from traditional canonist sources.[43] It was an illustration of the fact that a Reformed position could nonetheless go hand in hand with institutional conservatism.

Throughout the Reformation period, the church courts operated their inherited procedures, and the professional learning of their lawyers and officials continued to draw upon manuals produced by continental colleagues.[44] Those who administered the church were thus quite likely to be sceptical about the grander claims of common lawyers. As early as 1565, the impeccably Protestant Sir Thomas Smith (who as Professor of Civil Law at Cambridge had been a leading trainer of such people) had echoed Gardiner's argument that church courts, being royal courts, could not commit

[39] Felicity Heal, *Of prelates and princes: a study of the social and economic position of the Tudor episcopate* (Cambridge, 1980), 220–1.
[40] Hartley, *Proceedings*, II 51–2.
[41] Matthew Parker, *De antiquitate Britannicae ecclesiae et privilegiis ecclesiae Cantuariensis* (1572).
[42] MacCulloch, *Cranmer*, 533.
[43] Gerald Bray (ed.), *Tudor church reform: the Henrician canons of 1535 and the Reformatio legum ecclesiasticarum* (Woodbridge, 2000), lxvi–viii.
[44] Helmholz, *Roman canon law*, esp. 121–57.

the crime of *praemunire*.[45] By the early 1590s, Richard Cosin, Whitgift's principal legal adviser, was boldly maintaining, on similar grounds, that Magna Carta had no application to the procedures of church jurisdictions.[46]

The situation of the hierarchy thus tempted them towards some arguments that drove a wedge between them and the Protestant laity. It also drove them to associate with dubiously Protestant allies, for though the church's leaders were mostly unambiguously Reformed, the same was not yet true of the bulk of its clergy. There did exist some forces in the church prepared to argue, from whatever motives, for a more moderate form of Protestantism. The Convocation of 1563, which drew up the Thirty-Nine Articles of Religion, entrusted Article 28 'Of the Lord's Supper' to Bishop Edmund Guest of Rochester. The article that he drafted was later criticised for omitting the 42 Articles' denial of 'a real and bodily presence'. By his own account, the doctrine formulated 'did not exclude the presence of Christ's body from the sacrament, but only the grossness and sensibleness of the receiving thereof'.[47] There are ways of understanding this doctrine as Reformed, but it was certainly conciliatory. The same assembly reaffirmed, against Bullinger of Zurich and Calvin of Geneva, that Christ physically descended into hell;[48] and tinkered with the Article about predestination and election so as to give more prominence to the statement that 'we must receive Christ's promises in such wise as they be generally set forth to us in Holy Scripture' (a shift that may have been an accident, but which in the end encouraged the rejection of theories of limited atonement).[49] Perhaps most interestingly, the Lower House rejected a proposal to make it optional to wear the surplice that may have enjoyed at least tacit support from several of the bishops.[50]

Conservative forces in the church were thus not negligible. Their position was considerably strengthened by the debating strategy adopted by the church's most admired theologian. John Jewel's 'Challenge' sermon, first preached in November 1559, denied that a long list of Catholic claims could be supported from patristic writings of any of the first *six* centuries. From a logical point of view, this hardly implied an endorsement of every

[45] Smith, *De republica Anglorum*, 143–4.
[46] Richard Cosin, *An apologie for sundrie proceeding by jurisdiction ecclesiastical* (1593), 102.
[47] R. W. Dixon, *History of the church of England from the abolition of the Roman jurisdiction* 6 vols. (Oxford, 1902), v, 400–1n.
[48] Strype, *Annals*, I 519.   [49] Bray, *Documents*, 295.
[50] David Crankshaw, 'Preparations for the Canterbury provincial Convocation of 1562–3: a question of attibution' in Susan Wabuda and Caroline Litzenberger (eds.), *Belief and practice in Reformation England* (Aldershot, 1998), 60–93.

aspect of patristic practice (it was the *Catholic* attitude towards the primitive church that made Jewel's claims polemically useful), but even at the time a certain disquiet was expressed, on the grounds that his tactics encouraged an inappropriate reverence for the Fathers. His puritan biographer Laurence Humphrey regretted that he weakened his position by turning away from scriptural evidence.[51]

Uncertainty about the Fathers' status continued to be a source of difficulty. In a pamphlet that he wrote in 1580, the Jesuit Edmund Campion caused some embarrassment by an evocative memory of 1560s Oxford. He asked his close friend the Protestant Toby Matthew 'that he would plainly tell me, whether he that so diligently read the Fathers, could be of that side, whereunto he laboured to allure his audience. He replied [no], if he both read them and believed them.' Campion felt sure that 'neither he now, nor Matthew Hutton, who as I hear is a famous man, and bent much to study the Fathers, nor any of the adversaries which do the like, do otherwise think'.[52] It says much about the nature of the clerical elite that the two friends he chose to name both ended their careers as archbishop of York. It also says something important about the way that English thought developed that Matthew's frank admission would subsequently have been unthinkable.

When the high Calvinist William Whitaker replied to Campion the following year, he found himself reduced to saying lamely that 'in private and familiar conference we say many things, which we would not have further reported or dispersed'.[53] By 1589, the learned Thomas Cooper, bishop of Lincoln, had come to a carefully worded formulation that shifted the burden of proof, in matters of doctrine, to those who wanted to reject patristic evidence. 'What comfort is it', he affirmed,

to any church to have the grounds of their faith and religion so established upon the holy scriptures that for the interpretation of the same they have the testimony and consent of the primitive church, and the ancient learned fathers. From which consent they should not depart either in doctrine or other matter of weight unless it so fall out . . . that we be forced thereto, either by the plain words of the Scriptures, or by evident and necessary conclusions following upon the same, or the analogy of our faith.[54]

In time, this respect for the Fathers became the major cause of the Catholicising drift among the clergy's leaders.

---

[51] Laurence Humphrey, *Ioannis Juelli Angli Episcopi Sarisburiensis vita et mors* (1573), 212.
[52] William Whitaker, *An answere to the ten reasons of Edmund Campian the Jesuit*, tr. Richard Stock (1606), 122.
[53] Ibid, 146.   [54] Cooper, *An admonition*, 69.

But whatever the longer-range impact of patristic scholarship, the short-term future of the church was shaped by a political disagreement. It was political theology that drove otherwise conventional reformers into alliance with Platonists, church papists, Lutherans, and cultural conservatives. It is anachronistic to assume that this involved the trumping of religion by merely secular considerations. A judgement commonly made of sixteenth-century conformist writings is that their stress upon obedience involved them in a certain spiritual aridity; but the basis of this judgement is a modern attitude to the delimitation of the sacred. A better way of thinking about conformism (to the extent that it was principled) would stress the positive appeal of reverence for civil government.

At the beginning of the reign, this reverence was still 'republican' both in its character and its expression. Thus Matthew Parker's private correspondence reveals a cautious attitude to extra-legal power. Parker accepted that the queen both had, and ought to have, a power that enabled her to act outside the law, but his attempts to think about the church's situation led him towards some interesting distinctions. As he was well aware, he was particularly vulnerable to godly criticism when wielding his power of dispensation, a power (it may be remembered) conferred on him by a Cromwellian statute. As he explained to Cecil in 1569, 'I will not dispute of the queen's absolute power, or prerogative royal, how far her highness may do in following the Roman authority.' He nonetheless felt some uncertainty

> if any dispensation should pass from her authority to any subject, not advouchable by laws of her realm made and stablished by herself and her three estates, whether that subject be in surety at all times for afterward: specially seeing that there be parliament laws precisely determining causes of dispensations. Wherein, I have heard say, King Henry himself did use that authority in some of his own private causes.[55]

Parker acknowledged there would be occasions when there was no alternative to royal intervention: in those cases where unusual circumstances had made existing rules inapplicable 'I leave them to my prince, as I ought.' But his strategy for protecting his own authority involved exclusive stress upon the statute. The problem with invoking the royal absolute power was the long-term uncertainty created: 'during the prince's life, who shall doubt of anything that may pass from that authority? But the question is, what will stand sure in all times, by the judgement of the best learned?'[56]

At the end of his life, in 1574, he wrote a further letter, again to Cecil, in which he explained his legalistic standpoint. Like most conformists,

---

[55] Parker, *Correspondence*, 351.   [56] Ibid., 351–2.

he denied he cared 'for cap, tippet, surplice, wafer-bread or any such'; it was only 'for the laws so established I esteem them'. The corollary of this emphasis on laws was an unwillingness to go beyond them. He noted that 'her princely prerogatives in temporal matters be called into question of base subjects' and that 'whatsoever the ecclesiastical prerogative is, I fear it is not so great as your [Cecil's] pen hath given it her in the injunction'.[57] But at the time he wrote these words, his moderate and careful position was becoming less attractive. The period's nascent presbyterianism, with its stress on collective government of churches, struck Parker himself as politically subversive, for presbyterians did not just 'cut down the ecclesiastical state, but also give a great push at the civil policy', so much so, he feared, that 'we evidently see . . . a popular state to be sought'.[58]

It was the existence of such fears that doomed his unfortunate successor, Edmund Grindal (1519–83). In a notoriously ill-judged letter, despatched in December 1576 though possibly composed a little earlier, Grindal set out to challenge the royal policy of acting to suppress the 'prophesyings'. To someone whose priorities were primarily evangelical, these gatherings of ministers for public discussion of scripture seemed unambiguously beneficial, serving to raise the standards of the ministers themselves and to inform and edify lay hearers. At earlier and later periods, they generally involved a sermon or sermons followed by private clerical discussion,[59] but the prophesyings complained of in the 1570s appear to have been public disputations; Grindal himself described them as 'in effect . . . all one with the exercises of students in divinity in the universities; saving that [they are] done in a tongue understood, to the more edifying of the unlearned hearers'.[60]

It was these 'unlearned hearers' that made them vulnerable; Elizabeth was probably suspicious of any unnecessary meetings of her church's ministers, but the serious case against the prophesyings rested upon the airing of controversial views in the presence of uneducated laymen; Thomas Cooper, for example, was a defender of the institution who was opposed to the lay audience.[61] Unfortunately, Grindal felt committed to every aspect of these gatherings. Although his public statements stressed the good that they did to the clergy, he privately saw 'no reason why the people should be excluded, especially seeing that St Paul giveth great so commendation to that which

[57] Ibid., 478–9.   [58] Ibid., 434.
[59] Patrick Collinson, 'Lectures by combination: structures and characteristics of church life in seventeenth-century England', *Bulletin of the Institute of Historical Research* 48 (1975), 182–213.
[60] *The remains of Edmund Grindal*, ed. W. Nicholson, 385.   [61] Add. 29,546, fo. 42.

was used in the primitive church, especially for the benefit that groweth thereby to the hearers'.[62]

Still more unfortunately, he chose to defend his position by the more general claim that

When your Majesty hath questions of the laws of your realm, you do not decide the same in your court, but send them to your judges to be determined. Likewise for doubts in matter of doctrine or discipline of the church, the ordinary way is to refer the decision of the same to the bishops, and other head ministers of the church.[63]

Although the queen was not averse to appealing to the authority of bishops, especially when they were, in fact, just following her instructions, she could not let such claims be used against her. Faced with a challenge that attacked her power of controlling religion, she had no real option but to punish the archbishop; it is a mark of her timidity, in the face of the foreseeable disapproval of most of her immediate followers, that she procrastinated for five months before she actually suspended him.[64]

It was noticeable, however, that though the English hierarchy unanimously regretted the suspension (which had a disastrous practical effect), not all of them supported the primate's position. At least three senior bishops opposed the prophesyings, while the newly appointed bishop of London, John Aylmer, believed that Grindal had been misinformed.[65] We do not know John Whitgift's attitude, but it seems most unlikely to have been positive. Whitgift became archbishop in 1583. During his lengthy tenure (he died in 1604), a fear of 'popularity' eclipsed concern for missionary endeavours, and the defenders of the church began to see the merits of a vulgar monarchism.

III

Whitgift's ecclesiastical career exemplified the logic of the drift to Anglicanism. During the 1560s, his views had been impeccably Reformed. Although his Cambridge patron, Andrew Perne, was one of the few prominent clergymen who might legitimately be called an Anglo-Catholic, his doctoral thesis argued that the pope was Antichrist, and he felt sure that Zwingli's works were preferable to Luther's.[66] As late as 1566, he had opposed the

[62] Patrick Collinson, *Archbishop Grindal 1519–1583: the struggle for a Reformed church* (1979), 247.
[63] Grindal, *Remains*, 387.   [64] Collinson, *Grindal*, 247–8.
[65] Patrick Collinson, *The Elizabethan puritan movement* (Oxford, 1990), 195. For a list of those consulted, see Collinson, 'Lectures by combination', 202n.
[66] Strype, *Whitgift*, I 15, 64.

surplice, and even in his maturity, he personally disliked the use of wafers, on the grounds that 'it were to be wished, for the avoidance of superstition, that common and usual bread were used'.[67] He nonetheless presided, as archbishop, over a transformation in the church's self-perception.

The pivotal event in Whitgift's life was his polemical exchange with Cartwright, which began in 1570, in Cambridge, when Whitgift was Master of Trinity and Cartwright was his most distinguished Fellow. Whitgift had the advantage, in this conflict, that his opponent thought it obvious that the ideal church polity was mixed:

> For in respect of Christ the head, [the church] is a monarchy; and, in respect of the ancients and pastors that govern in common and with like authority amongst themselves, it is an aristocraty, or the rule of the best men; and, in respect that the people are not secluded, but have their interest in church-matters, it is a democraty or a popular estate. An image whereof appeareth also in the policy of this realm; for as in respect of the queen her Majesty it is a monarchy, so, in respect of the most honourable council, it is an aristocraty, and, having regard to parliament, which is assembled of all estates, it is a democracy.[68]

This conventional view, the view of Smith and Aylmer, encouraged the incautious observation that 'as the hangings are made fit for the house, so the commonwealth must be made to agree with the church'.[69]

Whitgift's ideas were rather different. He held that governments were named after the part which 'beareth the greatest sway' and that a popular government was 'the worst kind of government that can be'.[70] Armed with this preconception, he found Cartwright's stress on mixture sinister, remarking that 'the reasons that you use for popular or aristocratical government of the church, when they come among the people, will be easily transferred to the state of the commonweal'. Not surprisingly, he pounced on Cartwright's innocent remark that 'the commonwealth must be made to agree with the church'.[71] He also adopted a near-Henrician view about the authority enjoyed by 'Christian magistrates, who have the chiefty, power, the making of laws, and government, not only in profane matters but also in divine'.[72] The problem with Bezan presbyterianism was that

> it giveth unto [the prince] only *potestatem facti*, not *juris*, as the papists do; for the prince must maintain, and see executed, such laws, orders, and ceremonies, as the pastor with his seniors make and decree; but in making and appointing orders, and ceremonies he may in no case meddle.[73]

---

[67] Patrick Collinson, *Godly people: essays on English Protestantism and Puritanism* (1983), 325–33; *The works of John Whitgift, D.D.*, ed. John Ayre, 3 vols. (Cambridge, 1851–3), II, 84.

[68] Whitgift, *Works*, I 390.

[69] Ibid., III 189.   [70] Ibid., I, 393, 467.   [71] Ibid., II 239, 264; III 192, 211.   [72] Ibid., III 171.

[73] Ibid., III 210–11.

More strikingly, he was ready to affirm that Christian princes had authority 'in deciding of matters of religion, even in the chief and principal points'.[74] Whitgift had every reason to appeal to an increasingly high monarchism. It is, however, unfair to regard him as nothing but a royalist authoritarian or to assume that his ideas were necessarily unpopular. To begin with, his bark was considerably worse than his bite. At the start of his two decades as archbishop, he chose to adopt a policy of 'subscription', that is, of demanding a statement from beneficed clergy to the effect that nothing in the Articles or Book of Common Prayer was actually against the law of God. It would be difficult to show, however, that he expected to reduce the puritans to full conformity. As he himself protested, 'my proceedings are neither so vehement nor so general against ministers and preachers as some pretend'.[75] In practice, a vague undertaking to use the Prayer Book appears to have been enough to save a man from deprivation.[76] During the 1580s, this moderation probably arose from political weakness, but in the 1590s, when his position had become much stronger, he seems to have stuck to the same policy. He took decisive action against the separatists (including executions for sedition), but there is little evidence of new pressure on people who were merely scrupulous.

During the final decade of Queen Elizabeth's reign, the most striking single feature of the religious scene was the completeness of his victory. He had, to be sure, some invaluable help from the lunatic fringe of the godly; the genius who wrote the scurrilous Marprelate tracts (1588–9) and the millenarian prophet William Hacket (who was put to death for treason in 1591) were probably both instrumental in alienating moderate opinion. But the passivity of his opponents is nonetheless quite difficult to account for; in a period in which printed controversies were frequently uselessly lengthened by a love of the last word, the large-scale treatises of his supporters – most notably William Bridges, Matthew Sutcliffe, and Richard Hooker – went virtually unanswered by their targets. In the parliament of 1593, he managed to criminalise perfectly orthodox worship if it was deemed to have taken place outside the Church of England. Thereafter, his control of church affairs seems not to have been seriously challenged. Unlike the more divisive William Laud, he had relatively cordial relations with other members of the hierarchy. Perhaps most tellingly, he was a friend of the country's greatest Protestant military hero, Elizabeth's favourite the earl of Essex; though Essex had in most respects inherited the earl of Leicester's role, he seems to have been indifferent to presbyterianism.[77]

---

[74] Ibid., III 306.   [75] Strype, *Whitgift*, III 108.   [76] Collinson, *Puritan movement*, 264.
[77] Sir George Paule, *The life of the most reverend and religious prelate John Whitgift* (1612), 57, 69.

The curious collapse of political puritanism is a significant pointer to the movement's character. Its underlying impulse had always been a righteous indignation at policies that seemed to slow the process of conversion. But ministers whose over-riding purpose was the salvation of their godless neighbours were relatively easy to control; they would always, in the end, subordinate their hopes of institutional reform to the short-term requirements of a public ministry. Their unremitting focus upon preaching was also a more subtle handicap; it tended to encourage an indifference to ideas – even, to some extent, towards theology itself. Their greatest theologian, William Perkins (1558–1602), acquired a European reputation, but his rigidly predestinarian system directed the reader's attention to what his younger followers would soon call 'practical divinity'. His 'supralapsarian' position – he held that the decision to reject the reprobate was logically prior to God's knowledge of the Fall – was really a summons to godly introspection. The Perkinsite believer was primarily concerned with what one of his most famous tracts had called *A case of conscience, the greatest that ever was; how a man may know whether he be the child of God or no* (1592). This practical bias was probably one of the reasons why puritans paid fatally little attention to arguments discovered by their subtler enemies. Martin Marprelate's annihilating title *Oh read over D. John Bridges, for it is a worthy work* may well have ensured that few if any did, but it also left conformists in possession of an important type of battleground.

Even John Whitgift's own ideas encountered oddly little criticism. This was quite fortunate for the archbishop, for though his stated doctrines were Reformed, there are traces in his thinking of a religious style that had entirely different implications. A Reformer of John Jewel's generation would hardly have ventured the statement that 'there is no man of learning and modesty which will without manifest proof condemn any order, especially touching the government of the church, that was used and allowed during the time of the primitive church, which was the next 500 years after Christ'.[78] Whitgift also adopted a positive view of ceremonial worship, rejecting a proposal to muster his cathedral's vicars choral on the grounds that they were 'such as were occupied in the daily service of God'.[79] He thought that it was 'most untrue that God so severed his people from the Egyptians or other nations near adjoining that they had nothing in common with them, or no ceremonies like unto theirs', since it was clear that Israelite religion had very similar 'external rites'. There were, he added, 'divers learned men' who thought that 'God did prescribe unto the Israelites that solemn manner and

---

[78] Whitgift, *Works*, II 182.   [79] Strype, *Whitgift*, II 425.

form of worshipping him . . . that they, being therewith not only occupied, but also delighted, should have no desire to return into Egypt'.[80]

Propensity to value forms made his theology more sacramental. In 1574, he informed Thomas Cartwright, that 'your manner of doctrine is such that it maketh men think that the external signs of the sacraments are but bare ceremonies, and in no sense necessary to salvation'. In the case of infant baptism, this view had some importance, for it made him a defender of private baptism in urgent cases: 'what Christian', he asked, 'would willingly suffer his child to die without the sacrament of regeneration, the lack whereof (though it be not a necessary) yet may it seem to be a probable token and sign of reprobation?'[81] He even avoided condemning the private baptisms performed by midwives (a practice that archbishop Grindal was soon to be prevented by Elizabeth from banning).[82]

The importance of all this, from the perspective of our wider story, is that defence of Catholic survivals encouraged the use of Catholic arguments, while the fact that such survivals were embodied in a statute, Elizabeth's Act of Uniformity, gave the conformists a continuing stake in the authority of parliament. Though Whitgift stressed that it was for the monarch to make decisions about church affairs, he nonetheless expected her to take appropriate counsel. He was just as keen as Parker to maintain that

in matters of ornaments of the church, and of the ministers thereof, the queen's Majesty, together with the archbishop or the commissioners in causes ecclesiastical, have authority *by act of parliament* to alter and appoint such rites and ceremonies, as shall from time to time be thought by them most convenient.[83]

It would be wrong, in other words, to over-state the monarchism of the high conformists. One immigrant ideologue, the Fleming Hadrian Saravia, combined the belief that bishops were essential to the church with a political outlook that anyone would class as 'absolutist', but there is little evidence that his views were typical. The civilian Richard Cosin, who might have been expected to be a sympathiser, in fact had a largely conventional view of English monarchy, believing that 'the end' of Magna Carta 'was this, that the kings of this realm should not challenge an infinite and an absolute power'.[84]

Even the energetic Thomas Bilson (?1547–1616), the native thinker closest to Saravia about the status of episcopacy, was also the author of *The*

[80] Whitgift, *Works*, II 440.   [81] Ibid., II 538.
[82] Gerald Bray (ed.), *The Anglican canons: 1529–1947*, Church of England Record Society 6 (Woodbridge, 1998) 211 n. 4, 214; Whitgift, *Works*, II 540.
[83] Whitgift, *Works*, III 510.   [84] Cosin, *Apologie*, 102.

true difference between Christian subjection and unChristian rebellion (1585), which offered an extensive list of possible excuses for resistance:

If a prince should go about to subject his kingdom to a foreign realm, or change the form of the commonwealth, from imperie to tyranny: or neglect the laws established by common consent of prince and people, to execute his own pleasure: in these and other cases, which might be named, if the nobles and commons do join together to defend their ancient and accustomed liberty, regiment, and laws, they may not well be accounted rebels.[85]

This passage was later much quoted, especially, for obvious reasons, in parliamentarian pamphlets of the early 1640s, but such quotations usually obscured the salient fact that Bilson regarded the question of the scope for armed resistance as something to be settled by positive law; his theory actually *condemned* rebellion in England. His qualified backing for rebels in less fortunate polities was based on the presumption that local laws permitted such behaviour: 'because we do not exactly know what their laws permit, [we] see no reason to condemn their doings'.[86]

    This was a somewhat different position from the extremist view (condemned by Whitgift)[87] that there were ephoral magistrates in *every* polity; and it was perfectly harmonious with a conventional conformist stress upon the scope of the permissible. It draws attention to the fact that the arguments that really helped conformists, at this stage in the church's history, were ones that laid some emphasis on the variety of possible political arrangements. People within the English church with Catholic preferences had an incentive to defend the Catholic survivals as locally appropriate expressions of the God-given natural obligation to worship him in decency and order. The tendency of puritans to an exaggerated literalism gave the conformists an additional motive for stressing the significance of local circumstances. Though puritans naturally shied away from claiming that England was bound by all details of the Jews' 'judicial' laws (their non-ceremonial political arrangements), they were prone to see Old Testament institutions as normative for other polities. Thus Thomas Cartwright 'utterly denied' that 'any magistrate can save the life of blasphemers, contemptuous and stubborn idolators, adulterers, incestuous persons, and such like, which God by his judicial law hath commanded to be put to death'.[88] This rigorous stance was politically unwise – capital punishment for adultery had little

---

[85] Thomas Bilson, *The true difference between Christian subjection and unChristian rebellion* (Oxford, 1585), 520.
[86] Ibid., 520.   [87] Strype, *Whitgift*, II 16.   [88] Whitgift, *Works*, I 270.

appeal for the English landed class – and laid the godly open to the charge of judaising. Conformists were not slow to take their opportunity.

There was thus a natural harmony between conformism and the emerging intellectual structure of English constitutionalist thinking. Both stressed the creation of lawful institutions, conceived of as local attempts to interpret reason, by tacit or explicit acts of popular consent. It was therefore not surprising that it was a conformist, Richard Hooker (1554–1600), who was the first to integrate the claims of common lawyers into a general political theory.

IV

Parker and Whitgift were intelligent men whose views were in part a reaction to the needs of their position. Hooker was a pure intellectual who seems to have had few material ambitions, but put his astonishing literary powers at the service of religious impulses to which no previous writer had managed to give an adequate expression. From one point of view, it seems eminently fair to say that he 'invented Anglicanism';[89] he was the first to offer a thoroughly worked-out articulation of the intrinsic value of ceremonial observances. From another, the achievement of his unfinished *Of the laws of ecclesiastical polity* was to defend all aspects of the church's settlement in terms of a philosophy based on 'reason'; it thus reintegrated talk of decency and order into a *theological* position.

From the perspective of a book on constitutionalism, the main achievement of the *Laws* lay in its exploration of two related lines of argument. First, Hooker developed Henrician ideas, and showed how the church's arrangements could plausibly be seen as an authoritative interpretation of a divinely given but natural duty. The voice of reason was the voice of God, but reason had to be interpreted; moreover, compared to the 'public consent of the whole', the individual's judgement had a merely private status 'howsoever his calling be to some kind of public charge'.[90] Secondly, in the unpolished final book (which was not available in print till 1648), he showed that he had seen the implications of a consent-based legal theory.

The *Laws* was planned and started in the suggestive setting of the Temple, where Hooker was then Master – that is, in effect, the chaplain to two of the Inns. The Temple was also the background to his clash with William Travers, an episode that casts some light on his preoccupations.

[89] Peter Lake, *Anglicans and puritans? Presbyterianism and English conformist thought from Whitgift to Hooker* (1988), 227.
[90] Hooker, *Works*, I 34.

When Hooker arrived at the Temple in 1585, the puritan Travers occupied the post of Temple lecturer in divinity, John Whitgift having intervened to stop his appointment as Master.[91] Relations between the two men were never, perhaps, likely to be easy, but they got off to a bad start when Travers suggested that Hooker should seek a formal calling from the congregation.[92] Over the course of the next year, Travers accumulated grounds for doubting Hooker's basic orthodoxy. In particular, he was worried by the claims that human reason validated Scripture (orthodox Calvinists believed that scriptural truth was self-authenticating); that God willed everybody should be saved; and that ignorant but otherwise godly papists could nonetheless hope for salvation.[93] Each one of these then heterodox opinions would also find expression in the *Laws*.

Thus even before he wrote his masterpiece, Hooker seems to have been committed to a theology that valued reason, that insisted that Christ died for everyone, and that was charitable towards the ignorance of conservative believers. A sermon on this final point was printed in the more tolerant atmosphere of the next century. With the rhetorical ingenuity that made his works so brilliantly polemically effective, Hooker confessed that his ideas might be erroneous, but that 'if it be an error to think, that God may be merciful to save men, even when they err, my greatest comfort is my error. Were it not for the love I bear unto this error, I would neither wish to speak nor to live.'[94]

It should be stressed that such opinions were and remained both daring and unusual; even in the 1620s, Laud had trouble explaining away Hooker's remarkably unProtestant view that the authority of the church was the first motive for accepting scripture.[95] Travers was not exaggerating much when he said that Hooker's doctrines 'have not been heard in public places within this land since Queen Mary's days'.[96] What is interesting, for present purposes, is that he wrapped them up within a system that virtually escaped from criticism. The likely explanations of his strange immunity include the demoralisation of the godly, but he was also probably assisted by the fact that he bewilderingly changed the terms of the debate.

The essence of the hardline presbyterian position had been that matters of church government were not, as the bishops' defenders supposed, mere *adiaphora*; after all (it was asserted) a detailed scriptural recipe for organising churches could be consulted in the book of Acts. By the time that Hooker

---

[91] Ibid., v 196–7.   [92] Ibid., v 228.   [93] Ibid., v 189–210.   [94] Ibid., v 165.
[95] William Laud, *An answere to Mr Fisher's relation of a conference between a certaine B (as he styles him) and himselfe* (1624), 28–9.
[96] Hooker, *Works*, v 208.

was writing, these claims had started to provoke conformist counter-claims that rule by bishops could be proved by scripture. Even a moderate like Matthew Hutton, the last Elizabethan archbishop of York, would come to reject the previous orthodoxy (associated mainly with St Jerome) that bishops were simply a custom of the church, invented as a means to cope with schism.[97]

Hooker by contrast waived such arguments. Instead of separating laws of scriptural origin from laws that were devised by human beings, he held that the status of any particular rule should be determined by its subject matter. Not even a law delivered by God himself was necessarily forever binding. As early as 1586, he was detecting

a misconceipt that all laws are positive which men establish and all laws which God delivereth immutable. No it is not the author who maketh but the matter whereon they are made that causeth laws to be thus distinguished.[98]

Thus even if it were to be conceded that presbyterianism was scriptural, this fact would not be fatal to episcopalians; arrangements quite appropriate under Nero were not necessarily suited to a Christian monarchy.

This argument was not completely novel; it would have been familiar to an attentive reader of St German.[99] Its appearance in Hooker's polemical works raises the possibility that his experience of the Inns of Court contributed to the substance of his thinking. But whether or not he borrowed particular ideas, there were some striking parallels between his political doctrines and those of the most radical of godly common lawyers. Like Snagg and Morrice, though for different reasons, Hooker placed stress upon the force of popular consent. It was, he said, important to remember that 'in many things assent is given, they that give it not imagining they do so, because the manner of their assenting is not apparent'.[100] One of the examples offered of this phenomenon was that 'that which hath been received long sithence and is by custom now established we keep as a law which we may not transgress; yet what consent was ever thereunto sought or required at our hands?'[101] Hooker was keen to stress that

as any mans deed past is good as long as himself continueth: so the act of a public society of men done five hundred years sithence standeth as theirs who are presently of the same societies, because corporations are immortal: we were then alive in our predecessors and they in their successors do live still.[102]

[97] Strype, *Whitgift*, III 395.   [98] Hooker, *Works*, V 335.   [99] See above, 75.
[100] Hooker, *Works*, I 103.   [101] Ibid., I 103.   [102] Ibid., I 103.

This general view had a worrying implication: the people might mistakenly concede unfettered power. In such a case, Hooker said bleakly that 'such things . . . must be thought upon beforehand, that power may be limited ere it be granted'.[103] He accepted, furthermore, that 'kings by conquest make their own charter, so that how large their power either civil or spiritual is, we cannot with any certainty define further'.[104]

It might have been expected that Hooker would exploit this fact to draw authoritarian conclusions. But Hooker's interest in the power of custom – that is, the possibility of tacit legislation – led him in a quite different direction. Whatever a kingdom's original constitution, it could be moulded over time by general consent, that is, by 'whatsoever hath been after in free and voluntary manner condescended unto whether by express consent, whereof positive laws are witnesses, or else by silent allowance famously notified through custom reaching beyond the memory of man'. This type of 'after agreement' could take away the powers of conquerors:

it cometh many times to pass in kingdoms, that they whose ancient predecessors were by violence and force made subject do grow even by little and little into that most sweet form of kingly government which philosophers define to be regency, willingly sustained and endued with chiefty of power in the greatest things.[105]

There could be very little doubt that these remarks applied to Tudor England. Another passage had described law-governed monarchy in language that he borrowed straight from Bracton:

where the law doth give dominion, who doubteth but that the king who receiveth it must hold it of and under the law according to that old axiom *Attribuat Rex Legi quod lex attribuit ei potestatem et dominium.* And again *Rex non debet esse sub homine, sed sub Deo et lege.* Thirdly, whereas it is not altogether without reason that kings are judged to have by virtue of their dominion although greater power than any, yet not than all the states of those societies conjoined, wherein such sovereign rule is given them, there is not hereunto any thing contrary by us affirmed, no not when we grant supreme authority unto kings, because supremacy is no otherwise intended or meant, than to exclude partly foreign powers, and partly the power which belongeth in several unto others contained as parts, within that politic body over which those kings have supremacy.[106]

On the face of it, these statements were surprising – so much so as to justify the later high church theory that puritans had tampered with the text – for Hooker's general attitudes were anti-populist. The well-known opening sentence of Book One observed that a subversive agitator 'shall

---

[103] Ibid., III 339.   [104] Ibid., III 340.   [105] Ibid., III 340.   [106] Ibid., III 332–3.

never want attentive and favourable hearers';[107] a rather less-known passage compares the impact of such agitation to a pervasive form of mental illness:

the nature, as of men that have sick bodies, so likewise of the people in the crasedness of their minds possessed with dislike and discontentment at things present, is to imagine any thing (the virtue whereof they hear commended) would help them; but that most which they least have tried.[108]

At first sight, there appears to be a tension between the savagery of such remarks and his apparent faith in parliament:

the parliament of England together with the convocation annexed thereunto is that whereupon the very essence of all government within this kingdom doth depend. It is even the body of the whole realm, it consisteth of the king and of all that within the land are subject to him for they all are there present either in person or by such as they have voluntarily derived their very personal right unto. The parliament is not a court so merely temporal as if it might meddle with nothing but only leather and wool.[109]

This sympathy with parliament was matched by an aversion to the idea of an unfettered power. Most Aristotelian writers saw a place for *epieikeia*, but Hooker believed 'that in those very actions, which are proper unto dominion there must be some certain rule whereunto kings in all their proceedings ought to be strictly tied'. Surprisingly, he went on to find fault with the uncertain character of the Supremacy: 'which rule for proceedings in ecclesiastical affairs and causes by regal power hath not hitherto been agreed upon with so uniform consent and certainty as might be wished . . . the best established dominion is, where the law doth most rule the king'.[110]

The presence of such statements in this unlikely source has naturally influenced historians; given that Hooker had no obvious motive for parroting the views of his opponents, they have been tempted to assume that such ideas were quite conventional. But this assumption is in fact mistaken, for Hooker had a good religious reason for finding doctrines of this type attractive. From a secular political perspective, his emphasis on positive law enacted by consent put him in the same category as the most radical of puritans. But from the standpoint of church polity (the subject, after all, of his great work), the thrust of his whole argument looks rather different. There are signs that Hooker's attraction to government by laws arose from his antipathy to papal monarchy, especially, perhaps, as defended by Nicholas Sanders in his *De visibili monarchia ecclesiae* (1572).

---

[107] Ibid., I 56.   [108] Ibid., I 16.   [109] Ibid., III 401–2.   [110] Ibid., III 346.

Sanders took general arguments that favoured monarchy and used them to support the papacy;[111] Hooker felt an attraction to equally general arguments for government by laws. Though he acknowledged uniformity to be self-evidently desirable, he thought it was attainable without resorting to the dangerous method of giving a fallible agent an absolute power. 'Dissimilitude in great things' was certainly a thing to be avoided, but

the way to prevent it is not as some do imagine the yielding up of supreme power over all churches into one only pastor's hands, but the framing of their government especially for matters of substance every where according to the rule of one only law to stand in no less force than the law of nations doth to be received in all kingdoms, all sovereign rulers to be sworn no otherwise unto it than some are to maintain the liberties, laws, and received customs of the country where they reign. This shall cause uniformity even under several dominions without those woeful inconveniences whereunto the state of Christendom was subject heretofore through the tyranny and oppression of that one universal Nimrod who alone did all.[112]

This line of argument possessed a further implication. It gave the clergy norms they could appeal to that had a higher authority than English institutions: at the very least, the judgement of the universal church should have some influence on parliament. What was more, the monarch had a moral duty, created by her coronation oath, to protect the English church's privileges. This could hardly not imply a moral duty to stand behind its mode of government. It might be said that Hooker liked popular consent because it enabled the people to give their power away; he liked the consent of the visible church, expressed in general councils, because it committed his national church to relatively Catholic arrangements.

The reason for dwelling on Hooker at such length is not, or not simply, the intellectual power he brought to the dilemmas of the English. From the perspective of this book, the interest of his writings is that they show consent-based law was still politically innocent. Like Whitgift, Hooker treated his opponents as anti-monarchical crypto-democrats; it is revealing that he did not worry that his own theories might be thought politically subversive. Yet just a decade later, the English church's teaching on the subject had undergone a lasting transformation. The hierarchy would come to make a virtue of its disdain for theories that were based on an act of consent. Moreover, those thinkers who were most attached to the authority of the church Fathers would also be the most attached to unchecked monarchy.

---

[111] Nicholas Sanders, *De visibili monarchia ecclesiae* (1572), 104–23.   [112] Hooker, *Works*, III 355.

The shift was remarkably rapid. As early as 1606, the clerical assembly Convocation attempted to commit the church to patriarchalism, that is, to asserting that the patriarchs had in effect enjoyed the rights of kings (and therefore that even the earliest human beings were born into political subjection). The doctrines then ruled out included the statement

> That men at the first, without all good education or civility, ran up and down in woods and fields, as wild creatures, resting themselves in caves and dens, and acknowledging no superiority one over another, until they were taught by experience the necessity of government; and that thereupon they chose some among themselves to order and rule the rest, giving them power and authority so to do; and that consequently all civil power, authority, and jurisdiction was first derived from the people and disordered multitude; or either is originally still in them, or else is deduced by their consents naturally from them, and is not God's ordinance originally descending from him, and depending upon him.[113]

The position being denounced here was not, to be sure, available to literal-minded Christians; as educated readers would at once have recognised, its ultimate source is a passage by the pagan Cicero.[114] But the point of the assault upon the far-fetched non-scriptural view that men had once behaved like 'wild creatures' was to discredit the belief that power derived from the people; the canons repeatedly stress that kings, like fathers, govern by God's *immediate* appointment.[115] This sudden repudiation of a virtual commonplace was not, or not simply, the product of the change in dynasty; although the Stuart claim did not derive from parliament, James seems to have felt no need (as king of England) to justify his family's position. The novel factor in the situation was not so much his public political stance as the hopes stimulated by his personal religion.

[113] *Bishop Overall's convocation-book, 1606* (London, 1690), 3.
[114] Cicero, *De inventione*, ed. and tr. H. Hubbell (1949).
[115] *Overall's convocation-book*, 2–4, 7–8, 19, 21, 27–8.

CHAPTER 6

James, kingship, and religion

James liked to have a theory of his activities. His earliest published poems, collected as his *Essays of a prentise* (1584), were printed with *Ane schort treatise, containing some reulis and cautelis to be observit and eschewitt in Scots poesie*. Thus it was perfectly in character that after more than thirty years of reigning over Scotland, he should have written two short works about the role of kingship: *The trew law of free monarchies* (1598), addressed to all his subjects; and the more esoteric *Basilicon Doron* (1599), a treatise addressed to his elder son, Prince Henry, and entrusted to just seven courtiers (an expanded edition for general circulation was published in March 1603).

The English were quite sensitive to signs that James was likely to oppress them; an episode in his earliest weeks in England when he despatched a criminal without trial was the occasion of much criticism.[1] It thus seems quite significant that their response to these two works appears to have been rather favourable. The Form of Apology and Satisfaction, the statement produced by malcontent MPs at the end of his first parliamentary session, is famous for pronouncing that 'the prerogatives of princes may easily and do daily grow; the privileges of the subject are for the most part at an everlasting stand'.[2] But the Apology complimented James on 'your Majesty's most wise, religious, just, virtuous and gracious heart, whereof not rumour but your Majesty's own writings had given us a strong and undoubted assurance'.[3] Its authors can hardly have seen his ideas as a threat to existing arrangements.

At this point, any treatment of the monarch's attitudes confronts the difficulties raised by the idea of 'absolutism'. When handled with some caution, the term can function as a helpful shorthand for governments that had wrested back the right to levy tax from various representative assemblies. In the later middle ages, in most areas of the West, such bodies were the

---

[1] S. R. Gardiner, *History of England from the accession of James I to the outbreak of the civil war 1603–42*, 2nd edn 10 vols. (1883–4), I, 87.
[2] J. P. Kenyon, *The Stuart constitution: documents and commentary*, 2nd edn (Cambridge, 1986), 32.
[3] Ibid., 30.

usual means of making 'extraordinary' levies on the people; in the sixteenth and seventeenth centuries, as the English were increasingly aware, the vast majority of them were either tamed or bypassed. Their common fate is likely to have had some common causes, including, perhaps, the increased expense of warfare, the enhanced coercive power supplied by permanent professional armies, and the ideological purchase on the governed created by confessionalisation. But there is no good reason to believe that this development required an innovative 'absolutist' theory.

A king who wanted to expand his power had no particular need of new ideas; as even the writings of Fortescue suggest, the readily available resources of late medieval Aristotelianism provided all the arguments that an ambitious ruler really needed. All that was actually required to justify an absolutist state was an 'extraordinary' prerogative, that is, a right to invoke *epieikeia*, whenever, in the king's sincere opinion, the good of the whole realm demanded it. Thus the period's intellectual innovations were probably not the consequence of a desire to augment the monarch's legitimate powers; *The Trew Law* typified the works of many 'absolutists' in that the constitutional claims for which it has often subsequently been read were incidental to its true objective, which was to remove excuses for rebellion, especially in 'this our so long disordered and distracted commonwealth'.[4]

James's preoccupation with this question was influenced by his personal experience. In Scotland, he had suffered both Protestant and Catholic rebellion, though he was probably most scarred by the Protestant coup of 1582, misleadingly described as the Ruthven raid, that had led to the expulsion from the country of his favourite Esmé Stewart, duke of Lennox (d. 1583). The strength of the emotions that this episode stirred up is evident from his poem in the latter's memory, defiantly printed in 1584. The event informed his thinking about recent history, in which a small number of *politiques* were the unquestioned heroes, while presbyterians were consistent villains. This view of the past had practical importance, because, as *Basilicon doron* explained, he 'never found yet a constant biding by me in all my straits, by any that were of perfect age in my parents' days, but only by such as constantly bode by them; I mean specially by them that served the queen my mother'.[5] During his English reign, people who had, or seemed to have, the same characteristics would prosper, while those who had, or seemed to have, the characteristics of presbyterians would find themselves enduring royal disfavour.

---

[4] James VI and I, *Political writings*, ed. Johann Sommerville (Cambridge, 1994), 63.   [5] Ibid., 24.

As someone who was menaced on both religious flanks, but who felt more antipathy to ultra-Protestants, James found himself in just the same position as the defenders of French monarchy in a similar triangular situation, the most notable of whom was Jean Bodin (1530–96). Since *The trew law* concerned itself with one particular mode of government – the kind of state James called 'free monarchy' – it did not express a view of Bodin's theory that every 'commonwealth', by definition, includes a single undivided agent (which might, of course, be a collective, or even an assembly of the people), that wields unrestricted legislative sovereignty. Bodin's *Les six livres de la république* (1576), which was already a much-cited book, is nonetheless a helpful point of reference, partly because it offers an interesting parallel example of the mutation of political theory under the pressure of religious warfare.

Like James, Bodin was broadly *politique*; he may, for a time, have been a Calvinist, but he was not irrevocably committed to one of the competing orthodoxies. In the French situation, he seems to have wanted a monarch strong enough to impose a tolerationist solution. In his *Method for the easy comprehension of history* (1566), he was already hostile to the notion that ultimate authority was shared between more than one agent, but he was ready to concede a veto to suitably qualified national assemblies.[6] At some time in the next ten years, presumably as a result of reading Huguenot resistance theory, he moved to a more hardline attitude, defending instead the famous Bodinian thesis that any *république* must have an undivided legislative sovereign.

Given the type of theory that Bodin was opposing, there was a certain logic to this shift. Mainstream Reformed resistance theory derived from a sense of the duty of inferior magistrates to bridle their superiors' excesses; it therefore rested on the view that the difference between monarchs and lesser functionaries was one of degree, not of kind. In such a situation, the best way of asserting a starker difference, and therefore of discouraging rebellion, was to exclude subordinate officials from a defining act of sovereign power. One could of course coherently maintain that only the king could properly make law, but that to exercise his right he had to secure the conjunction of some such body as a parliament. But concession of a veto to assemblies not only gave rise to foreseeable practical problems – it also conveyed the impression that they shared supremacy. The best way of securing the irresistibility of monarchs was thus

---

[6] Jean Bodin, *Method for the easy comprehension of history*, tr. Beatrice Reynolds (New York, 1945), 178–9, 204.

to insist that their right to make laws could not be fettered by a human agent.

This view of what Bodin intended is confirmed by the persistence in his later theory of a range of other safeguards for the people's interests. The famous opening of his *République* encapsulates most of his principal assumptions: 'a commomweal is a lawful government of many families, and of that which unto them in common belongeth, with a puissant sovereignty'.[7] Lawful government means government in line with natural law – a qualification that implies that kings should keep their contracts and should subordinate their private ends to the promotion of the common good. Moreover, a right government 'of many families, and that which is in common between them' means a government that respects a private sphere, including rights of private property. Thus Bodin was quite justified in asking

What could be more popular than what I have dared to write – that even kings are not allowed to levy taxes without the fullest consent of the citizens? Of what importance is it that I have also held that kings are more strictly bound by divine and natural law than those who are subject to their rule? Or that they are obligated by their contracts like any other citizen? Yet almost all the masters of juristic science have taught the opposite.[8]

His boasts cast light both on his likely motives and on the general nature of his doctrine: they suggest that he wished to stop loopholes that might assist abuse of royal power; and that the sovereignty that he upheld was seen as a requirement of the natural principle that government should promote the common good. This general orientation towards the common good in turn explains why sovereigns were forbidden from abrogating beneficial laws, including the so-called 'fundamental laws' by which their office had been constituted (in the case of France, the Salic law restricting the succession to heirs male and the law that prevented the crown estate from being permanently alienated). Thus Bodin's best-known doctrine – the claim that the right to make positive laws was indivisible – was not intended to affect the content of the sovereign's obligations; he simply denied that such duties derived from man-made principles.

The relevance of this digression is not just that his *République* had acquired a canonical status, but that the structure of Bodinian theory resembled the structure of Jacobean thinking. Like Bodin, James thought

---

[7] Jean Bodin, *The six bookes of a commonweale*, ed. K. D. McRae (Cambridge, MA, 1962), 1.
[8] Jean Bodin, *On sovereignty: four chapters from the Six books of the commonwealth*, ed. J. H. Franklin (Cambridge, 1992), xxv–vi.

it important that sovereigns could legislate unaided: 'albeit the king make daily statutes and ordinances, enjoining such pains thereto as he thinks meet, without any advice of parliament or estates; yet it lies in the power of no parliament, to make any kind of law or statute, without his sceptre be to it, for giving it the force of a law'.[9] But like Bodin, he also accepted that he was loaded down with obligations, including obligations to keep beneficial laws and to protect his subjects' property.

He made no attempt, for instance, to use the words of Samuel about king-ship to justify extending royal power. Like Fortescue, he regarded Samuel's outburst as a prediction of the 'points of justice and equity their king will break in his behaviour unto them':

As if he would say; The best and noblest of your blood shall be compelled in slavish and servile offices to serve him: And not content of his own patrimony, will make up a rent to his own use out of your best lands, vineyards, orchards and store of cattle: So as inverting the law of nature, and office of a king, your persons and the persons of your posterity, together with your lands, and all that ye possess shall serve his private use, and inordinate appetite.[10]

The moral he drew from this story was not that kings enjoyed the right to govern as they pleased, but that their subjects were obliged to suffer patiently. Because the Jewish kingdom ought to be 'a pattern to all Christian and well-founded monarchies', there was an overwhelming scriptural case for holding that good Christians should put up with such abuses.[11] The prophet Jeremiah had after all forbidden the people of Judah to rise against Nebuchadnezzar; St Paul's injunction to obey applied to the Emperor Nero.[12]

When arguing against rebellion, James was thus happy to presume that property was sacred. *The trew law* also stated that 'every Christian monarch' swears to maintain 'all the lowable and good laws made by their predeces-sors'.[13] The adjectives 'lowable and good' suggest a possible loophole, but James was prepared, on occasion, to go further. In a well-received speech that he gave in 1610 (which was quoted with approval by John Locke),[14] he told the House of Commons to distinguish between 'the state of kings in their first original' and 'the state of settled kings and monarchs that do at this time govern in civil kingdoms'. Just as God had once spoken 'by oracles, and wrought by miracles', but later governed

---

[9] James, *Political writings*, 74.   [10] Ibid., 68–9.   [11] Ibid., 70.
[12] Ibid., 71.   [13] Ibid., 64–5.
[14] John Locke, *Two treatises of government*, second treatise, paragraph 200, ed. P. Laslett (Cambridge, 1988), 399–400.

his people and church within the limits of his revealed will. So in the first original of kings, whereof some had their beginning by conquest, and some by election of the people, their wills at that time served for law. Yet how soon kingdoms began to be settled in civility and policy, then did kings set down their minds by laws, which are properly made by the king only, but at the rogation of the people, the king's grant being obtained thereunto. And so the king became to be *lex loquens*, after a sort, binding himself by a double oath to the observation of the fundamental laws of his kingdom: tacitly, as by being a king, and so bound to protect as well the people as the laws of his kingdom; and expressly, by his oath at his coronation.[15]

From James's point of view, this was a generous concession, especially if he remembered that he had earlier told the same assembly that all of common law was 'fundamental' (in contrast to Scots fundamental law, which was restricted to the rules that governed the succession).[16] From the perspective of his audience, though, its implications may have seemed less satisfactory. For the most important claim that he was making – that royal obligations were not strictly speaking *legal* – was one that they found increasingly disturbing. To the extent that they assumed that royal power could be regulated, they were impelled to demonise some previously conventional assertions. It is because we are the heirs of constitutionalists that James is often classed as 'absolutist'. Full exploration of this point must wait till chapter 7. For the present, though, it seems worth emphasising that growing English worries about extra-legal power reflected, amongst other things, a new understanding of law. This is not to say, however, that these worries owed nothing to the king's behaviour. During the Jacobean period, the relationship of royal power to law was not, as we shall see, a simple matter, but it is clear that James upheld a newly sharp distinction between a duty *to* the law and a straightforward legal obligation; his reluctance to allow the two ideas to be conflated was in itself a troubling innovation.

There was also a more general novelty, perhaps to some extent derived from Bodin, in his whole attitude towards political institutions. To a remarkable degree, his thinking had been purged of Aristotelian teleology. Aristotle's moral theory had been much concerned with 'virtue', that is, with the habits appropriate to human flourishing. He had implied a history of the Greek city-state in which such cities coalesced from 'families' (that is, patriarchal households), but the virtues that most interested him were those that could only develop in a *polis*; it was indeed 'political' behaviour and the associated dispositions that constituted men as fully human. In contrast, Bodin could not see a qualitative difference between

---

[15] James, *Political writings*, 183.   [16] Ibid., 172.

the *polis* and the family. These units differed in their scale, but not in their essential character; both should be governed by a single head, enjoying a power of punishing by death.[17] This was of course the theory that was later popularised by the Bodinian Sir Robert Filmer. James was not prepared to go to Filmerian lengths, but he was ready to impute a kingly power to some primeval fathers; at all events, he told the House of Commons that heads of families once enjoyed the power of life and death, at least if they were 'such fathers of families as were the lineal heirs of those families whereof kings did originally come'.[18]

His willingness to accept this new idea was probably connected with its clear advantages for anyone who aimed to discourage rebellion. One was the breaking of the link between legitimate power and personal virtue. In Aristotelian thinking, the distribution of power in a given polity should track the distribution of the virtues; the point of the mirror-for-princes literature that Aristotelianism had generated was to instil in actual, fallible monarchs the qualities that made them properly kings. James's concerns were rather different. He was capable of saying, to be sure, that it was kingly to be virtuous (much of *Basilicon doron* is devoted to this theme), but not that the possession of right habits was constitutive of the kingly office.

The second advantage of this way of thinking was its potential usefulness in neutralising contract theories. Although James thought some polities were founded by agreement, he had a powerful motive for maintaining that there were non-consensual ways of setting up a kingdom. His tutor George Buchanan had defended armed resistance by an appeal to the terms on which a rational person would voluntarily leave a state of nature,[19] but James denied the relevance of all such speculations. As he dismissively remarked,

Although it be true (according to the affirmation of those that pride themselves to be the scourges of tyrants) that in the first beginning of kings rising among Gentiles, in the time of the first age, divers commonwealths and societies of men choosed out one among themselves, who for his virtues and valour, being more eminent than the rest, was chosen out by them, and set up in that room . . . yet these examples are nothing pertinent to us; because our kingdom and divers other monarchies are not in that case, but had their beginning in a far contrary fashion.[20]

In Scotland's case, the 'far contrary fashion' was conquest, but James appears to have grasped quite early on that Englishmen found talk about conquest

[17] Bodin, *Six bookes of a commonweale*, 16–17, 22, 29.   [18] James, *Political writings*, 182.
[19] George Buchanan, *De jure regni apud Scotos* (Edinburgh, 1846), 265.
[20] James, *Political writings*, 72–3

disturbing. In English circumstances, the point that power need not have stemmed from popular consent was most conveniently made by speaking of the kingly power of fathers.[21]

If the phrase 'the divine right of kings' has any meaning, it refers to the modernisation of monarchist theory resulting from this kind of breach with Aristotelian thinking. Abandonment of teleology meant that the very existence of strictly political power (especially the mysterious power of punishing by death) was seen as a problem demanding explanation. The usual response was to insist that power of this type was an immediate gift of the Almighty to those who had the sovereignty in any commonwealth.[22] The patriarchalist version of this claim – that God had given such a power to Adam in his capacity as the first father – had the advantage of appearing naturalistic, but the doctrine's implications were not dissimilar: the authority of sovereigns had a sacred character. Non-teleological political theory thus hastened the sacralisation of English monarchy.

A sense of the distinctiveness of monarchs must also have been encouraged by a more secular intellectual fashion: the vogue for disenchanted 'Tacitist' analysis of the behaviour of states and princes. As the essayist Sir William Cornwallyes remarked, this mode of thinking could be very crude: some readers 'converted his [Tacitus's] juice into as little variety or good use as "Beware by me, my good people".'[23] But vulgar republicanism was not the only possible response. Cornwallyes himself drew the different conclusion that 'as princes and private men differ in the outward magnificence, so in their inward minds. To a low fortune belongs simply the use of virtue. In the other she must often be changed, not into vice, but not to look always like virtue.'[24] These were, however, dangerous speculations; Cornwallyes also thought Tacitus 'so worthy that I wish he were as rare, for I hold no eye meet to wade in him that is not at the helm of a state'.[25]

James would have endorsed this latter principle. In some moods, he insisted that the sacredness of kings meant that their powers were too high to be discussed by subjects. It was therefore only fitting that his most widely read political treatise was a work addressed to his only social equal, his son and heir Prince Henry; *Basilicon doron* was that rare thing, a genuine advice book, whose title (best translated as 'An imperial gift') refers both to its donor and its recipient. It was also, of course, a work of propaganda,

---

[21] Johann Sommerville, 'Absolutism and royalism', in J. H. Burns (ed.), *The Cambridge history of political thought 1450–1750* (Cambridge, 1991), 358–9.
[22] Ibid., 356–8.
[23] *Essayes by Sir William Cornwallyes*, ed. D. C. Allen (Baltimore, 1946), 201.
[24] Ibid., 19. [25] Ibid., 42.

released into more general circulation immediately before his journey south; James must have believed that the work as a whole (he added a conciliatory preface) was likely to appeal to the English. This was an understandable belief, because the political programme it announced was one of making Scotland more like England. There are signs, in fact, that James VI of Scotland was not so much an 'absolutist' as an Anglophile; the sort of polity he wished to govern was one constructed on the English model.

His diagnosis of his kingdom's troubles revealed the envy that he felt for the more settled character of English institutions. In the secular sphere, this led him to maximise the power of royal judges at the expense of private jurisdictions. His heir was instructed to work towards suppressing 'these heritable Shirefdomes and regalities, which being in the hands of the great men, do wrack the whole country ... pressing, with time, to draw it to the laudable custom of England'.[26] In the religious sphere, his starting point was the belief that the Scottish Reformation 'being extraordinarily wrought by God' involved 'many things'

inordinately done by a popular tumult and rebellion, of such as blindly were doing the work of God, but clogged with their own passions and particular respects, as well appeareth by the destruction of our policy, and not proceeding from the prince's order, as it did in our neighbour country of England, as likewise in Denmark, and sundry parts of Germany.[27]

The 'parity' these malcontents established in the church was a dangerous example to the state. The remedy was to repeal 'that vile act of annexation', by which the bishops' lands had been removed from their possession, and 're-establish the old institution of three estates in parliament, which can no otherwise be done: But in this I hope (if God spare me days) to make you a fair entry'.[28] In other words, James was committed to strengthening royal power by strengthening two groups of royal servants, the judges and the bishops. It would be difficult to say which group was more important, but it will be convenient to take the bishops first.

I

When James rode south in 1603, he doubtless knew comparatively little about the personalities of England's higher clergy. There was, however, one bishop whose reputation was well-known to him. The most pugnacious of the high conformists, Richard Bancroft, the bishop of London, was

---

[26] James, *Political writings*, 29.   [27] Ibid., 25–6.   [28] Ibid., 27.

also the author of *Daungerous positions and proceedings published and prac-tised within the iland of Britain* (1593), a treatise whose curious title implied unusual interest in Scottish politics. Bancroft first came to James's attention in 1589, when he delivered a sermon at Paul's Cross outlining, on the gov-ernment's behalf, the principal objections to presbyterianism. The sermon was a moderate defence of episcopal rule (he nowhere states that bishops are a scriptural institution), but its otherwise routine arguments had one original feature: a well-informed if somewhat slanted passage about the recent history of Scotland, where Royal Supremacy on the English model had been established five years earlier (when James was just seventeen) over bitter presbyterian objections.

Much the most tactless element of Bancroft's argument was his insistence that the king (still only twenty-one) continued to be anti-presbyterian: 'the king he is not altered . . . his crown and their sovereignty will not agree together'.[29] This and other remarks provoked a printed answer, *D. Bancroft's rashnes in rayling against the church of Scotland* (1590), by the presbyterian John Davidson, who happened to be one of James's chaplains. As Davidson had access to James's personal copy of the sermon, he quoted the words that his master inscribed in the margin: 'my speaking, writing, and actions, were and are ever one, without dissembling, or bearing up at any time, whatever I thought'.[30] Perhaps to Davidson's genuine surprise, James was unwilling to pursue the matter and did his utmost to suppress his chaplain's publication.[31] The slur that the monarch had found objec-tionable was not the imputation of anti-episcopal views, but the suggestion he had hidden them. He can hardly have forgotten the affair in 1604, when he appointed Bancroft to the see of Canterbury.

A second vignette is even more revealing. At the conference he convened at Hampton Court to settle the religion of the English, James let slip a number of comments (including the notorious 'no bishop, no king') that seem to have been designed to draw attention to his pronounced hostility to presbyterianism. According to a puritan observer, he complained that 'at first the puritans were content to strengthen themselves against their oppo-sites with the countenance of my authority, but when they had overcome their opposites, they begun to question about my authority.' Although this was a misinterpretation, the garbling was quite understandable, for what he

---

[29] *A sermon preached at Paules Cross the 9 of Februarie* (1588–9), 75.
[30] I. D. [John Davidson], *D. Bancroft's rashnes in rayling against the church of Scotland* (Edinburgh, 1590), sig. A5v.
[31] *Calendar of state papers relating to Scotland and Mary, Queen of Scots 1547–1603*, vol. x, ed. W. K. Boyd and H. W. Meikle (Edinburgh, 1936), 409–10.

actually said was hard for an English Protestant to credit. William Barlow's semi-official *The summe and substance of the conference* (1604) reveals that James was not in fact referring to himself, but to his Catholic grandmother, the anti-English regent, Mary of Guise.[32]

Thus Scots history as James chose to understand it pitted rebellious puritans against a longsuffering crown. As *Basilicon doron* explained, the roots of the problem were traceable to Scotland's Reformation, when

some fiery spirited men in the ministry, got such a guiding of the people at that time of confusion, as finding the gust of government sweet, they begouth to fantasy to themselves a democratic form of government: and having (by the iniquity of the time) been overwell baited upon the wrack, first of my grandmother, and next of mine own mother, and after usurping the liberty of the time in my long minority, settled themselves so fast upon that imagined democracy, as they fed themselves with the hope to become *Tribuni plebis*: and so in a popular government by leading the people by the nose, to bear the sway of all the rule.[33]

One of his later anti-Catholic writings *A premonition to all most mighty monarchs, kings, free princes, and states of Christendom* (1609) indignantly rejected the suggestion

That I was a puritan in Scotland and an enemy to Protestants: I that was persecuted by puritans there, not from my birth only, but even since four months before my birth? I that in the year of God 84 erected bishops and depressed all their popular parity, I then being not 18 years of age? I that in my book to my son, do speak ten times more bitterly of them nor of the papists . . .?[34]

Though he exaggerated his own consistency, there seems no good reason for doubting that this was what he wanted to believe.

It was therefore not surprising that he decided to support the most conservative faction in the church. This aspect of his policy has nonetheless been much misunderstood, partly because historians have failed to grasp his standpoint. As James's views were not 'Arminian' – he had no time for the idea that God's decision to elect was in any way contingent on the believer's faith – he has been held to be a 'Calvinist', and this in turn has licensed the idea that his church policies were even-handed: that though he used high churchmen such as Bancroft for the important purpose of maintaining discipline, his real affinities were with the mainstream of Reformed opinion.

[32] R. G. Usher, *The reconstruction of the church of England*, 2 vols. (1910), II, 351–2; William Barlow, *The summe and substance of the conference* (1604), 81. For a similar but more extended account of the Hampton Court conference, see Alan Cromartie, 'King James and the Hampton Court conference', in Ralph Houlbrooke (ed.), *King James VI and I* (forthcoming).
[33] James, *Political writings*, 26.
[34] James VI and I, *The political works of James I*, ed. C. H. McIlwain (Cambridge, MA, 1918), 126.

This claim has had a major structural function in the best-known revisionist accounts of the coming of the English revolution, partly because it undermines the thesis – taken for granted by the Whig historians – of continuity of opposition. Thus in the influential view of Patrick Collinson, the political tensions arising from one monarch's oddities could be, and were, substantially resolved by the irenic policies pursued (with occasional lapses) by her astute successor. A 'rising tide of consensual, evangelical Calvinism'[35] submerged Elizabethan differences and made accommodation possible. Though a distinctive puritan tradition continued to exist, and even perhaps, in some areas, to gain ground on other styles of Protestant religion, its intellectual energies were largely focused on its pastoral mission till it was driven to revive its previous radicalism by the excesses of archbishop Laud. There was, to be sure, a growing clique of 'anti-Calvinists', but they were held in check by royal wisdom, at least until the last years of the reign. This outline of church history encouraged a simple conclusion: if James was 'Calvinist', but Charles was not, then an important variable shifted at some time in the later 1620s – important enough, certainly, to offer a plausible short-term explanation of why the Caroline regime proved unsustainable.

This general picture has some evident strengths: the Caroline church was clearly an unhappy institution, in which a number of moderate individuals, including members of the hierarchy, found that their previously mainstream views had come to be regarded with suspicion; while what they reasonably saw as almost Catholic doctrines had come to be permitted and even encouraged. It was noticeable, however, that such 'Calvinist conformists' reverted, almost to a man, to an uncomplicated loyalism before the outbreak of the civil wars; the rift between them and the puritans was evidently significantly deeper than the divide between them and the followers of Laud. This fact casts doubt on the idea that 1624–7 saw a complete religious revolution. As we shall see, a plausible case can be made that most, if not all, of the 'Laudianism' of the 1630s was a quite natural development of James's 1604 church settlement. If Charles was characteristically cackhanded in his pursuit of a well-ordered church, the outline of his policy was faithful to his father's preferences, and his probable long-term objectives were quite identical. The real discontinuity was not between the 'Calvinist' James and the 'Arminian' Charles, but the conservative Elizabeth and her actively reactionary successor.

---

[35] *Before the English civil war: essays on early Stuart politics and government*, ed. Howard Tomlinson (1983), 50.

The contrast was apparent from the outset. At the beginning of the reign, a neutral or irenic politician would have set out to minimise the difference between his national churches, but the effect of James's intervention was actually, if anything, to increase it. The event announcing the new dispensation, the conference that he held at Hampton Court, was meant to be a royal demonstration of confidence in the episcopate. James told the assembled prelates that 'he sent for them not as persons accused, but as men of choice by whom he sought to receive instruction'.[36] The upshot of proceedings suggests he was sincere, for few, if any, changes arising from the event were actively unwelcome to the bishops. Moreover, James personally vetted William Barlow's *The summe and substance of the conference*, a work that emphasised the king's endorsement of all the main priorities of post-Hookerian high churchmanship.[37] This pamphlet's flagrant bias has always been found so transparent that scholars have in general discounted Barlow's picture, but its detailed statements tally with those that can be found in other sources. In any case, the many words attributed to James are most unlikely to have been invented. Even if, as the historian Thomas Fuller later wrote, the conformists 'set a sharp edge on their own, and a blunt one on their enemies weapons',[38] Barlow was hardly likely to risk his monarch's wrath by falsifying royal utterances.

At all events, the conference was followed by policy changes whose tendency was unmistakable. The principal improvement James suggested, the abolition of excommunication for all but the most serious offences and its replacement by financial mulcts, seems not to have been seen as controversial: all parties freely admitted that it was scandalous that laymen pronounced sentences of excommunication, often for very trivial offences.[39] The problem, as he was shortly to discover, was not so much episcopal resistance as the impossibility of using parliament to set up a replacement mechanism.[40] In the liturgical sphere, James did insist on one reform to sacramental practice: he put an end to tolerance of baptism by laymen (and, more shockingly, laywomen) in a life-threatening emergency. But in this particular context, he had a motive for his troublemaking; the upshot of discussion was to confirm his view of the 'necessity' of baptism. After enjoyably minute debate, he admitted that

---

[36] Frederick Shriver, 'Hampton Court revisited: James I and the puritans', *Journal of Ecclesiastical History* 33 (1982), 59.
[37] Historical Manuscripts Commission, Salisbury XVI, 95.
[38] Thomas Fuller, *The Church-history of Britain* (1655), Book X, 21.   [39] Usher, *Reconstruction*, II 343.
[40] Shriver, 'Hampton Court revisited', 63.

he also maintained the necessity of baptism . . . and that he had so defended it against some ministers in Scotland; and it may seem strange to you, my Lords, saith his Majesty, that I, who now think you in England give too much to baptism, did 14 months ago in Scotland, argue with my divines there, for ascribing too little to that holy sacrament. Insomuch that a pert minister asked me, if I thought baptism so necessary, that if it were omitted, the child should be damned? I answered him no: but if you, being called to baptise the child, though privately, should refuse to come, I think you shall be damned.[41]

His actions revealed that his quip was serious. By canon 69 of 1604, he encouraged a high view of baptism by making it obligatory, on pain of indefinite suspension unless they promised not to re-offend, for ministers to baptise a dying baby.[42] As the puritan John Burges noted, 'our church's doctrine in this point is declining to that opinion of the simple necessity of that sacrament and grace annexed thereto which we formerly opposed'.[43] In more Protestant Scotland, James waited, but the 1618 Articles of Perth brought Scottish practice into line with English.

This shift away from godly norms was not an aberration; similar preferences can be detected in virtually all his personal contributions, including the two other questions that he placed on the agenda. The first was the Anglican practice of confirming catechumens by means of episcopal laying on of hands. When he discussed the matter with the bishops, he accepted the episcopal argument that this was a practice vouched for in the Bible. When he discussed it with the puritans, he told them that he was determined that bishops (as opposed to parochial clergy) should have a role examining the young; he therefore suggested a change in the name of the service to 'confirmation or examination of the young'. This change would have suited all parties, as it emphasised the point that the occasion was not sacramental. But the outcome revealed the true tendency of his opinions, for in the event, as a puritan complained, the 1604 Prayer Book was 'made worse: being now termed the confirmation or imposition of hands'.[44] Fourteen years later, the Articles of Perth introduced confirmation into Scotland. The second question that James raised was the Prayer Book's use of the word 'absolution', which puritans believed was suspiciously popish. But James was not only relaxed about the term; he even approved the formula for special absolution of the sick – 'by his authority committed to me, I

---

[41] Barlow, *Summe and substance*, 17.   [42] Bray, *Anglican canons*, 359.
[43] Peter Lake and Michael Questier (eds.), *Conformity and orthodoxy in the English church, c. 1560–1660* (Woodbridge, 2000), 188.
[44] Barlow, *Summe and substance*, 7, 11–12, 36; Add. MS 38,492, fo. 12; cf. Bray, *Anglican canons*, 351.

absolve thee from all thy sins' – that was already being used to bring back something not unlike confession.[45]

These details are of some significance. The policy that they inaugurated was the fostering of an intellectual culture that was essentially at odds with the historic character of English Protestantism. They were consistent with some other features of the religious outlook he revealed. One was a lack of sympathy with speculative predestinarianism, especially when it was fused (as in the works of Perkins) with heartfelt evangelical religion. At Hampton Court, the puritan leader John Rainolds wanted the 39 Articles revised 'for the avoiding of the errors of general grace'[46] – in other words in order to exclude the implication that Christ had in some sense atoned for every human being. He was also most unhappy about the statement that 'after we have received the Holy Ghost, we may depart from grace given and fall into sin, and by the grace of God we may arise again and amend our lives'.[47] The fact that James rejected both requests is not, of course, a reason for believing that he was secretly a 'Lutheran' (the word then used for the opinions soon to be thought of as 'Arminian'); but the record of the conference does suggest proto-Arminian anxieties.

Earlier English Protestants had taken it for granted, as the 39 Articles put it, that 'godly consideration of predestination, and our election in Christ, is full of sweet, pleasant and unspeakable comfort to godly persons'. Precisely because the Almighty had predestined his elect, his love for them could be assumed to be completely unconditional. A doctrine central to the faith was that a justifying grace, once given, is never completely extinguished in even the most sinful of believers. Thus if the murderer and adulterer David (the example most frequently raised) had happened to die before he had repented, he was nonetheless assured of his salvation. This was the principle upheld by Rainolds when he opposed the notion that 'we may depart from grace'. It was the principle implied by puritan dislike of the petition to be preserved from 'sudden' (that is, unexpected) death.

When he wrote *Basilicon doron*, James had no sympathy with this way of thinking. In a passage that came perilously close to treating human works as meritorious, he instructed his son that

I would not have you to pray with the papists, to be preserved from sudden death, but that God would give you grace so to live, as ye may every hour of your life be ready for death: so shall ye attain to the virtue of true fortitude, never being afraid for the horror of death, come when he list.[48]

---

[45] Barlow, *Summe and substance*, 12–13.   [46] Usher, *Reconstruction*, II 344.
[47] Barlow, *Summe and substance*, 24; Usher, *Reconstruction*, II 344–5.
[48] James, *Political writings*, 18.

It was therefore not surprising that his behaviour at Hampton Court suggested basic sympathy with the liberals. Thus he gave his support to John Overall, who was attacked by Rainolds for maintaining in the schools that though a man like David would 'finally' be saved, salvation was contingent on repentance.[49]

It may seem wrong to make too much of James's views on this particular question; Overall's deviation was somewhat recondite, and he had the considerable advantage (in dealing with a clever autodidact) that common sense supported his opinion. But in fact, this was a turning point in the whole history of English culture; it was the moment when anxiety about the social and political order came into collision with Calvinist orthodoxy. It is relevant that Whitgift's private view appears to have been rather similar and that the Lambeth Article which dealt with this difficult question had been considerably toned down from the first draft by the orthodox hardliners.[50] The way the wind was blowing was obvious from Bancroft's interventions. If Barlow's *Summe and substance* can be trusted, the future archbishop of Canterbury denounced the line of thought that gave predestination its pastoral usefulness:

We should reason rather *ascendendo* than *descendendo*, thus; I live in obedience to God, in love with my neighbour, I follow my vocation &c. therefore I trust that God hath elected me and predestinated me to salvation; not thus, which is the usual course of argument, God hath predestinated and chosen me to life, therefore, though I sin, never so grievously, yet shall I not be damned, for whom he once loveth, he loveth to the end.[51]

What Bancroft was attacking in this outburst was central to the heritage of English Protestantism and to the pastoral practice of a portion of its clergy. On the traditional view, the spirit could work through a sense of sinfulness, so even dejection verging on despair was often in fact a symptom of election (one of the central duties of a godly minister was pressing this point on members of his flock who showed anxiety about their status). But Bancroft showed no interest in this type of introspection; he wanted the believer to look at his works. He had no words of comfort for those who worried that their works might be inadequate.

During the next few decades, most high conformist clergymen continued to uphold a moderately Calvinistic doctrine, but such beliefs had lost

---

[49] For a register of this minor liberalisation, compare Thomas Rogers, *The English Creed* (1585), 62 with Rogers, *The faith doctrine and religion professed and protected in the realme of England* (Cambridge, 1607), 74.
[50] H. C. Porter, *Reformation and reaction in Tudor Cambridge* (Cambridge, 1958), 366, 369–71.
[51] Barlow, *Summe and substance*, 29.

their previous function as the affective heart of their religion. In the absence of vigorous efforts at dogmatic education, they were bound to be eroded, in the long term, by theories less potentially productive of a subversive antinomianism. The king's own contribution to this shift was his endorsement of the view (which he consistently upheld thereafter) that popular instruction should avoid these 'curious, deep, and intricate questions'.[52] At the conference, he promised to revise the Articles, but he seems to have regretted the undertaking; given that all the pressure for revision came from a hardline Calvinist direction, this breach of faith was in itself suggestive of the true nature of his sympathies.[53]

Perhaps by no coincidence, the conference also saw a shift to an alternative approach to controversial questions. The Hampton Court discussions presupposed that the practice of the earlier church Fathers was normative for seventeenth-century England. Thus James's dean of Chapel James Montagu (a prelate usually described as being 'Calvinist') reported that the puritans had failed to make a proper case against the alleged abuses: 'there was not any of them they could prove to be against the word, but all of them confirmed by the Fathers, and that long before popery'.[54] When James was informed that the sign of the cross was used in baptism as early as the reign of Constantine, Barlow records that he exclaimed: 'is it now come to that pass, that we shall appeach Constantine of Popery and superstition'?[55] The principal puritan account records him as remarking 'he might use it as well as Constantine did'.[56]

As these remarks implied, James was committed to the view that 'popery' had started to develop at some time after the fourth century. He thought this fact was crucial to confuting Catholics: 'I know not how to answer the objection of the papists, when they charge us with novelties; but truly to tell them that their abuses are new.'[57] It followed from this general position that 'no church ought further to separate itself from the church of Rome, either in doctrine or ceremony, than she had departed from herself, when she was in her flourishing and best estate'.[58] Puritans were uneasy about those practices and institutions they had in common with the Catholics, but James had effectively shifted the burden of proof. As he instructed his first parliament,

[52] Ibid., 44.
[53] For the initial promise, see Sir Ralph Winwood, *Memorials of affairs of state in the reigns of Queen Elizabeth and King James I*, 3 vols. (1725), II, 15. His general hostility to over-definition makes it extremely difficult to believe that he bore any responsibility for the hardline *Irish Articles* of 1615.
[54] Winwood, *Memorials*, II 14.   [55] Barlow, *Summe and substance*, 69.
[56] Usher, *Reconstruction*, II 350.   [57] Barlow, *Summe and substance*, 73.   [58] Ibid., 75.

if [papists] would leave, and be ashamed of such new and gross corruptions of theirs, as themselves cannot maintain, nor deny to be worthy of reformation, I would for mine own part be content to meet them in the mid-way, so that all novelties might be renounced on either side.[59]

II

In the short term, the importance of Hampton Court was its announcement of a policy that was certain, in the short to medium term, to cast him into alliance with one group among the clergy against a vocal segment of the Commons. Whitgift's excellent political judgement made him gloomy, so much so that he is reported to have hoped, in his last days, that he would die before the parliament.[60] It is not quite clear, however, if James himself expected any trouble. Unlike Elizabeth, he seems to have had no principled objection to parliament's involvement in religion; the government even introduced a bill intended to confirm the Prayer Book.[61] It must in consequence have been unpleasant to find that the House ignored his personal efforts. The admittedly rather scrappy *Commons Journal* contains no reference to the fact that James had consulted with interested parties, revised the liturgy, and issued a proclamation on the subject that was supposed to be definitive.

Instead, in early May, a Commons committee produced six demands for discussion, including a revision of the 39 Articles and an end to deprivations for ceremonial noncomformity. The upshot, by the start of June, was a collapse in the relationship between the Lower House and convocation, provoking the latter body to declare that the Commons had no right to intermeddle. This claim was later retracted by the bishops, but it provoked some counter-claims, including the gibe that a canon not confirmed by parliament was no more than a 'convocation pamphlet'.[62] In this mood, the Commons rejected 'an act for suppressing innovations in the church of England', whose 'effect was to take an oath to the government and ceremonies', and passed 'An act for disburdening of clergymen of such offices as hinder them in their divine callings and cure' and 'An act against scandalous ministers'.[63]

By the end of the session, the dispute had escalated further, so much so that the Apology denied that 'the kings of England have any absolute

[59] James, *Political writings*, 140.   [60] Barlow, *Summe and substance*, sig. A2.
[61] Chris R. Kyle (ed.), *Parliament, politics and elections 1604–48*, Camden Society, 5th series 17 (Cambridge, 2001), 22; N. R. N. Tyacke, 'Wroth, Cecil and the parliamentary session of 1604', *Bulletin of the Institute of Historical Research* 50 (1977), 120–5.
[62] Usher, *Reconstruction*, I 352.   [63] Kyle, *Parliament, politics and elections*, 87–9.

power in themselves either to alter religion (which God defend should be in the power of any mortal man whatsoever), or to make any laws concerning the same otherwise than as in temporal causes'.[64] The king was naturally enraged at this assault on his prerogative. As he complained during his final speech, 'I cannot enough wonder that in three days after the beginning of the parliament men should go contrary to their oaths of Supremacy.' He recalled that 'in my first speech I did lightly note those of that novelty [puritanism]; I did not think they had been so great, so proud, or so dominant in your House'.[65]

In fact, the monarch's perception of puritan dominance was almost certainly inaccurate. Some statements that may have been taken to represent the feeling of the House were actually just the effusions of a minority, including, as G. R. Elton showed, the Apology itself.[66] Like every assembly of the period, the parliament of 1604–10 was liable to sudden fits of anticlericalism, especially when the church could be portrayed as trespassing upon the temporal sphere; this did not mean, however, that a majority of its membership was even in a loose sense puritan. The Commons as a whole looked favourably on toleration for the conscientious, but there was clearly a group within the House that was actively devoted to the church's interests; a petition to dispense with ceremonies provoked a debate that defeated the note-taking powers of the clerk, who wrote that it had been 'opposed, disputed, and furthered by divers'.[67]

James should also have been capable of grasping that some of his opponents on secular matters were natural allies in church politics. In the debates about the Union, the House's leading 'opposition' speaker was probably Sir Edwin Sandys, who had been Richard Hooker's loyal pupil and who had recently composed a *Survey of the state of religion* (first printed 1605) that offered coded criticisms of high Calvinism.[68] In 1606 he was prepared to argue that 'no alteration should be of any substantial point of religion but by parliament with the advice and consent of the clergy in convocation' (a principle not respected in 1559), on the grounds that 'the papists would say, not without show, that we professed only a statute religion'.[69] There is no sign that his willingness to speak against the godly in any way diminished his personal influence.

---

[64] Kenyon, *Stuart constitution*, 32.   [65] Ibid., 37.

[66] G. R. Elton, 'A high road to civil war', in *Studies in Tudor and Stuart politics and government* 4 vols. (Cambridge, 1974–92), II 164–82.

[67] *Commons Journal*, I 238.

[68] *Europae speculum or a view or survey of the state of religion* (1638), 283–4, 320–1.

[69] *Commons Journal*, I 273; *The parliamentary diary of Robert Bowyer 1606–7*, ed. D. H. Willson (Minneapolis, MO, 1931), 52.

Perceptions were, however, quite important. It was unwise of Barlow to use the preface of the *Summe and substance* (whose publication was held back until the prorogation) to exult in the king's firmness in resisting Commons pressure. Resentment at the hierarchy's behaviour informed the politics of the following session, when members of the Commons renewed their representations about ecclesiastical grievances. Among other things, they pointed out that the whole of the episcopal court system was daily breaking statutory law. Whether by malice or by oversight, an omnibus statute of the previous session had had the effect of repealing the repeal of 1 Edward VI c.2 (this was the Edwardian law which had insisted that all the business of church courts should be conducted in the monarch's name). The king and Cecil wanted to resolve the situation by means of a brief explanatory statute, but this was evidently found to be politically impossible; their apparent inability to put through such a measure speaks volumes about the Commons' attitudes (as we shall see, it also had some inconvenient long-term consequences).[70] The Lower House also passed a bill 'to restrain the execution of canons ecclesiastical not confirmed by parliament'.[71] The following Sunday, a member of Convocation caused a scandal by telling his audience at Paul's Cross that parliament had no standing in the matter: 'doth the church totter? Let it totter; you have nothing to do withal.' As he was rumoured to have spent the previous night at cards, it was presumed that his remarks were scripted.[72]

This was the type of episode that would hereafter be a regular feature of English parliamentary politics. In the course of the same session, Richard Bancroft stoked the flames by telling Commons representatives that Samuel's bitter prophecy of royal misbehaviour was a description of the monarch's power.[73] He was also the probable draughtsman of the anticontractualist canons referred to at the end of the last chapter.[74] In 1610 he would defend his friend and adviser John Cowell's law dictionary *The interpreter* (1607), which held (under the title 'King') that

Though for the better and equal course in making laws he do admit the three estates, that is, lords spiritual, lords temporal, and the commons unto counsel: yet this in divers learned men's opinions is not of constraint, but of his own benignity, or by reason of his promise made upon oath, at the time of his coronation.[75]

---

[70] Bowyer, *Diary*, 144–6 and nn.   [71] *Commons Journal*, 1 305.
[72] Ibid., 1 313.   [73] Bowyer, *Diary*, 61.
[74] J. P. Sommerville, *Royalists and patriots: politics and ideology in early Stuart England*, second edn (Harlow, 1999), 78–9.
[75] John Cowell, *The interpreter* (Cambridge, 1607), s.v. 'King'.

This kind of ultra-monarchism owed little to direct encouragement; if anything, James seems to have rejected the ostentatious loyalty of his prelates. When he vetoed publication of the canons of 1606 (apparently on the grounds that they went too far in stopping resistance to *de facto* rulers), he commented that attitudes towards support for rebels appeared to have undergone some recent changes, for 'none of your coat ever told me that any scrupled about it in her [Elizabeth's] reign. Upon my coming to England, you may know that it came from some of yourselves to raise scruples about this matter.'[76] In a significant because public gesture, he even called in *The interpreter* for burning. He had not, of course, rejected Cowell's views, but he was probably sincere as well as politic in wishing to dampen this type of speculation.

James did not seek, in other words, the explicit support of the clergy and their associates. He did, however, shape their attitudes in ways that had far-reaching implications. The debate about the canons showed that only royal power could guarantee the English church its right to legislate. More generally, a clerical profession that was increasingly well educated and conscious of its corporate interests was bound to feel attracted to ideas that offered an appeal beyond lay-dominated legal institutions; an under-appreciated intelligentsia, believing that 'whatsoever cause comes into the common law for tithes must go against us',[77] could see the monarch as a natural ally against the aggression of the common lawyers.

James also had some personal influence on the theology of leading churchmen, especially when it impinged on attitudes to Roman Catholics. At a time when his Protestant subjects were easily convinced that popery inverted true religion, James was committed to the view that it was really a political error. This relatively tolerant view of Roman Catholic doctrines supplied the underpinning of his foreign policy, including his professed long-term objective of the reunification of the churches.[78] Even in the immediate aftermath of the Gunpowder Plot, when any monarch could have been excused an unreflective spasm of reaction, he insisted that the plotters were unrepresentative, and he redoubled efforts to separate the extremists from the majority. His chosen tool, a secular Oath of Allegiance, involved him in polemical exchanges in which his valued allies were other-wise orthodox French and Scottish Catholics. The result was to encourage a debate in which the papacy's political claims became the most important

---

[76] David Wilkins (ed.), *Concilia Magnae Britanniae et Hiberniae a synodo Verulamensi A.D.406 ad Londiniensem A.D. 1717*, 4 vols. (1737), IV, 405.
[77] Richard Eburne, *The twofold tribute* (1613), part 2, 16.
[78] W. B. Patterson, *James VI and I and the reunion of Christendom* (Cambridge, 1997).

point at issue, with the result that England's leading clergy acquired a stake in those political theories that minimised the prospect of resistance. Such theories had the additional advantage, from the perspective of advanced high churchmen, of making it respectable to argue in cold print that puritans were just as bad as papists.[79]

The needs of anti-Catholic polemic also did much to stimulate patristic scholarship. James lent his support to the project of telling Roman Catholics 'that their abuses are new' by recruiting the Huguenot scholar Isaac Casaubon, who was entrusted with the task of a minute dissection of the Catholic church historian Baronius. Meanwhile, the clergy's attitudes towards their order's past were growing steadily more sympathetic. The much admired Richard Field, for instance, had been sufficiently godly in his youth to have been summoned to Hampton Court as one of the puritan spokesmen. On that occasion he was oddly silent, but in a court sermon preached just six weeks later, he set out a considered justification for an attention to church history as an essential guide in matters of doctrine as well as church order and ceremonial practice: 'we shall be sure to find our saviour Christ and the doctrine of faith he left unto us, if we have an eye to them, upon whom no note of innovation or division may justly be fastened'.[80] Thus the corruption of the Western church during the Middle Ages would have been easily exposed if sceptical observers had 'cast their eyes upon the Eastern churches that then presently were, or the churches in former times'.[81]

As might have been expected, Field was not a 'Calvinist'; he thought most inter-Protestant disagreements were semantic, including those 'touching the losing, or non-losing of grace once had, and touching predestination', and he was later to deplore the needless controversy that was stirred up by lecturing against Arminians.[82] But even undoubted 'Calvinists' were busily citing the Fathers on matters of faith. The best example of the trend was Dr Robert Abbot, Regius Professor of Divinity at Oxford and brother of the archbishop of Canterbury (and also, incidentally, the lecturer of whom Field disapproved). Abbot had made his name by defending *A reformed Catholike* (1598), an anti-Catholic work by William Perkins, but his anti-Arminian treatise *De gratia et perseverantia sanctorum* (1618) was prefaced by an essay

[79] David Owen, *Herod and Pilate reconciled: or the concord of papist and puritan (against Scripture, fathers, councels, and other orthodoxall writers) for the coercion, deposition, and killing of kings* (Cambridge, 1610).
[80] Richard Field, *A learned sermon preached before the king at Whitehall* (1604), sig. C5.
[81] Ibid., C5v.
[82] Ibid., B6v; Nathaniel Field, *Some short memorials concerning the life of that reverend divine Dr Richard Field* (1716–17), 22.

that criticised Perkins's supralapsarianism. His preface concluded with a call for study of the Fathers.[83] James seems to have made no distinction between those people who employed such methods in order to defend Reformed positions and those, such as Field and Casaubon, who were more adventurous; there was, of course, a spectrum of opinion, but it probably did not occur to him that he was favouring a clerical party when he sent George Abbot to Canterbury instead of Lancelot Andrewes. The king does seem to have come to think, howevever, that Abbot was too soft on puritans. As early as 1615, the Abbot brothers were humiliated when they invoked his aid to crush the Oxford high churchmen John Howson and William Laud. It is not entirely clear what happened to Laud, but we know he was promoted, the next year, to the deanery of Gloucester (a post in which he followed Richard Field). Howson was brought into the royal presence where (by his own account) he said that

In my time there were never above 3 or 4 at once, that were suspected of popery, and there were 300 preachers who opposed them by sermons and disputations: contrary wise there were ever 300 supporters of puritanising, and but 3 or 4 to oppose: with both these assertions my Lord Grace [Abbot] was highly offended: and denied them.[84]

The Abbots' numerous charges against Howson did not include an imputation of Arminianism; it is evident, however, that one of the points at issue was what beliefs and practices should count as 'puritanising'. On this essential question, James seems to have agreed with Howson's view, as he dismissed the charges and offered a rebuke so mild that it amounted to a strong endorsement, saying only that '[Howson] had not done wisely, considering how clamorous the puritans were, and forward to accuse men of popery, in not preaching more often; against the papists and join them together'.[85] Howson's account must be in substance true, because James (who had never previously met him) was later to promote him to the bishopric of Oxford.

This extraordinary snub to the primate suggests a significant hardening of royal attitudes. In the next few years, such signs would multiply. In the winter of 1616–17, James wrote to both the universities enjoining the reading of 'the fathers and councils, schoolmen, histories, and controversies' at the expense of 'compendiums and abbreviatures', a phrase that was understood by friend and foe to discourage pedagogic use of Calvin's *Institutes*.[86]

---

[83] Robert Abbot, *De gratia et perseverantia sanctorum* (London, 1618), sig. C2, dv.

[84] 'John Howson's answers to Archbishop Abbot's accusations at his "trial" before James I at Greenwich', ed. N. Cranfield and K. Fincham, *Camden miscellany* 29 (1987), 330.

[85] 'Howson's answers', 340. The ambiguous punctuation is Howson's.

[86] Christopher Dow, *Innovations unjustly charged upon the present church and state* (1637), 32.

When he visited Scotland next summer (with an entourage including the recently promoted William Laud), he told the Scottish parliament that 'I have observed in England some remarkable good things.'[87] In the secular sphere, he gave justices of the peace the English power of binding over on recognisances.[88] Meanwhile, in the religious sphere, he equipped the royal chapel with an unprecedented range of ceremonial paraphernalia, revived cathedral chapters, and tried to extort a parliamentary statute entitling him to govern Scotland's Church without the assistance of General Assemblies. He seems to have wanted a replacement body that would resemble England's Convocation; in the event, the Assembly was permitted to survive, but only on condition that its moderate supporters committed themselves to what became the 'Articles of Perth', which brought in private baptism, confirmation, private communion, the observation of feast days, and lastly, fatally, kneeling at communion, a ceremony that turned out to be unenforceable.[89] On the way back through Lancashire, he made a gratuitous attack on English puritanism by issuing a 'Book of Sports' encouraging recreation on the Sabbath. His motive, as so often, was anti-Catholic; he was particularly troubled by 'the hindering of the conversion of many, whom their priests will take occasion hereby to vex, persuading them that no honest mirth or recreation is lawful or tolerable in Our religion'.[90]

By the time that James sent delegates to Dort, the international synod intended to condemn Arminius, the English drift away from orthodoxy had become obvious enough to cause embarrassment. James chose his delegation from the ranks of the more orthodox conformists (his favourite preacher, Andrewes, had vehement Arminian sympathies), but even this moderate group revealed some curious attitudes, perhaps most strikingly in their reluctance to speak about the Pope as Antichrist.[91] They were unanimously opposed to supralapsarian theories and quarrelled with the leading Dutch hardliners.[92] Moreover, they opposed condemning the view (which they acknowledged to be erroneous) that someone who was justified could nonetheless be ultimately damned.[93] So far from being uncritically 'Calvinist' partisans, they accepted Overall's teaching that justified sinners like David 'in respect of their present condition . . . lose (*amittunt*) their

---

[87] Bodleian Library, Tanner MS 74, fo. 88v.   [88] *The acts of the parliaments of Scotland*, IV, 535.
[89] John Spotswood, *The history of the Church of Scotland* (1655), 530–4.
[90] *Minor prose works of King James VI and I*, ed. J. Craigie, Scottish Text Society, 4th series 14 (1982), 105.
[91] *Golden remains of the ever memorable Mr John Hales* (1673) [second pagination], 157.
[92] Ibid., 124, 129–30.
[93] Peter White, *Predestination, policy, and polemic: conflict and consensus in the English church from the reformation to the civil war* (Cambridge, 1992), 198.

capacity to enter the kingdom of heaven'.[94] They even came around to
Hooker's view that Christ had in some sense intended that every individual
should be saved.

On both these last two controversial points, they may have been affected
by non-intellectual pressures. They must have been conscious of their king's
instruction to stick to the moderate terms of existing confessions, none
of which mentioned limited atonement, and to do nothing that would
jeopardise closer relations with the Lutherans (who took the more liberal
view on both these questions).[95] Their modification of limited atonement
was certainly developed on the spot. The man responsible, John Davenant,
stated that he was influenced by the knowledge that 'sundry of the most
learned bishops, and others in England do hold the same; and we doubt not
but if the tenents of sundry of the Contra-Remonstrants here were made
known unto them, they would disdain them'.[96] The unity of England's
church was evidently considered more important than that of international
Calvinism. Dort suggested that James still valued his position as much the
most important Calvinist prince, but it also showed that the anomalies
created by the other side of his religious practice were becoming ever harder
to contain.

During the 1620s, the outbreak of a European war revealed the extent
of the gulf between his worldview and that of his conventional Protestant
subjects. The crisis for his foreign policy arose from what most Englishmen
regarded as an intolerable humiliation, the dispossession of his son-in-law,
the Elector Palatine, by Habsburg-led Catholic forces. James's preferred
solution to this crisis, in line with his longstanding pacific preferences, was
to marry his son Charles to the king of Spain's daughter. Part of the price
that he was ready to pay was the issue of 'Directions' to his clergy, in 1622,
discouraging needless anti-Catholic preaching. The same set of 'Directions'
banned preaching on predestinarian topics.

A couple of years later, an elderly, exasperated James was tempted into
going even further. The occasion of his folly was an anti-Catholic pamphlet
by a writer he had previously encouraged: Richard Montagu's *A gagg for the
new gospel? No: a new gagg for an old goose* (1624). Richard Montagu was
an important figure: the man entrusted by the king with editing the great
Casaubon's literary remains. The novelty of his *New gagg* lay in its acceptance of something that anti-Catholic writers were inclined to minimise:

[94] *Suffragium collegiale theologorum Magnae Britanniae* (1626), 72.
[95] Fuller, *Church-history*, x 78; Bodleian Library, Tanner MS 74, fo. 196
[96] Hales, *Golden remains*, 190.

the existence, within English Protestantism, of serious doctrinal disagreements. Montagu's strategy was to insist that much within the English church that Catholics criticised was actually not Protestant but merely 'puritan'. As this approach completely coincided with James's understanding of how Catholicism should be opposed, it was not at all surprising that he supported Montagu against his many critics. It is possible that he did not exclaim (as Montagu later alleged) that 'if this be popery, I am a papist',[97] but he definitely licensed the printing of the sequel *Appello Caesarem* (1625).

All Montagu's positions were at the Catholic end of the permissible religious spectrum. In the ordinary sense of the word, there is no doubt he was 'Arminian' (although, like most Arminians, he had developed his ideas before he ever read Arminius);[98] nobody orthodox would have implied that it was a 'private fancy' that 'Peter was saved because that God would have him saved absolutely.'[99] But this incautious statement was unusual in having no respectable warrant in print. On other issues, he had hopes of finding some support in his enemies' writings; he asked his friend John Cosin to 'help me with some quotations' from the works of the Calvinist bishops Hall, Morton, and Ussher, along with any other mainstream figures who 'yet join in the things which I affirm'.[100] Even on some aspects of his claims about predestination, he had a *prima facie* case when he maintained that the ideas 'now styled Arminianism' were those advanced by Overall and Bancroft.[101] The arguments that he provoked on the status of sinners like David were a reprise of the debates at Hampton Court two decades earlier.[102]

The significance of Montagu's *New gagg* has be viewed within a wider context than disagreements on predestination. It is in fact unlikely that Montagu's leading supporters were in a narrow sense Arminian; it is difficult, for instance, to believe that James himself had suddenly converted to a wholly new position.[103] The bishop of Carlisle, Francis White, who acted as Montagu's principal defender at the beginning of the following reign, refused to speak up for the *New gagg*'s assertion that 'Peter was not saved

<hr/>

[97] *Proceedings in parliament 1625*, ed. Maija Jansson and William B. Bidwell (New Haven, CT, 1987), 325–6.
[98] *The correspondence of John Cosin, D.D.*, 2 vols., Surtees Society 52, 55 (1869–70), I, 90.
[99] *A gagg for the new gospel? No: a new gagg for an old goose*, 179.　　[100] Cosin, *Correspondence*, I 90.
[101] Richard Montagu, *Appello Caesarem: a just appeal from two unjust informers* (1625), 30–2.
[102] *The works of the right reverend father in God John Cosin*, 7 vols. (Oxford, 1845), II, 56–61.
[103] For his anti-Arminianism, see for instance the remark at Samuel Clarke, *A general martyrologie containing a collection of all the greatest persecutions which have be fallen the church of Christ from the creation to our present times*, 3rd edn (1677), [second pagination], 89.

without respect unto his believing and obedience.'[104] Though numerous writers, then and since, have had an incentive to do so, no one has yet come close to demonstrating that Laud himself was an Arminian. What really united these figures was not adherence to a novel doctrine so much as deep hostility to supralapsarianism, combined with a lax attitude to liberal innovations. It would have been hard to condemn the *New gagg* for a single foolish passage without discrediting a whole approach to which the king and others were committed.

The case for defending this *enfant terrible* did not in fact depend upon endorsing his opinions. The reasoning that was probably decisive was set out in a cogent memorandum signed by the high conformists Howson, Buckeridge, and Laud on 2 August 1625. This group were not defending the *New gagg* (with its incautious statement about Peter), but the more moderate *Appello Caesarem*. They admitted they were influenced by worries about antinomianism 'if such fatal opinions, as *some* which are opposite and contrary to these delivered by Mr Montagu, are and shall be publicly taught and maintained',[105] but avoided detailed comment on the substance of his views.

Instead, their argument relied upon two principles: first, that 'to make any man subscribe to school-opinions may justly seem hard in the church of Christ'; and secondly, that

when the clergy submitted themselves in the time of Henry the Eighth, the submission was so made that if any difference, doctrinal and other, fell in the church, the king and the bishops were to be judges of it, in a national synod of convocation, the king first giving leave, under his broad seal, to handle the points in difference.[106]

Their case was not, in other words, that Montagu was right in every detail, but that the issues that he raised were merely technical in character; and that such issues were, in any case, a matter to be settled by the church of England's clergy (acting, of course, with royal supervision). Both principles were well-established royal policy. They added 'that if the church be once brought down beneath herself we cannot but fear what may be next struck at' and applauded Charles's decision 'to refer it in a right course to church-consideration' (as opposed, of course, to parliamentary judgement).[107] Whatever motives underlay their stance, it would undoubtedly have been endorsed by the king's father.

[104] Ibid., 103; Nicholas Tyacke, *Anti-Calvinists: the rise of English Arminianism c. 1590–1640* (Oxford, 1987), 178–9.
[105] My italics. The letter is printed in full in Tyacke, *Anti-Calvinists*, 266–7.
[106] Tyacke, *Anti-Calvinists*, 266.   [107] Ibid., 267.

III

If this account of Jacobean religion is correct, it raises, in its turn, a further problem. James's behaviour was provocative, but the developments that he encouraged largely escaped from hostile criticism. The likely explanation is that the intellectual tide was running in his favour, perhaps because a shift towards more Catholic attitudes reflected a change in the nature of clerical culture. One sign that things were changing was the growing cult of Hooker.[108] By 1622, the *Laws* had reached its fifth edition. The second edition of 1604 had admittedly been subsidised by Sandys, but its handsome successor of 1611 was a commercial venture.[109] Enthusiasm for Hooker was not confined to anti-Calvinists. When his charitable sermon about Catholics was printed in 1612, its editor Henry Jackson was untroubled by Hooker's attitude towards the papists, but drew attention to the fact that the great man avoided 'some errors, which he hath been thought to have favoured', that is, that he was evidently not Arminian.[110] A daringly liberal text had been assimilated to the church's mainstream.

Meanwhile, a growing stress upon the role of the visible church supplied a way for alienated intellectuals to claim more adequate rewards and higher social status. The new preoccupation with the sin of 'sacrilege' (that is, with lay diversion of the church's property) appears to be one symptom of this general tendency. So too does the readily favourable reception of Richard Field's treatise *Of the church* (1606), which argued that medieval Western churches retained a minimum of orthodoxy, despite the efforts of the 'court' of Rome, until the moment of the Reformation.[111] Such claims could be defended by appealing to unimpeachably Reformed ideas, but almost all the adjustments to received opinion tended to make the church more Catholic. In early 1629, for instance, at the height of the furore about Arminianism, the 'Calvinist' Bishop Hall of Exeter explained to Sir John Eliot (his leading lay supporter) that he and his orthodox fellows Bishops Davenant and Morton were nonetheless upholders of 'that most innocent and true assertion of the true being and visibility of the Roman church'.[112]

---

[108] Diarmaid MacCulloch, 'Richard Hooker's reputation', *English Historical Review* 117 (2002), 773–812, sets out the facts but draws different conclusions.
[109] Hooker, *Works*, I xxi–ii.
[110] Richard Hooker, *A learned discourse of justification, workes, and how the foundation of faith is overthrowne* (1612), To the Christian reader.
[111] Anthony Milton, *Catholic and Reformed: the Roman and Protestant churches in English protestant thought 1600–1640* (Cambridge, 1996), 286–90.
[112] *De jure majestatis or political treatise of government and the letter-book of Sir John Eliot*, ed. A. B. Grosart, 2 vols. (1882), II, 41–2.

Although there were plenty of topics on which such figures disagreed with their higher-flying colleagues, it was only the predestinarian question that had the potential to create a serious and lasting division.

But whatever the truth in this picture of the development of conformist thinking, it hardly explains the puzzling lack of puritan resistance. The explanation seems to lie in a *modus vivendi* arrived at with the bishops, for Jacobean puritans had relatively little to complain of. Bancroft's methods were more rigorous than Whitgift's, but the purge at the beginning of the reign, based on renewed enforcement of 'subscription', resulted in fewer than ninety deprivations, of whom roughly a third suffered because of James's personal interference.[113] Although the hierarchy acquired a certain interest in moderation (the trivial number of victims was a good debating point), the puritans too had adapted in ways that minimised the scope for open clashes. Principled nonconformists could have comfortable careers in 'lectureships' (preaching posts with no liturgical obligations), but in any case some preachers of undoubted godliness conformed to the disputed ceremonies.[114]

Even puritan ecclesiology adapted to meet with episcopal requirements. 'Non-separating congregationalism', the principal intellectual innovation of these years, responded to the scandal of the church's national structures by focusing upon the parishes; in effect, it based the church's claim to be a church at all in the workings of its godly congregations. Thus the shift in the direction of congregationalism was not so much a radical departure as a conservative response to pressure for full separation. The most revealing statement of this general line of thought was William Bradshaw's *English puritanism: containing the main opinions of the rigidest sort of those that are called puritans in the realm of England* (1604). As his title indicated, Bradshaw bent over backwards to reassure the king that godly Englishmen were free of Scottish aspirations. He reserved the title 'church' for individual congregations, which were to be free of external interference from 'other churches or spiritual church officers'; there was to be no role, in other words, for Scottish-style General Assemblies. But none of this implied that congregations were exempt from interference by the English state; the souls of a heretical congregation were to be left to God, but their bodies could be punished by the 'sword and power of the civil

---

[113] B. W. Quintrell, 'The royal hunt and the puritans 1604–5', *Journal of Ecclesiastical History* 31 (1980).
[114] Tom Webster, *Godly clergy in early Stuart England: the Caroline puritan movement, c. 1620–1643* (Cambridge, 1997), 158–60.

magistrate', who was indeed 'alone upon earth' in having the right to do so.[115]

Although, in his capacity as a Christian, the king himself was subject to correction, the spiritual penalties involved could only be inflicted by the particular church that he had chosen; it is hard to imagine, in practice, that Bradshaw's version of a two-swords theory would ever have endangered royal power. As we shall see, the Church of England's bishops were actually more vulnerable to principled Erastian criticism. To a remarkable extent, the programme of even the 'rigidest sort' of English puritans was thus a complement, and not a threat, to the strengthening of the Anglo-Scottish state. If puritan cliques were successful in dominating some communities – especially such provincial towns as Dorchester, Exeter, and Coventry – the policies that they adopted when firmly in control were not dissimilar to those of conscientious but non-godly rulers.[116]

This is not to say, however, that they were in no sense culturally distinctive; to be a true 'professor' (an interestingly widespread self-description) was to be someone, after all, who had proclaimed his faith. Although the godly seldom used the label 'puritan', they often told each other to welcome such abuse as the foreseeable result of their behaviour patterns. The caricatures of the playwrights did have some basis in experience; the revered nonconformist John Dod could provoke helpless laughter because he sounded just like Ananias, the hypocritical grotesque who was the central figure in Jonson's comedy *The Alchemist*.[117] In godly but provincial Exeter, the puritan Alderman Ignatius Jordan was a dominating presence in local politics; at parliament in 1626, he was an isolated oddity who wanted to punish adultery by death.[118]

During the 1620s, this self-isolating group was largely unsuccessful in exploiting the crown's troubles; even in controversies about theology, their positions were essentially reactive. In the debate about Arminianism, they benefited from non-puritan allies whose moral support saved them from their own uncertainties; when they had to face the problem on their own, in the so-called Antinomian controversy (1637–8) that was to shake the peace of Massachusetts, they showed themselves surprisingly confused on

[115] *Puritanism and separatism: a collection of works by William Bradshaw*, ed. R. C. Simmons (1972), 'English puritanism', 37.
[116] Martin Ingram, 'Religion, communities, and moral discipline in late sixteenth and early seventeenth century England' in *Religion and society in early modern Europe*, ed. K. von Greyerz (London, 1985).
[117] Peter Lake, *The Antichrist's lewd hat: Protestants, papists, and players in post-Reformation England* (New Haven, CT, 2002), 609–10.
[118] Conrad Russell, *Parliaments and English politics, 1621–1629* (Oxford, 1979), 29.

questions of predestinarian doctrine. During the 1640s, the term 'Arminian' was much invoked, but it was generally used without much attempt at precision as a convenient shorthand for Laudian tendencies.

It seems unlikely, then, that the theology of grace had the capacity, in isolation, to stimulate a lasting political movement. In the last years of James's reign, in spite of the monarch's provocative behaviour, there was no real prospect of a broad-based coalition for a programme of religious reformation. It is manifest, however, that the advent of a war in which aggressive Catholics were initially victorious was likely to discredit the opinion that puritanism and popery were equal and opposite dangers. Conversely, godly writers could now present themselves as innocent victims of Spanish machinations. In a best-selling tract by Thomas Scott, significantly called *Vox populi* (1620), a secular-minded discussion of Spanish purposes (derived from the Italian Tacitist Traiano Boccalini) was fused with a defence of puritans

Which very name and shadow the king hates, it being a sufficient aspersion to disgrace any person, to say, *he is such*, and a sufficient bar to stop any suit, or utterly to cross it, to say, *it smells of, or inclines to that party*. Moreover, there are so many about him who blow this coal, fearing their states if parliament should enquire into their actions, that they use all their art and industry to withstand such a council; persuading the king, he may rule by his absolute prerogative, without a parliament.[119]

Here, evidently, a language had been found in which the godly could address non-godly sympathisers. But as the disapproving invocation of 'absolute prerogative' suggests, it also drew on secular and legalistic thinking.

[119] Thomas Scott, *Vox populi or newes from Spayne* (1620), 15.

CHAPTER 7

Law, politics, and Sir Edward Coke

After the Revolution, quite understandably, some writers saw law as intrinsically subversive. Thomas Hobbes's friend and patron the earl of Newcastle felt able to tell Charles II that 'after the Reformation, and dissolution of the abbeys, then the Law crept up, and at last grew to be so numerous, and to such a vast body, as it swelled to be too big for the kingdom, and hath been no small means to foment and continue this late and unfortunate rebellion'.[1] If the size of the profession was any sort of guide to its importance, then Newcastle's hypothesis was not unreasonable. During the 1520s, the number of active barristers was probably approximately fifty; a century later there may have been five hundred,[2] a figure that of course ignores the numerous 'attorneys', offering various informal services, who attached themselves to every jurisdiction.

The increase in demand for litigation affected all types of tribunal, including the church courts, but the two ancient courts of Westminster Hall appear to have been the most important beneficiaries. Suggestively, the period when expansion was most rapid was the prosperous early decades of Queen Elizabeth's reign; a speech made by Christopher Hatton in June 1588 remarked that 'there are now more at the bar in one House, than there was in all the Inns of Court, when I was a young man'.[3] All these new barristers had plenty of new business to cope with: between 1563 and 1580, the number of suits in King's Bench nearly quintupled. Admittedly, some of these cases would previously have gone to Common Pleas, but the latter court had little to complain of. In spite of the erosion of its dominant position caused by the King's Bench use of *latitats*, its business increased

---

[1] Thomas P. Slaughter, *Ideology and politics on the eve of Restoration: Newcastle's advice to Charles II* (Philadelphia, 1984), 24.
[2] Wilfrid R. Prest, *The rise of the barristers: a social history of the English bar 1590–1640* (Oxford, 1986), 7.
[3] H. Nicolas, *Memoirs of the life and times of Sir Christopher Hatton K.G.* (1847), 477.

between two and three times over the course of the same period. The rise continued at a slower pace until the outbreak of the civil war.

Nobody has an adequate account of this remarkable phenomenon, nor, for that matter, of the fall in levels of litigation during the final quarter of the seventeenth century. 'Peace and prosperity' (the explanation favoured by the lawyers) may well have been a trigger of this process, but the expansion in demand for legal services was clearly disproportionate to economic growth. It may be, indeed, that the use of the courts helped *constitute* a new economy; the ready availability of common law actions of debt (in local as much as in national jurisdictions) must, amongst other things, have had the effect of making working capital go further.[4] At all events, the consequence was a law-saturated polity. If population levels are allowed for, litigiousness peaked in about 1580, when law-suits seem to have been initiated at a rate approaching one per year per household.[5]

The trend towards formalisation of various types of social interaction was also expressed in the use of the queen's courts for punishing deviant behaviour. Here too, the shifting economic background provides, at best, a partial explanation. In the south-east of England, the number of indictments at the Assizes rose steadily throughout Elizabeth's reign until it peaked in the hard times of the mid 1590s (it was to reach another peak in the famine years of the early 1620s). But the willingness of magistrates to use the lesser weapon of binding people over to keep the peace appears to have risen in good times as well as in bad.[6] Their readiness to extend their power through formal, that is, legal mechanisms, reflected increasing attachment to their role as the custodians of legal order. In the first years of the Stuart period, a witty summary of received opinion could describe a 'country gentleman' as 'a thing out of whose corruption the generation of a justice of the peace is produced. He speaks statutes and husbandry well enough to make his neighbours think him a wise man.'[7]

As this implied, respect for law had probably never been greater, so much so that a legal education became a normal attribute of prosperous gentlemen. In the parliament of 1601, some 55 per cent of Commons members had attended one or other of the Inns – only a little less than the proportion

---

[4] Craig Muldrew, *The economy of obligation: the culture of credit and social relations in early modern England* (Basingstoke, 1998), esp. chapters 4 and 8.

[5] Ibid., 236.

[6] Steve Hindle, *The state and social change in early modern England, c. 1550–1640* (Basingstoke, 2000), 103.

[7] *A wife now the widdow of Sir Thomas Overburye . . . whereunto are added many witty characters* (1614), sig. E4.

(around 60 per cent) in the initial membership of the Long Parliament.[8] A study of county commissions of the peace, bodies predominantly drawn from the same social stratum, suggests that a little over half of country justices had also had this shared experience.[9] Though there is plenty of room for scepticism about the range and depth of legal knowledge acquired by most gentleman students, conventional wisdom insisted on its utility. Thus the Yorkshireman Sir Hugh Cholmley (1600–57) told his son that

> I was three years there and totally mis-spent my time, to my great regret since I came to be of riper judgment, and saw what advantage the study thereof might have been to me, in conducting and managing of affairs in the country, as well concerning my own private as the public, where every man that hath but a smattering of the law though of no fortune or quality, shall be a leader and director to the greatest and best gentlemen on the bench.[10]

Cholmley was not alone in this perception. In his post-revolutionary account of James's England, the Caroline bishop of Gloucester Geoffrey Goodman recalled that 'to be a lawyer . . . was indeed to be a governor of one's country. Thus, the recorders and town clerks governed corporations, the country lawyer is in Commission of the Peace, and gives charge at the quarter sessions and rules all there.'[11] In a yet more suggestive remark, the earl of Clarendon maintained that 'the nobility in all countries [i.e. areas] have much less interest, since they have taken such care that their eldest sons should know nothing of the law'.[12] Although his comment dated from the 1670s, his underlying assumptions were evidently derived from memories of the pre-war situation.

I

No one is likely to deny that the increased regard for law detected by contemporary observers was at least relevant to the emergence of constitutionalised politics. But the legalistic tone of social life is not a satisfactory explanation for the lawyers' own acceptance of expanded competence. Nor are the interests of puritans; as Hooker's exploitation of legal thinking

---

[8] P. W. Hasler (ed.), *The Commons 1558–1603*, 3 vols. (1981), I, 6; M. F. Keeler, *The Long parliament 1640–41* (Philadelphia, 1954), 27.

[9] J. H. Gleason, *The justices of the peace in England 1558–1640: a later Eirenarcha* (Oxford 1969), 86–8.

[10] *The memoirs of Sir Hugh Cholmley* (1787), 38.

[11] Geoffrey Goodman, *The court of James I*, ed. J. S. Brewer, 2 vols. (1839), vol. I, 294.

[12] Edward Hyde, earl of Clarendon, *Two dialogues: Of the want of respect due to age and Concerning education* in *The miscellaneous works*, 2nd edn (1751), 329.

shows, grand claims for the unwritten law were not a party doctrine, but a resource available to people of a wide range of opinions. Even (as we shall see) from the perspective of King James, they were less a limitation on the scope of royal power than part of the cultural background to English politics, creating opportunities as well as obstacles for those who wished to strengthen monarchy. They could hardly have achieved this kind of acceptance if they had been no more than a rationalisation of somebody's political objectives. It follows that their origins should probably be sought in the professional culture of the lawyers.

During the period down to 1580, the most important change within that culture was an increasing readiness to think of common law as general custom, that is, as a set of determinate rules, created by the people. This picture of the law was well adapted to limiting the powers of the monarch, but as Christopher St German had conceded, it faced a fairly obvious objection: most of the rules in question were unknown outside the courts. The notion of the law as populist custom was not derived from social observation; it was required by a theory that emphasised the law's consensual basis. As an account of what the judges did, especially when they appealed to 'reason', it was indeed less plausible than the extravagances of the 'Serjeant'.

An inability to cope with law's development is shared, of course, by many legal theories, and Tudor lawyers, as a group, were doubtless not much exercised about this type of question. But in the period around the accession of King James, there are some signs of an attempt to think a little harder about the basic character of their activities. The impulse to articulate the law's presuppositions owed something to the growth of a potential audience and something to what was in part an educational crisis. During the later sixteenth century, future professionals could train themselves by arduous private study, supplemented by post-prandial exercises, but there was no obvious body of strictly elementary information to meet the needs of diligent but less ambitious students; the abiding popularity of Littleton's fifteenth-century work on tenures was one of the symptoms of this situation.

In some respects, the efforts of the printers had the effect of making matters worse. The printing of the Year Books supplied a mass of legal information that it was difficult to ignore and even harder to assimilate. Printing conferred authority and uniformity on fairly disparate materials, encouraging a view of law as esoteric *knowledge* concealed in the medieval precedents. The rational student responded by relying on *Abridgements*, alphabetically ordered commonplace books that seem to have developed out of personal finding aids. In consequence, the major *Abridgements* in print – Sir Anthony Fitzherbert's and Sir Robert Brooke's – were more than simply short-cuts to the sources; they in effect defined the common law. Thus when the Marian judge Sir William Staunford wrote a short work about prerogative (that is, on the king's feudal rights), it took the form of *An exposition of the king's prerogative collected out of the great abridgement of Justice Fitzherbert* (1567). As Abraham Fraunce was to remark in 1588, 'we by a moot book and a Brooke's *Abridgement* climb to the bar and bar our selves utterly from the substance of the common law'.[13] Fraunce was an ardent Ramist, committed to bringing dichotomising 'method' to even the most unpromising material, but he was not eccentric in wishing 'the whole body of our common law to be rather logically ordered than by alphabetical breviaries torn and dismembered'.[14]

In the mean time, the profession required a theory explaining how legal conclusions could be drawn from this agglomerate of formless learning. The germ of such a theory emerged from Plowden's view that

there are two principal things from whence arguments may be drawn, that is to say, our maxims, and reason which is the mother of all laws. But maxims are the foundations of the law and the conclusions of reason and therefore they ought not to be impugned, but always to be admitted; yet these maxims may by the help of reason be compared together and set one against another (although they do not vary) where it may be distinguished by reason that a thing is nearer to one maxim than to another, or placed between two maxims.[15]

Thus reason generated rules that were in principle unchallengeable, but a continuing appeal directly to 'the mother of all laws' could not in practice be eliminated; the very existence of maxims gave rise to further puzzles – not least where those maxims apparently conflicted – that had to be resolved by reasoning.

In their development of Plowden's thinking, the lawyers followed St German in being aware of two opposing dangers. On the one hand, it was possible to claim too much for common law and lawyers, so much so that the very existence of statute began to seem like an anomaly. A *Treatise concerning statutes* probably written in the 1580s remarked that

Whereas I have said that some statutes are constitutive of new laws, and go to the enlargement of the common law, I cannot tell how it might be taken of some, who hold the law to be so perfect and so large, as reason is in every thing and beyond reason a man cannot go.[16]

---

[13] Abraham Fraunce, *The lawiers logike* (1588), fo. 61v.   [14] Ibid., 119v.
[15] Plowden, *Commentaries*, 27.
[16] Sir Christopher Hatton, *A treatise concerning statutes, or acts of parliament: and the exposition thereof* (1677), 24. This book is almost certainly not by Hatton.

The same work informs us that 'reason' as deployed by common lawyers was sometimes conflated with 'reason' as expounded in Cicero's dialogue *De legibus.*

The attraction of Cicero's treatment of the law was that it linked the *ratio* that was immanent in nature with the *lex* actualised by human beings. *De legibus* recorded that 'the most learned men' believed that '*lex* is the highest reason (*summa ratio*) implanted in nature, which commands those things which ought to be done, and prohibits the opposite things. The same reason when it is confirmed and fully developed (*confirmata et perfecta*) in the human mind, is *lex*. And so they believe that *lex* is practical wisdom (*prudentia*) . . .' Still more attractively to common lawyers, Cicero went on to contrast this view with the opinion of the mob that *lex* is a written command.[17] The author of the *Treatise concerning statutes* felt able to assume that all his readers were familiar with both Cicero and Plowden. He commented that

> I know that reason may be called the mother of the law and maxims the foundations, in respect of the more part of laws; and maxims may not be denied, but they may be compared, and must be reconciled in every case where they seem to differ; but all this negotiation bringeth us to a less matter than that which Tully *De legibus* speaketh of *Lex est summa ratio*, etc.[18]

But this anonymous writer was also anxious not to claim too little. Although he gave a role to the makers' intention in the interpretation of a statute, he noted that it was actually for judges to work out the true meaning of such laws. Even if all the legislators were to re-assemble 'for interpretation by a voluntary meeting', their views would be without authority,

> for the sages of the law whose wits are exercised in such matters, have the interpretation in their hands, and their authority no man taketh in hand to control; wherefore their power is very great, and high, and we seek these interpretations as oracles from their mouths.[19]

Thus the judges' reconstruction of the purpose of a statute had an authority denied to those who had actually made it. The author had also defended the bolder conclusion that 'if the words and mind of the law be clean contrary, that law or statute is void'. This principle enabled him to resolve 'one great doubt, which is, whether parliament may err or not': he held that 'when the matter is plain, every judge may esteem of it as it is, and being void, is not bound to allow it for good and forcible'.[20]

[17] Cicero, *De republica: De legibus*, ed. and tr. C. W. Keyes (1928), 316–17.
[18] Hatton, *Treatise concerning statutes*, 25–6.   [19] Ibid., 30.   [20] Ibid., 18–19, 20–1.

This final possibility was obviously important to the development of legal theory, but lawyers were more exercised in practice by the extent to which a judge could modify his rules by equity. They needed, in fact, to address St German's problem of how far *epieikeia* could be incorporated in the system. One thoughtful manuscript treatise of the later 1590s, Edward Hake's *Epieikeia*, was to discuss the question in some detail. Hake recognised the need for courts of 'conscience', employing extra-legal power to rectify the law's inadequacies, but he was anxious to maintain that 'the common law is not so severed from equity as amongst many hath been fondly conceived'. In consequence, 'the Chancery should not be resorted unto but upon some point of conscience, being helpless and succourless at the common law'.[21] Like St German, in fact, he thought of equity as something to a large extent internal to the law. This made him critical of Plowden's statement that 'equity is no part of the law, but a moral virtue which reformeth the law', on the grounds that 'no more can the words of the law without equity to direct it to the right sense thereof be said to be the law than the body of a man without reason to direct it in the actions of a man may be said to be a man'.[22] What was more, the close connection between equity and law was just as much an element of custom as of statute. If a puzzle arose about interpretation of a custom, it should be resolved by looking 'into the reason of the custom, and there you shall be satisfied (the same reason I mean as by the which by all likelihood the custom had his commencement)'.[23]

Though such statements directed attention to the origins of law, the 'reason' that he spoke of was its rationale as-understood-by-judges; it was to be politically important that in this type of thinking, as in Plowden's, the force of an implicit appeal to intentions was to expand, not to constrain, the scope of judicial discretion. Hake recognised that common law had limits – that there would be occasions on which the only remedy would be the making of new legislation – but the most striking feature of his work was the sheer scope that he allowed to equity internal to the system. The tendency of this process was to make the hidden explicit. Thus in the case of 'omission of continual claim . . . the righteousness of the law doth secretly minister an exception for infants'. Over time, such equitable adjustments to the rules, 'which in the beginning were *tacitae* and hidden . . . themselves become grounds or maxims as well as the principal grounds whereof they are exceptions', but they started as 'silent exceptions from the generality of the law'.[24]

---

[21] Hake, *Epieikeia*, 2.   [22] Ibid., 9, 12.   [23] Ibid., 19–20.   [24] Ibid., 50.

This plausible account of legal history was the foundation of his view of actions on the case. He quoted Justice Fairfax's remark 'that if such as were pleaders would bend their minds to the framing of actions on the case, and so maintain the jurisdictions of the courts of the common law, there would not then be so many *subpoenas*' and the principle *nullus recedat e curia Cancellariae sine remedio* ('let nobody come back from the court of Chancery without a remedy'), and daringly put the two ideas together. The main conclusion that he drew was that the *nullus recedat* tag referred to the Chancellor's 'ordinary' action in issuing common law writs:

> It were no offence (as I take it) to think that the said sentence or maxim might be also applied to original writs, as who should say the High Court of Chancery ought to be always so powerful and helpful as that a man might have from thence at all times an original writ for every particular wrong.[25]

Hake took this to be the force of Yelverton's statement that 'we must do even as the Sorbonnists and civilians . . . they resort to the law of nature . . . and therein out of that which is most for the commonwealth they make a law'.[26] As he correctly noted, there were 'sundry things which by divers and sundry statutes' were referred to the discretion of the judges, but 'other things that may be read in the reports of the common law to have been done by the only discretion of the judges'.[27] At times, this led them to consult with 'other sciences', but they were often led by preferences apparently implicit in the system: 'divers things which the common law itself is said to favour, as life, liberty, a woman's dower, infancy, coverture, privilege of arts and sciences . . and sundry other things'. Though judgements guided by these preferences 'may be said to be the favour of the judge', it would be equally appropriate to speak about 'the favour of the law'.[28]

Hake was a relatively subtle thinker who may indeed, in some respects, have been original, but many of the same tensions can be found in a much less ambitious work with a professedly educational purpose, William Fulbecke's *A direction or preparative to the study of the lawe* (1600). In Fulbecke's view, the common law was ultimately populist in basis: 'the common law ariseth from the people and multitude, but statute originally from the king'.[29] He seems to have been undecided, though, about the extent to which the legal system was fully comprehensible by laymen. On the one hand, he argued that law was rational in character: 'not without good reason', he wrote, 'is Bartolus reproved of the civilians, for that he denied reason to be of the essence of the law'.[30] This reason, what was more, was

[25] Ibid., 107.   [26] Ibid., 108.   [27] Ibid., 110.   [28] Ibid., 114–15.
[29] William Fulbecke, *A direction or preparative to the study of the lawe* (1600), 64v.   [30] Ibid., 31v.

'common reason . . . which doth *concludenter demonstrare* to the sense and understanding of the most part of men of indifferent capacity'.[31] On the other hand, he defended the opinion that the 'law is the invention of wise men, who would not make anything public without reason, though the reason of the law may be hid from him, from me, and from a number of men'.[32] He stressed that 'the law considereth things according to public respect, that is, inasmuch as concerneth the common weal', rather than 'according to their contingency *in facto*, which is every man's object and . . . needeth not any artificial understanding'; and therefore that 'the student's understanding must be . . . sequestered and refined from vulgar opinion'.[33]

The need for 'artificial' understanding, the understanding proper to a professional (the word derives from *artifex*: a craftsman) was to provide a central theme of Stuart legal thinking. Although its most famous expression is the thought of Edward Coke (which will be dealt with later in this chapter), its underlying logic is in some respects much clearer in writings by his colleague Sir John Doddridge. Doddridge's well-known book *The English lawyer* was posthumously printed in 1631, but it included some material (which must have been written by January 1604), entitled, in its earliest manuscript version, 'Le Methode de Monsieur Dodderige en son practize del ley dengleterre.'[34] Doddridge appears to have been dissatisfied with the available legal literature, for he remarked that 'to adhere . . . and wholly to respect particular cases without any observation of the general reasons and to charge memory with infinite singularities is utterly to confound and overwhelm the same'.[35] He aimed at a description of the law in terms of 'general rules' of the type that were known to the Year Books as 'principles', 'grounds', 'maxims', 'eruditions', or 'positive laws'. The notion captured by these various labels was 'a conclusion either of the law of nature or derived from some general custom used within the realm containing in a short sum the reason and direction of many particular and special occurrences'.[36]

Doddridge agreed with Plowden's view that 'there are two principal things on which arguments can be made our maxims and reason the mother of all laws'.[37] The latter basis for an argument involved him in considering 'consequences, mischiefs, and inconveniences, and such like'.[38] Thus the judges were to 'frame law upon deliberation and debate of reason . . . when present occasion is offered to use the same by a case then falling out and requiring judicial determination';[39] a system of this type addressed those difficulties that actually emerged, as opposed to those inaccurately foreseen

---

[31] Ibid., 35v.   [32] Ibid., 32.   [33] Ibid., 45.
[34] British Library, Additional MS 32,092, fos. 161–200.   [35] Ibid., 190.   [36] Ibid., 161v.
[37] Ibid., 190v.   [38] Ibid.   [39] Ibid., 185.

by more or less inexpert lawmakers. Doddridge was thus enabled to see advantages in being 'governed by an unwritten law, not left in any other monument than in the mind of man; and thence to be deduced by deceptation [disputation, discussion] and discourse of reason: and that when occasion should be offered, and not before'.[40] 'Hence it is', he explained

> that the law . . . is called reason; not for that every man can comprehend the same; but it is artificial reason; the reason of such as by their wisdom, learning, and long experience are skilful in the affairs of men, and know what is fit and convenient to be held and observed for the appeasing of controversies and debates among men, still having an eye and due regard of justice, and a consideration of the commonwealth wherein they live.[41]

Doddridge's claims for common law were thus in essence claims for the capacity of judges to act as experts on the common weal.

Such claims were undoubtedly 'constitutionalist' – they brought the powers of kingship within the legal sphere – but they were quite compatible, in practice, with highly 'absolutist' recommendations. As it happens, a good example of this possibility was that intelligent lawyer Francis Bacon (1561–1626), a man whose professional writings were for the most part perfectly consistent with the ideas that we have been describing. Bacon maintained that common law was reason, that is, a rational response to local circumstances, but he conceded that a rational system would sometimes need to delegate discretionary power. It would allow for uses, for example, 'for an use is no more but a general trust, when a man will trust the conscience of another better than his own estate and possession; which is an accident or event of human society which hath been and will be in all laws, and therefore was at the common law which is common reason'.[42] But reason dictated that practices founded in conscience needed a special conscience-based enforcement mechanism for settling the resultant disagreements; thus 'common reason doth define that uses should be remedied in conscience and not in courts of law, and ordered by rules of conscience and not by strait cases of law'.[43]

Although this line of thinking suggested that the courts had limitations, it actually entrenched the principle that common lawyers should decide when, and to whom, discretion should be granted; if conscience was a tool employed by reason, then it was obviously appropriate that 'the common

---

[40] Ibid., 185.   [41] Ibid., 185v.
[42] *The works of Francis Bacon*, ed. J. Spedding, R. L. Ellis, and D. D. Heath, 14 vols. (1857–74), VII 415.
[43] Ibid., VII 415.

law hath a kind of a rule or survey over the Chancery, to determine what belongs to the Chancery'.[44] This accounts for the fact that a loyal crown servant like Bacon could nonetheless hold that 'the king's prerogative and the law are not two things; but the king's prerogative is law, and a principal part of the law';[45] the conclusions reached by reason guaranteed the powers that were needed by the sovereign.

In the last years of Queen Elizabeth's reign, Doddridge himself began to write a treatise on the royal prerogative. Like Hake, he quoted Justice Yelverton's dictum that in unprecedented situations 'we do, as the Sorbonnists and civilians, resort to the law of nature, which is the ground of all laws, and thence drawing that which is most conformable for the commonwealth, do adjudge it for law'.[46] This statement has sometimes been cited as an appeal beyond the law of England, but Doddridge's view of the matter was almost certainly quite different. One clue to his general outlook is that he softened Yelverton's opinion; what Yelverton said was not 'adjudge for law' but 'make a positive law'. Doddridge's choice of language should be taken seriously; the act he was describing was in an ordinary sense a *judgement* and he was not departing from professional tradition, but offering a fairly conventional description of the development of law by reason.

II

By about 1600, then, professionals were able to express a view of law that emphasised its flexibility and therefore its capacity to address new social problems. As common law was made by crown employees, the government had much to gain from such a theory; it is noticeable that Hake's *Epieikeia* was presented to the two least 'popular' judges: the hardline anti-puritan Sir Edmund Anderson and the probable crypto-Catholic Thomas Walmsley.[47] But there were also dangers in the crown's resort to law, for growing expectations of the system conferred respectability on new varieties of opposition. At all events, the trend was a part of the background to the developments explored in Wallace Notestein's rightly famous lecture 'The winning of the initiative by the House of Commons'.

Notestein had set out to explain the process by which Privy Councillors ceased to guide the Commons and 'there came into power . . . a group of leaders, who had no official connection with the government, who had no

---

[44] Ibid., VII 415.   [45] Ibid., XIII 203.
[46] British Library, Harleian MS 5220, fo. 4v. He is quoting from the Year Book of M 8 Edward IV, fo. 12v, pl. 9.
[47] Hake, *Epieikeia*, xxviii.

common tie except those of the opinions and feelings that bound English country gentlemen together'.[48] Though much in his lecture seems dated, he rightly believed that the answer to this problem had something to do with the further observation that 'the late Elizabethan and early Stuart period saw in England a wider dissemination than ever before of legal knowledge and a wider interest in the nature of legal principles'. It was lawyers, he thought, who were the essential agents in the development of parliament, and legally educated antiquarians who found the legal precedents that tamed the monarchy.[49]

When sympathetically read, this thesis retains its attractions; the subsequent discovery that much Elizabethan 'opposition' was actually inspired by councillors has only confirmed the existence and importance of the perplexing puzzle it addresses. The Stuart House of Commons was not immune from outside interference (great claims have been made, for example, for the earl of Pembroke's influence on the sessions of the middle 1620s), but whatever the Stuarts themselves may have supposed, the sway exerted by the leading members did not depend on contact with noble malcontents; their leadership depended on their ability to give expression to the House's feelings. The very existence of many of our sources – the manuscript speeches and parliamentary journals preserved by private members and their heirs – suggests the emergence of new modes of parliamentary action. Though the tension between 'court' and 'country' was nothing like a clash of political parties, 'court' and 'country' did exist as social roles. In a parliamentary context, what gave the 'country' role legitimacy, placing Sir Edwin Sandys and Sir John Eliot in a quite different category from troublemakers such as Peter Wentworth or men of business like Thomas Norton, was a shift in members' own beliefs about the institution.

This shift has been obscured from many scholars by their decision to adopt a strangely apolitical perspective. Thus Elton's late work *The parliament of England, 1558–1581* (1986) treated the institution as part of the machine of government, 'a convenient and really rather ingeniously devised instrument for raising supply by consent and for making laws binding upon the agencies of enforcement'. This view was not the finding of empirical research, but the presupposition of his project: 'the rest', he pronounced, 'was pretence', though he promptly wrecked his case by the concession that 'that pretence could at times deceive the pretenders'.[50] What Elton was

---

[48] 'The winning of the initiative by the House of Commons', *Proceedings of the British Academy* 11 (1924), 126.
[49] Ibid., 172.   [50] G. R. Elton, *The parliament of England 1558–1581* (Cambridge, 1986), 379.

trying to do was to absorb the body's history into the history of administration. As a political actor, its independent power 'remained near zero in 1640, 1649 and 1688, though on each occasion the House [of Commons] provided a convenient battlefield for the contestants'.[51]

Elton's administrative functionalism was an extreme expression of attitudes detectable in less provocative writers. The unexpected plural in the title of Conrad Russell's *Parliaments and English politics* (1979) was one way of insisting that parliament was an 'event' and not an 'institution'. The Stuarts' problems *with* their parliaments were problems that had been reflected *in* them and the apparent surge in 'opposition' was really just a symptom of a wider 'functional breakdown': a royal inability to mobilise the nation to cope with the demands of modern warfare. From the perspective of the king, these gatherings were obsolete expedients, increasingly incapable of passing legislation, especially legislation to raise taxes to pay for national security. As their future was dependent on their usefulness to kings, their prospects were at best unpromising.[52]

The problem with this thesis is quite simple. In the opinion of its leading members, parliament was not just a legislature; it was also a court and a council. Where these two latter capacities were concerned, the parliamentary history of the period was a history of successful self-assertion, based partly on a growing sense that royal misbehaviour was *illegal*. This tendency was clearest in the debates about monopolies in the two final sessions of Queen Elizabeth's reign. It was already widely held that grants of this type were illegitimate if they promoted 'private' and not public interests. But the debates of 1601 witnessed an innovation when an MP called Lawrence Hyde demanded an 'exposition of the common law' declaring that monopolies were illegal.[53] It was at once objected that 'this bill may touch the prerogative royal, which . . . is so transcendent that the [thought] of the subject may not aspire thereunto',[54] and most of the House on reflection appear to have preferred the option of petitioning the Queen. They were influenced by the hopelessness of the alternative; the lawyer George Moore pointed out that 'admit we should make this statute with a *non obstante*, yet the Queen may grant a patent with a *non obstante* to cross this *non obstante*' and suggested that the House should proceed by petition.[55] In William Spicer's words, 'it is to no purpose to offer to tie her hands by act of parliament when she may loose herself at her pleasure'.[56]

---

[51] Ibid., 378.
[52] Conrad Russell, *Parliaments and English politics, 1621–1629* (Oxford, 1979), esp. 54, 64, 418.
[53] Hartley, *Proceedings*, III 363.   [54] Ibid., III 370.   [55] Ibid., III 370.   [56] Ibid., III 384.

Even in this pessimistic intervention, we can perhaps detect a significant shift; the very existence of prerogative (not simply its misuse) had come to be seen as presenting political problems. More turbulent spirits could respond by treating their sovereign as subject to ordinary law. The journal account of the debate enables us to document two different manoeuvres. The first was undertaken by a certain 'Mr Davyes', who took the Bractonian view that royal subjection to the law was actually inherent in the very conception of kingship. His starting point was Psalm 82 verse 2 ('I have said ye are Gods'), a text conventionally applied to monarchs:

> God hath given that power to absolute princes which he attributeth to himself, *dixi quod Dii estis*, and as attributes unto them he hath given majesty, justice, and mercy. Majesty in respect of the honour that the subject oweth to his prince, justice in respect he can do no wrong, therefore the law is 1 Henry VII that the king cannot commit a disseisin; mercy in respect that he giveth leave to subjects to right themselves by law, and therefore in the 43 Assize an indictment was brought against bakers and brewers for that by colour of [royal] licence they had broken the Assize. Wherefore, according to that precedent, I think it most fit to proceed by bill and not by petition.[57]

What was new here was not the charitable presumption that monarchs could not mean to be oppressive – Davyes no doubt believed that he was simply following Bracton – it was the use of episodes involving such presumptions (which obviously had their place in certain situations) as support for the more general position that monarchs were invariably controlled by positive law. It was understandable that Robert Cecil, the queen's chief minister and Commons spokesman, felt moved to complain that 'I am sure there were lawmakers before their laws.'[58]

A second and related opposition strategy was to assert that parliament could *judge* that royal misbehaviour was illegal. Hyde defended his bill by recounting 'one precedent in the 50 Edward III, what time one John Peache was arraigned at this bar in parliament for that he had obtained of the king a monopoly of sweet wines, the patent after great advice and dispute judged void and before his face in open parliament cancelled'.[59] Cecil subsequently responded by deploring the use of an 'ancient record of the 50 Edward III, likely enough to be true in that time, when the king was afraid of the subject'. The precedent offered no support for independent adjudicative action, because 'in former times all sat together, as well king as subject, and then it was no prejudice to his prerogative to have such a monopoly examined'.[60] This clash announced a central theme of

[57] Ibid., III 384–5.   [58] Ibid., III 385.   [59] Ibid., III 374.   [60] Ibid., III 386.

the political disputes of the next generation: the question of the nature and extent of parliament's adjudicative power. The crown's approach to these disputes was quite conciliatory; Cecil had not denied that such adjudication might be appropriate, so long as the monarch remained in control of the process. But it was royal policy, when pressed on the legality of the monopolies, to promise to refer them to the courts. In her well-crafted 'golden speech' to the session of 1601, Elizabeth protested that she had always aimed 'for a common good to the subject, as well as private benefit'[61] to the recipients. Robert Cecil had already promised that most (although not all) of the monopolies in question would be left to be examined by the judges.[62] In the test case of *Darcy* v. *Allen*, decided the same year, the troublemaking puritan Nicholas Fuller advanced a detailed argument that still survives in numerous manuscript copies. He started by maintaining that the case (which dealt with an exclusive right of selling playing cards) was 'such as may, yea ought, to be disputed and censured before competent judges . . . for I learn in Bracton . . . *ipse autem rex non debet esse sub homine, sed sub Deo et sub lege, quia lex facit regem, attribuat igitur lex regi quod lex attribuat ei'.* Among other exemplifications of this truth, he quoted Plowden's dictum that 'the law doth so admeasure the king's prerogative, that it shall not tend to the prejudice or hurt of the inheritance of any of his subjects'.[63] This much was probably quite widely accepted, but he went on to make some claims that may have been regarded as eccentric. It was common to regard monopolies as largely an offence against producers, in other words as an attack on the Protestant-humanist value of the sanctity of labour in a calling. The puritan Fuller went a great deal further in treating the Mosaic prohibition that 'thou shalt not take to pledge the upper or nether millstone, for it is his living' (Deuteronomy xxxiv 6) as being decisive for the law of England, apparently on the grounds that 'we are now the house of God and the people of God, the Jews being cut off to whom God was the lawgiver, and we being engraffed in their stead'.[64]

We do not know how much of this was found persuasive by the royal judges, because they prudently refrained from giving any reasons for their decision to strike down the patent.[65] According to Sir Edward Coke, they

---

[61] Ibid., III 290.   [62] Ibid., III 397.
[63] William Noy, *Reports and cases taken in the time of Queen Elizabeth, King James, and King Charles* (1656), 174.
[64] Ibid., 181, 174.
[65] J. I. Corré, 'The arguments, decision, and reports of Darcy v. Allen', *Emory Law Journal* 45 (1996), 1267, 1271.

did however reaffirm that there were two quite different types of royal prerogative: the 'ordinary', which was examinable by law, and the 'absolute', which, as Coke's notebook put it, was 'not examinable and determinable by any course of justice, but only by the king'.[66] The queen had not surrendered the important principle that certain royal powers escaped judicial scrutiny; indeed, if anything, she had entrenched it. Royal assurances about future monopolies continued to be useless to the subject right down to (and indeed beyond) the Monopolies Act of 1624. But the disappointing practical results of the Elizabethan agitation do not, of course, detract from its historical importance. The idea of parliament as declaring rights, as an assembly that could judge the law, and even perhaps annul a royal action, had become a significant factor in English politics.

III

This recent and deep-seated shift in cultural assumptions is one of the forces that helps to explain King James's difficulties. In his own estimation, James had the highest possible regard for common law and a properly kingly aversion to any action that would undermine it. One of his first considered proclamations made plain his distaste for the queen's misuse of her prerogative, especially her habit of issuing monopolies and 'protections'.[67] But his excellent intentions did not prevent him clashing with the English House of Commons as soon as it was possible to do so. Apart from the question of royal control of the church, the principal sources of tension in 1604 were *Goodwin* v. *Fortescue* and the proposals for a union. Both issues involved a collision between a new and foreign king and recently developed legalistic expectations.

In the *Goodwin* v. *Fortescue* affair, the Buckinghamshire member Sir Francis Goodwin, a 'popular' gentleman,[68] was excluded from the House by Chancery on the grounds that he was technically an outlaw. The beneficiary of this decision, his local opponent Sir John Fortescue, also happened to be a royal councillor, which probably explained why the resultant controversy acquired a symbolic character. In the event, a compromise was found, the upshot of which was that the House successfully asserted that it and it alone controlled elections. The intensity of feeling that the episode evoked was obviously connected with its sense of itself as representing England; if

---

[66] Ibid., 1297 and n.

[67] *Stuart royal proclamations*, ed. J. F. Larkin and P. L. Hughes, 2 vols. (Oxford, 1973–83), I, 11–14.

[68] On the local background, see Linda Levy Peck, 'Goodwin v. Fortescue: the local context of parliamentary controversy', *Parliamentary History* 3 (1984), 33–56.

the 'representative body' of the nation (the metaphor is corporal and pictorial) could not uphold its privileges against an alien head, then individual subjects were hardly likely to be more successful.

In this suspicious atmosphere, James made the mistake of remarking that 'since they derived all matters of privilege from him and by his grant, he expected they should not be turned against him'. More foolishly still, he had said that 'precedents in times of minors, of tyrants [*i.e.* usurpers], of women, of simple kings, not to be credited, because for some private ends', thus ruling out appeals to the actions of most of his immediate predecessors.[69] These remarks have duly been incorporated in standard Whig accounts of the affair; revisionists have tended to point out, with equal justice, that the matter was successfully smoothed over and seems to have had no long-term consequences. Less emphasis has been placed, though, upon an aspect of the case with genuinely far-reaching implications: the tensions it revealed between the Lower House and the judiciary. In a bid to settle the question, the king asked the House to consult with the common law judges (who had pronounced informally in favour of the Chancery position), but the Commons were unwilling to allow them any standing in the matter. Opposition to judicial intervention at once became the focus of discussion. The famous statement 'That now the case of Sir John Fortescue and Sir Francis Goodwin was become the case of the whole kingdom' has been repeatedly quoted; the Journal's next sentence 'That old lawyers forget, and commonly interpret the law according to the time' has never received the same level of attention, but it is arguably more important.[70] Someone summed up by noting 'the judges have judged, and we have judged. What need then of conference?'[71]

This was the real background to the Apology's assertion that the House of Commons was a court of record, 'and that there is not the highest standing court in this land that ought to enter into competency either for dignity or authority with these high courts of parliament'.[72] The plural 'high courts' is significant. It was of course a commonplace that parliament was in a sense a court, which claimed, like other important courts, a number of privileges for its members; the innovation was the claim that the unaided Commons had a legal jurisdiction. In the parliament of 1593, a similar case involving an outlawed knight of the shire led the lawyer William Brograve to pronounce that parliament 'for the dignity and highness of it hath privileges as all other courts have, and as it is above all other courts, so hath it privileges

---

[69] *Commons Journal*, I 158.
[70] Ibid., I 159. For the flavour of debate, see also Kyle, *Elections*, 35–7, 49–5.
[71] *Commons Journal*, I 160.   [72] HMC Salisbury XXIII 143–4.

above any court'.[73] But Brograve had also believed that 'we ought to desire instruction from the judges of the realm whether in these cases by law we can grant privilege or not'.[74] In 1604, by contrast, the Commons and the judges had become competitors.

Unfortunately, this altered self-conception made differences with the king more difficult to resolve. If the Commons had the competence to adjudicate on rights, then settled Commons demands (for restrictions on purveyors, for example) were not a matter for negotiation. Thus the Apology spurned the government's suggestion of 'a perpetual yearly revenue in lieu of the taking away of these oppressors [the purveyors], unto which composition neither know we well how to yield, being only for justice and due right, which is unsaleable'.[75] In the 1606 parliamentary session, this seems to have become the majority view, because the House of Commons passed a bill that its proponents thought to be 'no other in almost all points than the present law now requireth'.[76] Their stance brought them back into conflict with the judges, who held not only that the king had a right of compulsory purchase (this principle was accepted by all parties), but that he was allowed to buy on credit at sub-market prices. The numerous medieval statutes the Commons saw themselves as re-asserting (including one providing that he should pay in cash) were 'void according to the judges, because the denial of the subject does not prevent purveyance in so much as it is so necessary a prerogative'.[77] In a revealing statement of the new expectations, the letter-writer John Chamberlain commented that they had delivered 'one judgment in all men's opinions of dangerous consequence, that the prerogative was not subject to law but that it was transcendent above the reach of parliament'.[78] The prickliness so evident in the behaviour of the House of Commons reflected a shift in perceptions both of parliament and law.

One symptom of this shift was a widening gap between the king's and parliament's assumptions. James saw the common law as, for the most part, a feudally based body of positive law; his subjects believed it was reason as actualised in English circumstances. James saw his kingship as above the law (though bound to it by *moral* obligations); his subjects were beginning to regard the English crown as part of a complex of rational institutions. These differences between them extended to their attitudes to English history. When he wrote *The trew law of free monarchies*, James stressed that William the Conqueror had taken the country 'by force, and with a mighty army.

[73] Hartley, *Proceedings*, III 158.   [74] Ibid., III 158.
[75] HMC Salisbury XXIII 150.   [76] Bowyer, *Diary*, 122.
[77] 'The journal of Sir Roger Wilbraham', ed. H. S. Scott in *Camden miscellany* 10 (1902), 83–4.
[78] Bowyer, *Diary*, 134 and n.

Where he gave the law and took none, changed the laws, inverted the order of government, set down the strangers his followers in many of the old possessors rooms.'[79] He believed, what was more, that Scotland was the country that 'doth nearest of all others agree with the laws and customs of this state',[80] presumably on the grounds that both these countries had obviously feudal institutions. Though he was careful to avoid maintaining that he could wilfully transfer his subjects' property, he noted pointedly that every lordship was ultimately held of the Scots king, who was thus in a full sense the lord of the whole kingdom, '*dominus directus totius dominii*, the whole subjects being but his vassals'.[81]

This was, at all the events, the main assumption behind attempts to justify a union of laws. James had no reason to suppose that it was other than conventional. All editions of William Camden's great work *Britannia* (first published 1586) stated that

> the victorious William as a kind of monument of his victory abolished the greatest part of the ancient laws of the English, brought in Norman customs (the laws of the English being for the most part antiquated), and ordered that cases should be discussed in French; when the English had been excluded from their ancestral inheritance, he assigned lands and spoils to his soldiers, in such a way however that he reserved *dominium directum* to himself, and secured obedience through a client relationship to him and his successors, that is, so that all should hold in fee or in faith, and that no men except the king should be true lords but only fiduciary lords and possessors.[82]

While Camden did maintain (against Polydore Vergil) that juries had been used in Saxon times, he seems to have felt relaxed about the possibility of sharp discontinuity at the conquest. In the next twenty years, though, this view went out of fashion, and it became more usual to insist, as William Fulbecke did in 1601, that 'rather reason than sovereignty, and consent rather than command, was the principal agent in the alteration'.[83] The last edition of *Britannia* (1607) mentioned an episode in which the conqueror had respected pre-Conquest property; Camden remarked that this was an example that was urged 'by those would have him to have occupied England by compact and agreement, not by right of war'.[84]

---

[79] James, *Political writings*, 74.   [80] Ibid., 154.   [81] Ibid., 73.
[82] William Camden, *Britannia, sive florentissimorum regnorum Angliae, Scotiae, Hiberniae et insularum adjacentium ex intima antiquitate chorographica descriptio* (1586), 50. This passage is considerably toned down in Merlin Holland's 1610 translation.
[83] William Fulbecke, *A parallele or conference of the civill law, the canon law, and the common law of this realme of England* (1601), 'To the reader'.
[84] William Camden, *Britannia, sive florentissimorum regnorum Angliae, Scotiae, Hiberniae et insularum adjacentium ex intima antiquitate chorographica descriptio* (1607), 350.

Ever since J. G. A. Pocock's *The ancient constitution and the feudal law* (1957), this growing sensitivity has been understood to constitute a problem. One part of the solution is probably that the English feared absorption into a composite dynastic state, in which the common law would have the status of merely local rights and privileges; we have noticed that the similar threat presented by Philip of Spain appears to have evoked analogous worries. This was doubtless why some of the English delegation at the conference of lawyers about the union scheme surprised their visitor Sir Thomas Craig, the Scots historian of feudalism, by claiming that Scots and English law were 'diametrically opposed'.[85] Conversely, those who favoured a union of laws had an incentive to assert that the common law was feudal. It is not at all surprising to discover that this was the position of John Cowell, who understood the common law as 'nothing but a mixture of Roman and feudal law'. Cowell did his best to demonstrate this fact by writing a short volume called *Institutions of the law of England composed in the method and order of the imperial laws* (1605), whose stated purpose was to cleanse that law from the 'rotten filth' of English legal language: his aim was not to introduce 'a similarity of laws', but only to bring James's subjects to 'a knowledge of the existing similarity'.[86]

But the anxieties provoked by James's union scheme were probably, at most, a catalyst; they can hardly account for the permanent shift in English attitudes. As Pocock's solution still dominates most thinking on the subject, it seems worth pausing to assess his theory. In general, his model has worn extremely well. The subtlety of Pocock's view (not always understood by his admirers) was his refusal to explain an attitude to history in terms of constitutionalist political positions; he held that political fears, while relevant, were not in themselves an adequate explanation of the determination to deny the Norman Conquest that quite abruptly became characteristic of English antiquarian scholarship. Instead, he postulated a close link between this historical outlook and the English common law, the crucial connection being 'an assumption deeply rooted in "the common law mind" that all law was common law and all common law custom'.[87] Though he is often taken to have done so, Pocock did not assert that law was thought to be unchanging; and he was well aware that English custom was difficult to understand as strictly populist.[88] But he does seem to have believed that

[85] Thomas Craig, *Ius feudale*, ed. James Baillie (Edinburgh, 1732), vi.

[86] John Cowell, *Institutiones iuris Anglicani, ad methodum et seriem institutionum imperialium compositae* (1605), 4, 10.

[87] J. G. A. Pocock, *The ancient constitution and the feudal law: a study of English historical thought in the seventeenth century: a reissue with a retrospect* (Cambridge, 1987), 265.

[88] Ibid., 266.

the idea of common law as custom, as in some sense the product of the whole community, was fundamental to the legal system, while the idea of common law as reason was secondary and derivative.[89]

The model sketched out here largely endorses Pocock's theory, but it inverts this crucial emphasis. In the professional consciousness, at least until the later Tudor period, it was the idea of reason that was central, while the idea of custom was of less significance. It was the former notion that lay at the heart of the lawyers' professional thinking from Catesby's claim, in 1470, that common law was 'as ancient as the world', down to John Selden's statement, in his *Notes on Fortescue* (1616), that

All laws in general are originally equally ancient. All were grounded upon nature, and no nation was that out of it took not their grounds, and nature being the same in all, the beginning of all laws must be the same. As soon as Italy was peopled, this beginning of laws was there and upon it was grounded the Roman laws, which could not have that distinct name indeed till Rome was built, yet remained always what they were at first, saving that additions and interpretations in succeeding ages increased, and somewhat altered them, by making a *determinatio iuris naturalis*, which is nothing but the civil law of any nation.[90]

As the concluding phrases of Selden's statement show, this broad assumption could be made the basis of almost positivist attitudes; in spite of a vague reference to 'the merely immutable part of nature',[91] Selden appears to have resembled Hobbes (or a Hobbesian version of Hooker) in treating the right to determine natural law as an unfettered legislative power. He nonetheless remained within the framework supplied by the assumption that law is rational. To those who worked within this general framework, the threat presented by the Norman Conquest was not the possibility that James might be the heir to William's powers; as Pocock rightly pointed out, this was a claim no Englishman appears to have supported.[92] The shared presupposition that the Conquest might subvert was a conception of the law of England as a *continuous* rational response to English problems. Though Selden had no narrowly political incentive for stressing this unbroken history, the vision of the national past by which he was possessed was one of fairly seamless evolution.

The same could be said of the great Sir Henry Spelman, the most important feudalist in Pocock's narrative. Spelman was a high churchman and a high monarchist as well as a distinguished antiquarian, but though he

[89] Ibid., 35.
[90] John Selden, 'Notes upon Sir John Fortescue', 17 in Sir John Fortescue, *De laudibus legum Angliae* (1616).
[91] Ibid., 19.   [92] Pocock, *Ancient constitution*, 54.

believed that the conqueror had introduced a new tenurial system, he did not deny the existence of continuities across the Conquest. The Saxon mode of government was very different from the modern one 'yet can there be no period assigned wherein either the frame of those laws was abolished, or this of ours entertained'.[93] The foundation of the common law was German, but it was strongly influenced (at this point he cited Cowell), by principles borrowed by judges from the Romans, 'for I suppose they in those days judged many things *ex aequo & bono*, and that their judgments after (as *Responsa prudentum* among the Romans . . .) became precedents of law unto posterity'.[94] Even a brilliant scholar of broadly clericalist sympathies thus took it for granted that the legal system involved an unbroken professional tradition. Spelman also believed that some aspects of the Saxon frame of laws continued to apply in modern England; a recognition that some parts of common law were feudal was no bar to believing in an 'ancient constitution'. As might have been expected, he used this premise to the king's advantage. In 1639, he would explain that the Saxon kings' right of 'military expedition [conscription of men and equipment] and warding of the sea against enemies' was based in 'a fundamental law or custom of the kingdom'. This continued to be the basis of the 'naval expedition lately now revived', which was Sir Henry's learned euphemism for Charles's hated levy, Ship Money.[95]

All this suggests that Pocock was right to see his book as primarily 'a study of English historical thought'; during this early period of their development, the ideas he was concerned with did not imply the adoption of an oppositional stance. Beliefs about the English past were shaped by English law, but the deliverances of law were not necessarily threatening to the English monarchy. The notion of law as reason was a capacious one, compatible with a number of political positions, including positions that granted the king a virtually unlimited discretion. In practice, of course, a discretion that was granted by the law was hard to distinguish from extra-legal power. In July 1604, for example, the Speaker of a restless House of Commons offered his king the following sketch of England's legal system:

The laws whereby the ark of this government hath been ever steered are of three kinds: the first, the common law, grounded or drawn from the law of God, the law of reason, and the law of nature, not mutable; the second, the positive law, founded, changed, and altered by and through the occasions and policies of times; the third customs and usages, practised and allowed with time's approbation, without known beginnings. Wherein although we differ from the laws of other states' governments,

---

[93] *Reliquiae Spelmannianae: the posthumous works of Sir Henry Spelman Knt*, ed. Edmund Gibson (Oxford, 1698), 49.
[94] Ibid., 99.   [95] Ibid., 17–18.

yet have the authors thereof imitated the approved excellency of Plato and Aristotle, framing their laws according to the capacity, nature, disposition, and humour of the place and people.[96]

On this view, the prerogatives conferred by God or Nature were actually a part of the common law proper, more so indeed than the mutable arrangements brought in by subsequent positive regulations. But from a libertarian perspective, there was an obvious danger in this theory. High expectations of the legal system encouraged the belief that law could shield liberties, but precisely the same expectations could justify judges in giving legal sanction to those extra-legal powers by which the subjects' privileges were threatened. The judges' attitude to impositions was a perfect illustration of this point.

During a long and prosperous reign, in which the growth of import trades was the most striking index of her subject's new-found wealth, Elizabeth had barely used her sister's precedents for the creation of new customs duties. Such occasional adjustments as were made were mostly applications of commercial policy by levying retaliatory duties. In 1605, one duty of this type was questioned by a group of Turkey merchants who were importing currants via Venice. In 1606, the conflict reached the court of Exchequer as Bate's case, which was decided in the government's favour. This judgement's most disturbing single feature was its extension of the power of judges into what might be thought of as non-legal territory. Thus Baron Clarke noted '[the king's] intent to be, that this matter shall be disputed and adjudged by us according to the ancient law and custom of the realm', but he denied that ordinary legal principles could offer guidance in this situation. He brushed aside the acts of parliament cited as 'nothing to this purpose', insisting instead that 'the precedents of every court ought to be a direction to that court'. This meant, in effect, that precedents set by the executive were the appropriate authority on matters of 'the king's prerogative, his revenue, and government'.[97] In a notorious statement, Chief Baron Fleming's judgement for the crown spelled out the unusual character of the considerations to which he felt entitled to appeal:

these reasons are not extracted out of the books of law, but are only reasons of policy; for *rex est legalis et politicus*; and reasons politic are sufficient guides to judges in their arguments; and such cases and precedents are good directions in cases of judgment, for they are demonstrations of the course of antiquity. Whereupon my judgment shall consist upon reasons politic, and precedents.[98]

---

[96] *Commons Journal*, I 254.   [97] Cobbett and Howell, *State trials*, II 382.
[98] Ibid., II 388.

Two years later, the crown exploited this decision by issuing a replacement for the Marian Book of Rates. Legal sanction for increasing customs duties gave access to an income that was easy to collect and rose with national prosperity. In the medium term, these royal 'impositions' permitted the king to aspire to balance his budget, at least in time of peace, without resorting to a parliament. They also impelled disaffected spirits to articulate accounts of law that showed why the Exchequer was mistaken. The result, in the next parliamentary session, was a succession of well-reported speeches that wrestled with some fundamental questions. These speeches were remarkable for their variety. Apart from their agreement that the duties were illegal, they give no evidence of a consensus, but they supply a register of possibilities inherent in the new, more legalistic politics.

Perhaps the most pervasive theme was Fortescue's idea that the great privilege of the English people was freedom from taxation without consent, and that this privilege was the foundation both of their valour and their industry. The arguments defending this fortunate state of affairs were not, however, so traditional. Heneage Finch attacked one of his sovereign's most cherished principles by laying it down that matters of state were 'objects of our reason, not mysteries of faith' – in other words, that there were no such things as true *arcana regni*.[99] No absolute prerogative was more unquestionable than royal power of making war and peace, but this discretionary power was regulated by the royal judges, who could decide, for instance, 'whether the war be foreign or domestical, invasive or defensive'.[100] James Whitelocke preferred to emphasise the role of parliament: he believed that 'in point of the common right of the whole . . . the states would never trust any of the courts of ordinary justice with the deciding of them but assumed the cognizance of them unto the high court of parliament'.[101] Whitelocke mentioned the existence of absolute powers that could be exercised outside this context, but insisted that these were prerogatives that the king had 'time out of mind practised without the gainsaying and murmuring of his subjects'; in other words, they had received the tacit consent of the people.[102]

This was a thought that was developed further in an elaborate speech by William Hakewill. Hakewill noted that those arguing for the crown

[99] Elizabeth Read Foster, *Proceedings in parliament 1610*, 2 vols. (New Haven, CT, 1966), II, 235.
[100] Ibid., II 235.
[101] [James Whitelocke], *The rights of the people concerning impositions stated in a learned argument* (1658), 24.
[102] Ibid., 12.

had urged that the ancient custom upon wool (an apparently pre-statutory duty) 'must have his beginning either by the king's absolute power, or by a legal assent of the people, which can be nowhere but in parliament, and cannot but appear of record, but because no such assent can be shown, therefore they conclude that it began by the king's absolute power and infer that the same power remains still'.[103] His answer was that any such pre-statutory laws must be supposed to have been made by popular consent: 'who reduced all the known grounds of the common law to that certainty that now they are? . . . To say the truth, all these things began no man can say certainly when or how, but by a tacit consent of king and people, and the long approbation of time beyond the memory of any man.'[104] His argument thus exhibited a logic that led in the direction of consistent populism.

A notion of the law as fixed by popular consent was probably connected in his mind with a more curious consideration: a presumption that 'the common law of England (as also all other wise laws in the world) delight[s] in certainty'.[105] It followed that law 'giveth to the king . . . no perpetual revenue or matter of profit out of the interest or property of the subject, but it either limiteth a certainty therein at the first, or otherwise hath so provided, that if it be uncertain in itself, it is reducible to a certainty only by a legal course'.[106] He pushed this idea to unprecedented lengths. A common example of absolute power, in Fortescue's *De natura* and elsewhere, had been the power to react to a surprise invasion. Hakewill regarded even this as

very dangerous, for to admit this were by consequence to bring us into bondage. You say that upon occasion of sudden war the king may levy a tax; who shall be judge between the king and his people of the occasion? Can it be tried by any legal course in our law? It cannot: if then, the king himself must be the sole judge in this case, will it not follow that the king may levy a tax at his own pleasure, seeing that his pleasure cannot be bounded by law.[107]

Hakewill observed that the medieval law imposed on the subject a duty to serve at his own charge, 'the reason of which, in my opinion, was to no other end than that the king might have no pretence whatsoever for the raising of money upon his subjects at his own pleasure, without their common assent in parliament'.[108]

What was most interesting about all this was the emergence of an attitude that later became central to political debate: the idea that arbitrary power

---

[103] William Hakewill, *The libertie of the subject against the pretended power of impositions* (1641), 125.
[104] Ibid., 127.   [105] Ibid., 10.   [106] Ibid., 11.   [107] Ibid., 22.   [108] Ibid., 23.

was something of its very nature illegitimate. There was nothing new in holding that rule 'by will' (*arbitrium*) was unacceptable and that it stood in contrast to government 'by law', but medieval and Tudor uses of such language still made implicit reference to a psychology; somebody who governed by will (as opposed to by reason) was a disordered personality. At some stage in the seventeenth century (the question of the timing of the shift is difficult to settle by quotation), the objection to the 'arbitrary' changed in character. The psychological background began to disappear and the idea of arbitrariness came to refer to any power that was unchecked by binding regulations. In spite of Aristotle's ancient insights about the permanent need for *epieikeia*, the English began to believe that correct political behaviour could be dictated by a list of rules; conversely, they were easily persuaded that any loophole in such rules presented an intolerable menace.

On the face of it, this left no room for the kind of judge-made law that was produced by artificial reason. It was, however, possible to think about the system in ways that came close to combining these rival conceptions. This was the achievement of the synthesis suggested by the barrister Thomas Hedley. Hedley realised the treacherous nature of the idea that common law was reason:

> for though it be true that all law is reason, yet that is no convertible proposition, for everyone knows that all reason is not law. Some go a degree nearer and say, it is reason approved by the judges to be good and profitable for the commonwealth, yet that neither can be a true definition, for the statute laws of this realm are both reasonable and also good and profitable for the commonwealth . . . yet the judges nor the King himself without the parliament could never [*sic*] have made them laws, for then the parliament troubled itself about it in vain.[109]

His solution was both complex and ingenious. He declined to resolve the power of common law entirely into parliamentary power, if only on the grounds that parliament too derived its power from the legal system, 'for the parliament hath his power and authority from the common law, and not the common law from the parliament'. Though parliament had unlimited powers of piecemeal legislation, wholesale destruction of the law was quite impossible, 'for that were includedly to take away the power of the parliament itself'.[110]

In consequence, his theory did not rely on artificial reason, nor even on the reason of parliament itself, but only upon long-established custom:

---

[109] Foster, *1610*, II 173.   [110] Ibid., II 173–4.

'that then that can only try reason, and is the essential form of common law, in a word, is time, which is the trier of truth . . . such time whereof the memory of man is not to the contrary, time out of mind, such time as will beget a custom'.[111] The same idea was soon to be expressed in a populist form by his contemporary Sir John Davies in the celebrated preface to the latter's *Irish reports* (1615).[112] Davies provided a defence of an unwritten law that stressed its roots in popular experience: 'when a reasonable act once done is found to be good and beneficial to the people, and agreeable to their nature and disposition, then do they use it and practise it again and again, and so by often iteration and multiplication of the act it becometh a custom'.[113] As only beneficial acts developed into customs, the customary law of a nation was always rational.

Davies supplies an interesting contrast, because his writings demonstrate that populism in legal theory was not invariably associated with opposi-tional views in politics. Davies combined an eloquent defence of the merits of unwritten positive law with a continuing belief in the natural right of levying impositions.[114] Though Hedley was less populist, he was more 'popular'. Although he was committed to believing that all and every legal principle was ultimately traceable to custom, he 'would not be mistaken, as though I meant to confound the common law with custom, which dif-fer as much as artificial reason and bare precedents'.[115] All reasons in law could be traced to 'some primitive maxim, depending immediately upon some prescription or custom', but such reasons were digested and devel-oped by means of derivative secondary reasons, 'in which secondary reasons and consequence', he proudly remarked, 'appear as much art and learning, wisdom and excellency of reason as in any law, art, or profession whatso-ever'.[116] Hedley does not appear to have believed that even first-generation 'prescriptions or customs' were fully populist in character; the common law was not just any custom, but a 'reasonable usage, throughout the whole realm, approved time out of mind in the king's courts of record which have jurisdiction over the whole kingdom'.[117] Thus the crucial role was played by professional learning, but though Hedley believed in the wisdom of the judges, he nonetheless held that parliament was wiser than any particular gathering of sages of the law; it was parliament, and only parliament, of

---

[111] Ibid., II 175.
[112] Sir John Davies, *Le primer report des cases et matters en ley resolves et adjudges en les courts del roy en Ireland* (Dublin, 1615).
[113] Pocock, *Ancient constitution*, 33.
[114] Sir John Davies, *The question concerning impositions* (1656).   [115] Foster, *1610*, II 175.
[116] Ibid., II 176.   [117] Ibid., II 175.

which it could legitimately be said that 'there is . . . the whole wisdom of the whole realm'.[118]

The impositions debate of 1610 offers impressive evidence of the sheer range of arguments that common law had made available. The feelings of entitlement that they articulated account for the subsequent failure of the government's Great Contract, its final serious attempt to trade unpopular prerogatives for regular income from direct taxation. The same insistence upon legal rights ensured that the next national assembly, the 1614 'Addled Parliament', was doomed to acrimonious dissolution. But the verve with which some lawyers were working out a basis for constitutionalist politics could not disguise the fact that James had quite a strong position. His claims were studiously moderate; his representatives all stressed that impositions were not strictly taxes, but instruments of commercial policy, and that the government had no intention of tampering with property in England. As he himself remarked in 1614, he could hardly be accused of innovation:

When he came to the crown, he changed no counsellor, judges or other of Queen Elizabeth's and he was persuaded by the one that impositions were a great flower of his prerogative, and by the latter of the lawfulness thereof, as also by a judgment in the Chequer Chamber, that therefore he would die a hundred deaths before he would infringe his prerogative; yet notwithstanding that he would, if a writ of error should be brought, stand to the opinion of the judges.[119]

After a decade on the throne, James had adapted himself brilliantly to the peculiarities of English political culture. But his appeal to common law was not without its hazards. Although he paid the judges' salaries, he had to reckon with a strand in their professional thinking with a concealed potential for subversion. To grasp the hidden risks in his reliance on the bench, we must now turn to the thought of Edward Coke.

IV

Sir Edward Coke (1552–1634) has always divided opinion. To his admirers, he was a man who had excelled 'touts que va before him in that profession'.[120] From a technical professional point of view, he had undoubtedly deserved such praises, because his volumes of reports (1600–15) made the chaotic law of the Abridgments accessible and even teachable. As Francis Bacon (who hated him) confessed

---

[118] Ibid., II 175.
[119] *Commons debates 1621*, ed. Wallace Notestein, F. H. Relf, and Hartley Simpson, 7 vols. (New Haven, 1935), VII, 632.
[120] *The diary of Sir Richard Hutton*, ed. W. R. Prest, Selden Society supplementary series 9 (1991), 99.

Had it not been for Sir Edward Coke's *Reports* (which though they may have errors, and some peremptory and extra-judicial resolutions more than are warranted, yet they contain infinite good decisions and rulings over of cases) the law by this time had been almost like a ship without ballast; for that the cases of modern experience are fled from those that were adjudged and ruled in former time.[121]

The case against him was that this achievement concealed a political agenda. In 1616, just before his sacking, detractors among his colleagues commented that

It is to be observed throughout all his books that he hath as it were purposely laboured to derogate much from the rights of the church and dignity of churchmen; to disesteem and weaken the power of the king in the ancient use of his prerogatives; to traduce or else to cut short the jurisdiction of all other courts besides that court wherein himself doth sit.[122]

They claimed that he pursued his ends by highly tendentious reporting, 'oft times . . . setting down that for resolve[d], which he himself hales in upon the by, and tendeth nothing to the point in judgment'.[123]

Although such charges had some factual basis, they seem to have misjudged Coke's motivation. He had, to be sure, political attitudes; other things being equal (that is, when he was not retained by clients, including the crown, who happened to have opposing interests), his instincts were generally 'popular' and anticlerical. But these attitudes in turn were traceable to a consuming intellectual passion. He was not an attractive personality, but he was loyal, in most of his manoeuvres, to a compelling vision of the law. Coke had a humanist belief in the rewards of going to the sources; he held that 'the tumultuary reading of Abridgements doth cause a confused judgment',[124] while scrutiny of original court records and reports revealed an underlying harmony, so much so that he marvelled at 'the unity and consent of so many several judges and courts in so many successions of ages'. Like the group of extremists referred to by the anonymous author of the *Treatise concerning statutes*, he felt that this entitled him to borrow Cicero's language about the *ratio* immanent in the created order, and to apply it without reservation to every detail of the common law:

As in nature we see the infinite distinction of things proceed from some unity, as many flowers from one root, many rivers from one fountain . . . so without question *lex orta est cum mente divina*, and this admirable unity and consent in such diversity of things proceeds only from God, the fountain and founder of all good laws and constitutions.[125]

---

[121] Bacon, *Works*, XIII 65.
[122] British Library, Additional MS 14,030, fo. 91.   [123] Ibid., 91.   [124] Coke, *Fourth reports*, xi.
[125] Coke, *Third reports*, iv.

These claims were not just bursts of rhetoric; they were presuppositions that made his great achievements possible. As he himself noted, 'I affirm it constantly, that the law is not uncertain *in abstracto*, but *in concreto*, and that the uncertainty thereof is *hominis vitium* and not *professionis*.'[126] The function of a law report was 'to let in that gladsome light, whereby the right reason of the rule (the beauty of the law) may be clearly discerned'; in a metaphor borrowed from Plowden, he went on to say that 'it breaketh the thick and hard shell, whereby with pleasure and ease the sweetness of the kernel may be sensibly tasted'.[127] Reports were the best way of making legal truth accessible, because the law's most notable achievements were the result of a collective feat that 'no man alone with all his true and uttermost labours, nor all the actors in them themselves by themselves out of a court of justice, nor in court without solemn argument . . . could ever have attained unto'.[128] Thus the authority of law was the authority of a profession that was equipped, within a courtroom setting, to grasp the system's rationality. The wisdom of absolute reason became articulate in the decisions of the royal judges. This was his usefulness to James; it was also, in the long run, to make him dangerous.

Some radical possibilities concealed within his thought appear to have been present from the start. When he argued for the government in *Darcy* v. *Allen*, he nonetheless gratuitously conceded that 'such letters patents as tended to change the law, or course of any man's inheritance, or that was *contra commune jus*, or that tended to any general charge of the subjects, were void in law'.[129] Although his notes about the case admitted the existence of 'absolute power . . . not examinable or determinable by any course of justice but only by the king',[130] the tendency of his ideas restricted this power's deployment. Thus he endorsed the notion that the 'ordinary' power included all prerogatives that touched on 'arts or sciences or trade and traffic', a view that he associated with the Year Book tag that 'la ley est le plus hault inheritance que le roy ad'. He added (echoing Fuller) that 'with this agrees Bracton I viii: *ipse autem rex non debet esse sub homine sed sub deo et sub lege quia lex facit regem. Attribuat ergo rex legi quod lex attribuit ei viz. dominationem et potentiam quia sine lege non potest esse rex*.'[131] He also cited the Bractonian doctrine that 'it is characteristic of power to do justice, but of weakness to do injury'.[132] Like Fuller again, he had Protestant-humanist grounds for holding that the exercise of trades should be protected against interference; because they avoided 'idleness le bane del weal publique' and

---

[126] Coke, *Ninth reports*, xxxvii.   [127] Ibid., xxxviii.   [128] Ibid., xxxviii.
[129] Noy, *Reports and cases*, 175.   [130] British Library, Harleian MS 6686, 573.
[131] Ibid., fo. 573v. He is quoting P 19 Henry VI, fo. 63, pl. 1.   [132] Ibid., 573v.

exercised 'hommes in labour pur maintenance de eux et lour families', such trades were 'profitable pur le common weal'.[133]

In 1606, after fourteen years' work as Solicitor and then Attorney General, that is, as a government lawyer, Coke rose to the position of Chief Justice of Common Pleas. During this period of his career, he was a significant asset to the crown, if only because, in two important areas, he was a propagandist for royal policy. The first of these was the Supremacy. In 1605, Coke published a report on Cawdrey's case (usually bound up with his *Fifth Reports*) that gave a powerful account of the official doctrine. Cawdrey's case was an Elizabethan law suit about the legal powers of High Commission (Cawdrey himself had been a puritan who challenged his deprivation by that body), but Coke made use of it to write against the Catholics. He maximised his readership by writing in Latin and English rather than inaccessible Law French. As James would have wished, he explained that the successive Supremacy statutes were altogether declaratory in force and that the authority enjoyed by papal law in England depended entirely on local acquiescence (in this particular polemical context, he conceded rather more than he usually did to the role played by popular consent).

These claims provoked the Jesuit Robert Persons into a brilliant response that probed their weaknesses. Persons noted that '[Coke] runneth everywhere to this shift, that the pope's ecclesiastical and canon laws, being admitted to England, may be called the king's ecclesiastical laws for that they are admitted and allowed by him and his realm. In which sense', he shrewdly added, 'the evangelical law may also be called the king's law, for that he admitteth the Bible'.[134] The most memorable of many well-phrased jeers was addressed to Coke's heartfelt description of common law as an 'inheritance': 'will this patrimony of the law make them rich? Mr Attorney, and divers of his fellows, have had a good patrimony, and inheritance by them, but this is not every man's case.' It was difficult to admire a legal system in which the accused in a criminal trial had no access to a lawyer and the decisive role was played by venal and ignorant juries – practices that were so inequitable that Persons cruelly remarked that 'it may easily be believed, that they were indeed made by a Conqueror'.[135]

By the early seventeenth century, this disrespectful language was the mark of an outsider; the common law was part of the foundations of English structures of authority, in part because it could be seen as nature's

---

[133] Ibid., 573v.
[134] Robert Parsons, *An answere to the fifth part of reportes lately set forth by Syr Edward Cooke* (1606), 3.
[135] Ibid., 15.

law for England. There was, indeed, an element of truth in the quip about the 'admission' of the Bible; selective invocation of scriptural principles did have a legitimate part to play in legal reasoning. If Fuller's scripturalist approach was probably unusual, nothing in English legal theory excluded the use of this type of argument. Presuppositions such as Coke's permitted lawyers to invoke all kinds of principles – scriptural, political, or natural – so long as the use that was made of such ideas was guided by professional erudition. Thus the most famous showcase of Coke's method, his Latin and English report on Calvin's case (1608), treated the law of nature as 'part of the laws of England'.[136]

The purpose of this test case was to establish that so-called *post-nati*, the Scottish subjects of the king born after 1603, enjoyed the privileges of Englishmen. As it was obvious that such a claim was unacceptable to parliament, the principle could only be established by judges who discovered it within existing law. James was assisted by the fact that the lawyers had been put upon their mettle. The government's most formidable opponent, Sir Edwin Sandys, had argued that this was a question that should be settled by the law of nature, on the grounds that in unprecedented cases, resort must necessarily be made to natural reason. When the judges considered the question, both the Lord Chancellor and Coke referred to his opinion. In the former's view,

> it was truly said by a learned gentleman of the lower House, '*Deficiente lege recurrendum est ad consuetudinem: Deficiente consuetudine, recurrendum ad rationem.*' And so from the judges we shall have *responsa prudentum* to decide all such new cases and questions.[137]

Coke's attitude was very similar:

> if the said imaginative rule be rightly and legally understood, it may stand for truth, for if you intend *ratio* for the legal and profound reason of such as by diligent study and long experience and observation are so learned in the laws of this realm as out of the reason of the same they can rule the case in question, in that sense the said rule is true; but if it be intended of the reason of the wisest man that professeth not the laws of England, then (I say), the rule is absurd and dangerous.[138]

Here, as elsewhere within his published writings, Coke's main concern was to assert the adequacy of professional methods; new cases would from time to time arise, but they could always be resolved by principles implicit

---

[136] Coke, *Seventh reports*, Calvin's case, 4b.
[137] L. A. Knafla (ed.), *Law and politics in Jacobean England: the tracts of Lord Chancellor Ellesmere* (Cambridge, 1977), 220–1.
[138] Coke, *Seventh reports*, Calvin's case, 19a.

in the system. A passage whose sonorities proclaimed his depth of feeling denied that those who argued in favour of the Scots had any need to be original:

albeit they spake according to their own heart, yet they spake not out of their own head and invention . . . for we are but of yesterday (and therefore had need of the wisdom of those that were before us) and had been ignorant (if we had not received light and knowledge from our forefathers) and our days upon the earth are but as a shadow, in respect of the old ancient days and times past, wherein the laws have been by the wisdom of the most excellent men, in many successions of ages, by long and continual experience (the trial of light and truth) fined and refined, which no one man (being of so short a time) albeit he had in his head the wisdom of all the men in the world, in any one age could ever have effected or attained unto.[139]

All this was most convenient to James, but Coke's extreme self-confidence was not without its drawbacks. It may be that Coke exaggerated somewhat when he claimed that he had said to the king's face that the artificial reason of the judges had more authority, in legal matters, than James's personal opinions.[140] There is no doubt, however, that the great man had a habit of picking fights in which his own courts, courts of common law, were pitted against other vessels of the king's authority. Almost throughout his period on the bench, he was embroiled in jurisdictional conflicts, including battles with the bishops' courts, the court of High Commission, commissioners of sewers (statutory bodies with discretionary powers to organise flood defences), and the councils of the North and of the Marches. After 1613, when he was made Chief Justice of King's Bench, he turned to pursuing the feud with Lord Chancellor Ellesmere that climaxed three years later, in 1616, when he accused the Chancellor of committing *praemunire* for granting an injunction after judgement.

Coke seems to have been driven, in these conflicts, by something more than a desire to bring all possible business into the ancient courts; an exhaustive recent study of his use of prohibitions suggests that by the standards of his colleagues he was if anything a moderate.[141] The psychological mainspring of his activities appears to have been a conviction that every type of power should benefit from judicial supervision. Thus he allowed commissioners of sewers to levy rates, in an emergency, to put up flood defences 'and the reason thereof is *pro bono publico*, for *salus populi* is *suprema lex*'.[142]

---

[139] Ibid., 3b.   [140] Coke, *Twelfth reports*, 65.
[141] Charles M. Gray, *The writ of prohibition: jurisdiction in early modern English law* (2 vols.) (New York, 1994), I 67, 80; II 207.
[142] Coke, *Tenth reports*, 139b.

But he also drew attention to the fact that the discretion they enjoyed was ultimately subject to the law, for 'discretion . . . is *scire per legem quid sit iustum*' (to know by the law what is just).[143]

In the absence of a full biography, it would be most imprudent to be categorical, but on this, as on some other points, Coke seems to have become more radical in his eventful decade on the bench. The most extreme expressions of his thinking can be found in the eleventh of his volumes of reports, which was, by no coincidence, the last that he ever personally published. The final pages of this final volume were occupied by a report (Bagg's case) best known, then and since, for the staggering assertion that

To this court of King's Bench belongs authority not only to correct errors in judicial proceedings, but other errors and misdemeanours extra-judicial, tending to the breach of peace, or oppression of the subjects, or to the raising of faction, controversy, debate, or to any manner of misgovernment; so that no wrong or injury, either public or private, can be done but that it shall be here reformed or punished by due course of law.[144]

Ellesmere quite reasonably commented that 'in giving excess of authority to the King's Bench he doth as much as insinuate that this court is all sufficient in itself to manage the state'.[145]

Such claims are easy to present as drastic innovations, but Coke and those contemporaries who held him in uncritical reverence must have possessed some way of seeing them as something rather more conservative. In our present state of knowledge, they look like a further extension of the kind of professional thought examined in an earlier part of this chapter: the pattern of ideas derived from Plowden's *Commentaries* that surfaces in the *Treatise concerning the statutes*, Edmund Hake's *Epieikeia*, and 'Le Methode de Monsieur Dodderige'. Thinkers in this tradition did not believe that common law was perfect, but they do seem to have regarded it as being a kind of science of the English common weal, guided at every step by all the wisdom crystallised in the existing stock of legal maxims. The logic of Aristotelian *epieikeia* pushed them towards a stress upon intentions, but as we have seen, the effect of this manoeuvre was to expand the scope for judicial discretion. It tended to displace authority from actual to ideal legislators, figures devoted to the common good as understood by the professional experts. Thus parliament was formally supreme, but judicial

---

[143] Ibid., 140a.   [144] Coke, *Eleventh reports*, 98a.
[145] Knafla, *Law and politics*, 307.

application of statutory law was moulded by conceptions of the English common weal allegedly implicit in the system. This seems to have been the attitude that licensed Coke's high-handedness in dealing with the statutes. He was happy to envisage that a piece of legislation might cure a 'mischief and defect for which the common law did not provide', but he insisted that interpretation must rest on thorough knowledge of the previous state of affairs

And then the office of all the judges is always to make such construction as shall suppress the mischief and advance the remedy, and to suppress subtle inventions and evasions for the continuance of the mischief, and *pro private commodo*, and to add force and life to the cure and remedy, according to the true intent of the makers of the act, *pro bono publico*.[146]

Here, as elsewhere in Coke's judicial practice, the judges' own perception of what made for public good was evidently likely to determine their view of the makers' original intentions. In one of the best known passages from the *Eleventh reports*, he was to cite this dictum in defence of the much balder principle that 'the law will never make an interpretation to advance a private and to destroy the public, but always to advance the public and to prevent every private, which is odious in law in such cases'.[147]

Elsewhere in the same volume, this stress upon the public good was taken even further. Coke's belated report of *Darcy* v. *Allen* (which differs markedly from the notebook version) was taken to have limited the power of dispensation. This was politically sensational; it had after all been fear of dispensation that had frustrated Hyde's attempt at a declaratory Monopolies Act. Moreover, there was little need for Coke's report to deal with the subject; Darcy's monopoly of playing cards involved a dispensation with a statute that banned the importation of such products, but at the time this aspect of the case appears to have occasioned no discussion.[148] The likely reason for this total silence is that there was consensus on a well-established doctrine: kings were permitted to dispense with *mala prohibita*, actions forbidden by a positive law, but not with *mala in se*, actions forbidden by the law of nature.

There was, however, some authority for the belief that statutes made *pro bono publico* should also be immune from dispensation.[149] In a highly ambiguous sentence, Coke seems to have supported this tradition. He held that

---

[146] Coke, *Third reports*, 7b.   [147] Coke, *Eleventh reports*, 73b.   [148] Corré, 'Arguments', 1305–12.
[149] *Reports from the lost notebooks of Sir James Dyer*, ed. J. H. Baker, 2 vols., Selden Society 109–10 (1993–4), I, liii–iv.

when the wisdom of parliament has made an act to restrain *pro bono publico* the importation of many foreign manufactures, to the intent that the subjects of the realm might apply themselves to the making of the said manufactures &c. and thereby maintain themselves and their families with the labour of their hands, now for a private gain to grant the sole importation of them to one or divers (without any limitation) notwithstanding the said Act, is a monopoly against the common law, and against the end and scope of the Act itself.[150]

This complex statement could be read in several different ways, but one of them was certainly a rule to the effect that statutes made *pro bono publico* ought to be free from royal dispensation; in fields regulated by a statute, the judges' understanding of what made for public good was thus an absolute constraint on the prerogative. Lord Chancellor Ellesmere commented that

In point of dispensation it hath ever been allowed in all ages, and the difference taken between *malum in se et malum prohibitum*, the kings [*sic*] cannot dispense with the first, with the other he may. But that new difference invented by the reporter, that the king may dispense with *malum prohibitum* but cannot dispense with a statute made *pro bono publico*.[151]

Though Coke was not the first to have advanced this particular claim, it seems unlikely that his predecessors could have produced a form of words that was so craftily ambiguous. It was open to him to say that the idea of common good was not being used to over-rule the monarch so much as to interpret his and parliament's intention; the radicalism of Coke's jurisprudence was thus, as it were, hermeneutic, not substantive. A similar ambiguity is found in his notorious report on Bonham's case (1610), where Coke made the notorious assertion that the judges could declare a statute void if it were 'against common right and reason, or repugnant [self-contradictory], or impossible to be performed'.[152] Consensus has never been reached about the meaning of this passage, but the precedents he cited suggest that he thought that statutes could be void if they were construed so as to be 'repugnant'. If so, then he was saying nothing new; as we have seen, the *Treatise concerning statutes* had held that 'if the words and mind of the law be clean contrary, that law or statute is void'.[153] But it is clear that some contemporaries believed he was asserting a right of judicial review, 'advancing', as Ellesmere complained, 'the reason of a particular court above the judgment of all the realm'.[154]

---

[150] Coke, *Eleventh reports*, 88a.   [151] Knafla, *Law and politics*, 303.   [152] Coke, *Eighth reports*, 118a.
[153] Hatton, *Treastise concerning statutes*, 19–20.
[154] Charles M. Gray, 'Bonham's case reviewed', *Proceedings of the American Philosophical Society* 116 (1972), 51–3.

Thus the central motif of Coke's thought – the notion of an artificial reason – had no inherent connection with parliamentary supremacy, and tended, indeed, to militate against it. He was the heir to those Elizabethans, referred to in the *Treatise concerning statutes*, who should have found statute's existence so hard to account for. In basing his political claims essentially on the wisdom of a guild, it might be said that he was true to the medieval law as interpreted by people like the 'Serjeant'. But Coke's suspicion of statute was probably not in a crude sense politically driven; it was simply a further example of his dislike of power that he himself as judge could not control. It was characteristic of his legal theory that every form of governmental action was brought within the judges' jurisdiction. If, as he certainly appeared to hold, law was the science of the common weal, and if kingship was exhausted by the powers conferred by law, then kingship in turn was ultimately defined by the judges' own conception of the public benefit. To put the point another way, if *epieikeia* (the virtue embodied in personal rule) had been absorbed into the legal system, then there was nothing personal left in English monarchy. It was therefore not surprising that his culminating jurisdictional battle, which indirectly led to his dismissal, was over the power of Chancery, that vessel of personal rule, to issue an injunction after judgement. The clash was ultimately a disagreement about the scope, if any, for the unregulated use of royal natural reason.

The most interesting comment upon the whole affair was a manuscript defending Lord Ellesmere's position by the Chancery official Anthony Benn. In Benn's view, the Chancellor's equity was just as much *lex terrae* as any other legal principle. Though it was 'oft-times contrary to the law' (in the narrow and conventional sense of that term), it was still 'such as the king is bound by his oath and honour to administer to his people'. Benn was loyal, in fact, to the traditional view that it was the king's duty to 'do justice', the duty underlying all government by law, which generated an additional duty to moderate the law by equity.[155] He made the equally traditional point that Chancery never undermined existing legal judgements, but 'rectified the conscience [i.e. coerced the persons] of such as unconscionably take more than conscience or reason would'.[156] If the fifteenth-century dictum was correct that 'common law is as ancient as the world', it must surely refer to 'that law that is reasonable, equal, supple and mild, which is the law of nature'; if common law was 'universal reason', then it should be examined 'by that reason that is every man's reason'.[157] In any case, he was able to quote Plowden to the effect that 'it is the honour

---

[155] British Library, Stowe MS 177, fo. 190.   [156] Ibid., 191v.   [157] Ibid., 191v–2.

and commendation of the common law that it despiseth not other sciences and faculties'.[158]

James would have endorsed all these points. Just after Coke's dismissal, when he made a symbolic appearance in Star Chamber, he made a simple plea for common sense, 'for though', he told the assembled common lawyers

> the common law be a mystery and skill best known unto yourselves, yet if your interpretation be such, as other men which have logic and common sense understand not the reason, I will never trust such an interpretation.[159]

He had discerned the danger in leaving the task of defining what was legitimate to an essentially esoteric process. During the 1620s, that process would be turned against the crown.

V

The circumstances of the 1620s were bound to make life harder for the Stuarts, but it was not immediately clear that Coke and the ideas he represented would be the focus of their difficulties. Their troubles arose from the outbreak of a European war that made their attitudes seem alien: in the first fifteen years of his reign, James's pacific attitudes towards the Catholic powers had been politically unimportant, but after 1620, the troubles of his son-in-law, the Elector Palatine, drew attention to the gulf between his worldview and ordinary Protestant opinion. James and his subjects were agreed that the Palatinate should be recovered, but they had different ideas about the means adopted. James's preferred approach was diplomatic; he wanted a non-violent resolution of the problem, facilitated by a royal marriage between his son Prince Charles and a Spanish princess. This strategy reflected a realistic view of England's military capacities (though perhaps an overestimate of Spain's control over its German allies), but it was always likely to encounter opposition, not least because any such treaty was certain to involve *de facto* toleration for English recusants.

Unfortunately for the king, his policy also required the summoning of a national assembly; even a peaceful settlement was likely to demand the threat of an aggressive war, and it was conventional wisdom among those with whom he dealt that he would not be capable of waging such a war without the funds that parliament provided. The parliaments of the early 1620s thus had a much stronger position than any of their immediate predecessors. Both common sense and history led observers to expect this would

[158] Ibid., 194.   [159] James, *Political writings*, 212.

be very awkward for the monarch. Two well-known tracts of the preceding decade were meditations on the plight of an indebted king confronted with an angry parliament. The first, Sir Robert Cotton's *A short view of the long raign of Henry III*, was probably written just after the Addled Parliament. It described a king whose only real problems were 'such as are incident to all, the commons greedy of liberty and the nobility of rule',[160] but who had gravely weakened his position by generosity to foreigners. Henry had called a parliament in which he was informed he had 'undone the trade of merchants by bringing in maletolts [illegitimate duties] and heavy customs, and . . . hurt common liberty by *non obstantes* in his patents, to make good monopolies for private favourites'.[161] In return for confirmation of Magna Carta, he was given 'such a pittance as must tie him to their devotion for a new supply'.[162] Henry attempted to reform his conduct, but his continuing improvidence 'gave great assurance to the rebellious lords that they should now at the last have the sovereign power . . . and to bring it faster on, they desire nothing more than to see the king's extremity constrain a parliament, for at such time, princes are ever less than they should be, subjects more'.[163]

Given the clear analogies with James's situation, the later part of Henry's reign supplied an awful warning. When a parliament could no longer be avoided, Henry was forced to cede his power to a 24-man council, of whom half had been elected by the Commons; but even this arrangement proved to be inadequate to limit the ambitions of the magnates. The king was a helpless spectator to the baronial war that ended with the victory of de Montfort and he remained a prisoner till rescued by his valiant son, the future Edward I. At this point, however, he learned from his mistakes, reined in his indiscriminate lavishness, selected nobly born and honest advisers, and 'disposed affairs of most weight in his own person'.[164] He thus laid the foundations for the achievements of his son, who was 'the first that settled the law and state, deserving the style of England's Justinian, and freed this kingdom from the wardship of the peers'.[165] The moral of this story was fairly obvious; a parliament was not a panacea and might indeed exacerbate the king's political problems. The abiding threat to social peace was aristocratic faction and the solution was frugality. It is often assumed that what happened in the early 1640s was altogether unforeseeable, but Cotton's much-copied manuscript (unprinted until 1627) reveals he could imagine opposition that worked through parliamentary institutions and that made use of a financial crisis to gain control of royal government.

[160] [Sir Robert Cotton], *A short view of the long life and raigne of Henry the third* (1627), 4.
[161] Ibid., 22–3.   [162] Ibid., 25.   [163] Ibid., 27–8.   [164] Ibid., 44–6.   [165] Ibid., 49.

Cotton's *Henry III* provoked the second pamphlet on this politically urgent topic,[166] a work by the imprisoned Sir Walter Raleigh which also enjoyed a wide manuscript circulation before it was printed (in 1628) as *The prerogative of parliaments*. Raleigh's tract took the form of a dialogue between a 'Counsellor of Estate' and a 'Justice of Peace' – it was revealing in itself that these two roles should be assumed to generate antagonistic outlooks – in which the Justice argued that lively parliaments posed no real threat to English monarchy. The dialogue began by referring to the Addled Parliament, whose failure had been followed by a benevolence that stimulated legalistic grumblings. The Justice had no time for such complaints; he thought that the king had a right to impose and that 'all binding of a king by law upon the advantage of his necessity makes the breach itself lawful in a king'.[167] But he also believed it was pointless and counterproductive to waste political capital and intellectual effort on dreaming up non-parliamentary levies; the king would sooner or later require the 'great aid' that only parliament could provide him with and then 'the country will excuse itself in regard of their former payments'.[168] In the mean time, Raleigh feared that the imprisonments without trial by which the king responded to the Addled Parliament were likely, as he delicately put it, 'to dig out of the dust the long-buried memory of the subjects' former intentions with their kings'.[169]

Raleigh's epistle dedicatory to James advised him to 'leave the new impositions, all monopolies, and other grievances of the people to the consideration of the House; provided that your Majesty's revenues be not abated.'[170] Concessions of this type were well worth making, because 'it is far more happy for a sovereign prince that a subject open his purse willingly, than that the same be opened by violence'.[171] A survey of parliament's history exploded the myth that such national assemblies refused the king the taxes that he needed, but the medieval evidence did show that they habitually made three demands: confirmation of Magna Carta, appointment of some 'treasurers' to oversee the revenues they voted, and dismissal of unpopular councillors.[172] There was even a chance that the king could avoid confirming Magna Carta, because, as Raleigh cynically remarked, 'if the House press the king to grant unto them all that is theirs by the law, they cannot (in justice) refuse the king all that is his by the law'.[173] In the event of war, the use of parliament would have a further great advantage, for 'if the king

---

[166] See the shared quotation from Matthew Paris (Cotton, *Short view*, 27; Sir Walter Raleigh, *The prerogative of parliaments in England* (Middelburg, 1628), sig. A3v).
[167] Raleigh, *Prerogative*, sig. A3   [168] Ibid., 2.   [169] Ibid., 60.   [170] Ibid., A3.
[171] Ibid., 58.   [172] Ibid., 58.   [173] Ibid., 60.

had made the war by a general consent, the kingdom in general were bound to maintain the war, and they could not then say when the king required aid, that he undertook a needless war'.[174]

In the early 1620s, the Stuarts took Raleigh's advice, permitting legislation against monopolies and letting the Commons attack their unpopular servants. They even acquiesced in the rediscovery of parliament's adjudicative functions. In 1621, without much fanfare, the House of Lords resumed its former practice of hearing court cases submitted by petition; at the same time, James permitted the revival of impeachment, the disused medieval procedure by which the Commons could mount a prosecution in front of a court consisting of the peers. Though he retained a veto on this process, its very existence encouraged attacks on leading ministers. In 1621, the principal victim was Lord Chancellor Bacon; in 1624, more damagingly, Buckingham used it to displace the earl of Cranfield, the competent Lord Treasurer who had come close to balancing the budget.

As Conrad Russell has shown, the Commons initially responded well to this conciliatory handling; indeed, their tolerance surpassed Raleigh's most optimistic expectations. In a surprising show of self-restraint, the House of Commons of 1621 refrained from an attack on impositions; more surprisingly still, they deliberately ignored the intimidation of Sir Edwin Sandys, who had been persuaded to absent himself.[175] What they were not prepared to do was vote the degree of taxation that was required to prosecute a war. In Russell's view, the likely explanation was their parochialism and ignorance. For all their willingness to rage against the Antichrist, MPs had rather limited horizons, and most of them placed the convenience of their communities ahead of the country's military requirements. Parliament was essentially a congress of provincial magistrates and their apparent obstructionism was really just a function of their preoccupation with local government. In the later 1620s, it was the new administrative burden created by wartime conditions 'that brought relations between central and local government, *and hence between king and parliament* to the point of collapse'.[176]

Russell's classic revisionist treatment of this period thus rested upon the then-fashionable belief that the attachments of MPs were primarily to their native counties; administrative functionalism had been ingeniously fused with an exaggerated stress on local loyalties. It was further assumed that a provincial outlook was basically apolitical. The most significant advance of

---

[174] Ibid., 40.   [175] Russell, *Parliaments*, 123, 136.   [176] Ibid., 64 (my italics).

subsequent research has been the questioning of both assumptions. As the English country gentry were a homogeneous class, virtually all of whose political leaders had passed through Oxford, Cambridge, or the Inns, it would have been strange if their interests had been confined by county boundaries;[177] but in any case, a demonstrable feature of the decade was the intensity, across the country, of the attention that was paid to national and international news, especially when such news could be related to the apparent rise of Spanish power.[178] Hispanophobia helped to shape an outlook whose very terminology was worryingly subversive. This was the historical moment at which the title 'patriot' acquired the connotations (attachment to the 'commonwealth' ideals of public liberty and Protestantism) that the staunch church-and-king man Dr Johnson would see as the last refuge of a scoundrel.[179]

Not much of this language was used, of course, at Westminster itself – as revisionists have rightly emphasised, the Houses had a horror of 'party' or 'faction' – but this was the cultural background that made the period's controversies comprehensible. Support for international Protestantism was powerful enough to mute the voice of opposition, but it also bred suspicion of royal policies. Suspicion was entirely justified, for James's private attitudes were simply too unusual to give an adequate basis for sustained co-operation. Even his own advisers found them hard to understand. Thus the 1621 parliament collapsed when his chief minister Buckingham encouraged a petition that touched upon his foreign policy. It urged him to enforce the laws against the recusants, to embark upon a war against the Spanish monarchy, and to marry his son Charles to a non-Catholic princess. These suggestions were no more than conventional wisdom, but James reacted violently to every one of them, resenting 'great complaints of the danger of religion within this kingdom, tacitly implying our ill government in this point' and even deploring the commonplace assertion that 'he [the king of Spain] affects the temporal monarchy of the whole earth' on the grounds that 'there can be no more malice uttered against any great king'.[180]

James also provoked the Commons by asserting his right to punish 'any man's misdemeanours in parliament, as well during their sitting as after', thus inspiring them to make a Protestation, consciously modelled on the

---

[177] Clive Holmes, 'The county community in Stuart historiography', *Journal of British Studies* 19 (1980).
[178] Richard Cust, 'News and politics in early seventeenth-century England', *Past and Present* 112 (1986).
[179] Thomas Cogswell, *The blessed revolution: English politics and the coming of war* (Cambridge, 1989), esp. 83–105.
[180] *His Majesties declaration touching his proceedings in the late assemblie and convention of parliament* (1621/2), 18, 29.

Apology, that 'the arduous and urgent affairs [a conventional phrase from the parliamentary writs] concerning the king, state, and defence of the realm and of the Church of England, and the maintenance and making of laws, and redress of mischiefs and grievances which daily happen within this realm, are proper subjects and matters of counsel and debate in parliament', and that their privilege of free speech was therefore absolute.[181] James pointed out that the writs had been misquoted (they in fact refer to '*certain* arduous and urgent affairs') and commented that the whole Protestation was phrased 'in such ambiguous and general words, as might serve for future times to invade most of our inseparable rights and prerogatives, annexed to our imperial crown', including those 'actually possessed' by Queen Elizabeth (by which he evidently meant the right to imprison refractory MPs).[182]

After the dissolution, James did nothing to conciliate his critics. He punished a number of MPs, raised a benevolence, and let the recusants enjoy a level of *de facto* toleration that seems to have encouraged a stream of conversions. When the 1624 parliament assembled, the Speaker delivered a daring address that ventured to regret this course of action, but James made an instant and vigorous defence of his behaviour. He explained through the Lord Keeper that while benevolences might be regrettable, 'all the famous princes of this land' had made some use of them; and asserted that the 'suspension of some penal statutes against papists' reflected the fact that the king was 'like a horseman . . . the law the spur, reins, and bridle which are all in their due times to be used, now with slackness, now with straitness'.[183]

The history of the next year showed the depth of the distrust he had created. On the face of things, the parliament was successful, if only because Buckingham and the young Prince of Wales had come back empty-handed and embittered from the quixotic errand to Madrid by which they attempted to woo the Infanta in person. Their reaction to deserved humiliation was to co-operate with the 'patriots' to force James to abandon the Spanish alliance. Faced with this pressure from his intimates, he yielded a number of important principles, permitting some discussion of foreign policy, committing parliamentary revenue to 'treasurers' appointed by the Commons, and promising, in the event of war, not to make peace without consulting them. Unfortunately for the crown, the understandable caution

[181] Kenyon, *Stuart constitution*, 42.
[182] Larkin and Hughes, *Proclamations*, 1 533; *His Majesties declaration*, 62–3.
[183] 'The parliamentary papers of Nicholas Ferrar, 1624', ed. David R. Ransome in *Camden Miscellany* 33 (1996), 18–19.

of MPs precluded any lasting realignment. Thus a suggestion by the House of Lords that the Commons pass a motion that 'we will assist his Majesty with our persons and our fortunes according to our abilities as becometh good and well affected subjects' was strenuously and in the end successfully resisted.[184]

Russell held that the decision to ignore it revealed the fact that 'at the crucial moment, members' local loyalties had proved to be stronger than their national ones', but the decisive grounds for opposition appear to have been constitutional;[185] they feared, not without reason, that any such expression of a collective will would be exploited by the king to justify non-parliamentary taxes. The first speaker to respond described the motion as 'a kind of engagement of all our estates', and subsequent speakers on both sides addressed themselves to this anxiety. Sir John Saville remarked that 'it was a great engagement, and that having once passed it was not in our power to revoke it nor moderate it, but the king would be judge what we are able'.[186] Some wanted to save the proposal by adding the phrase 'in a parliamentary way' so as 'to avoid the imposing of benevolences and other kind of contributions', but even with the addition of such safeguards it turned out to be unacceptable.[187] Seven days later, they did pass a motion 'in a parliamentary way to assist your Majesty with our persons and abilities', but no great perspicacity was needed to notice that their 'fortunes' had been silently omitted.[188] This episode was a perfect illustration of the relationship between the constitutional conflicts and the state's functional inadequacies. As might have been expected, the members had been forcibly reminded that 'Rome and Spain would triumph at this day's work'.[189] The motives of those who nonetheless frustrated the proposal may well have been informed, to some extent, by localist myopia, opposition to the war, or a disinclination to pay taxes. But feelings of this nature could not have found respectable expression but for more fundamental disagreements.

The extent of the subjects' suspicion of the crown was shown by Charles's failure to surmount it. In 1625, when he came to the throne, Charles had been functioning for eighteen months as one of the leading proponents of a change in policy. Unlike his dead brother, Prince Henry, he was a pallid personality, an insignificant presence with a speech impediment, but his failure to make an impression should if anything have helped him; all that his subjects knew about his doings was that he had resisted the blandishments of Spain and had become, in consequence, an advocate of

[184] Ibid., 60.   [185] Russell, *Parliaments*, 182.   [186] Ransome, 'Ferrar papers', 61.
[187] Ibid., 64.   [188] Cogswell, *Blessed revolution*, 186.   [189] Ransome, 'Ferrar papers', 63.

war. As both these characteristics were very popular, he might legitimately have expected that there would be a period in which he would get the benefit of the doubt. In fact, the political tensions of 1624 persisted virtually uninterrupted.

Charles's imminent marriage to the French king's sister was a quite reasonable strategic step for somebody about to fight with Spain, but it involved him in the same concession as the negotiations with the Spanish: effective toleration for English recusants. In the first parliament he called, the atmosphere was tainted from the start by discontent about this situation, which seems to have been compounded by resentment that taxes voted for a naval war had been diverted for a war on land in Germany. Together, these feelings probably accounted for the House of Commons' refusal to vote taxes until an anti-Spanish war had actually begun. The Commons also threatened some essential revenue by failing to make a life grant of Tunnage and Poundage, that is, of statutory customs duties. As a stopgap solution, they offered Charles a one-year grant instead. When the Lords loyally refused to ratify this insult, he found himself obliged to levy these customs (which he could hardly operate without) by making use of his prerogative.

In retrospect, the failure to grant Tunnage and Poundage for life seems an extraordinary unforced error, which set the king upon a path of extra-legal action from which there was, in the end, no turning back. This counter-productive rigour is virtually unintelligible unless it is seen within a larger context. Two arguments appear to have been decisive. One was that the life grant of Tunnage and Poundage was a relatively recent innovation; during the time of the Lancastrians, the duties had been voted for a fixed period;[190] the influence of this antiquarian finding was in itself a symptom of the legal-istic spirit in which the Commons debates were now conducted. The other, which was clearly more important, was that Tunnage and Poundage (a levy upon wool) had been used in the previous session to justify 'the preter-mitted custom' (a Jacobean levy upon cloth).[191] MPs thus had reason to fear that the traditional legislation supplied an excuse for imposing further duties.

One problem, then, was that the narrow issue of whether or not to give Charles his Tunnage and Poundage had come to be entangled with the impositions question. But the underlying reason for the escalating clash was that the Commons were not disposed to seek a compromise. They

---

[190] *Proceedings in parliament 1625*, ed. Maija Jansson and William B. Bidwell (New Haven, 1987), 313, 314, 317.
[191] Ibid., 313, 317, 511.

rejected the crown's offer of a neutral saving clause, which would have made it clear that Tunnage and Poundage could not be used to justify related impositions.[192] Perhaps a genuinely neutral clause would have been difficult to formulate. But in any case, a section of the House was keen not only to restore the principle of consent but to devise a novel Book of Rates.[193] Thus it was not surprising that a temporary renewal struck MPs as an innocent expedient (as opposed to an affront to a new monarch); it shelved a difficult debate that would require some detailed preparation. Most MPs probably assumed that the whole customs issue required a comprehensive parliamentary settlement. But from the king's perspective, a *parliamentary* Book of Rates was a departure from existing practice for which it was quite reasonable to ask for compensation

There was, to be sure, a possible and statesmanlike solution: a confirmation of the *status quo* in return for royal acceptance of parliament's control of customs duties. In an inflationary period, Charles might have been foolish to accept this kind of settlement, but it would surely have attracted him. Unfortunately, it was never offered. For the rest of the 1620s, most of the Commons took the view that ratification of the impositions amounted to a grant of new taxation, which they were most unlikely to allow until the king had met their grievances. Charles was to summon three more parliaments before despairing of the institution, but in each of them, an indignant Lower House believed that it was doing no more than standing on its rights. In doing so, it shaped a reconstruction of its function. It took the labels that it found in the medieval sources and emphasised, in varying proportions, its role as a High Court and a Great Council.

In the assembly summoned in 1626, events encouraged stress upon the latter. Under the circumstances of that year, the patriots had a simple diagnosis of all the problems that the nation faced. Ever since 1621, they had, in their own estimation, offered excellent advice, which was as regularly disregarded. The natural conclusion to draw, as the MP Sir William Walter put it, was that 'the cause of all the grievances was for that all the king's counsel rides upon one horse'.[194] Unfortunately, Charles was most unlikely to concede the sacking of his closest friend and leading minister. When it became apparent that only the duke of Buckingham's impeachment was likely to lead to the granting of taxation, he let it be known he was tempted by another course of action.

---

[192] Ibid., 318.   [193] Ibid., 511.
[194] *Proceedings in parliament 1626*, ed. William B. Bidwell and Maija Jansson, 4 vols. (New Haven, 1992), II 324.

In what was widely taken to be an unofficial royal statement, Sir Dudley Carleton darkly warned that 'his Majesty's love to us is such that so long as we carry ourselves as fitting dutiful subjects towards so good a prince, he will not take new counsels'. In case anyone had missed what he was saying, he added that 'this kind of parliament has been formerly in most kingdoms, but in most monarchy is changed by new counsels, for when they changed their parliamentary liberty into tumultuary endeavours, it was changed by the sovereign to another form of government'.[195] In their last declaration to the king before the dissolution, the Commons reported that 'this intimation' had given them

just cause to fear that there were some ill ministers near your Majesty's sacred person that in the behalf of the said duke, and together with him who is so strangely powerful, were so much against the parliamentary course of this kingdom as they might, perhaps, advise your most excellent Majesty with such 'new counsels'.

They instanced the continuing exaction of Tunnage and Poundage as an 'apparent effect' of the counsels in question.[196] What for Charles was a regrettable short-term expedient appeared to them to be a sign that constitutional changes were already happening.

By the time of the next assembly, in 1628, the king had given them more evidence. During the intervening period, Charles and Buckingham had blundered into war against the French, thus committing themselves to fighting both the Continent's great powers. This absurdly overambitious undertaking was bound to require extensive new taxation, which was unlikely to derive from parliamentary sources. In the summer of 1626, for the first time since the Amicable Grant, a benevolence was successfully resisted, but the government recovered from this setback. It asked instead for a Forced Loan, which raised, in the end, the remarkable sum of £264,000 (the rough equivalent of five subsidies); the idea of a Forced Loan, even a loan on an enormous scale with no realistic prospect of repayment, appears to have been thought of as less objectionable than the assault on property involved in a forced gift. No one supposed, however, that the Loan could be repeated, and Charles paid a heavy political price for the relief afforded.

Things started to go wrong when the common law judges unanimously refused to give the policy their backing. It is in fact unlikely that all or even most of them were hostile to the levy (in their personal capacities, they not only paid the Loan, but actively encouraged others to do so),[197] but their

---

[195] Ibid., III 241–2. [196] Ibid., III 440. [197] HMC Buccleuch, III 307.

refusal to pronounce was liable to be seen as condemnation. They probably did not foresee this popular reaction; the idea that their opinions on such a point were crucial was in itself a relatively new development. Their silence may, however, have been responsible for triggering a fairly large-scale problem of principled refusal to pay up. As was to be expected, the government reacted by imprisoning its opponents. When five prominent protesters defended themselves by applying for *habeas corpus*, the royal lawyers told King's Bench that they had been imprisoned *per speciale mandatum domini Regis*. In the Five Knights case of 1627, the judges refrained from taking steps to free them, but did not actually endorse the government's right to imprison. Along with other grievances arising from the war (principally martial law and billeting), these imprisonments formed the background to the well-known debates that dominated the next parliament.

The radicalism disclosed by these debates owed something to the king's own intervention. His father's thoughtful speeches could usually be read in several ways; there was no misunderstanding Charles's statement that

the only intention of calling this parliament is for present [immediate] supply, and this way of parliament is the most ancient way and the way I like best; wherein, if you do use such speedy resolution as the business requireth and shall become the business of this House, I shall be glad to take occasion thereby to call you oftener together. And if it should so fall out, as God forbid it should, that you do neglect your duties herein, I must then be forced, for the preservation of the public, and that which by the folly of some particular men may be destroyed, to take some other course.[198]

With characteristic loftiness, he added that this was not a threat 'for I scorn to threaten any but my equals', but a 'friendly admonition from one that holds himself tied to preserve you'.[199] If Charles was often suspected of contempt for parliament, he only really had himself to blame.

But though the king could hardly have done better if he had tried to raise his subjects' hackles, the single most striking political fact about this parliament was the availability of common law ideas through which a lawyer-dominated Commons was able to articulate resistance. In the first of the speeches that made him the most prominent country leader, the Cornish MP Sir John Eliot gave powerful expression to their worries. Even in the fragmentary form of a note-taker's eloquent jottings, it gives a strong sense of the tone of political feeling. He spoke, he said, not only for himself, nor 'for the country [Cornwall] for which I serve', nor 'for us all and for the country which we represent [England]', but 'for the ancient glory of

---

[198] *Proceedings 1628*, II 8.   [199] Ibid., II 9.

the ancient laws of England'.[200] He went on to a summary of popular grievances:

The ancient law of England, the declaration of Magna Carta and other statutes, say the subject is not to be burdened with loans, tallages, or benevolences. Yet we see them imposed. Doth not this contradict the law? Where is law? Where is *meum* and *tuum*? It is fallen into the chaos of a higher power.[201]

To those who saw this as an over-reaction to 'money upon a particular occasion', he replied that 'this reflects on all that we call ours, those rights that made our forefathers free men, and they render our posterity less free'.[202]

This terror of the arbitrary both fed on and encouraged Sir Edward Coke's extremist attitudes. Coke's own first intervention insisted on two points: that prerogative was part of common law; and that 'the command of the king is in the King's Bench, which is there *coram rege*, and *per preceptum Regis* is the command of the judges of the King's Bench'. If a single claim epitomised his thinking, it was the Year Book dictum that 'the king hath distributed his power into his several courts'.[203] Authority in Coke's England was impersonal and legal, so much so that it left no space for extra-legal power. Coke's victory was not of course total; there were doubtless still some people in the Commons (and many more in the old-fashioned Lords) who clung to some version or other of the previous orthodoxy. We know, for instance, that on two occasions, the Queen of Bohemia's secretary Sir Francis Nethersole made diffident appeals to an out-dated common sense. On the second, he was careful to explain that

It is not my opinion that the king hath or ought to have any legal ordinary power to commit men in an ordinary judicial manner without cause, but in some time and in some rare cases we are to allow the king to commit men without setting down the cause of the commitment, and that from the law of nature that dispenseth with her laws to preserve things.[204]

But Nethersole's once-conventional position was instantly assaulted by a lawyer named John Browne, who insisted that the king of England's power was 'regular and regulated by laws, and therefore I deny that distinction of the absolute power and legal power'.[205] Browne tacitly admitted that there were precedents that pointed in a different direction, but noted that 'it is the modesty of the commonwealth not to complain for every cause'. Above all, he maintained that 'there is no danger but the law hath made provision

---

[200] Ibid., II 57. [201] Ibid., II 57. [202] Ibid., II 57.
[203] Ibid., II 107, citing YB M 8 Henry IV, pl. 13. [204] Ibid., II 172.
[205] Ibid., II 173. See also 173, 176, 180, 183, 185; the fact that these fragmentary accounts seem perfectly consistent shows that his argument was grasped by ordinary hearers.

for it'; one diarist summarised his point by saying 'What need reason of state when the law provides a remedy in all cases.'[206]

Browne's argument brings out a fact that scholars have often ignored, but that was crucial to the spread of legalistic thinking: that Cokean common law was not a precedent-bound system. It was after all Coke's frequently stated opinion that artificial reason had a wisdom that was denied to any man or any generation. He held that legal methods were capable of solving any problem but not that judges were exempt from error – indeed, his very faith in legal reason implied that judicial decisions could be *demonstrably* wrong. The role of precedents, for Coke, was to bring out law's underlying logic, and he was perfectly prepared to stigmatise earlier judgements as 'sudden', that is, ill-considered and therefore ill-founded. Under the circumstances of 1628, the opposition were obliged to make extensive use of this particular aspect of his thinking, not least because one precedent for imprisonment without cause had actually been set by Coke himself.[207]

The case presented to the House of Lords by four of the most learned common lawyers showed how post-Plowden common law jurisprudence could be adapted to construct a formidable position. It rested on the assumption, set out by Sir Dudley Digges, that 'the laws of England are grounded on reason more ancient than books, consisting much in unwritten customs, yet . . . full of justice and true equity'.[208] These laws had been 'confirmed' by the Confessor, and 'sworn unto' by William and his heirs.[209] It was an 'undoubted and fundamental point of this so ancient common law of England, that the subject hath a true property in his goods and possessions'. Edward Littleton took up the argument by leading his audience through the statute book, which showed that, in the later Middle Ages, these laws were reaffirmed by Magna Carta and several other acts of parliament 'the authority whereof is so great that it can receive no answer save by interpretation or repeal by future statutes'.[210] In a brilliant display of critical learning, John Selden went on to discredit the apparent weight of precedent in favour of the king.[211] He did so by asking for something most unlikely to be found: proof positive that the judges believed, as a matter of law, that people imprisoned by royal command ought not to be released. In effect, he was asking a question that could not have arisen a few decades earlier: did kings possess a *legal* right to act by extraordinary power? During the Middle Ages, this question made no sense; extraordinary power was a

---

[206] *Proceedings 1628*, II 173, 185.   [207] Ibid., II 191, 193, 197.   [208] Ibid., II 333.
[209] Ibid., II 333.   [210] Ibid., II 334–5.   [211] Ibid., II 342–56.

brute fact that lay outside the judges' jurisdiction. They could ignore this fact of life or tacitly approve it, but the very definition of extraordinary power excluded them from judging it to have a legal status. Selden's exhilarating tour de force of detailed antiquarian erudition was thus not a cause, but an outcome, of a complete conceptual transformation.

Lastly, Sir Edward Coke himself presented the Lords with three Commons resolutions condemning arbitrary imprisonment, which he supported by 'manifest and legal reasons which are the grounds and mothers of all laws'.[212] He offered nine 'general reasons', including the notions that arbitrary imprisonment was something only appropriate to villeins and that the king could not so much as fine his freeborn subjects 'but it must be done judicially, by his judges'.[213] Like almost everybody who pronounced upon the question, he held that English valour and industry, and hence security and prosperity, depended on the maintenance of freedom.[214] Lastly, and most importantly, he made appeal to three authorities. The first two said, in different ways, that judges should not recognise imprisonment by the king because a man wrongly arrested by the monarch would find himself with nobody to sue. The third, inevitably, was Plowden's maxim that 'the common law hath so admeasured the king's prerogative, as he cannot prejudice any man in his inheritance', a maxim Coke went on to gloss by saying that 'the greatest inheritance a man hath is the liberty of his person, for all others are but accessory to it'.[215]

It is clear that these 'legal reasons' were not exactly rules; they were priorities so deep within the legal system that they should govern all interpretation. Perhaps the least unhelpful way to think about their status is to regard them as ideas internal to a practice, the practice of the monarch 'doing justice' to his subjects through a coherent system of formal remedies administered by a specialised profession. In 1628, this royal practice absorbed his supplementary practices: the common law secured its place as the sole fountain of legitimacy. The Commons obtained acceptance (or so they believed) of a Petition of Right (as opposed to 'of Grace') that was a detailed statement of popular liberties (forbidding arbitrary imprisonment, the use of martial law and billeting, and the raising of non-parliamentary taxes, especially Forced Loans and benevolences). Their crucial triumph, in their own opinion, was the omission of a clause suggested by the peers 'to leave entire that sovereign power wherewith your Majesty is entrusted for the protection, safety, and happiness of your people'.[216]

---

[212] Ibid., II 356.   [213] Ibid., II 357.   [214] Ibid., II 357–8.
[215] Ibid., II 358.   [216] Ibid., III 563.

The arguments used to justify omission of this saving were laid out in a major speech, designed for circulation,[217] by the Lower House's spokesman Serjeant Glanville. In a move that would have many imitators, Glanville picked up the notion of a 'trust'. He conceded that 'there is a trust inseparable reposed in the kings of England', but he insisted that 'that trust is regulated by law'.[218] The example he chose was revealing. He pointed out that kings enjoyed the power of dispensing with statutes (unless they prohibited a *malum in se*), because 'by those statutes the subject has no interest in the penalties, which are all the fruit such statutes can produce, until by suit or information commenced he become entitled to particular forfeitures'.[219] In other words, the right of dispensation was limited by concrete 'interests', rights granted to specific individuals, such as the rights that certain laws conferred upon informers.

This was a well-established legal doctrine, clearly explained, for instance, in Sir Thomas Smith's *De republica Anglorum*.[220] The crucial move that Glanville made was to insist that liberties conferred in Magna Carta and elsewhere enjoyed the status of such interests. The Petition was founded, he said, upon

laws not inflicting mulcts or penalties upon offenders in *malis prohibitis*, but laws declarative and positive conferring or confirming *ipso facto* an inherent right and interest of liberty and freedom in the subjects of this realm as their birthright and inheritance, descendable to their heirs and posterity; statutes incorporated into the body of the common law, over which (with reverence be it spoken) there is no trust reposed in the King's sovereign power or prerogative royal to enable him to dispense with them, or to take from his subjects that birthright and inheritance which they have in their liberties by virtue of the common law and of those statutes.[221]

Thus the essential point about these laws was that they shielded an 'inheritance', an 'interest' that was enjoyed by every English subject severally. This was a more perspicuous idea than Coke's vague talk about the public good, and its emergence was, perhaps, a necessary feature of English constitutionalisation. A process by which a humble land law system came to provide the language of political debate inevitably projected upon the public sphere the habits of mind of private litigation: the common law existed to offer remedies, especially those remedies securing heritable property; if kingship was exhausted by its legal processes, then it existed to secure the 'interests' of the subject, especially those interests that fell within the traditional scope of the system. In short, the regal powers enjoyed by monarchs would stand

---

[217] Ibid., III 557.   [218] Ibid., III 565.   [219] Ibid., III 565.
[220] Smith, *De republica*, 86.   [221] *Proceedings 1628*, III 565–6.

revealed, sooner or later, as instrumental to 'inheritances', the property and property-like rights that were the system's primary concern.

In time, this intellectual upheaval would be followed by political events that partially worked out its implications. But in 1628 its principles were most unlikely to be implemented. The Commons opted to believe that Charles had simply accepted their demands, but in fact, he declared, as he did so, that he intended to 'confirm all your liberties, knowing (according to your own protestations) that you neither mean nor can hurt my prerogative'.[222] This was at best cold comfort, and it did nothing to resolve the much more significant problem of Tunnage and Poundage.

The obstacle here, as in 1625, was the determination of the Commons to oversee all details of the royal Book of Rates. On this better-reported occasion, it is clear the sticking-point was more than just a matter of abstract principle; there was a risk, if not a certainty, that the resultant level of customs duties would actually have reduced the royal income. The House had imprisoned a government official for saying, in a private conversation, that it might be best to double the pre-imposition rates.[223] As he was referring to a set of duties that mostly dated from the reign of Mary, this was hardly an unreasonable statement. It was therefore not surprising that Charles declined to give the House the time that it said that it needed to work through the required legislation.

In 1629, then, Charles showed some optimism (or possibly an unsuspected slyness) in giving his subjects one last chance to vote him Tunnage and Poundage. In a speech that gave 'great satisfaction', he asked that 'by passing the bill as my ancestors have had it', his past and future actions could be 'authorised'. He added that he presupposed that there would have been no objection 'if men had not imagined that I have taken these duties as appertaining to my hereditary prerogative, in which they are much deceived, for it ever was and still is my meaning, by the gift of my people to enjoy it'.[224] He took the precaution of sending them a bill he could accept, which was, however, denounced by Sir John Eliot as giving him 'power to lay impositions at pleasure'.[225] No other member supported this unlikely accusation, so Eliot presumably meant that the bill was traditional in form, and therefore gave no guarantees against the new exactions. Although the House then undertook to draft a better statute, no more was heard about such legislation.[226] The rest of the session would be dominated by efforts to attack 'Arminians' and to defend those merchants (who unluckily included

---

[222] Ibid., IV 182.   [223] Ibid., IV 406–9.
[224] *Commons debates 1629*, ed. Wallace Notestein and F. H. Relf (Minneapolis, 1921), 245, 11.
[225] Ibid., 108.   [226] Ibid., 109.

an MP), who were refusing to pay customs duties. To the puzzlement of many, then and since, the Commons seemed incapable of grasping that Charles could hardly cease to levy customs, and that it was desirable, from every point of view, that he should raise this income legally.

The most perceptive commentary on their behaviour was offered by one of Charles's few supporters, the courtier Sir Francis Kynaston, in his manuscript tract 'A true presentation of forepast parliaments to the view of present times and posterity'. It is clear that Kynaston blamed Coke for many of the king's troubles. He was unusual in his generation in wondering 'how Sir Edward Coke can prove our common municipal law of England for integrity and perfection to be next the law of God, and for antiquity equal, if not elder in time to all other',[227] and he disliked 'the title of the father of the law, which I have heard no less frequently than flatteringly bestowed upon him by many members of the House of Commons'.[228] But he also regarded Coke's status as a depressing sign of a more general development:

the greatest lawyers, to manifest their power, and to be counsellors in all things, insisted much that they were as members of the parliament the Gran Councell[229] of the Kingdom: that it was their function to advise and consult of the most important affairs of the Kingdom, that their summons was by writ, to treat of and resolve *de arduis et urgentibus negotiis &c.*, as if nothing were too high for them.[230]

In Kynaston's view, then, the lawyers were conflating the role of a professional 'counsellor' (that is, an advocate) with that of an adviser on matters of state. Professional erudition and legally minded antiquarian learning were playing an exaggerated role in politics.

Conflation of counsel and legal jurisdiction could have two different effects, both of them deleterious to royal interests. On the one hand, as we have seen, it tended to encourage a self-righteous stubbornness. But it could also ease the path of highly irregular actions. Thus when the Commons drew up a declaration denouncing the duke of Buckingham's misdeeds, it was objected that their charges rested on 'conjectures'. John Pym felt able to reply that 'we sit here as law makers, as counsellors, and as judges. This declaration is our counsel to the king and may very well and parliamentarily be upon probable grounds and conjectures'.[231] In the early 1640s, he was to make extensive use of similar conflations.

[227] Lansdowne MS 213, fo. 149v.   [228] Ibid., 149v.
[229] Counsel (advice), 'council' (an institution), and counsel (a legal adviser) were then interchangeably spelt.
[230] Lansdowne MS 213, fos. 151v–2.   [231] *Proceedings 1626*, III 434.

Both James and Charles were worried by the signs that some MPs believed themselves to be in essence judges. As early as 1621, James had attacked Sir Edward Coke by name for what he saw as an attempt to bring judicial business to the Commons.[232] Seven years later, his worst fears were shown to have been well founded, for Coke assured the Lower House that 'whatsoever the Lords House and this House at any time have agreed upon, no judge ever went against it. And when the judges in former times doubted of the law, they went to the parliament, and there resolutions were given to which they were bound.'[233] It was not surprising that Charles stressed, in his speech at the end of the session, that 'none of the Houses of parliament, joint or separate (what new doctrine soever have been raised), have any power either to make or declare a law without my consent'.[234] This was the obvious principle by which to resist the steady advance of Cokean jurisprudence; fourteen years later, it assisted him to find a party in a civil war.

[232] *His Majesties declaration*, 40–1.
[233] *Proceedings 1628*, III 628. See also 634.   [234] Ibid., IV 481.

CHAPTER 8

The constitutionalist revolution

The upshot of the complex shift this book has been describing can be encapsulated in a contrast. In the later 1550s, Queen Mary fought a war against the French. In doing so, she exercised her extra-legal powers – she raised forced loans, revised the Book of Rates, and made extensive use of martial law – but not even her Protestant subjects made public objections. In the later 1620s, when Charles I was waging war against the same opponent, he naturally resorted to the same expedients, but reactions were completely different. What had changed was not the government's behaviour but the political culture in which it operated.

Charles had few of the characteristics traditionally attributed to tyrants. He was a sane and virtuous man of no imagination whose anti-political craving for hierarchy and order cursed him with a debilitating sense both of his duties and his dignity. Close reading of the promises he was accused of breaking in general acquits him of the charge of perjury, though not, perhaps, of willingness to be misunderstood. He had the kingly quality of lack of interest in other people: when subjects were obedient, he showed no curiosity about their private motives; when they were disobedient, however, he jumped to the conclusion that their recalcitrance was part of a deliberate attack on monarchy. Although he was committed to personal rule, his major political weakness, under pressure, was not so much a failure to consult with his advisers as a calamitous tendency to vacillate between them.[1] As archbishop Laud was to put it after he had betrayed the earl of Strafford, he was 'a mild and gracious prince, who knew not how to be, or be made great'.[2] This well-meaning but inadequate politician inherited two major difficulties. One was the pervasive cultural transition, to some extent encouraged by the crown, for which 'the rise of common law' is probably the most convenient label. The other was the intellectual trend, largely, though

[1] Conrad Russell, *The causes of the English civil war* (Oxford, 1990), 189–211, offers an excellent analysis.
[2] *The autobiography of Dr William Laud*, ed. J. H. Bliss (Oxford, 1839), 271.

not exclusively, confined to the ranks of the clergy, that was revaluing the visible church. In both spheres, Charles's policies were virtually identical to his father's.

The most revealing of his early actions was an initiative he took in Scotland, the realm where he could govern without obvious constraints. As he was only twenty-four, convention allowed him to issue an 'act of revocation', recalling any grants of royal assets that had been made in his minority. A routine measure to this effect appears to have been drafted by crown servants within two months, at most, of his accession, but when the matter came to his attention, he chose to substitute some more ambitious legislation. This nullified all grants conferred by any previous monarch that were 'hurtful to the principality'.[3] At the same time, it reformed the teind (tithe) system by an enlightened compromise that lasted centuries, reasserted the crown's feudal rights as the ultimate landlord (even where feudal dues had been commuted), and paved the way for abolishing hereditary sheriffs.[4] These measures were a bold attempt at social engineering, but there was nothing new about his basic principles. In his explanatory declaration, Charles stated his intention to minimise extraordinary levies and to achieve the 'planting of the church and frieing of the gentrie from the bondage whairin thay are by the meanis of heretable offices and of teyndis'.[5] He hoped, in fact, to anglicise the country's social structure by strengthening the clergy and the gentry at the expense of the nobility. All of these aspirations were either expressed or implied in James's *The trew law* and *Basilicon doron*.

Where Charles differed from his father was in the sheer abruptness with which his policies were executed. He decided, for example, that it was undesirable for nobles to sit as judges in the court of session (the highest ordinary Scottish court), and therefore expelled them from its membership. When it was objected that this wholesale change was likely to disrupt the course of justice, he characteristically replied that 'it is better the subject suffer a little than all lie out of order'.[6] Charles was capable of grasping that such a policy was liable to prove unpopular; the point he had probably missed was that the principles on which he acted destroyed his own capacity to grant his propertied subjects peace of mind. He may have failed to understand

---

[3] *The register of the privy council of Scotland*, 2nd series, 8 vols. (1899–1908), I, 651. Allen I. Macinnes, *Charles I and the making of the covenanting movement* (Edinburgh, 1991), 52–3.
[4] David Stevenson, *The Scottish revolution 1637–1644* (1973), 35–40.
[5] *Register of the privy council of Scotland*, I 352.
[6] *Historical manuscripts commission report on the manuscripts of the Earl of Mar and Kellie preserved at Alloa House* 2 vols. (1904–30), I, 141.

that the polite objections that he faced, usually phrased as worries about less benign successors, concealed anxieties about his own behaviour.[7] He cannot seriously have intended to exercise the full range of the rights he was reviving, but he showed little interest in the political arts by which he might have reassured the anxious, inspired a grateful loyalty in those whom he had helped, and publicised his broadly constructive intentions.[8] The same high-minded disregard for popular perceptions would characterise the policies that he pursued in England.

I

In spite of Charles's earlier threats to govern by 'new counsels', the Personal Rule was not, in fact, particularly 'arbitrary' in nature. The eleven years without a parliament saw plenty of controversial royal actions, but a pedantic eagerness to insist upon the letter of the law was much more characteristic of his behaviour than a desire to evade or flout it. The crown's unenviable situation if anything encouraged it to show respect for law; in the absence of extraordinary aids, Charles had to wring all possible advantage from 'ordinary' or legal revenue. Old abuses like monopolies persisted, but virtually everything that the crown did was justifiable by precedents. Few of the government's measures were as hated as the entirely legal 'knighthood fines', the feudal penalties imposed on minor landowners for failing to present themselves to be knighted.

No such affront was greater than the disastrous judgement in the Ship Money case (1637–8), which seemed to have established both that Charles had a right to emergency taxation and that the monarch was sole judge of the existence of emergencies. But this conventional reading of the upshot of the case was actually an oversimplification. Like the Forced Loan and indeed the impositions, Ship Money was not technically a tax; 'shipping money', as the government liked to call it, was strictly speaking merely a cash payment in lieu of the provision of a vessel. In stressing this point, the government was narrowing its options, perhaps to the point of ruling out non-parliamentary aids such as the Jacobean benevolences; but it was undoubtedly wise to adopt a moderate position. The bench was to support the king by the narrowest of margins (seven to five), and most of the pro-government decisions held that the levy would have been illegal if it had been straightforwardly taxation.

It was hardly surprising, however, that qualifications of this type were lost upon the public. The episode was memorably discussed by Clarendon:

---

[7] Ibid., 140.   [8] Stevenson, *Scottish revolution*, 40–1.

It was an observation long ago by Thucydides, that 'men are much more passionate for injustice than for violence' . . . So when Ship Money was transacted at the council-board, they looked upon it as a work of that power they were always obliged to trust, and an effect of that foresight they were naturally to rely upon. Imminent necessity and public safety were convincing persuasions; and it might not seem of apparent ill consequence to them that upon an emergent occasion the regal power should fill up an hiatus or supply an impotency in the law. But when they saw in a court of law, (that law that gave them title and possession of all they had) apophthegms of state urged as elements of law; judges as sharp-sighted as Secretaries of State and in the mysteries of state; judgment of law grounded upon matter of fact of which there was neither inquiry or proof; and no reason given for the payment of the thirty shillings in question but what concluded the estates of all the standers-by; they had no reason to hope that that doctrine or the preachers of it would be contained within any bounds.[9]

In an acute and interesting discussion that quotes this particular passage, Glenn Burgess takes it to support his view that Charles confused 'the languages of civil law/divine right and common law' by introducing some ideas that were acceptable in other contexts into a legal setting in which they were much less appropriate.[10] Clarendon might have been content with such an exposition of his thinking. But if the metaphor of 'languages' is meant to suggest modes of discourse that were incompatible, then it is fundamentally misleading. As we have seen, developments internal to the law were making the judges receptive to arguments derived from other sources, including arguments from necessity.

The most revealing feature of Clarendon's account is actually its basic incoherence. On Clarendon's view, the principal objection to the judgement was that it gave a legal force to 'apophthegms of state'; but this objection presupposed a vanished political world in which such matters could be kept from entering a courtroom. Interestingly, Clarendon believed that if Ship Money 'had been managed in the same extraordinary way as the royal [*i.e.* the Forced] loan . . . men would much easier have submitted to it', which seems to imply that it would have been much better to have imprisoned Hampden and his lawyers. But the historian's own explanation of why the burden 'was borne with much more cheerfulness before the judgment for the king than ever it was after' depended on the assumption that people believed that the royal courts were open:

[9] Edward Hyde, earl of Clarendon, *The history of the rebellion and civil wars in England*, ed. W. D. Macray, 6 vols. (Oxford, 1888), I, 87–8.
[10] Glenn Burgess, *The politics of the ancient constitution: an introduction to English political thought, 1603–1642* (Basingstoke, 1992), 211.

men before pleasing themselves with doing somewhat for the king's service as a testimony of their affection, which they were not bound to do; many really believing the necessity, and therefore thinking the burden reasonable; others observing that the access to the king was of importance, when the damage to them was not considerable; and all assuring themselves that when they should be weary, or unwilling to continue the payment, they might resort to the law for relief and find it.[11]

Thus a satisfactory outcome from the royal point of view depended on people possessing a right to appeal to the courts but never actually exploiting it.

This type of incoherence was the intellectual fruit of constitutionalist royalism. As we shall see, most royalists understood the common law as basically a list of determinate rules with no capacity for adaptation; in consequence, they drew a sharp distinction between legal and non-legal arguments. The fact that modern scholars share their faith in this distinction explains the pro-royalist flavour of most modern narratives. It also explains why most scholars have failed to observe that Hampden's two principal lawyers, Robert Holborne and Oliver St John, had different theoretical approaches. Holborne's conception of the law placed emphasis upon its fixity. He stressed that legal questions depended on matters of fact: 'reason alone will not argue against a fundamental rule: for we are not now to examine on reason what is fit, and what not, but to see what is the truth'. The idea that the people's safety should be the highest law was a consideration in the legislative process, but from the lawyers' point of view 'the question is not, what are we to do by necessity, but what is the positive law of the land?'[12] Holborne agreed that there might be occasions – floods, fires, or foreign incursions – on which the king could interfere with private property, but he insisted that the right that justified such royal interference had nothing to do with the positive law of the land; the king was not invoking a royal prerogative – a right possessed in virtue of his status as the king – but appealing to the natural right of every human being to yield to 'absolute necessity'.[13]

St John by contrast stressed the omnicompetence of law. He took it for granted that national defence was 'a thing so necessary that it must needs be legal'[14] and therefore that the king enjoyed the powers that he needed for this purpose; 'the question', he remarked, 'is only *de modo*, by what medium or method this supreme power, which is in his Majesty,

<hr>

[11] Clarendon, *History*, 1 86–7.   [12] Cobbett, *State trials*, III 1011.
[13] Ibid., III 1012.   [14] Ibid., III 858.

doth infuse and let out itself into this particular'. At this point, however, his argument took a subversive turn. He pointed out that it is kings who judge, 'yet I conceive that his Majesty alone, without assistance of the judges of the court, cannot give judgement'.[15] The king's Great Council, parliament, was also a court-like vessel of an impersonal will:

If an erroneous judgement was given before the statute of 27 Eliz. in the King's Bench [which created a court of appeal] the king could not relieve his grieved subject any way but by writ of error in parliament: neither can he out of parliament alter the old laws, or make new, or make any naturalisations or legitimations, nor do some other things: and yet is the parliament his Majesty's court too as well as other his courts of justice.[16]

This vision of the English state, simultaneously impersonal and deeply monarchist, was to be somewhere near the heart of parliamentarian thinking, while Holborne's belief in a law that was composed of rigid rules was to be characteristic of moderate royalism.

In 1638, though, such differences were easy to ignore. From a practical political perspective, the only thing that mattered was that virtually all England believed that the payments demanded were indefensible. It is true the early levies were collected with relatively little difficulty, but there was reason to expect the subsequent spread of principled resistance; a payment that was justified by reference to a threat to public safety became more unacceptable, not less, each time it was exacted in peacetime conditions. The obvious analogy was not encouraging. During the previous decade, some gentlemen appear to have paid the Forced Loan out of a sense of loyalty to a beleaguered wartime government; in the peaceful 1630s, the government could not appeal to patriotic solidarity. Given that the mechanism of collection was an unpaid and overburdened sheriff whose term of office was a single year, the steadily mounting refusals of 1638–9 were virtually impossible to handle. Under ideal political conditions, the problem might perhaps have been contained, but the regime's authority was vulnerable to external shocks. In the event, the jolt that it received was caused by its provocative religion.

II

No sensible scholar has ever denied that Charles's religion had something to do with his downfall. But Charles did not invent the policy of giving royal support to high conformists, nor was it obvious that such a

[15] Ibid., III 861.   [16] Ibid., III 862.

stance was in itself inevitably disastrous; in the religious sphere, at any rate, he was swimming with the intellectual current. His problem was that the 'constitutional' and 'religious' spheres were not, in fact, entirely separate, and that the leakage ran in both directions. It has always been clear that his preference for uniform and ceremonious worship enabled his opponents (whatever their motives) to mobilise resistance through the cry of popery. But there was also a reverse effect: Charles managed to encourage a perception that bishops were a threat to secular order.

This perception was not altogether new; during his father's reign, there was no shortage of zealous or ambitious high church prelates who wanted to serve both the church and themselves by shows of loyalty. But one of the most impressive signs of James's superior guile was his reserved approach towards such clerical supporters. As we have seen, his personal religious attitudes aligned him with the highest of conformists, but he actively discouraged the like-minded from propagating 'absolutist' doctrines. One consequence of his sensible restraint was that the crown's unpopularity was not a threat to its preferred religion. In Jacobean parliaments, the constitutionalist opposition had mingled puritans like Nicholas Fuller with supporters of the church like Edwin Sandys. This may, to some extent, have harmed the monarch's interests; as secular and religious grievances could be dissociated, potentially quite serious theological disputes did not prevent MPs co-operating. But the great benefit to the church was that the bishops and their privileges were not an obvious target of secular-minded reform. The most serious of Charles's many mistakes was his abandonment of this advantage.

The symbol of his errors was archbishop William Laud, the man whose personality and tactics created a disastrous rift among the clergy's leaders. But though Laud must be central to any analysis of the collapse of Stuart monarchy, discussion of his impact has been much hampered by two preconceptions. On the one hand, he has sometimes been presented as a mere clericalist martinet, a figure whose primary commitment was to uniformity; on the other, he has been treated as a reactionary, the leader of an obscurantist counter-Reformation. In either case Laudianism was an external shock, a movement whose brief dominance of English church affairs was based upon the accident of Charles's inclinations. What neither of these approaches can explain is why this shock was such a threat to the church's episcopal structure. If it had been essentially an alien imposition, then its effects should surely have been reversible without a complete institutional upheaval.

A better understanding of the damage that Laud did and its connection with our wider story requires a grasp of his positive achievement. Laud was not just a high-handed bureaucrat; he was an intellectual who represented powerful cultural forces, most of which were to re-emerge, considerably strengthened, after the setback of the revolution. If he was initially slow to be promoted, his personality was found impressive; no one so cripplingly irascible and ostentatiously immoderate could have been so politically successful without a certain moral force and personal magnetism. Given his openness about his rigid attitudes, it is striking that he should have been admired by characters otherwise as different as the radical lawyer James Whitelocke,[17] the future archbishop of York John Williams[18] (a natural sympathiser with whom he later quarrelled), and the king's chief minister and favourite, the marquis (later duke) of Buckingham.

Laud's close relationship with Buckingham was probably more important than his influence on Charles in shaping subsequent developments. Though it is generally assumed that Charles was a convinced Arminian, there is not in fact much evidence that he was interested in such questions. When he was Prince of Wales, he had been noted for his piety, but his chaplains were drawn from the 'Calvinist' end of the court religious spectrum.[19] It was Buckingham, not Charles, who organised the York House conference (at a time when he was threatened with impeachment) and took the risk of backing Montagu instead of at least affecting to be neutral. The likely explanation of his conduct is that the favourite belonged to the *New gagg's* target audience: conservatives with a regard for ceremonial for whom Catholicism represented a possible form of religious seriousness. It is striking, for example, that when he chose a bride, he opted for a recusant who did not conform till the moment of her marriage. He also clearly had a taste for ritual; in January 1622, he led a group of courtiers in being 'confirmed or bishopt as children use to be . . . where they had choice music and all the ceremonies belonging to that action'.[20] Part of the rationale of Laudianism was its capacity to meet the pastoral needs of such people.

The event that created the Buckingham–Laud alliance was a crisis in the former's family that was also a revealing episode in the development of court religion. For much of 1622, Buckingham's mother dithered on the brink of

[17] James Whitelocke, *Liber famelicus of Sir James Whitelocke*, ed. John Bruce, Camden Society 50 (1858), 51, 77.
[18] Cobbett, *State trials*, II 1461.
[19] Peter MacCullough, *Sermons at court: politics and religion in Elizabethan and Jacobean preaching* (Cambridge, 1998), 195–208.
[20] John Chamberlain, *The letters of John Chamberlain*, ed. N. E. McClure, 2 vols. (1939), II 419–20.

a conversion to Catholicism. James took an interest in this situation, and even arranged a meeting with the missionary involved, a Jesuit who passed by the name of 'John Fisher'. The resultant disputation, which stretched over three days, was mostly conducted by Laud and Francis White (the man who was later to license *Appello Caesarem*). It resulted in two major publications: White's *A replie to the Jesuit Fisher's answer to certain questions propounded by his most gracious majestie*, and Laud's own *An answer to Mr Fisher's relation of a third conference* (that is, of the last day's proceedings), more usually known as his *Conference with Fisher*.

These works illuminate the situation that was to encourage the rise of Laudianism. Both were moulded by a shift in Catholic tactics. As White explained, '[the Catholics'] manner is, when they dispute with Protestants *viva voce*, to avoid all other controversies and to set up their rest upon the questions of visibility and authority of the church'.[21] Only a perpetually visible church, they argued, could give an infallible guarantee that Scripture's message was reliable. Their clinching piece of evidence was a statement by Augustine to the effect that only the authority of the church induced him to credit the message of the Bible. White offered two explanations of Augustine's troubling dictum (he was evidently reluctant to suggest that the great Father might have been mistaken). One was to note that 'some schoolmen hold that [Augustine] speaketh of acquisite or historical faith, which is an introduction to infused [i.e. justifying] faith . . . most men are first induced by external motives, to give credit to the Scriptures'.[22] The second referred to 'other learned papists' who held 'that St Augustine, in the place objected, understood the church wherein the Apostles themselves governed, and of which they were parts'.[23] Both of these moves were mildly controversial – a generation earlier, Hooker had been thought daring for treating reason as the 'key' to scripture and the authority of the church as an initial 'motive' to religion – but White had not abandoned the important principle that scripture was intrinsically self-authenticating.

Laud too regarded scripture as self-authenticating, but his discussion went a little further. His starting point was quite conventional; he stressed the need for an authority not just partially but 'absolutely divine' to show that scripture was infallible. This ruled out 'the testimony or voice of the present church: For our worthies prove [a marginal note cited Hooker] that

[21] Francis White, *A reply to Jesuit Fisher's answer to certain questions propounded by his most gracious majesty* (1624), sig. b3v.
[22] Ibid., 22.   [23] Ibid., 22.

all the church's constitutions are of the nature of humane law'.[24] But though the church was powerless to authenticate the Word, illumination was in practice granted within the context of this institution: 'no man may expect inward private revelation, without the external means of the church, unless perhaps the case of necessity be excepted, when such a man lives in a time and place, as excludes him from all ordinary means'.[25] Similarly, although he held that the workings of God's grace exceeded anything possible to reason, he thought of the two as intimately linked:

Grace is never placed but in a reasonable creature, and proves by the very seat which it hath taken up, that the end it hath is to be spiritual eye-water, to make reason see what by nature only it cannot, but never to blemish reason in that which it can comprehend . . . Reason then can give no supernatural ground into which a man may resolve his faith, That scripture is the word of God infallibly, yet reason can go so high as it can prove that Christian religion, which rests upon the authority of this book, stands upon surer grounds of nature, reason, common equity, and justice, than anything in the world, which any infidel or mere naturalist hath done, doth, or can adhere to against it.[26]

Thus though Laud's argument remained essentially Reformed, he laid unusual stress upon the role of the church and of reason. From a strictly theological point of view, he was a relatively cautious thinker. It is often supposed that his Eucharistic theory must have been scandalously Catholic, but there is little evidence that his ideas, in this respect, departed from the norm. As Thomas Morton quite correctly noted, the English church was very close to Calvin (the most sacramentally minded of non-Lutheran reformers), who held that 'we account not our sacraments mere signs, to represent the graces of God, but that they are also seals, to present and exhibit the truth of God's promises of grace, and to apply them to the hearts of faithful receivers'.[27] Laud's teachings on the Eucharist stood firmly in this Calvinist tradition. Like the indisputably godly William Perkins, he was happy to speak about a 'real presence', but this concession was entirely verbal. Perkins had stated that the phrase was unexceptionable, so long as the reality of the presence was understood not to be 'local, bodily, or substantial'.[28] Laud's exposition in *The Conference* was quite compatible with these principles, although his veneration for the altar did lend some credence to the charge that he believed the presence to be

---

[24] William Laud, *An answere to Mr Fisher's relation of a conference between a certaine B (as he stiles him) and himselfe* (1624), 18.
[25] Ibid., 20.   [26] Ibid., 21.
[27] Thomas Morton, *A defence of the innocencie of the three ceremonies of the church of England* (1618), 55.
[28] Perkins, *A reformed Catholike* (1597), 187.

'local'.[29] A generation later, the allegedly much more extreme John Cosin offered a lucid summary of Laudian beliefs:

We do not hold this celebration to be so naked a commemoration of Christ's body given to death, and of his blood there shed for us, but that the same body and blood is present there in this commemoration (made by the sacrament of bread and wine) to all that faithfully receive it: nor do we say, it is so nude a sacrifice of praise and thanksgiving, but that by our prayers also added, we offer and present the death of Christ to God, that for his death's sake we may find mercy, in which respect we deny not this commemorative sacrifice to be propitiatory.[30]

It is evident that Cosin's stress on the believer's role was wholly incompatible with transubstantiation, but it is also evident that the conciliatory talk of 'sacrifice' and 'presence' was likely to alarm an unreflective Protestant.

Buckingham must have been impressed by this theology, because Laud's diary records the growth of an intimate friendship. Shortly before the *Conference* (in May), Laud wrote for him a 'paper concerning the difference between the Church of England and Rome in point of salvation'. In mid-June, 'my Lord Marquess Buckingham was pleased to enter upon a near respect to me. The particulars are not for paper.' A week later, he became 'C.' (presumably 'Confessor') to the favourite, who then received communion at his hands.[31] Their chance affinity of temperament, probably coloured, on Laud's side, by sexual attraction,[32] had some important practical results, including Laud's emergence as the leader of the existing group among the clergy (previously led by Richard Neile of Durham) who disapproved of Abbot's Grindalian attitudes. In 1627, in a revealing episode, this group put an end to the archbishop's career as a national politician.

The occasion of their coup was his refusal to allow the printing of a controversial sermon. Its author, William Sibthorpe, was not a Laudian, but an intemperate self-publicist who railed at a long list of clerical bugbears (including, as it happened, sabbath-breaking). The questionable aspect of his rambling diatribe was his unqualified support for arbitrary taxation and in particular for the Forced Loan. In an embittered account of the affair, Abbot quite plausibly maintained that he had been sent 'Dr Sibthorpe's contemptible treatise' because his enemies foresaw that he would feel obliged to stop the sermon's publication.[33] It is obvious whom he blamed for his misfortunes. Laud was described as being 'the only inward counsellor with

[29] See the second edn, *A relation of the conference* (1639), 292–6. On locality, see Sir Thomas Aston, *The Short Parliament (1640) diary of Sir Thomas Aston*, ed. Judith D. Maltby, Camden Society, 4th series 35 (1988), 89.
[30] *The works of the right reverend father in God John Cosin*, v, 336.
[31] *Autobiography of Dr William Laud*, 9.   [32] Ibid., 43.   [33] Cobbett, *State trials*, II 1465, 1457.

Buckingham, sitting with him sometimes privately whole hours, and feeding his humour with malice and spite'. This pattern of malign behaviour had been established in his time at Oxford, where he 'picked quarrels in the lectures of the public readers' (including of course Abbot's brother Robert) and told 'the then Bishop of Durham, that he [Richard Neile] might fill the ears of King James with discontents against the honest men that took pains in their places and settled the truth (which he called puritanism) in their auditors'.[34]

But more was at stake in this contest than sectarian advantage; it also involved a practical disagreement about the best way forward for royal policy. Here Abbot was on relatively strong ground. He pointed out that Sibthorpe's argument had undermined the government's whole case by its admission that the Loan was actually a 'tribute' (this was corrected in the printed version).[35] More generally, Sibthorpe had broken with King James's attitudes. Abbot was able to recall an earlier episode when his episcopal colleague Samuel Harsnett had preached a sermon 'upon the text, "Give unto Caesar the things that be Caesar's", wherein he insisted that goods and money were Caesar's'. On that occasion, James 'calmed all' by saying that 'the bishop only failed in this . . . he did not add, they were his according to the laws and customs of the country wherein they did live'.[36] Abbot concluded with a pointed story about the chaplain who was asked to license the eventual printed version. The unfortunate official had signed the document, but then had second thoughts and consulted a lawyer, who

spake to this purpose: What have you done? You have allowed a strange book yonder; which, if it be true, there is no *meum* and *tuum*, no man in England hath any thing of his own: if ever the tide turn, and matters be called to a reckoning, you will be hanged for publishing such a book.[37]

According to Abbot, the chaplain then erased his signature. It would have been better for Laud and his supporters if they had manifested the same prudence.

Their disregard for lawyers was a natural consequence of their beliefs about their situation. Laud was above all else a champion of the interests of the clergy; as the epistle to the second edition (1639) of *The Conference* explained, he thought it was his duty to preserve their 'maintenance' as well as their 'doctrine and manners'.[38] In this he differed from Abbot, who had had a reputation for failing to stand up for his profession. According to the historian Thomas Fuller (who was no Laudian), the older man was

[34] Ibid., II 1460.   [35] Ibid., II 1460, 1464.   [36] Ibid., II 1463.
[37] Ibid., II 1465.   [38] Laud, *Conference*, Epistle dedicatory.

'consecrated bishop, before ever called to a pastoral charge, which made, say some, him not to sympathise with the necessities and infirmities of poor ministers'.[39] Laud by contrast was continuously aware of the collective interests of his order and of the practical difficulties it faced. He had no doubt at all who was to blame; the church, in his view, was 'so bound up in the forms of the common law, that it is not possible for me, or for any man, to do that good which he would, or is bound to do'.[40] When the puritan common lawyer Henry Sherfield took it upon himself to smash an image (a window that portrayed the Holy Spirit as a dove), Laud worked himself up to a disastrous outburst:

> This much let me say to Mr Sherfield and such of his profession as slight the ecclesiastical laws and persons, that there was a time when churchmen were as great in the kingdom as you are now; and let me be bold to prophesy, there will be a time when you will be as low as the church is now, if you go on thus to contemn the church.[41]

Such words could hardly have been better suited to feed what Clarendon would call 'the virulency and animosity expressed upon all occasions from many of good knowledge in the excellent and wise profession of the common law towards the church and churchmen'.[42] Resurgent clericalism was colliding with an increased regard for legal values.

As we shall see, this clash of attitudes would be disastrous for the hierarchy. But Laud's counterproductive aggression is comprehensible as a reaction to some shifts affecting most of the conformist clergy. A number of related trends were making a Grindalian church a less attractive option. It is striking, for example, that John Prideaux, who was the best-known 'Calvinist' in Oxford during the period of Land's dominance, was hostile to the single most powerful impulse of early seventeenth-century godly culture: its ever-increasing obsession with Sabbath observance.[43] Their fellow 'Calvinist' Joseph Hall not only believed, as we have seen, that Rome was a true church, but was eventually to write the standard defence of *jure divino* bishops.[44] Above all, a more positive view of ceremonies and of the visible church made tolerance of puritanism less defensible. The standard Jacobean defence of ceremonies was written by the 'Calvinist' Thomas Morton. It attacked the nonconformists on the grounds that 'by your detracting from the ordinances of the church, many take occasion

---

[39] Thomas Fuller, *Church-history of Britain* (1655), Book x, 87, 128.
[40] Laud, *Works*, vi 310.   [41] Cobbett, *State trials*, iii 553.   [42] Clarendon, *History*, i 404.
[43] John Prideaux, *The doctrine of the sabbath*, 3rd edn (Oxford, 1635).
[44] Joseph Hall, *Episcopacie by divine right asserted* (1640).

to neglect the outward worship of the church; whereupon their inward zeal and devotion soon cooleth, and in the end vanisheth away'.[45] If this argument were taken seriously, then it was right to place new stress upon conformity.

The idea that such figures were sharply distinct from more rigorous high churchmen is less attributable to the substance of their views than to the Laudians' own bigotry; it says more about Laud than it does about Hall that the former set a spy upon the latter.[46] There was, to be sure, a spectrum of opinion about the harder points of the theology of grace, but orthodoxy's boundaries were shifting. By 1624, the high conformist bishop Samuel Harsnett was in a position to recall that he had been in trouble in Queen Elizabeth's reign for preaching against absolute reprobation, but that Robert Abbot 'hath since declared in print that which he then preached to be no popery'.[47] Even in the controversy surrounding the *New Gagg*, the term 'Arminian' was invoked without much attempt at precision; when the concept became central to political debate (which was not until the parliament of 1628–9), it had become a shorthand for a range of grievances, including such events as Sibthorpe's sermon.

It cannot be assumed, then, that the Laudian position was founded on distinctive views about predestination. In the preface to the second, expanded edition of the *Conference with Fisher*, Laud insisted that his motives were anti-Catholic: 'no one thing hath made conscientious men more wavering in their own minds, or more apt, and easy to be drawn aside from the sincerity of religion professed in the church of England, than the want of uniform and decent order in too many churches of the kingdom'.[48] He added the Hookerian claim that 'external worship of God in his church is the great witness to the world that our heart stands right in [the inward] service of God', and stressed that 'these thoughts are they, and no other, which have made me labour so much as I have done for decency and an orderly settlement of the external worship of God in the church'.[49]

Laud could legitimately have pointed out that this was a position with little or nothing in common with Catholic thinking; precisely because Catholics believed their ceremonies to be efficacious, they wasted no time in general defences of the desirability of ritual. Peter Lake has rightly argued that whether or not the Laudians had a theology, they certainly had a distinctive 'style', one that insisted, among other things, on setting apart times and places for worshipping God in the context of established social

---

[45] Morton, *Innocencie of ceremonies*, 167.   [46] *Dictionary of National Biography*, s.v. 'Hall, Joseph'.
[47] Cobbett, *State trials*, II 1255–6.   [48] Laud, *Conference*, Ep. Ded.   [49] Ibid., Ep. Ded.

order.[50] One of the features of this style was that most modern of attitudes: self-conscious traditionalism. According to George Herbert, the 'country parson is a lover of old customs, if they be good, and harmless; and the rather, because the country people are much addicted to them, so that to favour them therein is to win their hearts'.[51] There are signs that such a willingness to work through popular culture (exemplified most obviously in the Book of Sports) would later help to stimulate plebeian royalism.[52]

Defence of this nostalgic mode of feeling did have some intellectual implications, but they were not particularly Catholic. To the extent that it implied that love of ceremony was natural, it also had affinities with the most rationalistic strands in seventeenth-century theology. John Pockling-ton referred to the 'instinct of nature' by which men in the Old Testament built altars.[53] Peter Heylyn agreed that 'sacrifices, priests, and altars were from the beginning by the light of nature'.[54] The Laudians' puritan-baiting choice of language could thus be justified, in part, by reference to natural religion. At times, they had a tendency to drift towards a creed in which the obligations of a Christian were in effect absorbed in social duties. In his defence of Laudian arrangements, *Innovations unjustly charged upon the present church and state* (1637), Christopher Dow pronounced that

> God doth not bring men to heaven by difficult questions; the way to eternity is plain and easy to be known: to believe that Jesus Christ was raised from the dead, to acknowledge him to be Lord and Christ, and to live soberly, righteously, and religiously in the present world is the sum of saving doctrine and Christian religion.[55]

The rationalist clergy of Restoration times would make exactly the same point in roughly the same language.

A further Laudian train of thought had similar implications. We have seen that Laud revalued both the visible church and the individual's reason. In the context of anti-Catholic polemic, the former emphasis required the latter. The Hookerian admission that papists could be saved laid moderate Protestants open to the dangerous argument that anybody risk-averse should be a Catholic. The only possible response was to argue that this charitable concession only extended to the ignorant; sophisticated people had

---

[50] Peter Lake, 'The Laudian style', in Kenneth Fincham (ed.), *The early Stuart church, 1603–42* (1993), 161–85.

[51] George Herbert, *A priest to the temple* (1652), 157.

[52] David Underdown, *Revel, riot, and rebellion* (Oxford, 1985), 66–8, 276, 279.

[53] John Pocklington, *Altare Christianum* (1637), 4.

[54] Peter Heylyn, *Antidotum Lincolniense: or an Answer to a book entitled Holy Table Name and Thing* (1637), section 2, 1.

[55] Dow, *Innovations*, 41.

a duty to exercise their rationality. In the later 1630s, this line of argument was pressed as far as it would go. In his famous *The religion of Protestants a safe way to salvation* (1638), Laud's godson William Chillingworth (a former convert of the Jesuit Fisher) abandoned the basic distinction between a merely human or 'historical' faith in the Bible and the infallible 'infused' or justifying faith that worked the salvation of Calvinist believers. In Chillingworth's view, 'God desires only that we believe the conclusion as much as the premises deserve, that the strength of our faith be equal or proportionable to the credibility of the motives to it.'[56] In practice, this meant that the Saviour's resurrection (the well-attested miracle that vouched for the truth of the Bible) deserved the faith elicited by well-established facts about geography and history: the existence of the city of Rome, for example, or of a Roman by the name of Caesar. In consequence, the ordinary Christian's sole duty was a sincere belief in the deliverances of scripture: 'he that believes the scripture sincerely, and endeavours to believe it in the true sense, cannot possibly be an heretic'.[57] The importance of sincerity led him to bite the bullet of religious toleration, on the grounds that 'nothing can be more evidently unjust, than to force weak men by the profession of a religion which they believe not to lose their own eternal happiness'.[58]

These ultra-liberal doctrines were a much deeper challenge to existing orthodoxy than recondite Arminian deviations, but by the 1660s they were conventional. They did not necessarily imply abandonment of *ceremonial* uniformity and their Laudian adherents had no particular grounds for changing their political opinions. The preface to Chillingworth's treatise applauded the church's commitment to 'the beauty of holiness', its emphasis upon patristic study, and even its willingness to 'use the names of priests and altars'.[59] As Hugh Trevor-Roper has shown, his attitudes were not at all unique; especially at Oxford, there were other staunch high churchmen and future royalists with highly rationalistic attitudes, including perhaps willingness to doubt the Trinity. Laud was himself intelligent enough to be suspicious of these new ideas, but he did nothing decisive to suppress them.[60] Unlike their nineteenth-century admirers, the Laudians were not consciously rejecting their culture's most distinctive innovations.

In the end, the great upheaval that swept away their church was triggered by one of their successes. One mark of that church's appeal to lively minds was its ability to attract some foreign sympathisers. In Scotland too,

---

[56] William Chillingworth, *The religion of Protestants a safe way to salvation* (Oxford, 1638), 36.
[57] Ibid., 'Preface', s.43.　　[58] Ibid., 297.　　[59] Ibid., 'Preface', ss.22, 24–6.
[60] Hugh Trevor-Roper, *Catholics, Anglicans, and puritans* (1987), 187–8, 230 and n, 207.

an intellectual movement, proportionately much smaller but if anything more extreme, had been encouraged by patristic study in a Reformed episcopalian setting. In the Scottish situation, matters were complicated by the rational fears of owners of church lands; the apparently growing power of the Scottish hierarchy was seen in the light of the worries provoked by the earlier Revocation. But in Scotland as in England, the bishops might have got away with purely intellectual innovations, had they not drawn attention to their programme by changes that they made to public worship. In England, these included the revival of an altar at the east end of the church in place of a Reformed communion table. The English were affronted by the altar policy in much the same way that the Scots had been affronted by James's insistence on kneeling at communion: here was a symbol anyone could grasp of a regression to Catholicism. But the offence created by the altar policy was mild compared with the backlash that Charles caused when he imposed a Prayer Book on Scotland that took as its model the English book of 1549 with its conservative communion service. The effect on mainstream Scots opinion was to discredit the idea of government by bishops.

In a political culture quite different from England's, not least in being influenced by sixteenth-century resistance theories, a national 'covenant' against such changes provided a firm basis for a comprehensive movement. Once this movement was firmly established, there was no way, short of military invasion, that Scots episcopacy could be protected, but Charles proved characteristically unable to stick to a consistent course of action. After marching an army to the Scottish border, he lost his nerve before entering the country and ended the first brief war about the matter with the 'Pacification of Berwick' of June 1639, an agreement by which he promised to accept that 'all matters ecclesiastical shall be determined by the assembly of the kirk'.[61]

What happened next casts useful light on Charles's political failings. His private instructions to the earl of Traquair, his representative at the assembly, allowed the latter to sanction the abolition of episcopacy, 'so as the conclusion seem not to be made in prejudice of episcopacy as unlawful, but only in satisfaction to the people, for settling the present disorders, and such other reasons of state'. But he insisted that the church assembly was not to 'meddle with anything that is civil, or which formerly hath been established by act of parliament'.[62] Charles thought of the Pacification

[61] Gilbert Burnet, *The memoires of the lives and actions of James and William Dukes of Hamilton and Castleherald* (1677), 141.
[62] Ibid., 150.

as a tactical withdrawal. With the pedantry that many of his opponents regarded, understandably, as mere duplicity, he clung to a narrow reading of his promise that 'matters ecclesiastical' should be decided by the church assembly. He appears to have distinguished between the abolition of bishops by the kirk (in which he was prepared to acquiesce) and the destruction of the privileges that had been granted by the Scottish state. As a subsequent letter insisted, he would not rescind 'those acts of parliament, which our father with so much expense of time and industry established, and which may hereafter be of so great use to us'.[63] He was following James's example in working to preserve a secular structure that would in time facilitate the bishops' restoration. But though there was a rationale for his behaviour, it was politically suicidal. Scottish episcopacy did have a few convinced supporters, especially in the north-east of the country; the only actual battle of the first Bishops' War took place at the Bridge of Dee, near Aberdeen. Charles had betrayed such people without acquiring any new adherents. Only a man of some intelligence could have devised the brilliantly deceptive undertakings by which he had misled the covenanters; only a man of no political wisdom could have supposed that they supplied a workable fallback position.

About a fortnight after he had signed the Pacification, the desperate situation of the Scottish monarchy was spelled out in a cogent memorandum. In this incisive document, his leading Scots adviser, the marquis of Hamilton, predicted, quite correctly, that the assembly would abolish bishops and that parliament would ratify its verdict. At this point, if the king employed his veto, the result would be 'a certain loss of civil authority'. The king must either 'give way to the madness of the people' or else attempt a military conquest, but war against Scotland would require an English parliament. His conclusion was stark:

So all may be summed up in this; Whether to permit the abolishing of episcopacy, the lessening of kingly power in ecclesiastic affairs, the establishing civil authority in such manner as the iniquity of the times will suffer and to expect better; and what will be the consequence of this if way be given thereto: or to call a parliament in England and leave the event thereof to hazard and their discretion, and in the interim Scotland to the government of the Covenanters.[64]

When Hamilton's predictions were fulfilled, the king preferred the second of these options, and summoned the Short Parliament that met in April–May of 1640. The events of that assembly corroborate the view that Laudianism, though unpopular, had gained significant ground upon its

[63] Ibid., 158–9.   [64] Ibid., 145.

critics. Arminianism in the narrow sense seems not to have been a serious concern and indignation centred on the altar policy. But even the Laudian altar had open partisans, including the future royalists Viscount Falkland, Edward Hyde, and Edmund Waller;[65] in spite of the offence to conventional instincts that had undoubtedly been caused by high church innovations, there was certainly none of the witchhunt atmosphere that dominated the first months of the Long Parliament. Above all, a fairly substantial group of members was quite prepared, in principle, to help Charles to restore the Scottish bishops in return for constitutional concessions. As Conrad Russell noted, the division of opinion on this question 'was not greatly different from the division of opinion of August 1642'.[66] All this suggests that Laud may have evoked much discontent and radicalised puritan opinion, but that the implementation of puritan ideals was not yet a potentially popular programme. The history of the next twenty years, a period in which military upheavals proved powerless to affect the national culture, suggests it was never likely to become so. To grasp how the bishops nonetheless provoked catastrophe, we must return to Laudian clericalism.

III

It goes without saying that Laud was a believer in a strong church in a strong monarchy, but if he had been asked to choose between these loyalties, there could be little doubt of his decision. Unlike his mentor, Hooker, who had denied that parliament was purely secular, Laud was convinced, in principle, that churches should be governed by their clergy. Thus he believed that clerical assemblies enjoyed an unrestricted power to legislate for churches, though (as he put it in a private letter) 'when and where these synods shall be limited by the statute laws of any kingdom, then I conceive the law must be submitted unto, till it may be helped'.[67] Even in a document that he intended to be considered by the House of Lords, he was entirely open about his attitude:

I will not dispute it here what power a lay assembly (and such a parliament is) hath to determine matters of religion, primely and originally by and of themselves, before the church hath first agreed upon them. Then, indeed, they may confirm or refuse. And this course was held in the Reformation. But originally to take this

[65] *The Short Parliament (1640) diary of Sir Thomas Aston*, ed. Judith D. Maltby, Camden Society, 4th series 35 (1988), 88, 90.
[66] Conrad Russell, *The fall of the British monarchies, 1637–42* (Oxford, 1991), 121.
[67] Laud, *Works*, VII 580.

power over religion into lay hands is that which hath not been thus assumed since Christ to these unhappy days.[68]

Not surprisingly, then, he attached significance to securing a judicial declaration that bishops were fully entitled to hold courts in their own names. When the judges obliged, in 1637, he doubtless thought they had affirmed the proper theological position: bishops enjoyed inherent jurisdiction enabling them, if necessary, to excommunicate, although the 'exercise' of such a power both could and should be scrutinised by monarchs. It says much about the assumptions of the majority of English laymen that whenever this notion came to their attention they found it deeply shocking and unacceptable. A rare exception to this rule was the parliamentarian writer Henry Parker, who noted that almost all Protestant divines 'hold princes incompetent for spiritual [as opposed to ecclesiastical] regency' and that it was for this reason that 'our prelates' style is *providentia divina*, not *gratia Regis*, and as they issue writs in their own names, so they use their own arms in their seals, and not the king's'.[69] But Parker was a writer of some learning and great candour, and it was commoner to imply that Laud's opinions were somehow novel. The articles of impeachment that the archbishop faced included the charge that 'the said archbishop claims the king's ecclesiastical jurisdiction as incident to his episcopal and archiepiscopal office in this kingdom, and doth deny the same to be derived from the crown of England'.[70] By 1642, some people believed that the English bishops' practice of holding diocesan courts in their own names was actually a recent innovation.[71] Laud's mischief-making enemy, John Williams, bishop of Lincoln, knew just what he was doing when he associated his attack upon the Laudian altar with an insistence that 'power in matters ecclesiastical' belonged to God alone, 'before it came (by his and his only donation) to be vested in the king'.[72]

The fatal mistake that Laud made in 1640 was to encourage the anxiety to which the subtle Williams had appealed. In the Short Parliament, the House of Commons did not dispute that convocation had the right to formulate laws for the clergy, but it was worried by the news that Charles had empowered the assembly to proffer new canons, 'the rather because of the innovations brought in and practised before the grant of this commission'.[73]

[68] Ibid., VI 142.   [69] Henry Parker, *The true grounds of ecclesiasticall regiment* (1641), 12.
[70] *The speech or declaration of John Pymm . . . upon the delivery of the articles* (1641), 9
[71] Oliver St John, *Master St John his speech in parliament* (1642), sig. A3. It is doubtful if St John is the true author of this text.
[72] John Williams, *The holy table name and thing* (1637), 24.
[73] *Commons Journal*, II 11; *Aston Diary*, 50–3.

This worry proved well founded. When the Short Parliament had been dissolved, Charles ordered convocation to keep sitting. The clerical body then voted him clerical taxes, and passed a succession of canons, including a canon imposing an oath, *inter alia*, not to consent 'to alter the government of this church by archbishops, bishops, deans, and archdeacons &c.'[74]

Even if it had not implied that the office of archdeacon was too sacred to be abolished by a human agent, this oath would have been a serious mistake. It confirmed what many moderates suspected: that Laudian ecclesiology supplied an absolute constraint on the Supremacy. The future royalist militant George Digby regarded the oath as a 'covenant against the king for bishops and the hierarchy, as the Scottish covenant is against them, only so much worse than the Scottish, as they [the Scots] admit not of the Supremacy in ecclesiastical affairs, and we are sworn unto it'.[75] The future parliamentarian Nathaniel Fiennes concurred that it was

against the law of the king's Supremacy, in that it maketh archbishops, bishops, deans, archdeacons etc. to be *jure divino*, whereas the law of this land hath annexed to the imperial crown of this realm not only all ecclesiastical jurisdiction, but also all superiority over the ecclesiastical state . . . it is against the oath of Supremacy established by law point blank, for therein I am sworn not only to consent unto, but also to assist and to the uttermost of my power to defend all jurisdictions, pre-eminences etc. annexed to the imperial crown of this realm.[76]

Thus Laudianism was more than just a challenge to the religious practice of the English; it was also a threat to the nation's political structure. In some minds, of course, there was barely a distinction; as William Lamont was able to show in his study of William Prynne, there were those to whom the royal Supremacy was a fanatically held religious principle.[77] But what divided Laud and Charles from natural supporters such as Digby was the perception that the rule of bishops had come to pose a constitutional problem to which extensive church reform would be the best solution.

In a parliamentary setting, the canons played a crucial role in making a puritan programme once more legitimate. They fitted into an analysis that treated the recent excesses as the foreseeable result of processes inherent in an unreformed church order. Thus the first of the regular 'fast sermons' to the House, preached by the puritan Cornelius Burges, declared that

[74] Bray, *Canons*, 568.
[75] George Digby, *The speeches of the Lord Digby in the high court of parliament concerning grievances and the triennial parliament* (1641), 5–6.
[76] *A second speech of the honourable Nathaniel Fiennes* (1641), 12.
[77] William Lamont, *Marginal Prynne, 1600–1669* (1963).

'the perfecting of the reformation of [the church]' was the only way of stopping the dynamic by which 'the power of godliness will soon generate into formality, and zeal into lukewarmness, but popery, Arminianism, Socinianism, profaneness, apostasy and atheism itself will more and more crowd in upon us'. Burges proposed a covenant with God, while cautiously stressing that 'my meaning extends not to engage you in any civil covenant and bond for defence of your municipal laws and liberties'. He did not fail to point out, however, that 'that late ecclesiastical oath and covenant' was 'little less than a combination and conspiracy against both king and state'.[78]

One of the great advantages of those who thought like Burges was that their viewpoint positively encouraged a thoroughly reductionist account of 'popery'. Because the Roman Catholic faith was simply a fraud by the clergy, its elements could be borrowed by non-papist ministers with similarly selfish purposes. There was no need, it followed, to hold that Laudians were actually secret Catholics. Nathaniel Fiennes explained that 'one party had some need of their [the papists'] principles to maintain their hierarchy, together with their worldly pomp and ceremonies, which are appurtenances thereunto'.[79] If a historical analogue was needed, Laud was in general compared to Cardinal Wolsey, not to Cardinal Pole; his excesses were presumed to have arisen from quite intelligible worldly motives. As one popular pamphlet put it, 'the Cardinal's ambition was to be pope, the archbishop strove to be patriarch'.[80] Such an analysis could be accepted by moderate and sophisticated people. Clarendon's friend and ally Viscount Falkland was careful to avoid support for old-fashioned puritan scruples, but thought that 'some have evidently laboured to bring in an English, though not a Roman popery. I mean not only the outside and dress of it, but equally absolute a blind dependence of the people upon the clergy and of the clergy upon themselves, and have opposed the papacy beyond the sea, that they might settle one beyond the water.'[81] It is striking that these were *concessions* that prefaced a convinced defence of bishops. When even the church's supporters decided to endorse such hostile language, the puritans had clearly found a promising line of attack.

---

[78] Cornelius Burges, *The first sermon preached to the honourable House of Commons now assembled in parliament at their public fast Novemb. 17 1640* (1641), sig. A3v–4, 56–7.
[79] Nathaniel Fiennes, *A speech of the honourable Nathanael Fiennes . . . in answere to the third speech of the Lord George Digby* (1641), 9.
[80] *A true description, or rather a parallel between Cardinall Wolsey, arch-bishop of York and William Laud arch-bishop of Canterbury* (1641), 7.
[81] Viscount Falkland, *A speech made to the House of Commons concerning episcopacy* (1641), 7.

IV

We are now in a position to speak about the nature of the crisis that led to a war between crown and parliament. It seems worth stressing, at the start, that disagreements on this complex question are not, on the whole, concerned with points of fact, but with the motives that inspired well-documented actions. It is common ground that when the Long Parliament met the English were astonishingly united in opposition to their government. In November 1640, virtually no one seriously defended the secular policies symbolised by Ship Money and personified by Thomas Wentworth, earl of Strafford, or the religious policies symbolised by the practice of bowing to the Altar and personified by archbishop William Laud. Scholars are also generally agreed that the first open threat to unity was the Root and Branch petition against episcopacy delivered in December 1640, but not discussed in parliament till 12 February.

Unfortunately, the divisions that the Petition caused are not at all straightforward to interpret. Not all its supporters were culturally godly; it cannot be assumed, though, that a non-godly member who favoured Root and Branch was broadly 'secular' in motivation. The body of the Petition was cleverly drafted as an attack on *lordly* prelacy, and there were certainly episcopalians who disapproved of bishops who wielded secular power. It does seem clear, however, that the *etcetera* oath had given a new legitimacy to puritan proposals. Though the petitioners themselves were clearly puritan (the schedule of complaints annexed was an old-fashioned godly document), the starting point of the Petition proper was actually an erastian statement:

That whereas the government of archbishops and lord bishops, deans and archdeacons, etc., with their courts and ministrations in them, have proved prejudicial and very dangerous both to the church and commonwealth, they themselves having formerly held, that they have their jurisdiction or authority of human authority, till of these later times, being further pressed about the unlawfulness, that they have claimed their calling immediately from the Lord Jesus Christ, which is against the laws of this kingdom, and derogatory to his Majesty and his state royal.[82]

In consequence, they requested that 'the said government, with all its dependencies, roots and branches, may be abolished, and all laws in their behalf made void and the government according to God's word may be rightly placed among us'. It was clear that they had called for the destruction of the church's apparatus of deans, chapters, and church courts; it was not,

[82] Kenyon, *Stuart constitution*, 154.

however, obvious that 'government according to God's word' was necessarily incompatible with some kind of reduced episcopacy. This probably explains the curious fact that the petition was brought in by the episcopalian MP Sir Edward Dering, who later plausibly explained that he did so 'to expedite the progress of another bill against the secular jurisdiction of the bishops'.[83]

Support for Root and Branch was not, then, necessarily a sign of a commitment to ultra-Protestant theology. Conversely, opposition to the measure was typically less an expression of devotion to the bishops than of a hostile attitude to cultural godliness, especially when it could be seen as crypto-democratic. From one possible perspective, the popular enthusiasm for further Reformation could be a reason for resisting it; thus Edmund Waller struck a sensitive nerve when he said that 'I look upon episcopacy as a counter-scarf, or outwork, which if it shall be taken by this assault of the people, and withal this mystery once revealed, that we must deny them nothing when they ask it thus in troops . . . we may have as hard a task to defend our propriety.'[84] Anxieties of this general type proved valuable allies for Charles; one mark of the great cultural success of England's conservative-minded reformation is that the godly gained and kept a radical reputation when they had done so little to deserve it.

What makes the power of such fears particularly striking is that the members of the House of Commons continued to agree on other issues, including the need for Charles's minister, the earl of Strafford, to be found guilty of committing treason. The law involved in Strafford's trial was somewhat intricate, in part because so much of the feeling against him rested upon his conduct in his time in Ireland, but two conclusions can be drawn from a confusing story. One is that the focus of loyalty was shifting. It was widely agreed that attacks upon laws could be treason, if only because laws supplied 'the very subsistence of kings'.[85] It could indeed be said without much fear of contradiction that 'treason against the person of a prince is high treason . . . but it falls short of this treason against the state'.[86]

The other is that proceedings against Strafford depended on a flexible conception of the law and willingness to emphasise the Houses' court-like status. It is well known that the Commons switched their tactics,

---

[83] *A collection of speeches made by Sir Edward Dering* (1642), 3.
[84] Edmund Waller, *A speech made by Master Waller Esquire in the honorable House of Commons, concerning episcopacie* (1641), 4.
[85] *In answer to the earle of Straford's conclusion* (1641), 1.
[86] *Mr Maynards speech before both Houses in parliament* (1641), 3.

moving from a conventional impeachment towards the more direct approach involved in an act of attainder. But though the earl had mounted a formidable defence of his behaviour, the shift in approach was probably not caused by an access of doubt that he was in a technical sense guilty. The Commons explanation of what was happening (delivered, as it happens, by Oliver St John) insisted that 'the legislative power is not used against my lord of Strafford in the bill; it's only the jurisdiction of the parliament'.[87] This actually made life more difficult for any Commons member with conscientious qualms; it involved their House assuming shared responsibility for an adjudicative course of action. There was little attempt, however, to challenge their adoption of this function. When Lord George Digby tried to rescue Strafford, he admitted that even the Commons had 'a double power of life and death by bill, a judicial power and a legislative', but complained that the two powers were being conflated.[88]

In the end, the matter hinged on a technical question. The declaratory statute of 25 Edward III, the basis of the English law of treason, included a clause that provided 'that because many other like cases of treason might fall out which are not there declared, therefore it is enacted, That if any such case come before the judges, they shall not proceed to judgement till the case be declared in parliament'. Interpretation of this clause provided a sensitive index of legal attitudes. To Strafford's opponents, it seemed obvious that this residual parliamentary power was in itself a part of common law; a mechanism of this sort would be a necessary part of any legal system. As an answer to Digby explained

To deny unto that representative body the high court of the kingdom a liberty to do anything not unjust in itself (though not as yet legally declared to be just) for the preservation of that greater body it represents, when according the sincere and dispassionate judgement of prudence and policy, it cannot be sufficiently secured by laws already made, is neither agreeable to the law of nature, nor of the land, nor of God.[89]

The point seemed clear to anyone whose view of common law prioritised the thought that law was reason above the thought that reason is expressed in rigid rules. However, a number of qualified observers insisted that the crucial clause was merely a proviso, an element of the statute that had been subsequently superseded. They included Robert Holborne, and also,

[87] Oliver St John, *An argument of law concerning the bill of attainder of high-treason of Thomas earle of Strafford* (1641), 69.
[88] Sir George Digby, *The lord George Digby his last speech against the earle of Strafford* (1641), 11.
[89] *An answer to the Lord Digbies speech in the House of Commons* (1641), 17.

more remarkably, the future parliamentarian John Selden, a man who is unlikely to have been motivated by personal sympathy with the accused.[90] Their relatively positivist view of common law, a picture of the system as a list of determinate rules forever established by popular consent, would subsequently play a significant part in forming constitutional royalism.

But in spite of the existence of these doubts, the list of fifty-nine 'Straffordians' who voted against the attainder excluded Sir John Colepeper, Edward Hyde, Viscount Falkland, and numerous other future royalists. Colepeper was a leading advocate of the decision to proceed by statute.[91] Hyde and Falkland seem to have felt no great discomfort at the idea that parliament could *judge* the common law. Hyde was quite ready to condemn the judges on the grounds that '[impositions] had long been debated in parliament undetermined and [were] therefore not within the conusance of an inferior court'.[92] Falkland not only intervened against the earl of Strafford, but professed his belief in 'parliamentary treason' on a completely different occasion. When he was presenting the charges against Lord Keeper Finch, the man most widely blamed for Ship Money, he held that an attack upon the fundamental laws was treason in the fullest possible sense:

The highest kind and in the highest degree of parliamentary treason . . . a treason as well against the king as against the kingdom, for whatsoever is against the whole is undoubtedly against the head, which takes from his Majesty the ground of his rule, the laws (for if foundations be destroyed, the pinnacles are most endangered), which takes from his Majesty the principal honour of his rule, the ruling over free men.[93]

This was roughly the theory of treason defended by John Pym.[94]

Over the next few months, these people nonetheless emerged as a distinct episcopalian party that was ready to co-operate with Charles. In the later months of 1641, the king and these new allies were steadily gaining ground on his opponents, not least because he could rely upon the House of Lords. While the bishops were present and voting, the royal position seemed to be secure, especially after he filled four vacant sees with academic 'Calvinist' conformists. Most temporal peers were probably indifferent or hostile to these colleagues, but they were unwilling to vote for the prelates' removal for fear of hastening more radical changes. The earl of Northumberland

[90] *A briefe and perfect relation of the answeres and replies of Thomas earle of Strafford* (1647), 68.
[91] Russell, *Fall*, 288.
[92] Edward Hyde, *Mr Edward Hyde's speech at a conference between the two Houses* (1641), 7–8.
[93] *The speech or declaration of the Lord Falkland to the Lords of the Upper House* (1641), 7.
[94] Compare *The speech or declaration of John Pym Esquire after the recapitulation or summing up of the charge of high-treason against Thomas earle of Strafford* (1641).

remarked that the passing of Bishops' Exclusion was 'very doubtful, unless some assurance be given that the voting out of the function is not afterwards intended'.[95] Given this situation, the king would have had every prospect of outmanoeuvring his enemies but for the sudden outbreak, in October, of a rebellion in Ireland, an event that might have been designed to restore parliamentary cohesion on the basis of anxieties about a popish plot. But horror at this evidence of Catholic machinations was insufficient to erase the growing bitterness. It did not, for example, prevent resistance to the Grand Remonstrance, an authoritative statement (the term did not invariably connote a mere complaint) of all the injuries endured since 1625. This was a powerful account of a conspiracy theory that traced all possible ills to popery, but it proved to be exceptionally divisive and passed through the House (on 22 November) by a majority of just eleven. No one supposed that such a document would be accepted by the peers and bishops.

At the end of the year, then, Charles had every reason for a recovered long-term optimism. While he controlled the House of Lords, there was little that his enemies could do; what was more, the attempts of hostile crowds to intimidate the peers were liable to alienate conservative opinion. Unfortunately for the royal cause, the bishops then made a political mistake that totally destroyed the crown's position. After a couple of days in which the mob had hindered them from reaching parliament, they sent a letter asking that the votes passed in their 'forced and violent' absence should be struck down as being 'null and void'. The Lords chose to regard this as a breach of privilege, and the House of Commons sent them to the Tower with a view to prosecuting them for treason. This remarkable over-reaction says much about the power of erastian attitudes. The bishops who protested were not the hated Laudian inner circle; most of them would conventionally be classed as 'Calvinists', and the protestation was drafted by Laud's great enemy John Williams. They had explicitly disclaimed the view that valid parliamentary proceedings required an episcopal presence.[96] Yet their abandonment by the secular peers 'seems to have been due to a change of heart, rather than to differential absence';[97] it was a visceral response to clerical claims to secular influence.

This was a pivotal moment. The sudden loss of royal control over the Upper House was probably the trigger of an attempted coup: the king's descent on Westminster, on 4 January, accompanied by several hundred well-armed cavaliers, to arrest five members on a charge of treason. Within

[95] Russell, *Fall*, 424.
[96] John Hacket, *Scrinia reserata: a monument erected to the great deservings of John Williams* (1691), 557.
[97] Russell, *Fall*, 443.

a week of failing in this mission, the king had departed from London, apparently in fear for his family's safety. From that point on, the Houses had reason to believe that he intended, if he could, to get his way by military action. But this cluster of unnecessary misjudgements was more than an unlucky accident; it had revealed a fact about the shape of politics. Though defence of the religious *status quo* was potentially extremely popular, defence of the church's secular power was not. On 5 February, some nobles who were otherwise habitual crown supporters must have voted for the Bishops' Exclusion Bill to which the king assented nine days later.[98] In doing so, he had finally freed his cause from the dead weight of Laudian clericalism.

v

The main conclusion to be drawn from this admittedly quite tangled story has to do with the sheer power of legal values. The first nine months of the Long Parliament witnessed the final victory of English common law as the criterion of authority: a constitutionalist revolution. Commitment to the common law united future members of both sides; the episcopalian 'party' (as their critics began to call them) were if anything disproportionately active in the extensive programme of secular reform completed in the summer months of 1641. This legislation had included a Triennial Act, allowing parliament to meet whether or not the king had summoned it, an act declaring Ship Money illegal, and statutes that completely or effectively abolished such non-common law institutions as Star Chamber, the court of Requests, the councils of the North and of the Marches, the court of High Commission, and the whole of the episcopal court system. As scholars who have examined the actual workings of these institutions have on the whole strongly defended their basic usefulness, their downfall is a symptom of the pervasiveness of some tyrannical presuppositions.

Under these circumstances, the king's ability to find a party depended on his willingness to redescribe his role. But once he had dismantled the Tudor monarchy, he found himself in a transformed position. His evident devotion to the church made him the natural leader of episcopalians; his newly legalistic rhetoric enabled him to paint himself as the defender of existing law against unprecedented innovations. These accurate perceptions have been the intellectual foundation of much revisionist analysis, especially when it has stressed the salience of the religious issues; after all, if Charles had settled the constitutional questions, the nature of English religion was

[98] Ibid., 471, 475.

all that there was left to fight about. As Conrad Russell put it, 'Charles, with whatever reluctance, decided to conciliate men . . . who put legal issues first, when he chose not to conciliate men like Pym or Sir Robert Harley, who put religious issues first.'[99]

There is much to be said for this theory, which has, indeed, to some extent, been strengthened by the material presented here. If the narrative just offered is well founded, the bishops were unpopular while they appeared to threaten legal order, but as the illusory threat to law receded, religious differences reappeared. These divisions were sufficiently deep-seated to survive the trauma of the Irish insurrection. Moreover, abundant evidence suggests that when the two parties attempted to describe their enemies, it was religious stereotypes they grasped for: parliamentarians were really Brownists, while royalists were Jesuits and papists.[100] There is nothing absurd in Anthony Fletcher's suggestion that 'two groups of men became the prisoners of competing myths that fed on one another'.[101]

The limitation of this whole tradition is not so much its stress upon religion as the self-confidence with which it isolates 'religious' motivation. The objection to this confidence is not that religious ideas were unimportant, but that attitudes were relatively fluid, and that more 'secular' considerations could shape and divert 'religious' loyalties. In a theistic culture that had been shaped by Protestant-humanist efforts to moralise and sacralise social relations, the secular–religious distinction was in any case quite difficult to draw. Outside the ranks of the culturally godly, virtually nobody could boast of a preformed political position, and few can have experienced impulses that pointed in a uniform direction. It was possible, though probably very unusual, to be a thoroughgoing nonconformist for whom the duty to obey the king took precedence over suspicion of his motives.[102] It may have been quite common to be a former patron of godly ministers whose sympathy with conscience and dislike of lordly bishops was trumped by loyal feelings or a fear of anarchy.[103]

Moreover, reverence for the law was strong enough to over-ride distaste for puritans. The governor of Hull, Sir John Hotham, whose brave refusal to admit the king was the first act of military defiance, was 'manly for the defence of the liberty of the subject and privilege of parliament, but not at all for their new opinions in church government'.[104] Hotham was not

[99] Ibid., 527.   [100] Ibid., 528.
[101] Anthony Fletcher, *The outbreak of the English civil war* (1981), 415.
[102] Edward Symmons, *A loyall subjects beliefe* (Oxford, 1643), Ep. Ded.
[103] *Sir George Sondes his plain narrative* (1655), 19–20.
[104] *The diary of Sir Henry Slingsby*, ed. Daniel Parsons (London, 1836), 92.

unique. Out of 90 MPs identified by Russell as being positively opposed to 'further reformation', 10 nonetheless supported parliament.[105] These people were not just deluded. The Nineteen Propositions, the final parliamentarian demands, asked only 'that such a reformation be made of the church government and liturgy as both Houses of Parliament shall advise; wherein they intend to have consultation with divines'.[106] It is true that after the royalists withdrew, most of the Commons, from whatever motive, were ready to vote for further reformation, but 'the strength of true godliness in the Lords was very small',[107] and it was reasonable to hope that a representative body of non-Laudian divines would favour a set liturgy and even some form of reduced episcopacy. In the event, the Westminster Assembly was boycotted by moderate conformists, but many of those who attended were undecided on church government, and the list of those originally invited included men of known episcopalian convictions.[108] The leading New England divines, the heirs of the Elizabethan radical tradition, saw little point in crossing the Atlantic 'to agree', as one of them put it, 'with three men'.[109]

Thus parliamentarianism was more than simply a 'religious' cause. The exaggerated stress upon the church that dominates much recent scholarship is really founded on a false assumption. The secular-minded historian Thomas May gave an acute account of the whole process:

That frequent naming of religion, as if it were the only quarrel, hath caused a great mistake of the question in some, by reason of ignorance, in others, of subtlety; whilst they wilfully mistake, to abuse the parliament's cause, writing whole volumes in a wrong stated case; as, instead of disputing whether the parliament of England lawfully assembled, where the king virtually is, may by arms defend the religion established by the same power, together with the laws and liberties of the nation, against delinquents, detaining with them the king's seduced person: they make it the question, whether subjects, taken in a general notion, may make war against their king for religion's sake.[110]

The lasting victory won by royal controversialists has been the belief that the Houses had no legal case at all when they employed an 'ordinance' to find themselves an army. The standard compilation of relevant sources states that 'on any academic judgement, there can be no doubt that the

---

[105] Russell, *Causes*, 224–6.   [106] Kenyon, *Stuart constitution*, 224.   [107] Russell, *Fall*, 473.
[108] R. S. Paul, *The assembly of the Lord* (Edinburgh, 1985), 90–1, 106–10, 546–53.
[109] Stephen Foster, *The long argument: English Puritanism and the shaping of New England culture, 1570–1700* (Chapel Hill, 1991), 169.
[110] Thomas May, *The history of the parliament of England which began November the 3 1640* (1647), 117–18.

King had won this legal and constitutional debate'.[111] But to contemporary common lawyers, this claim was very far from obvious; the two most senior lawyers with the king, Lord Keeper Littleton and Chief Justice Bankes, both took the view the ordinance was arguably legal.[112] The probable reason they did so was that no legislation was involved; the ordinance was simply an administrative expedient in an unprecedented situation. Amongst other things, it had no legal sanction; defaulters were 'to answer their neglect and contempt to the Lords and Commons in a parliamentary way and not otherwise'.[113] Like any such unprecedented measure, it drew whatever authority it had from omnicompetent fundamental laws.

The parliamentarians believed that parliament (without the king) had power to interpret those laws. On 15 March, the Houses had both voted 'that the kingdom hath been of late and still is in so evident and imminent danger, both from enemies abroad and a popish and discontented party at home; that there is an urgent and inevitable necessity of putting his Majesty's subjects into a posture of defence'.[114] After noting that the king had declined to assent, they went on to resolve 'that in this case of extreme danger, and of his Majesty's refusal, the ordinance agreed on by both Houses for the Militia, doth oblige the people and ought to be obeyed by the fundamental laws of this kingdom'.[115] The ultimate basis of their whole position was thus not legislative sovereignty, but an adjudicative supremacy. As another vote the following day explained,

When the Lords and Commons in parliament which is the supreme court of judicature in the kingdom nation shall declare what the laws of the land is, to have this not only questioned and controverted, but contradicted, and a command that it should not be obeyed, is a high breach of the privilege of parliament.[116]

Perhaps the clearest statement of their consistent view was a further declaration of 19 May:

if the question be whether that be law which the Lords and Commons have once declared to be so, who shall be the judge? Not his Majesty, for the king judgeth not of matters of law but by his courts, and his courts, though sitting by his authority, expect not his assent in matters of law; not any other courts, for they cannot judge in that case because they are inferior: no appeal lying to them from parliament, the judgement whereof is in the eye of the law, the king's judgement in his highest court, though the king in his person be neither present nor assenting thereunto.[117]

---

[111] Kenyon, *Stuart constitution*, 183.
[112] George Bankes, *The story of Corfe Castle* (1853), 135; *Lords Journal*, v 134.
[113] Gardiner, *Constitutional documents*, 247.   [114] Edward Husbands, *An exact collection* (1643), 112.
[115] Ibid., 112.   [116] Ibid., 114.   [117] Ibid., 206–7.

Given the importance of the claim that parliament, in one capacity, effectively excluded the king's person, it was not at all surprising that the most famous of the king's replies, *The Answer to the Nineteen Propositions*, made the otherwise inexplicable concession that monarchy was one of the three estates. This startlingly sudden revival of an obsolete idea was a powerful way of asserting that while King, Lords, and Commons were functionally differentiated, the monarch had just the same status as the Houses in fully parliamentary proceedings. Thus the matters described by the two Houses as 'fit to be transacted only in parliament' were either no concern of theirs at all or else the proper object of a tripartite legislative action. 'What,' asked the *Answer*

concerns more the public, and is more (indeed) proper for the High Court of Parliament than the making of laws? Which not only ought there to be transacted, but can be transacted nowhere else; but then you must admit Us to be a part of the parliament.[118]

It was also not surprising that parliamentarian talk of emergency powers reminded every royalist of an analogy. The slogan 'Ship Money again'[119] both emphasised the king's new-found commitment to the law and redescribed his enemies as lawless.

Even a few of parliament's supporters accepted that the parallel was just. Philip Hunton's *A treatise of monarchie* (1643) would ask why mainstream parliamentarians were ready 'to give all that to the two Houses which ere while they would not suffer when the judges in the case of Ship Money had given it to the king'.[120] He was inspired by his doubts to develop a new theory of co-ordinate sovereignty, according to which disagreements between the three estates could only be resolved by violence. Hunton has been admired by modern scholars, partly because his pamphlet is a miracle of lucid exposition, but mainly because the theory he presents is recognisably concerned with ultimate control of legislation. His willingness to make this kind of case was certainly an interesting straw in the wind; it suggests that the kind of radical Cokean theory expressed in St John's argument for Hampden was losing ground to attitudes much closer to his colleague Robert Holborne's.

No doubt the political crisis helped concentrate the mind by showing that Cokean theory could lead to unforeseen conclusions. But this should not obscure the fact that Cokean ideas were still widely accepted. To royalists,

---

[118] Ibid., 317.   [119] *An answer to a printed book intituled Observations* (1642), 43.
[120] Philip Hunton, *A treatise of monarchie* (1643), 70.

the common law was basically a list of determinate rules; to parliamentarians, by contrast, it was both richer and less well-defined, something closer to
a body of resources implicit in the national experience. The parliamentarians appealed to 'fundamental laws', which royalists could describe as 'laws
in the clouds . . . which no men ever read or heard of but yourselves'.[121] The
royalists preferred to stress 'known laws', a phrase that became so successful that they could be accused of having 'invented and used a new name
for our laws, calling them "known laws".'[122] When royalists appealed to
precedent, the parliamentarians emphasised that the Houses were not just
a court but a 'court of law and counsel', ideally equipped to cope with an
emergency[123] it was of course characteristic of parliamentarianism that it
conflated the idea of counsel with that of strictly legal jurisdiction. Both
sides could plausibly lay claim, it followed, to the legitimacy derived from
the support of legal institutions.

The point of reconstructing this ambiguity is not to show that parliament's case was evidently superior, but only that its arguments were a
development of earlier constitutionalist thinking. The continuities can be
traced through the successive works of Henry Parker, the best-known of
the Houses' propagandists. The first of these, *The case of Ship Mony* (1640),
had followed St John's argument in conceding that 'rather than a nation
should perish anything shall be held necessary and legal by necessity'.[124]
It also granted that the king was 'supreme and consequently sole judge in
all cases', though not 'as to the exercise and restraint of judgement'.[125] The
object of *The case of Ship Mony* was simply to prove that the king and his
private advisers were less equipped than parliament to judge necessity. As
'national laws are made by consent of prince and people both, and so cannot
be conceived to be prejudicial to either side', the prince alone should never
be permitted to judge in his own cause.[126] Instead, it should be presupposed
that

> there is more favour due to the liberty of the subject than to the prerogative of the
> king, since the one is ordained only for the preservation of the other; and then to
> solve these knots our dispute must be what prerogative the people's good and profit
> will bear, not what liberty the king's absoluteness or prerogative may admit.[127]

This argument foreshadowed the case that Parker made in his famous
Observations on some of his Majesty's late answers and expresses (1642). Again,

---

[121] William Cavendish, earl of Newcastle, *A declaration of the right honourable the earle of Newcastle his
excellency &c. in answer of six groundless aspersions* (1643), 3.
[122] *Knowne lawes* (1643), 1.   [123] Husbands, *Collection*, 304.
[124] Henry Parker, *The case of Ship Mony briefly discoursed* (1640), 7.
[125] Ibid., 20.   [126] Ibid., 5.   [127] Ibid., 4–5.

the central line of thought was really hermeneutic. Given that 'all rule is but fiduciary', it followed that 'we must not think it can stand with the intent of any trust that necessary defence should be barred and natural preservation denied to any people'.[128] Parker insisted, above all, upon a single natural, but still *legal*, principle:

the transcendent *acme* of all politics . . . the paramount law that shall give law to all human laws whatsoever, and that is *salus populi*. The law of prerogative itself, it is subservient to this law, and were it not conducing thereunto, it were not necessary nor expedient.[129]

This principle has tended to be read by modern scholars as a decisive step away from common law ideas. From a biographical standpoint, there may be something to be said for this interpretation; Parker was free with language about parliament's 'absolute' power.[130] But what is most important, for present purposes, is that his argument developed smoothly out of a constitutionalist position.

Readers still sceptical about the naturalness of this train of thought are referred to the private letters of Sir Cheney Culpeper (a cousin of the royalist Sir John), who was a man with no direct political involvement. During the second winter of the war, Culpeper jotted down some principles ('a taste in matters of law which I have *ex tempore* set down') that showed he had internalised the case for parliament. The tone was set by the first three:

1. Whether the law be not the only rule as well to the king's prerogative as to the subject's liberty 2. Whether the judicial judgement of the legally constituted courts be not the only binding rule to which all parties are to submit for their knowledge of or their obedience to the law 3. Whether a judicial declaration of law in any inferior court of justice (though perhaps erroneous, as in the case of Ship Money) be not (by all parties that acknowledge themselves subject to the law) to be submitted to till legally reversed by the judgement of the same or some superior legally constituted court.[131]

These principles would all have been accepted by constitutionalist royalists (unless they rejected the evident implication that the decision in *R. v. Hampden* made it immoral to refuse to pay their Ship Money). What made Culpeper a parliamentarian was his belief that parliament (without the king)

---

[128] [Henry Parker], *Observations on some of his Majesty's late answers and expresses*, the second edition corrected (1642), 20.

[129] Ibid., 3.

[130] Michael Mendle, *Henry Parker and the English civil war: the political thought of the public's 'privado'* (Cambridge, 1995), 87–8.

[131] 'The letters of Sir Cheney Culpeper, 1641–57', ed. M. J. Braddick and Mark Greengrass in *Camden Miscellany* 33, Camden Society 5th series 7 (1996), 189–90.

enjoyed a court-like status. In the next question that he chose to frame, he broke the link connecting that court's authority with the professional expertise of judges:

4. Whether this great trust and power of dispensing law and justice be reposed in the judges as either infallible or incorruptible and not rather grounded (as in all voluntary arbitrements) upon these two principles: (i) general consent (ii) ut sit finis litium [that there may be an end to law-suits].[132]

Culpeper had taken the same route as Parker towards a justification of parliament's actions. Unlike Parker, however, he left no room for doubt that his ideas were strictly speaking legal. He vigorously disapproved of 'a most pestilent doctrine of the people's denying active or passive obedience to the civil magistrate upon a supposition of a remote possibility of the magistrates abusing their power to the ruin of a people in case they had not that help left them'.[133] But this commitment to the rule of law was not at all a mark of moderation; it was the intellectual foundation on which he based a radically innovative position. He disapproved, for instance, of the monarch's 'negative voice', that is, his right to veto legislation. In December 1644, he asked

if then this supreme [judicatory] shall judge either concerning the crown itself as it hath often done or against the negative voice, what earthly legal power can recall the judgement, and from this ground I have often thought that the supreme power and legislative power are inseparable.[134]

In Culpeper's mind, a picture of the state as, in its essence, a judicial structure had in effect absorbed the personal role of monarchy.

The argument could indeed be taken further. When Charles was executed, the Rump adjusted with surprising ease to its completely novel situation. Less than a fortnight later, the assize judge Serjeant Thorpe told the Yorkshire grand jury that kingship was essentially a trust, created by the people for the common benefit, which could legitimately be revoked as soon as kings 'did alter the peoples *rempublicam* into the governor's *rem privatam*'.[135] But abolition of the kingly office (and of that other obstacle, the Lords) required no further changes in the constitutional framework. As Thorpe explained, the 'name and word king' was 'frequently used to set forth the public interest of the people; so we call it the king's peace, the king's coin, the king's highway and the like'.[136] This was the view that

---

[132] Ibid., 189.   [133] Ibid., 197.   [134] Ibid., 205.
[135] *Serjeant Thorpe, judge of assize for the northern circuit, his charge* (York, 1649), 7.
[136] Ibid., 15.

underlay the 'Act abolishing the kingly office', which modestly provided that 'the office of a king in this nation shall not hereafter reside in, or be exercised by, any one single person'.[137] Where the term 'king' had previously been used in legal documents and court proceedings, the commonwealth chose to substitute 'the keepers of the liberties of England', a term that captured their ideas about the monarch's function. The elaborate declaration in which they justified their kingless state assured the reader that the courts were largely unaffected, 'the name of king being used in them for form only'.[138] Coke might have been appalled at this conclusion, but there was a respectable case for saying that they had pursued the logic of his thinking.

VI

There is a striking irony in these developments. If anything made plausible high claims for common law, it was the Cokean idea of *artificial* reason. But when the omnicompetence of sages of the law came to be exercised by parliament, this way of thinking ceased to have much purchase. The High Court of parliament's claim to have discerned the common good was plainly not dependent on its learning, but rather on what might be called its microcosmic or pictorial status: its claim to be a faithful *representation* of the nation, the 'representative body [as opposed to the head] of the kingdom', and therefore to be well equipped to register the public interest.

This laid the Houses open to two counter-arguments. The first, which gained increasing force with every month that passed, was to question whether those at Westminster were genuinely representative. Royalist propagandists would soon be making points about Old Sarum that furnished the staples of all such agitation the whole way down to 1832.[139] The second counter-argument was still more damaging. It pointed out that the considerations by which the Houses justified ignoring the king's views had inconvenient further implications. The *Answer to the nineteen propositions* had gloomily predicted that 'the second estate [the Lords] would in all probability follow the fate of the first'.[140] The clearest of numerous royalist variations on this theme pointed out that

if the Commons shall adjudge that the Militia for repelling danger ought to be put into such a way as dislikes the king and major part of the Lords . . . yet ought

---

[137] Kenyon, *Stuart constitution*, 306.
[138] *A declaration of the parliament of England, expressing the grounds of their late proceedings* (1649), 24.
[139] *A view of a printed book intituled Observations upon his Majesties late answers and expresses* (Oxford 1642/3), sig. D2.
[140] Husbands, *Collection*, 322.

the House of Commons being virtually the whole kingdom to be obeyed by the people against the will and command of king and Lords, and against the desire of the minor part (perhaps by two votes) in the House of Commons.[141]

The logic could be indeed taken further:

The Lords vote in respect of their baronies . . . the Commons vote in right of their electors whom they represent, at least nine parts of the kingdom neither do or may vote in their election . . . power being (you say) nothing else but that might and vigour which a society of men contains in itself, why should the might and vigour of these being far the major part, be overmastered and concluded by the votes of those that are deputed by a minor number of the people?[142]

These claims were not just the dark fantasies of a besieged authoritarian movement; they registered an obvious implication of what might be called the logic of *epieikeia*, the habit of construing legal rules in the light of hypothetical intentions. The Leveller John Lilburne, for instance, made frequent reference to a compilation – Edward Husbands' comprehensive *Exact collection* (1643) – of messages passed between king and parliament. He was particularly struck by a brief pamphlet called *A question answered: How laws are to be understood, and obedience yielded* (April 1642), a work that Husbands reproduced because the king complained about its message. *A question*'s anonymous author resorted to Plowden's ideas to explain that

There is in laws an equitable and a legal sense . . . So that when there is certain appearance or grounded suspicion, that the letter of the law shall be improved against the equity of it (that is, the public good, whether of the body real or representative) then the commander going against its equity, gives liberty to the commanded to refuse obedience to the letter: for the law taken abstract from its original reason and end is made a shell without a kernel, a shadow without a substance, and a body without a soul.[143]

From 1645 onwards, Lilburne repeatedly invoked this passage to attack the Houses' use of the discretionary power derived from the idea of 'privilege'.

'It cannot be imagined', he remarked, 'that ever the people would be so sottish as to give such a power to those whom they would choose their servants, for this were to give them a power to provide for their woe, but not for their weal'.[144] It was only a small further step to such assertions as that (in Richard Overton's words) 'the equity of the law is superior to the letter' and that

---

[141] *View of a printed book*, 22.   [142] Ibid., sig. D2 (n.p.).   [143] Husbands, *Collection*, 150.
[144] [John Lilburne], *England's birth-right justified against all arbitrary usurpation, whether regall or parliamentary* (1645), 4 (*A question* is alluded to at ibid., 2.)

all authority is fundamentally seated in the office and but ministerially in the persons; therefore the persons in their ministrations degenerating from safety to tyranny, their authority ceaseth, which is only to be found in the fundamental original, rise, and situation thereof which is the people the body represented.[145]

The thinking of the Levellers falls outside this chapter's scope. It does seem worth noting, however, that it is characteristic of all the main Leveller writers that they could never quite decide if they were rejecting the law as a whole or if they were appealing to its spirit. No puritan had to be told, least of all by a lawyer, that while the letter killeth, the spirit giveth life, but Leveller oscillations between the rights of man and the peculiar rights of Englishmen were eased by ambiguities within the lawyers' thinking. Moreover, it seems striking that even a man like Overton chose to assert the dignity of individuals by the metaphor of a 'self propriety'.[146] The great Marxist C. B. Macpherson notoriously believed that Overton was letting slip assumptions that underpinned the Levellers' beliefs:[147] like the much deeper thinkers Hobbes and Locke, he was articulating a view of human nature formed (and required) by a market order. Though there are difficulties with Macpherson's theory (the existence, for example, of market-dominated polities that make no use of such a metaphor), the well-aimed attacks of its critics have never quite extinguished its attractions. But the perspective opened by this book permits a better reading of Macpherson's evidence. Overton's phrase can now be seen as a slight variant on an already popular manoeuvre: if all political claims were really claims at common law, then every kind of liberty was an 'inheritance'.

On the sectarian fringes, then, the idea that law was reason could give legitimacy to positions that were too democratic to be acceptable; this was doubtless a contributory cause of the post-Restoration disappearance of Coke's variety of legal theory. But in more mainstream politics the effect of veneration for the law's deliverances was paralysingly conservative. The pre-war parliamentarian proposals assembled in the Nineteen Propositions of 1642 involved few fundamental innovations; the Propositions were a scheme to neutralise the monarch by giving parliament control of councillors and officers of state. The idea would have been perfectly familiar to any reader of Sir Robert Cotton's *A short view of the long life and raign of Henry the third*. A large majority of MPs stayed loyal to this programme; the parliamentarian conviction that the problem lay with Charles, not with

---

[145] *Leveller manifestoes of the puritan revolution*, ed. D. M. Wolfe (1944), 162–3.   [146] Ibid., 163.
[147] C. B. Macpherson, *The political theory of possessive individualism: Hobbes to Locke* (Oxford, 1962), 139–41.

his office, was obvious from the terms that he was offered when he was comprehensively defeated. These furnish a conclusive demonstration that Lords and Commons did not think they had, or ought to have, control over English military forces or an inherent legislative power. The Houses' 1646 Newcastle Propositions demanded that Charles govern through a parliamentarian council and that he *give assent* to a number of laws, including one that granted them control of the militia. But after only twenty years, the latter power – the power over which the civil war was fought – was to return into the monarch's hands. The only exception to royal control of military forces was that 'in all cases wherein the Lords and Commons shall declare the safety of the kingdom to be concerned', the Houses were allowed to make arrangements or acts that would 'have the force and strength of an act or acts of parliament' whether or not the monarch had assented.[148] All that this really amounted to was royal confirmation that the Militia Ordinance had been legal. It left the monarch well equipped for any future crisis in which he retained the support of the majority of his lords.

While common law retained its grip on the imagination, the constitutional puzzle remained insoluble. It was unthinkable, for practical reasons, to allow the king capacity for independent action, but equally unthinkable, for theoretical ones, to cut the Gordian knot by deposition. Charles was arguably safer on his throne in 1648 than 1640; a party that had fought in the king's name and that protested its concern for his best interests was not in a position to destroy him. Virtually all the parliamentarian members of the traditional political class had further limited their future actions by the incautious promise – part of the Solemn League and Covenant of 1643 – 'to preserve and defend the king's Majesty's person and authority'.[149] Only the Army generals possessed the will to take decisive action, in part because their actions derived legitimacy from their perception of the will of God. The coup they eventually mounted, Pride's Purge, had a simple, illegal objective: its providentially validated mission was vengeance on 'that man of blood Charles Stuart'. But the Army had no real wish to govern by the sword, and power passed, if only by default, to that minority of Commons members who were prepared to acquiesce in the new kingless order.

There was no reason to expect that this residual body would wipe away the framework that made sense of politics. As we have seen, the Act abolishing the 'kingly office' had emphasised the dangers in entrusting so much power to 'any one single person'.[150] The elimination of this dangerous office was not a fundamental revolution but a reactionary expedient, which would

[148] Gardiner, *Documents*, 295–6.　　[149] Kenyon, *Stuart constitution*, 240–1.　　[150] Ibid., 306.

enable 'this nation (if God see it good), to return to its just and ancient right of being governed by its own representatives or national meetings in council, from time to time chosen and entrusted for that purpose by the people'.[151] 'The king' was replaced by 'the keepers' in legal documents, but there was no adjustment to the powers of government; the council controlling the monarch envisaged by the Nineteen Propositions was succeeded by a kingless Council of State, but the essential functions of the 'executive' (a word just entering the English language) were virtually completely unaffected. As the republican Sir Harry Vane was later to remark, 'the commonwealth would not put the executive power out of their hands. For this reason they set up those shadows, the keepers of the liberties of England, as an executive power to distinguish it from the legislative.'[152]

Vane's statement was completely accurate; the Rump did not abolish the English monarchy so much as temporarily relocate it. The experiment lasted for almost five years until the Instrument of Government of 1653 restored 'supreme legislative authority' to 'one person, and the people assembled in parliament'. The Instrument provided that 'all writs, process, commissions, patents, grants, and other things, which now run in the name and style of the keepers of liberties of England, by authority of parliament, shall run in the name and style of the lord protector'.[153] It also admittedly stated that parliament could over-ride this king-like figure's veto, but even the removal of the veto could be defended upon legal grounds.[154] In any case, the subsequent protectoral constitution, the Humble Petition and Advice of 1657, continued the process of creeping Restoration, reviving government by 'three estates' (the third was a nominated 'Other House'), and providing for monarchical government 'according to this Petition and Advice in all things therein contained, and in all other things according to the laws of these nations, and not otherwise'.[155]

One of the implications of this statement was the reversal of reforms to parliament itself. The Instrument of Government had abolished rotten boroughs and given additional seats to the populous counties; but the House of Commons of 1659 (the third and last protectoral parliament) reverted to its previous composition. Faced with a choice between the law and even the most defensible political adjustments, the English took what

---

[151] Ibid., 306.

[152] Thomas Burton, *The diary of Thomas Burton*, ed. J. T. Rudd, 4 vols. (1828), III, 179.

[153] Kenyon, *Stuart constitution*, 308.

[154] This was William Prynne's view in *The soveraigne power of parliaments and kingdomes, or the second part of the treachery and disloialty of papists to their soveraignes* (1643), 73–4 (copies of this work often have inconsistent pagination; this refers to George Thomason's copy: British Library E248 [2]).

[155] Kenyon, *Stuart constitution*, 325.

seemed to them the line of least resistance, 're-imposing the yoke so lately cast off', as a non-constitutionalist republican complained, 'that this pack etc. [the lawyers] may not alter the style and form of their writs'.[156]

VII

Considered as a part of English history, the triumph of the lawyers is, or ought to be, a fact on which we can achieve a certain distance; whether the narrative is made to end with St John's pyrrhic victory over Holborne, with Cromwell's effective surrender to the constitutionalists, or with the reassertion of Holborne's point of view in Clarendon's legalistic Restoration, it lends itself to treatment as a finished episode recounted, according to personal taste, as a false dawn or a cautionary tale. But there is in fact a moral to be drawn that is significantly more disturbing. When politics is absorbed within a positive law system, the methods and priorities of that system inevitably condition the substance as well as the language of political debate. A law whose primary purpose was the protection of 'inheritances' required that the objectives that politicians seek should be presented as a form of heritable possession.

Not every existing political aim could be accommodated in this fashion. The Protestant-humanist impulse to sacralise the state was largely concerned with encouraging the 'exercise of virtue', that is, with promoting the habits that constituted a good human being. The politics that triumphed with the lawyers had no inherent link with such objectives. 'Law' still, of course, meant many things, including the suppression of vice and maintenance of religion, but the concerns of common law were really narrower; if government was in essence a *common* law device, it was an instrument to secure a simple aggregation of purely private liberties and exclusions. The role that was attributed to individual rights was thus internal to the law as Coke and others came to understand it. Coke's theory soon ceased to be persuasive, but Anglo-Saxon rights-talk has persisted; the idea that rights should structure social order survived the professional practice within which that idea was presupposed. The first of numerous attempts to fill the gap created was the political theory of Locke's *Two treatises*.

---

[156] William Sprigge, *A modest plea for an equal commonwealth* (1659), 8.

Epilogue: the constitutionalism of John Locke

At the end of Locke's life, a clerical admirer took down the great philosopher's 'Extempore Advice' about the reading for a 'gentleman'. The guidance that Locke offered was interestingly shaped by social and political assumptions. A gentleman, he held, was a man

whose proper calling is the service of his country; and so is most properly concerned in moral, and political knowledge; and thus the studies which more immediately belong to his calling, are those which also treat of virtues and vices, of civil society, and the arts of government, and so will take in also law and history.[1]

To be a gentleman, in fact, was properly to have a public function, but Locke's conception of the role left space for literary composition; he held that 'the greatest part of [a gentleman's] business and usefulness in the world is by the influence of what he says or writes to others'.[2] The writing of *Two treatises* was thus a form of gentlemanly action. So too, perhaps, if rather less directly, was the detailed under-labouring of *An essay concerning human understanding*, a work whose title page ascribed its author the needless honorific 'John Locke, Gent.' But at all events, the subject that he knew as 'politics' was manifestly central to a gentleman's concerns.

When the 'Extempore Advice' came to discuss the topic, it started by distinguishing two largely independent enterprises: 'politics contains two parts very different the one from the other. The one containing the original of societies, and rise and extent of political power, the other, the art of governing men in society'. Within the former category, Locke mentioned 'the first book of Mr Hooker's *Ecclesiastical polity*', his own *Two Treatises*, and Pufendorf's '*De jure naturali et gentium*, which last is the best book of that kind'.[3] An earlier essay 'Some thoughts concerning education' had taken the same view of Pufendorf (whom he described as marginally better than Grotius), and stressed the importance of this kind of study: 'this general

[1] John Locke, *Political essays*, ed. Mark Goldie (Cambridge, 1997), 350.
[2] Ibid., 349.   [3] Ibid., 351–2.

part of law and history' consisted, he thought, in 'studies which a gentleman should not barely touch at, but constantly dwell upon, and never have done with'.[4] Such passages reveal that modern scholarship is right to see Locke's political thinking as at least analogous to Grotius's *De jure belli ac pacis* (1625) and Pufendorf's *De jure naturali* (1672); this is, no doubt, how Locke himself would have preferred his writings to be studied.

But exclusive concentration on the natural law tradition yields an unbalanced picture of his thinking; it neglects the other part of 'politics' discussed in the 'Extempore Advice'. This was 'the art of government, that I think is best to be learned by experience and history, especially that of a man's own country'. As might have been expected, Locke's own historical opinions were shaped by his political commitments; thus he treated the *Modus tenendi parliamentum* (a description of the Saxon parliament treated with reverence by Sir Edward Coke but shown to be a forgery by John Selden) as a significant authority.[5] His personal specialisation in the 'general part of law and history' was perfectly consistent with acceptance of the most vulgar Whig accounts of England.

One historical work that he favoured has a special interest. This was John Sadler's pamphlet *Rights of the kingdom; or, customs of our ancestors* (1649), in which, Locke thought, '[a gentleman] will find the ancient constitution of the government of England'.[6] His choice of guide was telling, because Sadler's little book was an attempt to justify King Charles's execution. It set out to do so, however, in a strictly constitutionalist fashion. As Sadler noted at the start,

> it may seem a short work, and soon said: when the king breaks his trust, the parliament must judge him. And when the Lords refuse, then the Commons might and must, because it was necessity. But I am loth to hide myself in a dark chaos. I had rather see it cleared in the open sun. For if necessity be not rightly stated and well limited, I know not how it may [not] prevail against our greatest rights, and strongest laws.[7]

Sadler's book was self-indulgent and poorly organised, so much so that Locke's high regard for it suggests that he was powerfully attracted by its doctrines. These included the assertions that monarchy was elective in Saxon, and indeed Plantagenet, times and that 'it might be possible for future parliaments to reduce succession to election'.[8] Sadler also believed that legislative and judicial power had both originated in the Commons

---

[4] Ibid., 349.   [5] Ibid., 352.   [6] Ibid., 352.
[7] John Sadler, *Rights of the kingdom; or, customs of our ancestors* (1649), facing sig. Aa.
[8] Ibid., sig. Ii4v.

(and therefore that the recent abolition of the Lords was not a fundamental alteration).

If Locke was sympathetic to this vision of the past, then his political instincts were quite adventurous. But much in Sadler's pamphlet was a development of fairly conventional parliamentarian thinking, including the claims that 'allegiance was *ad legem*, to the laws, the kingdom and the kingdom's good or profit, rather than unto the king'[9] and that 'there is a trinity, which all our laws do seem to worship, here on earth: estate, liberty, and life'.[10] Sadler's arguments were particularly insistent on parliament's adjudicative role. His starting point was the belief that 'by the law of nature, there liveth not a man, in England, or in all the world, but ought, and must, submit himself to man's judgement'.[11] He went on to note that

through all this parliament, the Commons have joined with the Lords in judging Lords and Commons. Nay, in judging the king himself. For upon his withdrawing from parliament, refusing to return, and setting up his standard, both Houses proceeded, jointly together, in adjudging it treason against the state, or kingdom.[12]

The maxim that 'the king can do no wrong' was said to show 'that he can do nothing but by law; and what he may, by law, can do no wrong'. His personal acts not justified by law could 'be reclaimed and recalled, that I say not corrected, by the courts of justice, or the council of the kingdom'.[13]

During the 1680s, when he was writing his *Two treatises*, Locke placed a comparable stress upon adjudication. He believed that all rational adults had a natural right to judge, while the criterion of the existence of a 'political society' was the existence of a *common* judge: 'a judge on earth, with authority to determine all the controversies, and redress the injuries, that may happen to any member of the commonwealth; which judge is the legislative, or magistrates appointed by it'.[14] The power of this legislative, moreover, was established 'only with an intention in every [= each] one the better to preserve himself, his liberty, and property', which meant that it must govern 'by established standing laws' interpreted by 'indifferent and upright judges'.[15] In practice, this object was best secured by placing legislative power in 'collective bodies of men, call them senate, parliament, or what you please'.[16] Locke disapproved of monarchies in which the king himself played an essential part in legislation, 'so that he is no more subordinate than he himself shall think fit, which one may certainly conclude will be but very little'.[17] Like Sadler, however, he stressed that even in such

---

[9] Ibid., sig. Cc3v.   [10] Ibid., sig. Y.   [11] Ibid., sig. Aa.
[12] Ibid., sig. Ll2.   [13] Ibid., sig. Kk2v.   [14] Locke, *Two treatises*, II §89.
[15] Ibid., II §131.   [16] Ibid., II §94.   [17] Ibid., II §152.

monarchies, allegiance was owed to the monarch in his capacity as the 'supreme executor of the law, made by a joint power of him with others; allegiance being nothing but an obedience according to law, which when he violates, he has no right to obedience'.[18]

A further marked affinity between Locke's thought and Sadler's was the importance both attached to the idea of trust. We have seen that the foundation of the parliamentarian case was the idea that common law was not a list of rules (the 'known laws' of the moderate royalists), but rather something closer to a body of resources from which the nation could evolve solutions to its problems. The notion that kings were entrusted with discretionary power was actually demanded by this theory. It was not surprising, then, that Locke believed in 'power to act according to discretion, for the public good, without the prescription of the law, and sometimes even against it'.[19] In the early 1680s, though, he faced the difficulty that parliament was incapable of acting as the judge of whether this kind of irregular conduct was legal; unlike his father, Charles II controlled the House of Lords and had retained the power of dissolution. In any case, Locke doubted the body's representative credentials, no doubt because the 'Cavalier' House of Commons of 1661–78 had been vociferously intolerant. He went so far, indeed, as to maintain that '*salus populi suprema lex*' could justify 'the executive, who has the power of convoking the legislative, observing rather the true proportion than fashion of representation'; he would have preferred the Cromwellian Instrument of Government to the more legalistic Petition and Advice.[20] It was therefore not surprising that he took the Leveller view that even parliament's own power was revocably trusted by the people.

In some respects, indeed, Locke went beyond the Levellers: he vested an inalienable right of armed resistance in every rational person with a grievance. His grounds for claiming that this right would seldom be abused were simply that it was 'impossible for one or a few oppressed men to disturb the government, where the body of the people do not think themselves concerned in it'.[21] In practice, a people would only rebel if its rulers had shown beyond doubt that they were attempting to gain themselves absolute power. In such a situation, the rulers had themselves 'rebelled', that is, had brought about a state of war. It was a basic principle of Locke's political theory that 'he who attempts to get another man into his absolute power does thereby put himself into a state of war with him; it being understood as a declaration of a design upon his life'.[22] Even if such people caused no

---

[18] Ibid., II §151. [19] Ibid., II §160. [20] Ibid., II §158.
[21] Ibid., II §208. [22] Ibid., II §17.

actual harm, it was 'lawful for me to treat him as one who has put himself into a state of war with me, *i.e.* kill him if I can'.[23]

From one perspective, then, *Two treatises* is evidently the work of an extremist. Locke had inherited a stress upon adjudication, not least in regulating the king's use of his discretion, but he removed the right to judge both from the lawyers and from parliament and gave it to the individual's reason. His book has survived the objections to such a theory because it solved a more important problem: he gave a philosophical account of constitutionalist expectations. In particular, he found a novel means of justifying the established slogan that protection of 'lives, liberties and estates' (the rights that he significantly described as 'property') was the whole purpose of the legal order. As we have seen, the original justification for the priority of property was that this preference was in fact embedded within the practice of the common lawyers; when common law was treated as omnicompetent, the privileges attributed to an 'inheritance' became attached to all the rights of subjects. But this transition had relied on Coke's account of artificial reason. In Locke's generation, the Cokean view was virtually extinct, and Englishmen who thought about these questions regarded the law as a system of rules that had been framed by popular consent. They thus agreed with Pufendorf and Grotius that property was ultimately founded upon contract. But if property and kingship had the same contractual basis, then it was very hard to see why contracts that created rights to private property should have interpretative precedence over those contracts that created monarchs.

Locke was forced to find an answer to this problem by his antagonist Sir Robert Filmer. Filmer had rightly pointed out that a pre-political contract abolishing community of goods would have required the consent of every individual human being. Locke tacitly accepted this objection. The question that he set himself was 'how men might come to have a property in several parts of that which God gave to mankind in common, and that without any express compact of all the commoners'.[24] His detailed answer started out from a theology: 'men being all the workmanship of one omnipotent and equally wise maker; all the servants of one sovereign master, sent into the world by his order and about his business, they are his property, whose workmanship they are, made to last during his, not one another's pleasure'.[25] *An essay concerning human understanding* tells us that his abortive moral philosophy would have rested on a similar assumption: 'the idea of a supreme Being, infinite in power, goodness, and wisdom,

---

[23] Ibid., II §18.   [24] Ibid., II §25.   [25] Ibid., II §6.

whose workmanship we are, and on whom we depend; and the idea of our selves as understanding, rational beings'.[26] Locke seems to have thought that it followed from these notions that we are charged, as individuals, with making use of industry and reason: God gave the world, in a notorious phrase, to 'the use of the industrious and rational'.[27]

If rational, industrious beings were to flourish, or even survive, God must have provided a method by which a given individual could make a given consumable 'so his, *i.e.* a part of him, that another can no longer have any right to it'.[28] As labour is 'the unquestionable property of the labourer', Locke drew the conclusion that 'no man but he can have a right to what that is once joined to, at least where there is enough and as good left in common for others'.[29] Once separated from the common stock, such labour-generated property might pass into the hands of wealthy idlers, but all such property retained the status of a divinely chosen way of giving human beings sustenance. The creation of the Lockean magistrate does not involve the transfer of control of property, but only of the right to judge and punish infringements of that property by others; that is why, when a government ceases to exist, the rights it regulates survive unaltered. There is, of course, a problem, which Locke never squarely faced, raised by the need to find a clear distinction between the regulation of private ownership and actions that appear to over-ride it; he did permit taxation to pay for the expenses of 'protection',[30] and he occasionally implied, conventionally enough, that positive laws should promote the common good. But Locke's idea of common or public good appears to be a mere agglomeration of individual private interests; when he says, for example, that 'the power of the society, or legislative constituted by them, can never be supposed to extend farther than the common good; but is obliged to secure every one's property', he seems to have seen no tension between this common good and the entrenchment of proprietors.[31] Security of property was what Locke knew as 'freedom', for 'law in its true notion, is not so much the limitation as the direction of a free and intelligent agent to his proper interest';[32] thus law's object was not 'to abolish or restrain, but to preserve and enlarge freedom', understood as freedom 'from restraint and violence from others'.[33] Lockean law does nothing but police the boundaries behind which rational agents pursue what they rationally want; it is exhausted by its mechanisms for helping the possessor to exclude.

[26] Locke, *Essay*, IV iii 18.   [27] Locke, *Two treatises*, II §34.   [28] Ibid., II §26.
[29] Ibid., II §27.   [30] Ibid., II §140.   [31] Ibid., II §131.   [32] Ibid., II §57.   [33] Ibid., II §57.

This characterisation of some aspects of Locke's work yields no conclusive picture of his motives; it does not, for example, show that he had
democratic inclinations or that he consciously set out to justify his class's
privileges. It does, however, cast some light on his presuppositions. One
way of thinking about Locke's achievement would be to say that he had put
a constitutionalist politics on the basis of a rationalist religion. For Locke,
as for all thinkers in the rationalist tradition that ultimately stemmed from
Richard Hooker, the voice of reason was the voice of God. But Hooker's
legacy was ambiguous. Epistemologically speaking, his system was extraordinarily individualist; he believed that every kind of moral knowledge,
including the first 'motive' to believe in revelation, would be accessible,
in principle, to an unaided individual. Politically speaking, of course, he
was authoritarian; in the wide sphere of things apparently 'indifferent', he
thought that it was ultimately for the magistrate to say what was (and was
not) rational. Except in his earliest writings (which stressed the government's power in things indifferent), Locke emphasised the first strand of
this dual legacy.

An essay drew attention to the fact that the word 'reason' had a number of
meanings, but that his philosophical attention was devoted to 'a faculty in
man'.[34] This faculty played much the role a puritan might have attributed
to conscience.[35] If weight is given to its definition as 'natural revelation,
whereby the eternal father of light, and fountain of all knowledge com-
municates to mankind that portion of truth, which he hath laid within
the reach of their natural faculties',[36] then Locke's near-anarchist individualism becomes more readily intelligible. A God who willed his creatures,
as individuals, to be both rational and industrious, *obliged* them to secure
the property that was to be their means of preservation, and secondarily to
secure the property of others. Because we have no right to harm ourselves,
'reason . . . teaches all mankind, who will but consult it, that being all equal
and independent, no one ought to harm another in his life, health, liberty, or possessions'.[37] As 'freedom from absolute, arbitrary power' was 'so
necessary to, and closely joined with a man's preservation, that he cannot
part with it, but by what forfeits his preservation and life together', there
was a duty to avoid enslavement, if only because 'he that cannot take away
his own life, cannot give another power over it'.[38] As Locke additionally
held that wilful removal of 'any part of the subjects' property, without their

[34] Locke, *Essay*, IV xvii I.
[35] A crucial passage on the 'appeal to heaven' stresses that Locke is 'judge in my own conscience' of
whether resistance is permissible (Locke, *Two treatises*, II §21).
[36] Locke, *Essay*, IV xix 4.   [37] Locke, *Two treatises*, II §6.   [38] Ibid., II §23.

own consent . . . would be in effect to leave them no property at all', he had conferred on *every* right to private property the backing of the duty to self-preservation.[39]

There is much to be said for a reading of this theory that emphasises its religious basis. Though some might place less stress on the Hookerian character of Locke's exaggerated faith in reason, few scholars would doubt that assumptions about God are necessary to his argument. But one advantage of approaching Locke through English constitutionalist thinking is that it makes available an equally helpful perspective. In claiming for the details of English property rights the privileges of the law of nature, Locke was simply reasserting what Sir Edward Coke believed; conversely, when he extended the concept 'property' to cover lives and liberties as well as mere 'estates', he was uncritically taking over the idea that personal liberties are an 'inheritance'. This is not to maintain that he held Coke's beliefs for Coke's reasons – only that Cokean beliefs supplied what modern writers would probably want to call his 'intuitions'.

Above all, when he took it for granted that an individual's labour is 'the unquestionable property of the labourer', the *obviousness* of the idea that we can own our labour derived from constitutionalist sources. So did the obviousness of the claim (to be found in *An essay*'s discussion of a demonstrable ethics), that 'where there is no property, there is no injustice, is a proposition as certain as any demonstration in Euclid . . . the idea of property being a right to any thing; and the idea to which the name injustice is given being the invasion or violation of that right'.[40] If Locke was much more confident than any of his precursors that natural law's content consisted in property-like rights (that is, in private spaces from which all non-proprietors are excluded), he owed his confidence in the metaphor to a tradition that believed that power, where legitimate, was essentially judicial. Thus the exclusiveness of property in labour could not supply an independent basis for the exclusive character of property in general; Locke's premise was a borrowing from the very practices his argument set out to justify.

---

[39] Ibid., II §139.   [40] Locke, *Essay*, IV iii 18.

Bibliography

This bibliography lists only sources referred to in the text or in the notes. As in book titles in the text (to aid computer searching), spelling has been respected, but other accidentals have been modernized. If no place is supplied, printed works were published in London.

PRIMARY SOURCES

MANUSCRIPT

Bodleian Library, Oxford

Laud Miscellaneous MS 616 Roger of Waltham's *Compendium*
Tanner MS 74 Correspondence about Synod of Dort

British Library, London

Additional MS 14,030 Report on Coke's writings
Additional MS 29,546 Correspondence about prophesyings
Additional MS 32,092 Doddridge's 'Methode'
Additional MS 38,492 Puritan reaction to Hampton Court
Cotton MS Cleopatra E 6 'Collectanea satis copiosa'
Egerton MS 3376 Morrice on prerogative
Hargrave MS 27 Materials relating to impositions
Harleian MS 849 Plowden's succession tract
Harleian MS 4990 Hales's 'Commendation of laws'
Harleian MS 5220 Doddridge on the prerogative
Harleian MS 6234 'Itinerarium and Windsor'
Harleian MS 6686 Coke's notebook account of *Darcy* v. *Allen*
Lansdowne MS 68 Cartwright response to interrogatovies
Lansdowne MS 213 Kynaston's 'True presentation'
Royal MS 18 A 50 Henrician proposal for codification
Stowe MS 177 Benn's Treatise on chancery

PRINTED

Abbot, Robert, *De gratia et perseverantia sanctorum* (1618).

An abstract, of certaine acts of parliament: of certaine her Majesty's injunctions: of certaine canons, constitutions, and synodalless provinciall (1584).

The acts of the parliaments of Scotland, 12 vols. (Edinburgh, 1814–75).

Acts of the Privy Council, new series, ed. J. R. Dasent, 32 vols. (1890–1907).

Aegidius Romanus, *The governance of kings and princes: John Trevisa's Middle English translation of the De regimine principum of Aegidius Romanus*, ed. D. C. Fowler, C. F. Briggs, and P. G. Remley (New York, 1997).

An answer to a printed book intituled Observations (1642).

An answer to the Lord Digbies speech in the House of Commons (1641).

Aquinas, Thomas, *Opuscula omnia necnon opera minora*, ed. J. Perrier, 3 vols. (Paris, 1949).

The Armbrugh papers, ed. C. Carpenter (Woodbridge, 1998).

Aston, Sir Thomas, *The Short Parliament (1640) diary of Sir Thomas Aston*, ed. Judith D. Maltby, Camden Society, 4th series 35 (1988).

Aylmer, John, *An harborowe for true and faithful subjects* (Strasburg, 1559).

Bacon, Francis, *The works of Francis Bacon*, ed. J. Spedding, R. L. Ellis, and D. D. Heath, 14 vols. (1857–74) [NB. Spedding, *Life and letters* is volumes VIII–XIV of this publication.]

Baker, J. H. (ed.), *The reports of Sir John Spelman*, 2 vols., Selden Society 93–4 (1977–8).

Readings and moots at the Inns of Court in the fifteenth century, vol. II, Selden Society 105 (1989).

An introduction to English legal history, 3rd edn (1990).

Reports from the lost notebooks of Sir James Dyer, 2 vols., Selden Society 109–10 (1993–4).

Reports of cases by John Caryll, 2 vols., Selden Society 115–16 (1998–9).

Bancroft, Richard, *A sermon preached at Paules Cross the 9 of Februarie* (1588/9).

Daungerous positions and proceedings published and practised within the iland of Britaine (1593).

Barlow, William, *The summe and substance of the conference* (1604).

Barnes, Robert, *A supplicatyon made by Robert Barnes* (1531).

A supplication unto the most gracyous prince H. the viii (1534).

Bayne, C. G. and Dunham, W. H. (eds.), *Select cases in the council of Henry VII*, Selden Society 75 (1956).

Bekinsau, Joannes, *De supremo et absoluto regis imperio* (1546).

Bilson, Thomas, *The true difference between Christian subjection and unchristian rebellion* (Oxford, 1585).

Bodin, Jean, *Method for the easy comprehension of history*, tr. Beatrice Reynolds (New York, 1945).

The six bookes of a commonweale, ed. K. D. McRae (Cambridge, MA, 1962).

On sovereignty: four chapters from the Six books of the commonwealth, ed. J. H. Franklin (Cambridge, 1992).

The boke of justyces of peas (1506).

The Boke of Noblesse: addressed to King Edward IV on his invasion of France in 1475, ed. J. G. Nichols (Roxburghe Club, 1860).

Botero, Giovanni, *The travellers breviat* (1601).

Bowyer, Robert, *The parliamentary diary of Robert Bowyer 1606–7*, ed. D. H. Willson (Minneapolis, MO, 1931).

Bracton on the laws and customs of England, ed. G. E. Woodbine, tr. S. E. Thorne, 4 vols. (Cambridge, MA, 1968).

Bradford, John, *The writings of John Bradford, M.A.*, ed. A. Townsend, 2 vols. (Cambridge, 1848–53).

Bradshaw, William, *Puritanism and separatism: a collection of works by William Bradshaw*, ed. R. C. Simmons (1972).

Bray, Gerald (ed.), *Documents of the English Reformation* (Cambridge, 1994).

The Anglican canons: 1529–1947, Church of England Record Society 6 (Woodbridge, 1998).

Tudor church reform: the Henrician canons of 1535 and the Reformatio legum ecclesiasticarum, Church of England Record Society 8 (Woodbridge, 2000).

A briefe examination for the time of a certain declaration lately put in print in the name and defence of certain ministers in London (1566).

A briefe and perfect relation of the answeres and replies of Thomas earle of Strafford (1647).

Britton (1540).

Brooke, Sir Robert, *La graunde abridgement* (1573).

Buchanan, George, *De jure regni apud Scotos* (Edinburgh, 1846).

Burges, Cornelius, *The first sermon preached to the honourable House of Commons now assembled in parliament at their publique fast Novemb. 17 1640* (1641).

Burnet, Gilbert, *The memoires of the lives and actions of James and William Dukes of Hamilton and Castleherald* (1677).

Burton, Thomas, *The diary of Thomas Burton*, ed. J. T. Rudd, 4 vols. (1828).

Calendar of letters, despatches, and State Papers relating to the negotiations between England and Spain, 11 vols. (1862–1916).

Calendar of state papers and MSS relating to English affairs existing in the archives of Venice, ed. Rawdon Brown, 6 vols. (1864–84).

Calendar of state papers relating to Scotland and Mary, Queen of Scots 1547–1603, 13 vols. (Edinburgh, 1898–1969).

Camden, William, *Britannia, sive florentissimorum regnorum Angliae, Scotiae, Hiberniae et insularum adjacentium ex intima antiquitate chorographica descriptio* (1586).

Britannia, sive florentissimorum regnorum Angliae, Scotiae, Hiberniae et insularum adjacentium ex intima antiquitate chorographica descriptio (1607).

Britain, or a chorographicall description of the most flourishing kingdomes, England, Scotland, and Ireland, and the islands adjoining, out of the depth of antiquitie, tr. Philemon Holland (1610).

Cardwell, Edward (ed.), *Synodalia: a collection of articles of religion, canons, and proceedings of convocations* (Oxford, 1842).

Cartwright, Thomas, *Cartwrightiana*, ed. A. Peel and L. H. Carlson (1951).

A catechism written in Latin by Alexander Nowell Dean of St Paul's together with the same catechism translated into English by Thomas Norton, ed. G. E. Corrie (Cambridge, 1853).

Cavendish, William, earl of Newcastle, *A declaration of the right honourable the earle of Newcastle his excellency &c. in answer of six groundless aspersions* (1643).

Cecil, William, *The execution of justice in England for maintenance of publique and Christian peace* (1583).

A collection of state papers . . . left by William Cecill Lord Burghley, ed. S. Haynes, 2 vols. (1740).

Chamberlain, John, *The letters of John Chamberlain*, ed. N. E. McClure, 2 vols. (1939).

Chillingworth, William, *The religion of Protestants a safe way to salvation* (Oxford, 1638),

Cholmley, Sir Hugh, *The memoirs of Sir Hugh Cholmley* (1787).

Chrimes, S. B. and Brown, A. L., *Select documents of English constitutional history 1307–1485* (London, 1961).

Cicero, *De republica: De legibus*, ed. and tr. C. W. Keyes (1928).

Clarke, Samuel, *A general martyrologie containing a collection of all the greatest persecutions which have befallen the church of Christ, from the creation to our own times*, 3rd edn (1677).

Cobbett, W. and Howell, T. B., *A complete collection of state trials*, 33 vols. (1809–26).

Coke, Sir Edward, *The third part of the institutes of the laws of England* (1644).

The reports of Sir Edward Coke, Knt, ed. J. H. Thomas and J. F. Fraser, 6 vols. (1826).

Commons debates 1621, ed. Wallace Notestein, F. H. Relf, and Hartley Simpson, 7 vols. (New Haven, CT, 1935).

Commons debates for 1629, ed. Wallace Notestein and F. H. Relf (Minneapolis, 1921).

Commons Journal. Journals of the House of Commons, vols. I–IV (1742).

Cooper, Thomas, *An admonition to the people of England* (1589).

Cornwallyes, Sir William, *Essayes by Sir William Cornwallyes*, ed. D. C. Allen (Baltimore, 1946).

Cosin, John, *The works of the right reverend father in God John Cosin*, 7 vols. (Oxford, 1845).

The correspondence of John Cosin, D.D., Surtees Society 52, 55 (1869–70).

Cosin, Richard, *An apologie for sundrie proceeding by jurisdiction ecclesiastical* (1593).

Cotton, Sir Robert, *A short view of the long life and raign of Henry the third* (1627).

Cowell, John, *Institutiones iuris Anglicani, ad methodum et seriem institutionum imperialium compositae* (1605).

The interpreter (Cambridge, 1607).

Craig, Thomas, *Ius feudale*, ed. James Baillie (Edinburgh, 1732).

Cranmer, Thomas, *The works of Thomas Cranmer*, ed. Edmund Cox, 2 vols. (Cambridge, 1846).

Cromwell, Thomas, *Life and letters of Thomas Cromwell*, ed. R. B. Merriman, 2 vols. (Oxford, 1902).

Culpeper, Cheney, 'The letters of Sir Cheney Culpeper, 1641–57', ed. M. J. Braddick and Mark Greengrass in *Camden Miscellany* 23, Camden Society 5th series 7 (1996).

Cyvile and uncyvile life (1579).

Davidson, John, D. *Bancroft's rashnes in rayling against the Church of Scotland* (Edinburgh, 1590).

Davies, Sir John, *Le primer report des cases et matters en ley resolves et adjudges en les courts del roy en Ireland* (Dublin, 1615) *The question concerning impositions* (1656).

A declaration of the parliament of England, expressing the grounds of their late proceedings (1649).

Dering, Sir Edward, *A collection of speeches made by Sir Edward Dering* (1642).

Digby, Lord George, *The speeches of the Lord Digby in the high court of parliament concerning grievances and the triennial parliament* (1641).

The lord George Digby his last speech against the earle of Strafford (1641).

A discourse of the commonweal of this realm of England, ed. M. Dewar (Charlottesville, VA, 1969).

A discourse upon the exposicion and understandinge of statutes, ed. S. E. Thorne (San Marino, CA, 1942).

Diversite de courtz (1523).

Dow, Christopher, *Innovations unjustly charged upon the present church and state* (1637).

Dudley, Edmund, *The tree of commonwealth*, ed. D. M. Brodie (Cambridge, 1948).

Dyer, Sir James, *Les reports des divers select matters et resolutions des reverend judges et sages del ley* (1688).

Eliot, Sir John, *De jure majestatis or political treatise of government and the letter-book of Sir John Eliot*, ed. A. B. Grosart, 2 vols. (1882).

Elton, G. R., *The Tudor constitution: documents and commentary*, second edn (Cambridge, 1982).

Elyot, Sir Thomas, *The Boke named the Governour*, ed. H. H. S. Croft, 2 vols. (1880).

Erasmus, Desiderius, *The correspondence of Erasmus*, vol. VIII, tr. R. A. B. Mynors (Toronto, 1988).

Falkland, Lucius Cary, Viscount, *The speech or declaration of the Lord Falkland to the Lords of the Upper House* (1641).

A speech made to the House of Commons concerning episcopacy (1641).

Ferne, John, *The blazon of gentrie* (1586).

Field, Nathanael, *Some short memorials concerning the life of that reverend divine Dr Richard Field* (1716/17).

Field, Richard, *A learned sermon preached before the king at Whitehall* (1604).

Of the church (1606).

Fiennes, Nathaniel, *A speech of the honourable Nathaniel Fiennes in answere to the third speech of the Lord George Digby* (1641).

A second speech of the honourable Nathaniel Fiennes (1641).

Fitzherbert, Anthony, *Magnum abbreviamentum*, 3 vols. (1514–17).

The new natura brevium (1652).

Formularies of faith put forth by authority during the reign of Henry VIII, ed. C. Lloyd (Oxford, 1856).

Fortescue, Sir John, *Sir John Fortescue, Knt, his life, works and family history*, ed. Thomas Fortescue, Lord Clermont, 2 vols. (1869).

The governance of England: otherwise called The difference between an absolute and limited monarchy, ed. Charles Plummer (Oxford, 1885).

De laudibus legum Angliae, ed. S. B. Chrimes (Cambridge, 1942).

Foster, Elizabeth Read (ed.), *Proceedings in parliament 1610*, 2 vols. (New Haven, CT, 1966).

Fox, Edward, *The true dyfferens betwen ye regall power and the ecclesiasticall power*, tr. Henry Lord Stafford (1548).

Fraunce, Abraham, *The lawyer's logike* (1588).

Fulbecke, William, *A direction or preparative to the study of the lawe* (1600).

A parallele or conference of the civill law, the canon law, and the common law of this realme of England (1601).

Fuller, Thomas, *Church-history of Britain* (1655/6).

Gardiner, Stephen, *The letters of Stephen Gardiner*, ed. J. A. Muller (Cambridge, 1933).

Gardiner, S. R. (ed.), *Constitutional documents of the puritan revolution*, third edn (Oxford, 1906).

Gilson, J. P. (ed.), 'A defence of the proscription of the Yorkists', *English Historical Review* 26 (1911), 512–25.

Glanvill, *The treatise on the laws and customs of the realm of England commonly called Glanvill*, ed. G. D. G. Hall (Oxford, 1993).

Goodman, Geoffrey, *The court of James I*, ed. J. S. Brewer (1839).

The great charter called in latyn Magna Charta with divers olde statutes (?1540).

Grindal, Edmund, *The remains of Edmund Grindal D.D.*, ed. William Nicholson (Cambridge, 1843).

Hacket, John, *Scrinia reserata: a monument erected to the great deservings of John Williams* (1691).

Hake, Edward, *Epieikeia: a dialogue on equity in three parts*, ed. D. E. C. Yale (New Haven, CT, 1953).

Hakewill, William, *The libertie of the subject against the pretended power of impositions* (1641).

Hales, John, *Golden remains of the ever memorable Mr John Hales* (1673).

Hall, Edward, *Hall's chronicle* (1809).

Hall, Joseph, *Episcopacie by divine right asserted* (1640).

Hartley, T. E. (ed.), *Proceedings in the parliaments of Elizabeth I*, 3 vols. (1981–95).

Hatton, Sir Christopher, *A treatise concerning statutes, or acts of parliament: and the exposition thereof* (1677).

Herbert, George, *A priest to the temple* (1652).

Heylyn, Peter, *Antidotum Lincolniense: or an Answer to a book entitled Holy Table name and thing* (1637).

His Majesties declaration touching his proceedings in the late assemblie and convention of parliament (1621/2).

Historical manuscripts commission calendar of the manuscripts of the most honourable the Marquess of Salisbury, 24 vols. (1883–1976).

Historical manuscripts commission report on the manuscripts of the Duke of Buccleuch and Queensberry, 3 vols. (1899–1926).

Historical manuscripts commission report on the manuscripts of the Earl of Mar and Kellie preserved at Alloa House (1904).

Hooker Richard, *A learned discourse of justification, workes, and how the foundation of faith is overthrowne* (1612).

The Folger Library Edition of the Works of Richard Hooker, ed. W. Speed Hill, 7 vols. (1977–98).

Horne, Robert, *An answeare made by Rob. Bishoppe of Wynchester to a booke entituled the declaration of such scruples* (1566).

Howson, John, 'John Howson's answers to Archbishop Abbot's accusations at his "trial" before James I at Greenwich', ed. N. Cranfield and K. Fincham, *Camden Miscellany* 29 (1987).

Humphrey, Laurence, *The nobles or of nobilitye* (1563).

Ioannis Juelli Angli Episcopi Sarisburiensis vita et mors (1573).

Hunton, Philip, *A treatise of monarchie* (1643).

Husbands, Edward, *An exact collection of all remonstrances, declarations, votes, orders, ordinances, proclamations, petitions, messages, answers, and other remarkable passages betweene the king's most excellent Majesty and his high court of parliament* (1643).

Hutton, Sir Richard, *The diary of Sir Richard Hutton*, ed. W. R. Prest, Selden Society supplementary series 9 (1991).

Hyde, Edward, *Mr Edward Hyde's speech at a conference between the two Houses* (1641).

The history of the rebellion and civil wars in England, ed. W. D. Macray, 6 vols. (Oxford, 1888).

Hyde, Edward, Earl of Clarendon, *Two dialogues: Of the want of respect due to age and Concerning education* in *The miscellaneous works*, 2nd edn (1751).

In answer to the earle of Straford's conclusion (1641).

The institution of a gentleman, second edn (1568).

Institutions in the lawes of Englande (?1540).

Isidori Hispaliensis episcopi etymologiarum sive originarum libri xx, ed. W. M. Lindsay, 2 vols. (Oxford, 1911).

James VI and I, *The political works of James I*, ed. C. H. McIlwain (Cambridge, MA, 1918).

Minor prose works of K James VI and I, ed. J. Craigie, Scottish Text Society, 4th series 14 (1982).

Political writings, ed. Johann Sommerville (Cambridge, 1994).

Janelle, Pierre, *Obedience in church and state: three political tracts by Stephen Gardiner* (Cambridge, 1930).
John of Salisbury, *Policraticus: of the frivolities of courtiers and the footprints of philosophers*, ed. and tr. C. J. Nederman (Cambridge, 1990).
Justinian, *The Digest of Justinian*, ed. T. Mommsen and P. Krueger, tr. A. Watson, 4 vols. (Philadelphia, 1985).
Justinian, *Justinian's Institutes*, ed. P. Krueger, tr. P. Birks and C. McLeod (1987).
Kekewich, M. L., Richmond, C., Sutton, A. F., Visser-Fuchs, L., and Watts, J. L., *The politics of fifteenth-century England: John Vale's Book* (Stroud, 1995).
Kenyon, J. P., *The Stuart constitution: documents and commentary*, second edn (Cambridge, 1986).
Knafla, L. A. (ed.), *Law and politics in Jacobean England: the tracts of Lord Chancellor Ellesmere* (Cambridge, 1977).
Knowne lawes (1643).
Knox, John, *On rebellion*, ed. Roger A. Mason (Cambridge, 1994).
Kyle, Chris R., *Parliament, politics and elections 1604–48*, Camden Society, 5th series 17 (Cambridge, 2001).
Lambarde, William, *Archeion, or a discourse upon the high courts of justice in England*, ed. C. H. McIlwain and Paul L. Ward (Cambridge, MA, 1957).
William Lambarde and local government; his Ephemeris and twenty-nine charges to juries and commissions, ed. Conyers Read (Ithaca, NY, 1962).
Larkin, J. F. and Hughes, P. L., *Stuart royal proclamations*, 2 vols. (Oxford, 1973–83).
Laud, William, *An answere to Mr Fisher's relation of a third conference betweene a certaine B (as he stiles him) and himselfe* (1624) [NB this edn is meant unless otherwise stated].
Laud, William, *A relation of the conference between William Laud, then, Lord Bishop of St David's, now, Lord Arch-Bishop of Canterbury and Mr Fisher the Jesuite* (1639).
Laud, William, *The autobiography of Dr William Laud*, ed. J. H. Bliss (Oxford, 1839).
Laud, William, *The works of the most reverend father in God, William Laud D. D.*, 7 vols. (Oxford, 1847–60).
Letters and papers, foreign and domestic, of the reign of Henry VIII, ed. J. S. Brewer, J. Gairdner, and J. S. Brodie, 23 vols. (1862–1932).
Leveller manifestoes of the puritan revolution, ed. D. M. Wolfe (1944).
Liber assisarum, ed. Johannes Rastell (1514).
Lilburne, John, *England's birth-right justified against all arbitrary usurpation, whether regall or parliamentary* (1645).
Locke, John, *An essay concerning human understanding*, ed. Peter H. Nidditch (Oxford, 1975).
Two treatises of government, 2nd edn ed. P. Laslett (Cambridge, 1988).
Political essays, ed. Mark Goldie (Cambridge, 1997).
Lords Journal, Journals of the House of Lords, vols. i–v (1767).

Marshall, William, *The form and manner of subvention or helping for poor people devised and practised in the City of Ypres* (1535).

May, Thomas, *The history of the parliament of England which began November the 3 1640* (1647).

Maynard, John, *Mr Maynards speech before both Houses in parliament* (1641).

Memorials of the rebellion of 1569, ed. C. Sharp (1840).

Montagu, Richard, *A gagg for the new gospel? No: a new gagg for an old goose* (1624). *An appeal from two unjust informers* (1625).

More, Sir Thomas, *Utopia: Latin text and English translation*, ed. G. M. Logan, R. M. Adams, and C. H. Miller (Cambridge, 1995).

Morton, Thomas, *A defence of the innocencie of the three ceremonies of the church of England* (1618).

Noy, William, *Reports and cases taken in the time of Queen Elizabeth, King James, and King Charles* (1656).

Overall, John, *Bishop Overall's Convocation-Book, 1606* (1690).

Overbury, Sir Thomas, *A wife now the widdow of Sir Thomas Overburye . . . whereunto are added many witty characters* (1614).

Owen, David, *Herod and Pilate reconciled or the concord of papists and puritans (against Scripture, fathers, councels, and other orthodoxall writers) for the coercion, deposition, and killing of kings* (Cambridge, 1610).

Paget, William, 'A critique of the Protectorate: an unpublished letter of Sir William Paget to the duke of Somerset', ed. B. L. Beer, *Huntington Library Quarterly* 34 (1971).

'The letters of William, Lord Paget of Beaudesert, 1547–63', ed. B. L. Beer, *Camden Miscellany* 25 (1974).

Parker, Henry, *The case of Ship Mony briefly discoursed* (1640). *The true grounds of ecclesiasticall regiment* (1641). *Observations on some of his Majesty's late answers and expresses*, 2nd edition (1642).

Parker, Matthew, *De antiquitate Britannicae ecclesiae et privilegiis ecclesiae Cantuariensis* (1572). *Correspondence of Matthew Parker D.D.*, ed. J. Bruce (Cambridge, 1853).

[Parsons, Robert], *An answere to the fifth part of reportes lately set forth by Syr Edward Cooke* (1606).

Paule, Sir George, *The life of the most reverend and religious prelate John Whitgift* (1612).

Perkins, William, *A reformed Catholike* (1597).

Plowden, Edmund, *The commentaries or reports* (1761).

Pocklington, John, *Altare Christianum* (1637).

Prest, Wilfrid R., *The rise of the barristers: a social history of the English bar 1590–1640* (Oxford, 1986).

Prideaux, John, *The doctrine of the sabbath*, 3rd edn (Oxford, 1635).

Proceedings in parliament 1625, ed. Maija Jansson and William B. Bidwell (New Haven, CT, 1987).

Proceedings in parliament 1626, ed. William B. Bidwell and Maija Jansson, 4 vols. (New Haven, CT, 1992).

Proceedings in parliament 1628, ed. R. C. Johnson, M. F. Keeler, M. J. Cole, and W. B. Bidwell, 6 vols. (New Haven, CT, 1977–83).

The progresses and processions of Queen Elizabeth, ed. John Nichols, 3 vols. (1823).

Prynne, William, *The soveraigne power of parliaments and kingdomes, or the second part of the treachery and disloialty of papists to their soveraignes* (1643).

Pym, John, *The speech or declaration of John Pymm . . . upon the delivery of the articles* (1641).

The speech or declaration of John Pym Esquire after the recapitulation or summing up of the charge of high-treason against Thomas earle of Strafford (1641).

Queen Elizabeth's defence of her proceedings in church and state, ed. W. E. Collins (1942).

Raleigh, Sir Walter, *The prerogative of parliaments in England* (Middelburg, 1628).

Ransome, David R. ed., 'The parliamentary papers of Nicholas Ferrar, 1624', *Camden Miscellany* 33 (1996).

The register of the privy council of Scotland, second series, 8 vols (1899–1908).

A relation or rather a true account of the island of England, tr. C. A. Sneyd, Camden Society 37 (1847).

Rogers, Thomas, *The English creed* (1585).

The faith doctrine and religion professed and protected in the realme of England (Cambridge, 1607).

Rotuli parliamentorum ut et petitiones et placita in parliamento, 6 vols. (1767–77).

Sadler, John, *Rights of the kingdom; or, customs of our ancestors* (1649).

St German, Christopher, *An answere to a letter* (1535).

A treatyse concerninge the power of the clergye and the laws of the realm (?1535).

St German's Doctor and Student, ed. T. F. T. Plucknett and J. L. Barton, Selden Society 91 (London, 1975).

St John, Oliver, *An argument of law concerning the bill of attainder of high-treason of Thomas earle of Strafford* (1641).

Master St John his speech in parliament (1641/2).

Sanders, Nicholas, *De visibili monarchia ecclesiae* (1572).

Sandys, Edwin, *Europae speculum or a view or survey of the state of religion in the Westerne parts of the world* (1638).

Scott, Thomas, *Vox Populi or newes from Spayne* (1620).

Selden, John, 'Notes upon Sir John Fortescue' in Sir John Fortescue, *De laudibus legum Angliae* (1616).

Select cases in the Exchequer Chamber before all the Justices of England, vol. II: 1461–1509, ed. M. Hemmant, Selden Society 64 (1945).

Slaughter, Thomas P. (ed.), *Ideology and politics on the eve of Restoration: Newcastle's Advice to Charles II* (Philadelphia, 1984).

Slingsby, Sir Henry, *The diary of Sir Henry Slingsby*, ed. Daniel Parsons (1836).

Smith, Sir Thomas, *De republica Anglorum*, ed. Mary Dewar (Cambridge, 1982).

Snagg, Robert, *The antiquity and original of the court of Chancery and authority of the Lord Chancellor of England. Being a branch of Serjeant Snagg's Reading* (1654).

Sondes, George, *Sir George Sondes his plain narrative* (1655).

Spelman, Sir Henry, *Reliquiae Spelmannianae: the posthumous works of Sir Henry Spelman Knt*, ed. Edmund Gibson (Oxford, 1698).

Spotswood, John, *The history of the Church of Scotland* (1655).

Sprigge, William, *A modest plea for an equal commonwealth* (1659).

Statutes of the realm, 11 vols. (1810–28).

Strype, John, *The life and acts of John Whitgift D.D.*, 4 vols. (Oxford, 1822).

   Annals of the Reformation and establishment of religion and various other occurrences in the Church of England during Queeen Elizabeth's happy reign, 4 vols. (Oxford, 1824).

Stuart royal proclamations, ed. J. F. Larkin and P. L. Hughes, 2 vols (Oxford, 1973–83).

Suffragium collegiale theologorum Magnae Britanniae (1626).

Symmons, Edward, *A loyall subjects beliefe* (Oxford, 1643).

The teaching of Roman law in England around 1200, ed. F. de Zulueta and P. Stein, Selden Society supplementary series 8 (1990).

Thorpe, Francis, *Sergeant Thorpe, Judge of Assize for the Northern circuit, his charge* (York, 1649).

A true description, or rather a parallel between Cardinal Wolsey, Archbishop of York and William Laud Archbishop of Canterbury (1641).

Tunstall, Cuthbert, *A letter written by Cuthbert Tunstall* (1560).

Two Italian accounts of Tudor England, tr. C. V. Malfatti (Barcelona, 1953).

A view of a printed book intituled Observations upon his Majesties late answers and expresses (Oxford, 1642/3).

Waller, Edmund, *A speech made by Master Waller Esquire in the honorable House of Commons, concerning episcopacie* (1641).

Whitaker, William, *An answere to the ten reasons of Edmund Campian the Jesuit*, tr. Richard Stock (1606).

White, Francis, *A reply to Jesuit Fisher's answer to certain questions propounded by his most gracious majesty* (1624).

Whitelocke, James, *Liber famelicus of James Whitelocke*, ed. John Bruce, Camden Society 50 (1858).

[Whitelocke, James], *The rights of the people concerning impositions stated in a learned argument* (1657/8).

Whitgift, John, *The works of John Whitgift, D.D.*, ed. John Ayre, 3 vols. (Cambridge, 1851–3).

Wilbraham, Sir Roger, 'The journal of Sir Roger Wilbraham', ed. H. S. Scotts *Camden Miscellany* 10 (1902).

Wilkins, David (ed.), *Concilia Magnae Britanniae et Hiberniae a synodo Verulamensi A.D. 406 ad Londiniensem A.D. 1717*, 4 vols. (1737).

Williams, John, *The holy table name and thing* (1637).

Winwood, Sir Ralph, *Memorials of affairs of state in the reigns of Queen Elizabeth and King James I*, 3 vols. (1725).

The writings and speeches of Oliver Cromwell, 4 vols. (Cambridge, MA, 1937–47).

Year Books of Edward IV: 10 Edward IV and 49 Henry VI, ed. N. Neilson, Selden Society 47 (London, 1931).

Year Books, *Annalium tam regum Edwardi Quinti, Ricardi Tertii, et Henrici Septimi, quam Henrici Octavi* (1679).
Year Books, *Les reports de la cases conteinus in les ans vint primer et après (anno 21, 22, 27, 28, 29) in temps del Roy Hen le Siz* (1679).
Year Books, *Les reports del cases en ley que furent argues en le temps de tres haut princes les roys Henry le IV et Henry le V* (1679).
Year Books, *Les reports des cases en ley que furent argues en temps du roy Edward le Quart* (1680).
The Zurich letters comprising the correspondence of several English bishops and others with some of the Helvetian reformers during the early part of the reign of Queen Elizabeth, ed. Hastings Robertson (Cambridge, 1842).
The Zurich letters comprising the correspondence of several English bishops and others with some of the Helvetian reformers during the reign of Queen Elizabeth, ed. Hastings Robertson, second series (Cambridge, 1845).

SECONDARY SOURCES

Abbott, L. W., *Law reporting in England, 1485–1585* (1973).
Alford, Stephen, *Kingship and politics in the reign of Edward VI* (Cambridge, 2002).
Archer, Ian, *The pursuit of stability: social relations in Elizabethan London* (Cambridge, 1991).
Baker, J. H., *The law's two bodies: some evidential problems in English legal history* (Oxford, 2001).
The Oxford history of the laws of England, 12 vols. (Oxford, 2003–), vol. VI.
Bankes, George, *The story of Corfe Castle* (1853).
Bean, J. M. W., *The decline of English feudalism, 1215–1540* (Manchester, 1968).
Bennett, H. S., *English books and readers 1475 to 1557* (Cambridge, 1970).
Bernard, G. W., *War, taxation and rebellion in early Tudor England* (Brighton, 1986).
Blatcher, Marjorie, *The court of king's bench, 1450–1550* (1978).
Bowers, Roger, 'The Chapel Royal, the first Edwardian Prayer Book, and Elizabeth's settlement of religion 1559', *Historical Journal* 43 (2000), 317–44.
Boynton, Lindsay, *The Elizabethan militia 1558–1638* (1967).
Burgess, Glenn, *The politics of the ancient constitution: an introduction to English political thought, 1603–1642* (Basingstoke, 1992).
Bush, M. L., *The government policy of Protector Somerset* (1975).
Cargill Thompson, W. D. J., 'The sixteenth-century editions of A supplication', *Transactions of the Cambridge Bibliographical Society* 3 (1960).
Chrimes, S. B., *English constitutional ideas in the fifteenth century* (Cambridge, 1936).
Cogswell, Thomas, *The blessed revolution: English politics and the coming of war* (Cambridge, 1989).
Coleman, C. and Starkey, D. (eds), *Revolution reassessed: revisions in the history of Tudor Government and administration* (Oxford, 1986).

Collinson, Patrick, 'Lectures by combination: structures and characteristics of church life in seventeenth-century England', *Bulletin of the Institute of Historical Research* 48 (1975), 182–213.

Archbishop Grindal 1519–1583: the struggle for a Reformed church (1979).

Godly people: essays on English Protestantism and Puritanism (1983).

'The Jacobean religious settlement: the Hampton Court conference' in *Before the English civil war: essays on early Stuart politics and government* (1983), ed. Howard Tomlinson, 27–52.

The Elizabethan puritan movement (Oxford, 1990).

'The monarchical republic of Elizabeth I' in *Elizabethan essays* (1994).

Corré J. I., 'The arguments, decision, and reports of Darcy v. Allen', *Emory Law Journal* 45 (1996).

Craig, John, *Reformation, politics, and polemics: the growth of Protestantism in East Anglian market towns, 1500–1610* (Aldershot, 2001).

Crankshaw, David, 'Preparations for the Canterbury Convocation of 1562–3: a question of attribution', in Susan Wabuda and Caroline Litzenberger (eds.), *Belief and practice in Reformation England* (Aldershot, 1998).

Cromartie, Alan, 'Common law, counsel and consent in Fortescue's political theory', in *The fifteenth century* 4 (2004), 45–67.

Cust, Richard, 'News and politics in early seventeenth-century England', *Past and Present* 112 (1986), 60–90.

Davis, Ralph, *The rise of the Atlantic economies* (1973).

Dietz, F. C., *English public finance 1558–1641* (New York, 1932).

Dixon, R. W., *History of the church of England from the abolition of the Roman jurisdiction*, 5 vols. (Oxford, 1902).

Doe, Norman, *Fundamental authority in late medieval English law* (Cambridge, 1990).

Duffy, Eamon, *The stripping of the altars: traditional religion in England, c. 1400–c. 1580* (Yale, 1992).

Dunham, W. H., 'Regal power and the rule of law: a Tudor paradox', *Journal of British Studies* 3 (1963–4).

Eburne, Richard, *The twofold tribute* (1613).

Elton, G. R., 'Evolution of a Reformation statute', *English Historical Review* 64 (1949), 174–97.

Reform and renewal (Cambridge, 1973).

Studies in Tudor and Stuart politics and government, 4 vols. (Cambridge, 1974–92).

The parliament of England 1558–1581 (Cambridge, 1986).

Fisher, R. M., 'The Inns of Court and the Reformation 1530–1580'. Unpublished Cambridge PhD dissertation 1974.

Fletcher, Anthony, *The outbreak of the English civil war* (1981).

Foster, Stephen, *The long argument: English Puritanism and the shaping of New England culture, 1570–1700* (Chapel Hill, 1991).

Gardiner, S. R., *History of England from the accession of James I to the outbreak of the civil war 1603–42*, second edn, 10 vols. (1883–4).

Gilbert, Felix, 'Sir John Fortescue's dominium politicum et regale', *Medievalia et humanistica* 2 (1944).

Gleason, J. H., *The justices of the peace in England 1558–1640: a later Eirenarcha* (Oxford, 1969).

Graves, M. A. R. *Thomas Norton: the parliament man* (Oxford, 1944).

Gray, Charles M., 'Bonham's case reviewed', *Proceedings of the American Philosophical Society* 116 (1972), 35–58.

The writ of prohibition: jurisdiction in early modern English law, 2 vols. (New York, 1994),

Guy, John, 'Henry VIII and the praemunire manoeuvres of 1530–31', *English historical review* 97 (1982), 481–503.

The court of Star Chamber and its records to the reign of Elizabeth I, Public Record Office Handbook 27 (1985).

Christopher St German on Chancery and Statute, Selden Society Supplementary series 6 (1985).

'Wolsey and the parliament of 1523' in *Law and government under the Tudors*, ed. C. Cross, D. Loades, and J. J. Scarisbrick (Cambridge, 1988).

Harrison, C. J., 'The petition of Edmund Dudley', *English Historical Review* 87 (1972), 82–99.

Hasler, P. W. (ed.), *The Commons 1558–1603*, 3 vols. (1981).

Heal, Felicity, *Of prelates and princes: a study of the social and economic position of the Tudor episcopate* (Cambridge, 1980).

Heinze, R. W., *The proclamations of the Tudor Kings* (Cambridge, 1976).

Helmholz, R. H., *Roman canon law in Reformation England* (Cambridge, 1990).

Hindle, Steve, *The state and social change in early modern England, c. 1550–1640* (Basingstoke, 2000).

Holmes, Clive, 'The county community in Stuart historiography', *Journal of British Studies* 19 (1980), 54–73.

Hoyle, R., 'War and public finance' in D. MacCulloch (ed.), *The reign of Henry VIII: politics, war and piety* (Basingstoke, 1995).

Ingram, Martin, 'Religion, communities, and moral discipline in late sixteenth and early seventeenth century England', in *Religion and society in early modern Europe*, ed. K von Greyerz (1985).

Ives, E. W., *The common lawyers of pre-Reformation England* (Cambridge, 1983).

Jones, Norman, *Faith by statute: parliament and the settlement of religion 1559* (1982).

Jordan, W. K., *Edward VI: the young king* (1968).

Kaeuper, R. W., *War, justice, and public order: England and France in the later Middle Ages* (Oxford, 1988).

Keeler, M. F., *The Long Parliament 1640–41: a biographical study of its members* (Philadelphia, 1954).

Kelley, Donald R., '"Second nature": the idea of custom in European law, society, and culture', in *The transmission of culture in early modern Europe*, ed. A. Grafton and A. Blair (Philadelphia, 1990).

Kelly, M. J., 'Canterbury jurisdiction and influence during the episcopate of William Warham, 1503–32'. Unpublished Cambridge PhD dissertation 1963.

Kiralfy, A. K., *The action on the case* (1951).

Knowles, David, *The religious orders in England*, 3 vols. (Cambridge, 1948–59).

Lake, Peter, *Anglicans and puritans? Presbyterianism and English conformist thought from Whitgift to Hooker* (1988).

The Antichrist's lewd hat: Protestants, papists, and players in post-Reformation England (New Haven, CT, 2002).

'The Laudian style' in Kenneth Fincham (ed.), *The early Stuart church, 1603–42* (1993).

Lake, Peter and Questier, Michael (eds.), *Conformity and orthodoxy in the English church, c.1560–1660* (Woodbridge, 2000).

Lamont, William, *Marginal Prynne, 1600–1669* (1963).

Loades, D., *The reign of Mary Tudor: politics, government and religion in England, 1553–58*, 2nd edn (1991).

Lockwood, S., 'Marsilius of Padua on the royal ecclesiastical supremacy', *Transactions of the Royal Historical Society*, 6th series, 1 (1991), 89–119.

Logan, F. D., 'Thomas Cromwell and the vicegerency in spirituals: a revisitation', *English Historical Review* 103 (1988), 658–67.

MacCaffrey, Wallace, *The shaping of the Elizabethan regime* (1969).

MacCulloch, Diarmaid, 'Richard Hooker's reputation', *English Historical Review* 117 (2002), 773–812.

MacCulloch, Diarmaid, *Suffolk and the Tudors: politics and religion in an English county 1500–1600* (Oxford, 1986).

Thomas Cranmer: A Life (New Haven, CT, 1996).

Tudor church militant: Edward VI and the Protestant Reformation (1999).

MacCullough, Peter, *Sermons at court: politics and religion in Elizabethan and Jacobean preaching* (Cambridge, 1998).

Macinnes, Allen I., *Charles I and the making of the covenanting movement* (Edinburgh, 1991).

McIntosh, M. K., *Controlling misbehaviour in England, 1370–1600* (Cambridge, 1998).

Macpherson, C. B., *The political theory of possessive individualism: Hobbes to Locke* (Oxford, 1962).

Maddern, P. C., *Violence and social order: East Anglia 1422–1442* (Oxford, 1992).

Marshall, Peter, 'Mumpsimus and sumpsimus: the intellectual origins of a Henrician bon mot', *Journal of Ecclesiastical History* 52 (2001), 512–20.

Mendle, Michael, *Henry Parker and the English civil war: the political thought of the public's 'privado'* (Cambridge, 1995).

Metzger, Franz, 'The last phase of the medieval Chancery' in Alan Harding (ed.), *Law-making and law-makers in British history* (1980).

Milsom, S. F. C., *Historical foundations of the common law*, 2nd edn (1981).

Milton, Anthony, *Catholic and Reformed: the Roman and Protestant churches in English protestant thought 1600–1640* (Cambridge, 1996).

Muldrew, Craig, *The economy of obligation: the culture of credit and social relations in early modern England* (Basingstoke, 1998).

Nicolas, H., *Memoirs of the life and times of Sir Christopher Hatton K.G.* (1847).

Notestein, Wallace, 'The winning of the initiative by the House of Commons', *Proceedings of the British Academy* 11 (1924), 125–75.

Ormrod, W. M., 'The origins of the sub poena writ', *Historical Research* 61 (1988), 11–20.

Patterson, W. B., *James VI and I and the reunion of Christendom* (Cambridge, 1997).

Paul, R. S., *The assembly of the Lord* (Edinburgh, 1985).

Peck, Linda Levy, 'Goodwin v. Fortescue: the local context of parliamentary controversy', *Parliamentary History* 3 (1984), 33–56.

Peltonen, Markku, *Classical humanism and republicanism in English political thought, 1570–1640* (Cambridge, 1995).

Pocock, J. G. A. *The ancient constitution and the feudal law: a study of English historical thought in the seventeenth century: a reissue with a retrospect* (Cambridge, 1987).

Porter, H. C., *Reformation and reaction in Tudor Cambridge* (Cambridge, 1958).

Post, J. B., 'Equitable resorts before 1450', in E. W. Ives and A. H. Manchester (eds.), *Law, litigants, and the legal profession* (1983).

Powell, Edward, *Kingship, law, and society: criminal justice in the reign of Henry V* (Oxford, 1989).

Putnam, B. H. *Early treatises on the practices of justices of the peace in the fifteenth and sixteenth centuries*, Oxford studies in social and legal history 7 (Oxford, 1924).

Quintrell, B. W., 'The royal hunt and the puritans 1604–5', *Journal of Ecclesiastical History* 31 (1980), 41–58.

Read, Conyers, *Mr Secretary Cecil and Queen Elizabeth* (1955).

Richmond, Colin, *The Paston family in the fifteenth century: the first phase* (Cambridge, 1990).

Russell, Conrad, *Parliaments and English politics, 1621–1629* (Oxford, 1979).

The causes of the English civil war (Oxford, 1990).

The fall of the British monarchies, 1637–42 (Oxford, 1991).

Scarisbrick, J. J., *Henry VIII* (1968).

Shagan, Ethan H., *Popular politics and the English Reformation* (Cambridge, 2003).

Shriver, Frederick, 'Hampton Court revisited: James I and the puritans', *Journal of Ecclesiastical History* 33 (1982), 48–71.

Simpson, A. W. B., *Legal theory and legal history: essays on the common law* (1987).

Slack, Paul, *From reformation to improvement* (Oxford, 1999).

Sommerville, Johann, 'Absolutism and royalism' in J. H. Burns (ed.), *The Cambridge history of political thought 1450–1750* (Cambridge, 1991).

Sommerville, J. P., *Royalists and patriots: politics and ideology in early Stuart England*, 2nd edn (Harlow, 1999).

Starkey, David, 'Intimacy and innovation', in Starkey (ed.), *The English court: from the Wars of the Roses to the Civil War* (Harlow, 1987).

Stein, Peter, *Regulae iuris: from juristic rules to legal maxims* (Edinburgh, 1966).
Stevenson, David, *The Scottish revolution 1637–1644* (1973).
Trevor-Roper, Hugh, *Catholics, Anglicans, and puritans* (1987).
Tyacke, Nicholas, *Anti-Calvinists: the rise of English Arminianism c. 1590–1640* (Oxford, 1987).
Tyacke, N. R. N., 'Wroth, Cecil and the parliamentary session of 1604', *Bulletin of the Institute of Historical Research* 50 (1977), 120–5.
Tyndale, William, *Doctrinal treatises and introductions to different portions of the holy scriptures,* ed. Henry Walter, Parker Society 32 (Cambridge, 1848).
Underdown, David, *Revel, riot, and rebellion* (Oxford, 1985).
Usher, R. G., *The reconstruction of the church of England,* 2 vols. (1910).
Virgoe, R., 'The benevolence of 1481', *English Historical Review* 104 (1989), 25–45.
Walsham, Alexandra, *Church papists: catholicism, conformity, and confessional polemic in early modern England* (London, 1993).
Webster, Tom, *Godly clergy in early Stuart England: the Caroline puritan movement, c. 1620–1643* (Cambridge, 1997).
White, Peter, *Predestination, policy, and polemic: conflict and consensus in the English church from the reformation to the civil war* (Cambridge, 1992).
Whiting, Robert, 'Local responses to the Henrician Reformation', in *The reign of Henry VIII: politics, policy and piety,* ed. D. MacCulloch (1995).
Williams, Penry, *The Tudor regime* (Oxford, 1979).
Wolffe, B. P., *The Crown lands 1461 to 1536: an aspect of Yorkist and early Tudor government* (1970).
Yale, D. E. C., 'Of no mean authority: some later uses of Bracton' in *Of the laws and customs of England,* eds. M. Arnold, T. Green, S. Scully, and S. White (Chapel Hill, NC, 1981).

Index

IDEAS IN CONTEXT

Edited by QUENTIN SKINNER (*General Editor*),
LORRAINE DASTON, DOROTHY ROSS, and JAMES TULLY

QM LIBRARY
(MILE END)

WITHDRAWN
FROM STOCK
QMUL LIBRARY

WITHDRAWN
FROM STOCK
QMUL LIBRARY

Lightning Source UK Ltd.
Milton Keynes UK
16 December 2010

164487UK00001B/97/P